YOU COULDN'T
MAKE IT UP!

JOHN DEARNLEY COLLINS

PROLOGUE

Welcome to the life of John Victor Wattley – to my life. That's me in the pram - a vintage 'Cockney Sparra'. We're a dyin' breed, you know – but not just yet 'cos that kid was a survivor and I've still got a story to tell. It seems I was born to survive – first fosterin', then the Great Depression, evacuation, the Blitz, ill health, National Service and whatever else life had to throw at me – and all before I was 21. And, take it from me, the roller coaster ride didn't stop there, as you'll see, if you care to read on.

I'm writin' – or to be more precise, recountin' this at the tender age of 83 years with the help of my friend – my best buddy, John. With a bit of coaxin', I amaze myself with the clarity of the sights, sounds and yes, the smells I can recall, even from my very early years. I guess I've always been impressionable and lookin' back, maybe I have lived through more impressionable times than most kids. In any event, the more I opened up to John, the more convinced he became that my story needed to be recorded – needed to be told – not least because sadly, although I'm not 'Little Jack' any more, it seems I am now the last survivin' Ardingly boy evacuee.

The sharp ones amongst you might be thinkin' I've already lost the plot. 'Little Jack', what's all that about?. The fact is, whilst I was christened John, as far back as I can remember, even mum and dad always called me Jack. Everyone did except Roy, my big brother, who for some reason always called me Willie and carried on, right up until the day he died. To everyone else though, I was Jack. Apparently it all started because I had a cousin called John – Auntie Annie's lad – and his father was called Jack. As I recall we weren't together all that often, but the story goes they decided to call me Jack to save confusion! It seems nothin's been straightforward in my life – not even my name, but no matter, havin' a cousin John had its advantages. In particular, because he was that bit older, Auntie Annie would sometimes pass down his toys to me. I'll tell you about some of 'em later.

If you only ever read one biography in your life, make an old man happy, make it this one. My hope is that as you read on you'll get inside my skin, see things as I saw them, hear the sounds, smell the smells, experience the life, my life, as I remember it. It's written as I speak, a Cockney lad, rather than in perfect Queen's English, but that's because I want you to 'feel' you're me, or at least that you're livin' it with me. Be warned, sometimes it can be a 'bumpy ride', but then, that's life, isn't it? It never runs smooth all the time. It's full of 'ifs' and 'buts', well 'ifs' anyway. See for yourself, it's there, right in the middle, L if e, so there's no gettin' away from 'if's, but take a tip from me, avoid litterin' your life with 'if onlys' – with regrets. You can never change what's happened, so don't dwell on regrets. Learn from your mistakes, from your experience of life and as the song says, "Always look on the bright side." Trust me, you'll be much happier that way.

That I survived at all is somethin' of a minor miracle 'cos I was such a sickly kid and as a teenager lyin' in a hospital bed, I vividly recall mum bein' told well within earshot – "He'll never work, you know." Evidently the doctors thought my asthma was so bad I'd be incapable of holdin' down a proper job. Little did they know.

Mind you, by rights I should be dead! In fact I did die once. Take a tip from me, if you're goin' to die and you want to live to tell the tale, then do it in a hospital – but make sure it's a good 'un like St Thomas' in London.

Since then I've had a heart by-pass supported by 18 stents – with 2 more to come it seems. Guess I'll have a full set soon! Then there's the diabetes to compound the asthma and, take it from me, by the time you get to 83 – well, "bits start droppin' off you know!"

As for you – well, you've read this far – now put it down or buy it, borrow it, pinch it if you must – but read it and see what you think. You never know – you might learn somethin' and have a few laughs and maybe shed a few tears along the way.

My Birth Certificate, Oct 4th, 1933, St James Hospital, Balham, London.

Me in a pram – a vintage 'Cockney Sparra'. Take a good look at the pram – very Victorian. A sturdy old thing, built to last. A fair few kids in a fair few families would have had use of it before me and doubtless after.

CHAPTER 1

From the Beginnin'

Now I've got pretty good recall – for events, happenin's, even conversations, but I have to hold my hands up – I don't recall bein' born. But it is recorded – October 4th 1933, St James' Hospital, Balham, South London. Not great timin' – slap bang in the middle of the Great Depression.

My mother was Joyce Wattley, aged 21 and my father was Roy Wattley, aged 36. You're probably thinkin' that's quite a big age gap – and you'd be right. Mother had been born on 10th February 1912. That makes it memorable for me, but you may know it better as the year the unsinkable Titanic hit an iceberg on its maiden voyage and, despite its size and strength, was holed and sank. Dad on the other hand had been a soldier throughout most of the First World War. So yes, there was quite a big age gap and as time went on I'm afraid it showed more and more. On top of that, dad was quite a serious, educated man, whereas mum hadn't had the same opportunities. Mind you, when it came to money matters and organisin' the household, dad preferred to take a back seat and it was always mum who came to the fore.

I already had a brother – Roy – born out of wedlock in 1930. Back then this was considered shameful, so granddad, (dad's dad) drummed them out of Sidmouth and parcelled them off to dad's sister's, Auntie Annie's place in London – and of course there was a 'shotgun' weddin'. Otherwise, chances are mum would have been 'obliged' to give our Roy up for adoption. That's how it was in those days. None of the benefits system we have today which supports and some would say practically encourages single parents to the extent that some seem to make a career of it. Mum made a career out of sheer hard work – nothin' came easy, but more of that later.

When Roy and I were born, mum and dad worked mainly in service – hotels and the like – dad as a chef and mum as a chambermaid although, if you look back at my birth certificate, you'll see it shows dad workin' as a gardener and mum, as you might expect, had no employment at the time of my birth. Times were hard and they were grateful for any job they could get. Trouble was, children weren't allowed in service so in 1934 when Roy was not quite 4 and I was only about 8 months old, the pair of us were fostered out with a spinster called Miss Raithby. I don't need to tell you that fosterin' can be hit and miss. You'll learn, as my story unfolds, that Miss Raithby and her family were to have an enormous impact on my life which went well beyond the fosterin'. Whether it was by luck – or judgement on my parents' part – I don't know, but we couldn't have wished for a better foster parent. She was no relation, but to us she was Aunt Raithby. She was very kind to us and I have nothin' but fond memories of her. She lived in a rented property in Sandfield Road, Thornton Heath, which was a suburb of Croydon.

Sadly, the only photo I have of her was taken over a decade later at Olga's weddin'. Olga was her 'adopted' daughter. It's amongst those at the end of Chapter Five if you want to see it now. To you she may look rather strict and austere. True enough, we did have to behave ourselves – but then, kids generally did in those days. But she never hit or ill-treated us in any way and my eyes are glazin' over as I'm tellin' you this, because we were happy with her – in fact I should tell you we loved her and I don't doubt that she loved us and you can't wish for more than that – can you? She never married and we were the children she never had.

Aunt Raithby was a lady with high standards, but very limited means. Money was always short, but she was a very respectable lady – Victorian in appearance. She always wore black dresses with a lace bodice. Havin' prepared the evenin' meal, she would always go upstairs at around 4 o'clock to change for dinner – always into another black dress. Of course we never saw her changin', but I do remember her bedroom was very Victorian with a washstand and a jug and bowl on it.

As I remember it, the front of the house was more or less onto the street with just some iron railin's and a bit of pavin' between. We never sat in the front room, but Aunt Raithby took me in there from time to time to water the aspidistra. It had a Victorian air about it – with a chaise longue. At the back of the house there was a scullery with a gas stove and a sink. In the daytime I'd spend most of my time in the kitchen, which was really the livin' cum dinin' room, playin' with my toys on or under the table. Our Roy was usually at school. There was a big black clock with pillars on the sideboard next to the fireplace. Today I'd recognise it as a typical black marble Victorian mantel clock, except this one was special because it was a 'police clock' which had been presented to Aunt Raithby's father who I believe had been quite a high-rankin' police officer.

Upstairs was let to a bachelor called Edgar who I think must have been a carpenter because there was always a lovely aroma of wood shavin's. He was also a good gardener and looked after the garden, which was at the back. I had a little 'Mickey Mouse' tricycle (I think it was a Triang) and although it was very small, so was I and for a long time I couldn't manage the pedals so I'd scoot up and down the pavement instead. Aunt Raithby, very smartly dressed as she always was – particularly in public, would stand at the gate keepin' a watchful eye on me. That's me on my tricycle aged about 2 years.

Sometimes she'd give me a halfpenny for a sweet treat and still under her watchful eye, I'd run up to the greengrocer's at the top of the street to buy a bag of hundreds and thousands. That shop had a very distinctive smell and if I concentrate, even after all these years, I can smell it now. I guess they were really cake decorations, and thinkin' back, it seems a rather strange product for a greengrocer's to sell. Still, it was a treat for me. I used to wet a finger and dab it in to get it coated – same as you would sherbet or lemonade powder.

Roy went to Egger Street Infants School in Thornton Heath and I'd go with Aunt Raithby to collect him. When I was big enough, I'd scoot along the pavement on my tricycle. Other than that Aunt Raithby rarely went anywhere, but occasionally, maybe once every 4 or 5 weeks, whilst Roy was at school she would take me on a No. 159 bus to the Clock Tower at Thornton Heath and then on the No. 42 tram to Kennards, which was a real treat. I vividly recall the tram was the overhead type rather than the 'plough type' which operated in the City south of the river (Thames) where mum and dad lived. It stopped right outside Kennards (now Debenhams) which then, as now, was a department store sellin' almost everythin'. You could spend half a day there just lookin' – which is mostly what we did. It was a magical place and one big difference was that Kennards had a white pony which gave rides up and down the pavement. You have to remember that back then there was very little traffic to contend with. Whenever we went, I always knew that just before we left Aunt Raithby would make sure I had a 6d ride. I loved it. The only problem – not so much for me, but for Aunt Raithby – was that to get to the pony ride we had to walk through a tunnel under the store. At one end was a cage with a talkin' parrot which fascinated me. Imagine, a bird that could talk just like a human bein'. I was entranced by it. Trouble was, it swore like a trooper and so she always tried to scuttle me past its cage. Funny – the things you remember.

After my pony ride we'd always walk up to buy bacon at a shop in Surrey Street renowned for quality, variety and value. Afterwards, we'd walk on to Surrey Street market to buy veg and sometimes fruit before headin' back home the way we'd come. Eighty years on that bacon shop is still there today! And Surrey Street Market is still goin' strong. You can buy more or less anythin' there. Check it out for yourself if you get the chance.

In those days nobody – leastways nobody I knew – had a bathroom or an inside toilet. When I was young it was a case of standin' in the scullery sink and sittin' on the drainin' board for a 'bath' and usin' a potty in front of the fire. Quite a luxury really – compared to a freezin' cold outside privy which you had to use as you got bigger. Tin baths stored hangin' on an outside wall at the back were common, but Aunt Raithby had a built-in bath off the scullery. We'd have a bath about once a fortnight – always before bed. In winter it was a teeth-chatterin' experience 'cos there was no heatin' but at least havin' been washed we could scuttle into the kitchen to get dry in front of the kitchen cum livin' room fire and then straight into pyjamas and ready for bed.

When Roy and I arrived to be fostered, Aunt Raithby already had a much older foster daughter called Olga, who was 16 or 17. Olga's father was a sea captain and Olga had been placed with Aunt Raithby from a young age. I was later to learn that this had become permanent when Olga was about 12 years old and her father announced that he no longer wanted her back. Olga called Aunt Raithby 'mum' and I don't think she could have had a better mum. I don't know if she was legally adopted – but that didn't matter. What was important was the bond that existed between them – between us all.

Aunt Raithby had an older sister, Mrs (Kate) Donaby, who we called Grandma. She lived with her husband (granddad) and 4 grown-up children in Thornton Heath, Surrey (now more or less part of Croydon). They had 3 daughters and a son – Doris, Gracie, Kate and Fred. Their other son, Harry, had died of TB. As I remember it, Aunt Raithby never went anywhere outside Thornton Heath except for our monthly trips to Kennards. Our trips to Grandma's were still in Thornton Heath. Roy and I loved goin' to grandma's on a Sunday, not least because we always came away rich! All the children worked and they'd all give us 3d or 6d and sometimes we'd come away with as much as half a crown! Believe me, for kids like us, that was a small fortune.

'Grandad' never actually seemed to sit in the house but would come in for meals and a funny thing – he would always have a slice of bread and butter with treacle on afterwards. Not just sometimes – always. To this day, I can't see a tin of Tate & Lyle's without thinkin' back to 'Grandad'. I know he wasn't my real grandad, but he was the only grandad I ever knew.

Grandma was more or less house-bound and her legs were always bandaged up. To help her with housework – cleanin' and vegetable preparation, she had 'a lady who does'. I never knew her name. I only knew her as 'the lady who does' from listenin' to conversations. I might have been only 3 or 4 years old, but I never missed much and still don't. If there are any youngsters readin' this, then take a tip from me. It pays to sit quiet and keep your eyes and ears open. You can learn a lot from eavesdroppin' on adults' conversations. I know I did.

My first recollection of a trip to the seaside was when Olga (then about 18) took Grace and me to Eastbourne. The trip, includin' the train ride from East Croydon Railway Station, was a great adventure for a 3-year old. As with subsequent trips to the seaside, I returned badly burnt. The days always seemed to be hot and sunny then, but no-one had suntan lotion or knew about the dangers of sunburn.

Aunt Raithby never came with us, but she was always ready with the calamine lotion when we got back and I was smothered from head to toe with the stuff.

I don't know why, but that expression - 'head to toe'- has just made another little memory pop into my head – the chimney sweep comin' to call. I guess it's because he was black from head to toe. To start with we'd have to get up early to help prepare for the big event – well, it was to us. It was the kitchen chimney he'd come to sweep because the kitchen fire, with its polished fender, was the only fire Aunt Raithby could afford to light and havin' it workin' properly was important because it was the only form of heat in the house. We'd have to help cover everythin' over with sheets to try to keep the soot off and, of course, cold or not, there'd be no fire lit that mornin'. The chimney sweep would put his brush in the fire place with the rod end pokin' out through a black sheet with a hole in the middle. The sheet was taped to the fire surround to keep the soot from putherin' out but, inevitably some did anyway, especially after the sweepin' when the soot was bein' shovelled into a bag – there were no vacuum cleaners in those days. Before that though, the chimney sweep would screw one piece of rod after another onto his brush, all the while pushin' the brush head further up the chimney. That would be the cue for Roy and me to dash outside. We'd stare up at the chimney pot in anticipation and when soot puthered out followed by this great big round brush, we thought it was hilarious, especially when it kept disappearin' and reappearin' as the sweep pulled it back in and pushed it back out so as to give the chimney a proper clean. I suppose you could say 'small things amuse small minds' but I was fascinated by it – we both were.

From time to time a Mr Cornish would call on Aunt Raithby. I'm not sure, but I think he may have come to collect the rent. Anyway, we always had to be very quiet and good whenever he came and hide away under the kitchen table until he'd gone. It was one of the few times Aunt Raithby used her front room. I don't know, but perhaps Aunt Raithby wasn't supposed to take in foster children.

It's funny the things you remember as a kid and one abidin' memory, which I would have put about 1937, but history recounts it was actually November 1936, is when the Crystal Palace burnt down. So I'd have been precisely 3 years and one month old. Normally at that time Roy and I were bein' fostered out with 'Aunt Raithby' but now and again we'd spend a few days with mum and dad and this was one of those days. They were livin' in rooms above a disused printers in Tyneham Road. The place had been abandoned and there was lead typeface strewn all over the floor. Very temptin' for us kids, but we weren't allowed to go in and get any. There's a block of flats on the site now because durin' the War the whole block was blown to smithereens – but that's me, digressin' again when I should be tellin' you about the Crystal Palace.

It was evenin' time and what I remember was all these people rushin' up the Tyneham Road shoutin', "The Crystal Palace is on fire – it's burnin' down." Truth be told, I didn't know what the Crystal Palace was. I'd never seen it – but I could see it now, lightin' up the sky. And the fire engines – we could hear the fire engines rushin' to the scene. All very excitin' to a kid like me.

That's all I remember because watchin' from the street was as near as I got, but since it was such a momentous day in the history of London, I think I ought to say a bit more about it. For starters, the Crystal Palace was a giant, iconic, cast iron and plate glass structure designed by Joseph Paxton and originally built in Hyde Park for the Great Exhibition of 1851. Later it was moved to Sydenham. I've read about it and I've seen pictures of it, but I never saw it for myself – only this great glow in the sky. Bein' an iron and plate glass buildin' you'd think it wouldn't succumb to fire, but apparently it had tinder-dry wooden floors and lots of flammable stuff stored inside and by misfortune, the 30th November 1936 was a very windy night. Bein' so big, it took a good while to burn, but apparently the flames spread so quickly that even the 400 firemen and 89 fire engines in attendance couldn't stop it bein' completely destroyed.

Close up it must have been quite a spectacle and it's said that over 100,000 people stood on Sydenham Hill that night to watch it burn. Among them was Winston Churchill who, whilst witnessin' the devastation reputedly said, "This is the end of an age" not an era an age. I suppose he was his own man – Mr. Churchill. Sadly, apparently part of the buildin' complex was bein' used to house a large exhibition of exotic birds, but the heat was so fierce that even the fire fighters couldn't get in to rescue them and later one is quoted as sayin', "All that could be heard above the fire was the poor parrots screamin' as they perished." From what I've heard and read I wish I'd seen the Palace in all its glory, but back then the first I'd heard of it was that fateful night and all the commotion it caused in the street and what looked to me like a beautiful glow in the sky. I had no sense of the loss or destruction, but then I was only three.

I've mentioned 'grandma' (Mrs Kate Donaby), but Aunt Raithby was actually one of three sisters. They'd originated from Lincolnshire and the third sister, Aunt Pattie, still lived there. It seems Grandma and Aunt Raithby had moved to London in search of work. Anyway, Aunt Pattie would come and stay with Aunt Raithby about once every 6 months. She'd arrive at Kings Cross and take the train down to Thornton Heath. I always knew when she was comin' because Aunt Raithby would take up her customary stance, standin' with her hands on the table, to announce her sister's impendin' arrival. At such times I knew to be on best behaviour. Whilst stayin' with Aunt Raithby, Aunt Pattie would always ply between Aunt Raithby's and grandma's place in Kitchener Road about a mile away. We always had to play I Spy when Aunt Pattie came. I think it was the only kids' game she knew.

I'd often accompany my two 'aunts' up to 'grandma's'. Late in the afternoon, grandma would say, "Fred (her son) will be comin' home from work soon" and that would be my cue to walk up the pavement to the top of Kitchener Road and wait for him comin' off the bus. It was quite a long way and I was only 4, but it was quite safe. I knew to stop on the pavement and there weren't many cars about in those days.

If you ask me, Fred was a very interestin' chap. He'd left school at 14, which most kids did in those days, and gone to work at Croydon Airport, then London's premier airport, and run I think by Imperial Airways and later BOAC. Anyway, one day before the war when I'd be 4 or maybe just 5, Fred told us about an open day at the Airport and mum and dad took Roy and me along. As Fred had said, we were able to walk around the airport, see the aircraft and some of what went on in the hangars and workshops where Fred worked. Goin' to an airport was a pretty big deal because only business people or the very rich could afford to fly and so ordinary folk never got to see inside an airport. On the open day, which thinkin' about it was, I'm pretty sure, only a few months before the outbreak of war, I can remember dad pointin' out these two German planes sittin' on the runway –

11

distinctive with their crosses on. They weren't really big planes like you see today, just small planes to carry maybe 8 or 10 passengers. I've got it in my mind that one of 'em had a swastika on it, but I can't be sure of that, but I clearly remember dad tellin' me to keep an eye on 'em because they might take off in a minute and, sure enough, one did. We must have seen lots of planes, but it's the German ones I remember, I guess because within a few months we'd be at war with Germany and everybody would be talkin' about 'em then.

I'm gettin' a bit ahead of myself because, before then, somethin' momentous happened that I need to tell you about. Like many ordinary workin' folk during the 1930s Depression, mum and dad were in and out of work. That's why, around the middle of 1938, with no money to pay for fosterin', they took Roy and me back to live with them. Roy had to change schools, but I still wasn't old enough to go to school. At that time they were still livin' in those rooms over the abandoned printer's shop in Tyneham Road. Whilst we never went back to Aunt Raithby's for fosterin', Roy and I were glad to go back for visits and holidays and later on, as a teenager, I'd go and do jobs for her like cuttin' the hedge, but I'll come to all that later. When she died in 1963, she would have been in her late '80s. It was a very sad day for me. She was no relation at all, but she was my Aunt Raithby and she'd been like a mother to me and I really felt the loss.

When we were taken back 'home' (although for me at least, home had been with Aunt Raithby), dad was on the dole, drawin' less than ten bob a week. He would lose even that if mum worked. Men were seen as the breadwinners and with so many men out of work, women workin' was generally frowned upon. Nevertheless, to help make ends meet, mum would go off out to work under the cover of darkness so no-one would see. She used to go out cleanin' in what we called 'the big houses'. She was paid a pittance, but that bit of money was needed to help keep us. Mum was always a worker – often to be seen with a bucket of hot water, scrubbin' floors on her hands and knees. Dad would keep an eye on us whilst mum was out doin' her 'secret jobs'.

Our upstairs 'flat' had two bedrooms, a kitchen and a livin' room with a gas mantle over the fireplace. It was a pretty spartan affair with a shared privy out the back. Most of the time we used a guzunder. There was a tin bath on the wall outside, but I don't recall ever usin' it. In fact I don't recall a lot about our time in Tyneham Road – I guess nothin' much memorable happened. One thing I do recall was the milk! We had one and a half pints delivered and Roy and I were sent to fetch it from the bottom of the stairs. I was allowed to carry the half pint but Roy, bein' much bigger, was quicker down the stairs than me and very often would carry both bottles up. This upset me, but, not to be outdone, I'd carry my half pint all the way back down just so I could carry it back up myself! Daft, I know, but I didn't like bein' out-done even then. If dad was in, Roy might get a tellin' off, not so much for 'pinchin' my job but for the noise he'd make dashin' down the stairs. The thing was, we couldn't afford stair carpet and our shoes would always have 'blakeys' in 'em. In case you don't know, they're a sort of metal stud and dad would always hammer 'em into the heels and soles of our shoes, to make 'em hard wearin', to make 'em last. As you can imagine, leather soles and heels reinforced with blakeys made a right racket on the bare wooden stairs if we weren't careful and dad always hated noise.

Some of the kids made carts out of old boxes and pram wheels and a bit of rope washin' line for steerin'. Our street – Tyneham Road – was quite a steep hill and so made a good cart track. We didn't have a cart ourselves, so mostly we'd have to be content with watchin' but, if we were lucky, we'd get to ride in the back of one sometimes. I would have liked a go up front doin' the steerin' but beggars couldn't be choosers.

Now and again Roy and his friends would take me up to Clapham Common. If you've never been, then I can tell you it's really big and there are three ponds and a bandstand. Near the bandstand people used to play chess on collapsible tables, sittin' on fold-up green chairs. Even today I think people still meet up there to play chess. Bein' only 4 or 5, I didn't understand it then. In fact I've never really got the hang of chess. The players seemed to take it very serious. Sometimes we'd watch for a few minutes, but then we'd get bored and move on to somethin' more interestin' like fishin'.

A trip to the Common usually meant we'd be goin' fishin' or playin' football or, if we had money, goin' in a canoe on the boatin' pond. That was in the biggest pond – well a small lake really. Half of it was used for rowin' boats and canoes and the other half was for fishin'. We always went in the canoes 'cos they were cheaper – four pence for half an hour. It was two per canoe, so tuppence each. When our half hour was up we'd always come over all "mutton jeff". When the boatman got more insistent, sometimes we'd even put our fingers in our ears, but then we'd have to come in before he got really mad for fear he'd remember us and not let us out next time. Mind you there probably wasn't much chance of that because our visits to the park with money in our pockets were few and far between. Mum and dad just didn't have the money to give us.

As I say, the other half of the pond was for fishin'. Some of the bigger kids would take their shoes and socks off and jump in with potato sacks – one kid on each end. Then they'd drag the sack to the island and back. I think you'd be surprised by how many fish they managed to catch that way. They'd put 'em in a big jar and then try sellin' em for a few pence each. There'd usually be kids tryin' their luck fishin' with nets off the bank. They were never that successful, so sometimes would make good customers rather than goin' home empty handed.

A second, smaller pond with an island in the middle was called 'the mount pond'. I never did know why. Some folk fished in that as well, but I never did. The third pond was a boatin' pond where those lucky enough to have a sailin' boat or better still, a model motor boat, could set it goin'. We never had one, but it was nice to watch sometimes. It wasn't just kids – there were adults doin' it.

Clapham Common was free to go on, but it was run by the LCC and patrolled by Park Keepers in smart brown uniforms and a cap with a big brass badge on it. There were loads of 'em and each had their own number. I hadn't been long at school when the war started, but I can still remember many a time kids bein' caned by the headmaster because they'd been reported by one of the Park Keepers for misbehavin' on the Common or in Battersea Park. It was nothin' too serious. Maybe they'd broken a branch while climbin' a tree or maybe for gettin' in the pond and fishin' with sacks 'cos that was forbidden really. Most times though the kids would just run away when anyone saw a Park Keeper comin'.

Pre-war London was quite a lively, colourful place and twice a year somethin' really special arrived in our street – a group of street performers complete with a hurdy gurdy and a group of oxen to pull them. Imagine that in central London today! They would arrive as if from nowhere, but with great pomp and ceremony. Clad in very colourful outfits and dresses, there would be a man with an accordion and women singin' and dancin' – a bit like flamenco dancers. For the short time they were there they would transform the street into a lively theatre. People would hang out of their windows, applaudin' and throwin' coppers. All too soon they would suddenly stop, pack up and be gone as suddenly as they came – off to do a repeat performance in a nearby street.

A while ago I told you there was nothin' much to recount about my time livin' back with mum and dad in Tyneham Road but, those street performers, they were special and now a vivid memory of Christmas Eve has just popped into my head that I want to share with you. Lavender Hill is very close to Tyneham Road and so we'd often go shoppin' there with mum. Dad never went shoppin'. In those days – 1938/39, it was almost all food shops, mainly butchers. The only other shop I recall there was Godbolls, a big clothin' and haberdashery store with somethin' rather special inside that I'll tell you about in a minute. First though, it's the atmosphere on Lavender Hill on Christmas Eve that I want to share with you because it was magical, it really was, especially to a five year old like me.

On Christmas Eve those shops would stay open very late to around 11 pm. but I was never allowed out that late. In fact, on Christmas Eve, I'd have long been tucked up in bed dreamin' of Santa and what he might bring, but I clearly remember mum did take Roy and me up Lavender Hill after dark to savour the atmosphere whilst she checked out the prices. There'd be lots of activity. Loads of people wanderin' about doin' last minute shoppin' or like us, just lookin', and the trams would be noisily trundlin' up and down. The shops had canopies and awnin's out with bars from which to hang their wares – all manner of meat, poultry and game - rabbits, geese and colourful pheasants jostlin' for space with chickens and turkeys. Some shops had electric light bulbs danglin' off wires, but most of the atmospheric light came from gas lamps in the street. The noise, the bustle, the lightin', enough to see by but that was about all, created an atmosphere that somehow heightened the magic that was Christmas.

You have to remember that these were the days before refrigeration, so everythin' was fresh and that's why the shops would stay open so late because they had to clear everythin' before closin' for Christmas. Folk with money would take their pick and buy early. Poorer folk and those wantin' a bargain would bide their time waitin' for the prices to fall. I never saw it, but apparently, in the end the shop keepers would auction things off to clear 'em. Mum was always one for a bargain.

Godbolls wasn't the sort of store you could just walk in to as a kid, but it was where mum used to take Roy and me to buy trousers – always grey flannel, lightweight for summer, heavyweight and a bit itchy for winter. I didn't get to go in many times but, whenever I did, it always fascinated me because of the way they took money and gave receipts. There were about six assistants and, havin' been helped to find what you needed, they'd make out a bill and you'd give 'em the money, but unlike most shops, they didn't have a till or a drawer to put the money in. Instead they'd put the bill and your money in a sort of canister cage and attach it to an overhead wire. Each assistant had their own station, so there'd be half a dozen or so of these overhead wires, all leadin' to a sort of upper level mezzanine area where a lady cashier sat. The shop assistant would pull a lever and the canister would go whizzin' along the wire to the cashier. She would then send a receipt and any change due back to the assistant to give to the customer. As a four or five year old, I was mesmerized by these flyin' canisters. I suppose the idea was to relieve assistants from the responsibility or temptation of handlin' money, but to me they were just great fun to watch.

My only other really vivid memory of our time in Tyneham Road was a visit from Uncle Vic – dad's twin brother. The story goes that in 1914, fed up with them chasin' girls around Sidmouth, their father marched both dad and his brother down to the army recruitin' office and made them sign on. Both saw action in the First World War and Uncle Vic stayed on. By 1938 he was an army officer – I'm not sure what rank – but I clearly remember him arrivin' in an MG sports car, havin' driven up from Salisbury with a pair of brown army boots for dad. At the time an able-bodied man could get a job with Battersea Borough Council if he had a good pair of boots! So it was that dad got a job sweepin' the streets and, when the weather was really bad, 'snow bashin' – basically clearin' the streets of snow. Back then, a job, any job, with the Council was considered to be 'a job for life' and so it would turn out to be for dad. He worked for Battersea Borough Council for 27 years until he retired in 1965 at the age of 67 years. (He was allowed to do 2 years extra). Whilst he started off sweepin' the streets, he finished up as an administrator. He didn't drive – he always used the bus – but havin' secured 'an office job' he would always look smart in his blue serge suit and Anthony Eden trilby hat. (There's a photo of Dad with his trilby hat taken at my weddin' in December 1954 at the end of Chapter Seven.) But there I go, gettin' ahead of myself, way ahead because I'm barely 5 and it's still the late 1930s.

Bearin' in mind that dad's first job with Battersea Borough Council was as a road sweep, I suppose you could say he started at the bottom, but it was a job and you were glad of any job in the 'Depression'. He had four bins on his barrow and sometimes he'd tip one up on end so I could sit on it and he'd wheel me around. There was a bin store – a sort of big tin box affair – near the gates of Tennyson Street School. It held four bins and when dad's bins were full he'd take them there and it would be a case of four in and four out and then on he'd go again. Dad was an intelligent man, but work was work and he was glad of it. There was no welfare system to speak of, not like there is today. Nobody sweeps the streets anymore and just look at the state of 'em. On the whole, our welfare system is a good thing but if you ask me, we should never have got ourselves into a situation in which able bodied people of workin' age are given money week in week out without havin' to do anythin'. Not when there's lots of work in and for the community they could be doin'. What's more, how often do you hear it said that a person won't take this or that job because they'd be no better off workin' than not. If you ask me, the system has all but destroyed the work ethic. It's crazy and I don't see how it can continue to be sustainable especially now that more and more old folk like me are survivin' longer.

I'm not sure where all that came from but anyway, that's enough from me, spoutin' from my soap box when I should be tellin' you about my life back in London as a four goin' on five year old. One little incident that springs to mind, is when I decided to ask this policeman for help. It was before I started school so I guess I must have been 4. I was in Queenstown Road and I can clearly remember goin' up to this policeman on Belisha Beacon duty. Belisha Beacons were a sort of orange globe light on the top of a black and white striped pole to mark pedestrian crossin's. They were the forerunners of the Zebra Crossin's we see today. The thing was, I'd dropped my farthin' down a drain and I'd been told that if ever I was in trouble I should ask a policeman for help. I was small for my age and he was big and a bit intimidatin' with this cape slung over his shoulder but I'd lost my farthin' and I wanted to buy a toffee bar – 'golly bars' they were. Anyway, very politely, I asked him if he'd mind puttin' his hand down the drain to get my farthin' back. When I stop to think about it now he could easily have given me a clip round the ear and told me to clear off, couldn't I see he was busy. But he didn't. Whether it was the tears in my eyes or the quiverin' lip that swung it I don't know but he dutifully lifted the drain cover and retrieved my farthin' for me. Only a little thing I know but the memory has stuck with me and doubtless helped to give me the respect I still have for the police.

Dad's brother had given us 'a leg up' enablin' dad to get a job in 1938 and not long after in 1939, the family got another 'leg up' courtesy of dad's sister, Auntie Annie. She was a schoolteacher and Uncle Jack worked on the railway. They lived in a rented property, No 34 Montefiore Street, London SW 8, but in 1939 they decided to buy a place of their own in Harewood Road, Tooting. So it was that we were able to move out of our dingy rooms above the derelict printers and move into No 34 Montefiore Street. It was still rented, but by comparison, it was posh. The property was divided into two flats which shared the same front door, but the upstairs flat had a separate door down the passage. There was a shared toilet in the back yard. Ours was the ground floor flat, private rented via an agent called Edwin Evans in Lavender Hill opposite the Town Hall. Few ordinary workin' people could afford to buy a house or flat in those days. Most rented and whilst I don't know what our rent was, I clearly recall that rents generally fell into three bands – 9/6, 10/6 and 12/6 a week. As I've said, I learnt a lot from listenin' to adults' conversations.

Whilst dad didn't seem bothered either way, it's fair to say that mum was thrilled with our 'new house'. Ok, it wasn't 'new', but it was new to us and much more spacious than our rooms in Tyneham Road and really it was a flat and not a house, but from the outside it looked like a house and so that's how we thought of it. Inside there was only one bedroom, a kitchen, a scullery and a front room. It was common in those days for the front room or sittin' room to be kept for best and used only at Christmas or on special occasions, but out of necessity, ours also had to double up as a make-do bedroom for Roy and me. We shared a 'put-you-up bed' which could be folded away when visitors came and mum wanted the room to look smart.

Mostly, if we were in the house and not in bed, we'd be in the kitchen because that's where the fire would be lit if we had one. Whilst we called it the kitchen, really it was more of a livin' cum dinin' room. It had a range and a table and chairs. The 'scullery' at the back was where the sink, the copper and the cooker were and so that's where the washin' and food preparation was done. The sink in the scullery was very basic – a shallow, brown, pot sink with just a cold tap on the end of a lead pipe, set back in an alcove. The cooker was a sort of mottle grey enamel on legs. Because we had what was then considered to be quite a modern gas cooker in the scullery, the range oven in the kitchen was only ever used for keepin' sticks dry ready for makin' up the fire the next day. We did often use the top of the range to boil a kettle though, when the fire was lit, otherwise we'd boil it on top of the cooker. We didn't use the copper for boilin' water that often because that was more expensive.

When I say that the washin' was done in the scullery, I mean people as well as clothes because there was no bathroom. Mondays was always wash day and it was just that, a day's job. There was none of this stickin' the washin' into a machine and flickin' a switch and lettin' it get on with it. Before washin' powder came in, it was sunlight soap and a scrubbin' board. Omo, that was the first washin' powder, leastways it was in our house. It went on for years so I'm bettin' a lot of you will remember Omo. Whether it was soap or wash powder, mum still had to scub the washin' in the tin bath, then, after the rinsin', mangle it to get most of the water out before hangin' it on the line in the back yard – weather permittin'. Mum's mangle was a heavy thing that she had to fix to the end of the kitchen table before she could use it. The fixin's were rather like large versions of those you get on a mincer if you've ever seen one of those. Then it was a case of feedin' the wet wahin' into the rollers whilst turnin' the handle at the side which turned the rollers via a system of cogs.

Washin' done, mum used to scrub the whole house out with the soapy water finishin' with the front door and step. Washin' dry, then of course there was the ironin'. You used to hear it said that "a woman's work is never done" and it was true, it really was.

The upstairs was let to Mrs Cleve, who to me at the time seemed an elderly lady. She was probably in her 60s and lived alone, but she used to go out to work very early in the mornin' and come back in the afternoon at about 4pm. We didn't see much of her. She was a very quiet person and we never heard her upstairs. About the only time we'd see her to speak to would be on a Saturday mornin' when she'd always offer Roy and me a piece of butterscotch from a paper bag. We always took it and I can't say I really liked it – but over 75 years on, I can taste it now and re-live the feelin' it gave me. I suppose it was a bit too grown-up for me. It always left a bit of a dry feelin' in my mouth. Mind you, it couldn't have been that bad, could it, because I always took it when offered. I knew better than 'to look a gift horse in the mouth'.

Our flat only had one official bedroom where mum and dad slept. Roy and I always slept together in the same put-you-up bed in the front room. In those days that didn't matter because hardly anyone ever went in the front room except on Christmas Day! In any case, bein' a put-you-up bed it could be folded up and returned to bein' a parlour again if visitors were expected. Sometimes, when the weather was bad, provided it wasn't too cold, we'd play in there and the bed would be folded up to give us more space. Only the two of us mind. We were never allowed to have friends to play in the house. Often as not though, it would be just too cold for us to play in there, so we'd play in the kitchen, tryin' not to get under anyone's feet.

You remember I told you havin' older cousins was a good thing because Auntie Annie would sometimes pass on their toys to Roy and me. Well, I have particularly fond memories of this Hornby clockwork train set. It had a round track and a lovely green engine and two carriages. It may have only gone round and round, but I loved it, and I played with it time and again, especially on wet or cold winter days when I couldn't be outside. I'm sayin' it only went round and round, but actually, the engine had a switch so I could make it go backwards as well as forwards and settin' it up, gettin' all the track just right, that was part of the fun to me. If I close my eyes I can still see and imagine the sound of my 'hand me down' train chuggin' round and round on the kitchen floor in front of the fire. They were happy times.

The kitchen was the place the family ate and more or less lived except at Christmas or the odd special day when visitors were expected and mum or dad would make a fire up in the front parlour.

Mostly though, there would only ever be a fire lit in the kitchen range and then only when it was cold. We just couldn't afford to have more than one fire lit except at Christmas. At the very back, we also had a scullery with a sink and a gas cooker in it, but there was no fire in there and at times it was freezin' I can tell you, especially in winter when we were bein' washed in the sink. We had an outside toilet which we shared with upstairs, but no bathroom, just a big tin bath on a nail on the wall outside. Sometimes we'd get the tin bath in and we'd wash in front of the kitchen fire, which was a real treat. Mostly though, it would be in the stone sink in the scullery. When the bath came in, us kids would get bathed first and then the water would get topped up from the kettle and re-used. We only had the one cold water tap. Roy and I would be put in our pyjamas and put to bed in the front room whilst mum and dad had their baths.

I remember thinkin' that compared to Tyneham Road, how smart our new street looked with iron railin's runnin' the whole length on both sides. They had what I called 'scout tops' (fleur de lys) and dad was proud of the colourful flower garden he created out front. I'll come back to that later, but for now, in pre-war London, I'm just rememberin' our street and how fine it looked and how the sun always seemed to shine so us kids could go out and play. We just played then. We didn't smash things or spray graffiti – we just had fun. But, make no mistake – we were street-wise. With my big brother Roy and three or four pals we'd often take ourselves off to Clapham Common. Roy would be maybe 7 goin' on 8 and I'd be 4 goin' on 5. One such trip – in the summer of '39 – stands out. I would have been 5 by then. We'd gone for a bit of a picnic and I was lyin' down arms outstretched when 'Billy Bunter' came and sat on my left arm and broke it! And yes, we really did call him Billy Bunter 'cos he looked just like the comic cartoon character, especially when he had his cap on. Anyway, I didn't dare tell anyone for two days, but I was actin' a bit miserable and mum finally wheeled it out of me. That was it – off to hospital – St George's on Hyde Park Corner. They didn't put a cast on it but I came out with a sling and all the street cred that goes with it. I kept it on for ages – long after I really needed it.

When we could, Roy and me would go off to Saturday mornin' pictures – on the No 77A bus up to the Grenada. Kids could go on their own in those days if they were showin' two 'U's like Old Mother Riley and Laurel & Hardy (certificate U's were deemed suitable for children). We'd get on at the top of Silverthorne Road and travel the length of Wandsworth Road to Clapham Junction. Most buses stopped there but the 77A went on further up the hill and stopped right outside the Grenada Cinema. It was wonderful. Newly built as a theatre as well as a cinema in about 1937. Sometimes they'd have talent shows on there includin' big stars like Jonny Ray from America. More often, before the films started, an organist would rise up like a phoenix at the front of the stage and words would come down on a big screen to encourage us kids to sing along. I rather liked it but most of the boys wanted him off – they just wanted the Cowboys and Indians to come on. It was mainly Cowboys and Indians in those days with stars like Buck Jones, Roy Rogers, Gene Autry and Rin Tin Tin. Minor breakdowns were quite frequent, but the projectionist was usually quick to splice it and get goin' again. There'd always be a bit of murmerin', but if ever it took a while, then there'd be uproar, slow clappin' and booin' and bangin' on the seat backs, all orchestrated by the bigger boys who I guess were keen to show their bravado. As for the films themselves, well I suppose they were pretty corny by today's standards. Deep down we knew the 'goodie' would always win but we still got really caught up in it along with all the other kids.

When we came out, we'd still be 'buzzin' and, maybe inspired by the film, we'd save the penny bus fare and gallop home on our horses! I'd use my penny to buy a lead soldier from Woolworths. I loved my soldiers. Trouble was, by the time I'd got home sometimes the head was already off – what with all the gallopin' and slappin' my side to get my horse to giddy up.

Not very often, but sometimes, as a special treat, we'd have fish and chips on a Saturday after comin' back from the Pictures. Roy and I would fetch 'em from Gray's Fish and Chip shop down the bottom of Robertson Street. We'd always ask for 4 'two and fours' – two pennorth of chips and a fourpenny fish. You could get 'three and sixes' as well but we always had 'two and fours'. They'd come wrapped in a sheet of grease proof paper and wrapped again in newspaper. Then, with our two packs each, we'd run home before they got cold, me strugglin' to keep up 'cos Roy was bigger.

In those days, London was a lovely, colourful place. Not many cars but loads of buses and trams. It wasn't just the colour, but the noise – and the activity in the streets, especially the trams. They'd rattle along – steel wheels on steel rails. You couldn't really get run over by one – not unless you were deaf or drunk! For me, those clatterin' trams echoed a sense of belongin'. They were part of what made London special. I was, am, proud to be a Londoner, born and bred but, goin' back now, somehow the city, the people, they're not the same.

It's not just the trams that have gone. Today we have supermarkets and all the vast variety and so-called convenience they offer, but if you ask me, somehow, somewhere in the process we've lost somethin', somethin' rich, somethin' precious. I'm not just talkin' about the corner shops like Maceys, I'm talkin' about the street traders. When I was a kid in pre-war London, there were loads of colourful characters walkin' the streets, hawkin' their wares. Now, in truth, we hardly ever bought anythin' from any of 'em, partly because we didn't have the money, but partly because mum liked the Co-op and the divi, so I suppose you could say she was a supermarket fan. Mind you, the Co-op mum knew was nothin' like the supermarkets we see today.

Anyway, I'll just tell you about a few of the characters who used to walk the streets. For starters there was the Muffin Man. He'd come wanderin' down Montefiore Street with a flat cap on his head. I expect it was a special cap because on top of that he'd carry this big wicker tray stacked high with muffins. In some parts of London they'd be ringin' a hand bell to announce their presence, but as I recall, ours just yelled out 'Muffins!' as he strolled along.

Then there was the 'Pine Man'. He'd be pushin' a cart with some sort of disinfectant stuff in it. Hand carts were commonplace in those days and quite a few street traders would use 'em, includin' flower sellers and the like. Others would pedal a three-wheeled tricycle with a box on the front carryin' their wares and a bell on the handlebars, not just the normal bicycle bell, but a distinctive one so folk would know it was them in the street. Walls Ice Cream was sold like that, not so much cornets in those days as ice lollies and ice cream wafers. The knife sharpener had a cart with two different grades of grindin' wheel on it. When he was set up to grind, the pedals would turn one or other of the grindin' wheels dependin' on whether it was knives or shears or whatever he was wantin' to sharpen. I used to like watchin' him, especially when he made sparks fly. I'm not sure if all knife sharpeners did, but ours used to repair cane chairs as well.

Then there were the rag and bone men. Now they were a colourful bunch. Some would push a hand cart and others had a horse and cart which would come clip-cloppin' up the street. I got into trouble once for tradin' with them – big trouble! They had these goldfish and when you're four a goldfish is a big temptation. Mum had made these giant pom-poms for us and, lovely as they were, I swapped 'em for a goldfish. When mum got home, she wasn't best pleased. I think she'd spent a long time makin' 'em and she wanted 'em back, so she took off and scoured the streets, but I think it must have been in vain because I never remember seein' 'em again. I got to keep my goldfish. The up-side was dad had this big empty glass sweet jar which made a lovely home for my fish and Roy and I went up to Clapham Common to get pond weed to decorate it. I think even mum had to admit it looked nice. She never did stay mad for long, didn't mum. Not with us kids anyway. It just wasn't her way.

My favourite street trader, apart from Jim our milkman who I'll tell you about in a bit, was the Cockle & Mussel Man. On a Sunday afternoon, dad would either pack Roy and me off on our walk to Chelsea Bridge or get us both to sit outside waitin' for the Cockle & Mussel Man. It didn't take both of us, but he'd insist we both went out early, just in case. He'd say him and mum were goin' for a bit of a lie down. I didn't realise at the time, but now I see he wanted us out of the way so he could have a bit of 'quality time' with mum. Anyway, the Cockle & Mussel Man used to walk around the streets shoutin' out his wares, a bit like Molly Malone. He'd be pullin' a cart which was a smaller version of a horse and cart with him in place of the horse. A lot of street traders used what I call 'London Carts' in those days. They might be painted – decorated differently, but the one's I remember were all painted green and all the same basic design – smaller and narrower than a normal cart and made to fit a person pullin' it and they always had wooden rails around the sides and back to stop stuff fallin' off. Whether it was just his Sunday outfit I don't know, but he was always smartly dressed was our Cockle & Mussel Man, in a blue suit and a bowler hat. Come rain or shine, he always wore that hat. I hope you can picture him nearly as clearly as I can with his blue suit and bowler hat and all his wares in big enamel bowls covered by muslin cloths.

We'd have to sit and wait for him and make sure he stopped outside, but we'd have to fetch mum out to do the actual buyin'. I think she thought he might palm two kids off with rubbish or short measures and she wasn't havin' that. She'd usually get a selection, I think mainly dependin' on what dad wanted. Shrimps she'd buy by the pint. They were ready cooked, but still had their heads on. I always used to think there wasn't much left by the time I'd pulled the head off. There were winkles and we'd use a needle to get them out, same as we would with cockles, and sometimes we'd have whelks, which were already out of their shells when you bought 'em. I didn't care for them much. I thought they were tough and I couldn't chew 'em but you have to bear in mind, at the time I'm talkin' about I was only 4 or 5, which is why I'd be forever askin' Roy if it was winkle day or not 'cos half the time, I couldn't remember which Sunday it was. We'd have them every other week.

I have to say we ate well in those days. I don't think we ever had much money, but mum loved her food and makin' sure we were well fed was always a priority for her. On Sundays we would usually have a roast dinner, which dad would do, although on the odd occasion he'd do a stew instead, maybe when we were a bit short, I'm not sure. Tea would be down to mum and she'd always have the table set for High Tea on a Sunday and the best cups and saucers would come out. If it was a shellfish Sunday – 'winkle day' to me, mum would set the table out as usual except each place settin' would have a long pin or needle threaded into the cloth beside each plate and mum would have bought a pint of this and a half pint of that accordin' to what dad fancied or maybe just what we could afford. We always ate 'em cold with bread and butter and we'd put our own vinegar on. If the man had any celery left by the time he got to us, mum would buy a stick of that as well. I remember Roy used to try and play a joke sometimes. After he'd eaten the winkles he'd put the little 'head' back in and sneak the shell back in the bowl for mum, dad or me to get, but dad didn't always see the funny side. Thinkin' about it now, you don't even see winkles for sale these days. I suppose all the street sellers have gone and even the wet fish shops. Perhaps you can still get 'em at the seaside, but I think that's about it. Anyway, after we'd eaten all the winkles or whatever, we'd fill up on more bread, butter and jam and cakes if we'd got any. Havin' eaten all that Sunday Dinner (back then we didn't call it 'lunch'), I don't know where we used to put it all. Mum, especially, would never waste anythin'. I guess that's why as time went on, active as she was, she was the only one of us to put on weight. Mind you, if you could see me now you'd think as time went on I took after her, and you'd be right.

The goldfish incident apart, I've probably given the impression we were well behaved and generally we were – but we weren't angels – we did get up to mischief sometimes. One thing we liked to do was to go into Arding and Hobbs (now Debenhams). It was a department store that sold everythin' – a lovely buildin' with a clock tower on it. Anyway, it had a lift to all departments and we'd keep usin' it – just for the ride until the lift attendant twigged and told us to clear off. I can picture that lift attendant now. He had a gammy leg. He used to stand on one leg and rest his gammy leg on a stool. (Incidentally, I went back there some 30 years later and believe it or not that man was still there. He looked exactly the same. He hadn't changed a bit. He didn't look a day older).

In those days there was a posh Garden Restaurant on the top floor – but as kids on our own, we couldn't go in there. Our favourite place was the basement, where they had a big toy department. The displays at Christmas were just magical. We were allowed in but then the staff would watch us like hawks. They didn't really need to 'cos by today's standards we were cherubs. Mind you, they knew how to handle kids in those days – put one foot out of line and you'd get a clip round the ear.

My road to hell has always been paved with good intentions and once when mum and dad were both out at work I thought I'd do them a good turn and clean the range. I think I thought if I did a good job they'd give me money to go to the pictures. Trouble was I thought I could use a bucket of water and a scrubbin' brush – I didn't realise you had to use black lead. Before long it was glowin' but not quite like I'd hoped. It was glowin' red with rust! And the more I rubbed at it, the worse it got. When mum got back, havin' got over the shock, I think she was pleased with me for tryin', but as she set to with the black lead, I was told never to do it again. Some kids would have been belted for that but I can honestly say our parents never laid a finger on Roy or me – not once. Mind you, we knew we had to behave and we never dreamt of answerin' back – not like the kids of today. Havin' set to with the black lead, mum soon had it glowin' shiny black like I'd intended. Talkin' of intentions, I think I'd thought of askin' for some money for the cinema for my 'good deed' but seein' how it had turned out, I just kept stum. Well, at least you 'live and learn' don't you. As in life, I never made the same mistake twice.

As kids, we were never allowed to have friends in the house to play. They only ever got as far as the front door and that was it. In Montefiore Street I had a particular friend who used to come to call. His name was Jonny Gray. I think he was an only child. We particularly liked to play with my fort and toy soldiers. I used to bring it out onto the front path along with my lead soldiers. I used to keep addin' to my soldier collection with a new penny soldier that I'd buy on a Saturday after the pictures. Sometimes the heads would fall off and we'd put bits of matchstick in the neck to try to keep the broken head on. Pre-war, I can remember havin' loads of soldiers to play with on our doorstep. We had a bit of garden at the front. A mass of flowers it was. People used to stop to admire 'em. Dad was very proud of his flowers and so Jonny and I had to be very careful not to damage any of 'em.

I never remember Jonny comin' up the pictures with us on a Saturday mornin', but he would always be sittin' on our wall waitin' for me when I got back – to see my new soldier. Then I'd get my fort and soldiers out and we'd play. Johnny lived at the top of the street, but I never went to his house – he always came down to play with me and if I was called in for a meal or for any reason, he'd often sit out on the pillar between the railin's waitin' for me. Sadly, unlike me, Jonny wasn't born to survive. You'll understand later why I'm tellin' you this. There's a picture with Jonny in the background, sittin' on our wall at the end of Chapter Two.

I had another friend called Philip. He lived up the top end of Montefiore Street. He had a pile of sand in his back yard so sometimes I'd go and play with him in that. His mum was Polish but I never saw his father. I don't think he lived there because I remember hearin' it said that there wasn't a man in the house. I used to learn a lot from listenin' to adults' conversations.

I've said I was a sickly kid – prone to catchin' anythin' that was goin' round, and family used to joke that I had more German Measles than the Germans! So it was that just before Easter 1939 I was in bed with German Measles. I remember it was Easter 'cos eventually I was carted off to hospital with an Easter Egg in my lap – that I wasn't allowed to eat! I was 5. Anyway, Grandad Wattley was ill and dad decided it was time to build bridges. They hadn't seen one another since 1930. If you remember dad had been more or less banished from Sidmouth in disgrace on account of gettin' mum pregnant out of wedlock. Grandad had never seen his grandchildren and the plan was to take Roy and me down to see him. Trouble was I caught the measles, but it was touch and go with grandad so dad decided to dash down from London without me. Dad and Roy were to go from Paddington, but somehow they missed the train. I don't know where dad got the money from, but they took a taxi to Waterloo and went from there instead. In those days takin' a taxi was unheard of in our family. I don't know what happened in Sidmouth, but at some point dad must have taken Roy to the beach 'cos he came back with a bunch of shells for me. I hadn't been carted off to hospital yet – I was still in our 'put-you- up' bed in the parlour at home. Grandad soldiered on, but died the followin' year in 1940. I never did get to see him or grandma, but there is a picture of 'em at the end of this first chapter.

I never got to see mum's parents either come to that. Her mum had died young and apparently grandpa was a miner who worked down the pits near Wrexham. I believe he died quite young too. He couldn't have had a very good education because I was told he couldn't read or write and signed his name with an X. Sadly, I don't even have a picture of him or grandma.

Oh – just in case you were wonderin' – if you were taken to hospital with measles in those days, then they kept you in a darkened room on your own for about a week. Not much fun when you're only 5.

Now that we lived in a ground floor flat, there was no more carryin' milk bottles up the stairs, but no matter, for me, the milk delivery by United Dairies was now a much more excitin' event. Our milkman was Jim, who had a horse and cart and was always rather distinctive and really rather smart in his uniform. A white shirt, dark trousers and a jacket, a blue and white stripy apron and a peak cap. He was a lovely man – always whistlin', always jolly. Best of all, Jim would let us kids take it in turns to ride on his cart. As soon as his cart entered our street we'd be there. When it was my turn, because I was so small, he'd lift me up onto his seat. I wasn't allowed to touch the reins, but perched up there I felt on top of the world and the horse would move on whenever Jim gave a special whistle for him to do so. Jim was a real character – as well as whistlin', on pay day he used to yodel. I guess it was his way of tellin' the women to get their purses out. On other days he just put the bottles on the doorstep. When he'd finished his round Jim used to fairly fly back down our street. I can still hear those crates of empties chinkin' and clatterin' in his wake. I know it's silly, but I loved those rides and as I'm recountin' this, I wish I could turn the clock back and be little Jack ridin' high again, just one more time.

Later that year, when war was about to break out, Roy and I were told we would have to go away for a while because London might not be a safe place for children. It wasn't the goin' away from mum and dad that upset me – it was the fact that it was my turn to ride on Jim's cart! No amount of protestin' on my part made any difference – I was goin' and that was that.

Olga with me on her knee and 'big' brother Roy standin' beside her. Taken at Thornton Heath in 1934, this must have been soon after Roy and I were first fostered out.

Me with mum on a visit to Auntie Annie and Uncle Jack's house, 34 Montefiore Street, London SW8. I was fostered out at this stage and mum and dad were livin' in rooms above a derelict printers in Tyneham Road.

Me on a visit to Auntie Annie's at 34 Montefiore Street. Note the lovely iron railin's, later all ripped out for the war effort.

One of my earliest recollections – me on my tricycle in Sandfield Road where 'Aunt' Raithby lived. Taken in 1935 when I was maybe 18 or 20 months old. As you can see, little boys were often dressed more or less the same as little girls in those days and with my long curly blonde hair, I could just as well have been a girl! At that stage, I couldn't really manage the pedals, so I remember I used to just scoot along.

Me aged about 2 – 2 ½ years, possibly on a trip to Eastbourne. I don't recognize the settin', but it's the sort of outfit I'd wear to the seaside includin' the knitted shorts, which mum would have made for me.

Portrait photos of Grandad and Grandma Wattley.

Outside Grandma and Grandad's house in Peasland Road, Sidmouth. Grandad on the left, Grandma seated with Auntie Annie behind her and Uncle Dick in his submariner's uniform. Remember Uncle Dick because he'll feature later.

CHAPTER 2

Life As An Evacuee

And so it was that on 1ˢᵗ September 1939, my brother Roy and I were packed off to the country. We thought it would be for a couple of weeks – in the end it was 5 years! We were very young – but like many London kids in the '30s, we were already very streetwise for our age.

Nevertheless, we'd do a lot more 'growin' up' in those 5 years and we'd learn a lot of new skills in an environment which was completely alien to us. Lookin, back, they were certainly character-buildin' years.

I was 5 and quite small for my age with a mass of blonde curly hair like a blonde gollywog! I should have been a girl really – but grown ups thought I was cute and I dare say I made the most of that. Our Roy was 8, much bigger and with straight dark hair – at least he looked like a boy.

I don't remember anyone tellin' us why we were bein' evacuated or where to or for how long, but I suppose mum must have said somethin'. Maybe she just told our Roy – because he was bigger and she didn't want to frighten me. I do remember evacuation day though. Mum made sure we were dressed smartly in our best school uniform – white shirt, school tie, blazer with a hanky in the breast pocket, grey shorts, held up with an 'S' belt in school colours, long grey socks and sandals and she insisted on checkin' us over one last time before usherin' us out of the front door and takin' us hand in hand off up the road. Dad had written our names on the labels we'd been issued and they were already tied to our lapels. We didn't have far to walk because all the kids from our area were 'mustered' in the playground of Tennyson Street School. It was only at the end of the street, but it was the first time I'd been in the 'big school' playground. When war broke out we were both pupils at Heathbrook School. I remember there were lots of tears that mornin', but not from Roy or me. At that stage I think we thought of it as a bit of an adventure and I guess havin' been fostered out from a young age, bein' separated from mum and dad didn't seem like such a big deal to us. After all, we were only goin' for a few weeks, or so we thought.

Havin' said our goodbyes, we were assembled in the school hall and lined up to be examined in turn by 'Nitty Nora' as us kids called her. She was lookin' for head lice, which were quite rife in those days. Those with lice were sent to one side for special treatment. Fortunately she didn't find any on Roy or me – in fact I was lucky and I never caught them.

From the school it was only about a 10-minute walk down to Battersea Park Railway Station, but parents weren't allowed to go. You can imagine the long snakin' lines of kids marchin' two by two a bit like animals into the ark! Although I remember our Roy sayin', "Don't worry Willie – I'll look after you", none of us kids had got a clue that we wouldn't be seein' our parents again for a very long time.

Once at the station we were assembled together in groups waitin' for one of the Special Evacuee Trains to come for us. Lots had been laid on. It seemed like the whole of London was bein' evacuated that day. I didn't really know what an 'evacuee' was, but I knew I was one. At least we had a good day for it 'cos it was a beautiful, bright, sunny day. Funny how everythin' always seems better when the sun is shinin'.

You may be surprised to learn that it was an electric train – the Brighton line operated by Southern Electric. Most of Britain didn't get electric trains 'till much, much later. The carriages had side corridors with compartments off with space for about 10 kids in each sittin' opposite one another in rows of 5. Although I was one of the youngest kids on the train, compared to many I was a seasoned traveller because I'd been on a train before – to the seaside at Eastbourne with Olga and Gracie. What's more, I'd seen cows in fields before, but to many of the kids this was a whole new world so you can imagine the atmosphere of excitement and apprehension which ran through the train. For some of the kids it all became a bit too much and there were more than a few tears. I think that's why Miss Jones came and sat in our carriage for the latter part of the journey. Prior to that we'd just been kids on our own as there weren't enough teachers for every compartment. This was my first meetin' with her and I remember thinkin' she was a bit strange and a rather ugly woman. Much later, when I moved up to the juniors, she was to teach me and I came to like and rather admire her, which just goes to show you should never judge a book by its cover. For now she just seemed a bit strange – not least because she kept her hat on. Mind you, I never ever saw her without that hat –she wore the same one all the time she was teachin'. She never took it off, not even in class.

*

Bein' a special train, we went straight through to Haywards Heath without stoppin' at Clapham Junction, Streatham, East Croydon, Purley, Gatwick, Three Bridges or Balcombe. I hope you're impressed that I know all the stations! In truth, I didn't know 'em then, but I've ridden that line a fair few times since. I guess the journey took about 45 minutes. Once off the train, we were marched across the road and assembled on the forecourt of Griffins Garage. There were quite a lot of tables set out and some sort of documentation was goin' on. Each child was given a paper carrier bag containin' emergency rations. It had paper handles which weren't very strong and we were warned to be careful. We thought it was for us, but it wasn't. We were to hand it over to the lady at our billet to help keep us in the first few days. Evacuee? Billet? – that was another new concept for us to get acquainted with. Apart from this stuff in a paper bag which we weren't allowed to touch, I don't remember bein' given anythin' to eat or drink. I just remember havin' to stand around on the forecourt waitin'. We didn't know what we were waitin' for, but eventually a number of green and cream South Down buses arrived – there were 4 or 5 – I can't be sure. Anyway, Roy and I were put on the last one to leave. Just our luck, and as it turned out, a portent of things to come.

The journey to our destination in Ardingly was about 5 miles and took about 15 minutes. We pulled up on the forecourt of the village hall – Hapstead Hall – except there wasn't enough room for all the coaches so ours was stickin' out a bit. I remember pokin' my head out of the window to get a better look at the clock tower and a voice from the front said clearly and firmly, "Would that little boy with the curly hair please put his head back inside the window." He was nice about it really – but I remember thinkin', "We've only just got here and I'm in trouble already."

All the kids from all the buses were filed into the village hall and told to sit cross-legged on the floor. It was now around 1pm. We each had our little case or bag of belongin's and our paper bag of 'emergency rations' which we weren't allowed to eat! Talkin' of eatin' – I remember we were given a drink of milk but I don't recall gettin' anythin' to eat. Soon people came to choose children and take them away to their various 'billets'. Not very nice really, a bit like choosin' slaves, except we weren't slaves, we were 'evacuees' waitin' to be 'billetted'.

It was a beautiful, warm sunny day. We could see the sun was blazin' and we kids didn't want to be stuck inside. Some of us got restless, not least 'cos after sittin' cross-legged for an hour or more, the buckle on your sandals starts to dig in. But we got no sympathy – just told to stop fidgetin' and sit still. As time went on, we'd have gone with anybody just to be allowed to get up off that floor – not that we were the ones doin' the choosin'. If you've ever been the last ones to be picked for a team at school because no-one really wants you, then you'll have some idea of how Roy and I felt because in the end there was just the two of us sittin' cross-legged on that floor. I think even the Billetin' Officers were gettin' fed up with the waitin'.

Eventually a Mrs Honeybun came, but there was rather a commotion because she'd come for two girls. She had two daughters of her own and felt girls would fit in better. But there were no girls left – only Roy and me – a rather girly-lookin' boy. In the end she was persuaded to take us but just for the weekend and the billetin' officers would sort out alternative accommodation for us on Monday. It was now almost 4pm and Roy and I had been sittin' cross-legged on that floor with our sandal buckles diggin' in for nearly 3 hours.

Thinkin' back now – I don't know why Roy and I kept bein' passed over. I don't think it's because they didn't like the look of us 'cos, as I've said, mum had made sure we were well turned out in our best school attire, blue blazers with a hanky in the breast pocket, grey shorts and sandals. Maybe it was because I was only 5 and little for my age and Roy was 8 and big for his. Maybe they thought we'd be a difficult combination to deal with. I just know how we felt bein' left 'till last and, even at 5, it wasn't a very nice feelin'.

It looked like our first billet was goin' to be a very short affair, but I think we'd have gone anywhere with anybody just to be allowed to get up off that floor. Although not exactly pleased to have us, or over-welcomin', Mrs Honeybun was kind enough to take the pair of us and, together with her two daughters, June and Hazel, we trotted off down through Ardingly Village to their house. That was our first 'nice surprise'. I remember it was the end one of a row. I thought it was a Council house, but later discovered it belonged to the Church. It was brick built – probably in the 1920s – and had a bathroom downstairs off the scullery and a separate inside toilet beside the front door. To us that was luxury indeed. We'd never had a bathroom or an inside toilet.

We were shown to our bedroom and put our cases on our beds. I think it was all a bit strange for Mrs Honeybun because she wasn't used to havin' boys in her house. It was still a beautiful, warm, sunny day and rather than gettin' us to unpack our few belongin's, Mrs Honeybun suggested the girls take Roy and 'little Jack' out to play in the cornfield. I guess Mrs Honeybun decided to call me 'Little Jack' because I was so small and maybe she was beginnin' to warm to me and, as I say, with my mop of curly hair, I did look a bit like a girl. From then on, everyone in Ardingly was to call me Little Jack – except Roy of course, who continued to call me Willie. I never did know why. Whilst we were playin' in the cornfield, a motorbike and side car drove up towards the house and June said, "Here's dad – come and meet my dad." Later I learnt his name was Cyril and that he worked for a local builder before bein' called up, but that came later. Anyway, all four of us ran over and, perhaps seein' the surprise on her dad's face, June said, "We've had to have 2 boys because there weren't any girls left." He didn't seem bothered – he just smiled at us. I thought he was a nice man and that opinion never changed. Both he and Mrs Honeybun must have decided boys weren't so bad after all 'cos when Monday came round, rather than parcel us off to be re-billetted, they decided we could stay. And that cornfield, it was to become our favourite playground, easy to reach through a gap in the wire fence at the bottom of the garden. We'd often play in 'our' cornfield. It wasn't like today. Back then they'd cut the corn and bind it into sheafs to dry in the sun. Best of all, they'd stack the sheafs in groups just like a whole lot of tents and we'd play in them. We were in our own little world of innocent dreams and fantasies and at such times the war was a million miles away. Unless of course we were playin' war games and then it was right there, in our field.

Our teachers had travelled down with us from London and were also billeted in the village. All the children had been evacuated – infants, juniors and 'big boys' and girls. In those days you left school at 14. You were considered to be a man – or woman – then, so as soon as you reached 14, you were sent back to London to get a job – never mind the bombs!

I didn't know it then, but I know now that the Government suggested parents shouldn't come to see evacuees too soon in case we got homesick. We should be 'allowed to settle in' first. Havin' lived through it, I can't say that I agree with that strategy, but anyway it was 2 months before mum came down to see us. Generally, it seems, parents weren't allowed to visit their children's billets – they had to meet them elsewhere. Mrs Honeybun was different and in my experience the only billet to welcome mum to her home. I can remember the day as if it was yesterday. It was a rainy day, but that didn't dampen our spirits. Our mum was comin' to see us. Towards the end of her visit, I remember, mum played darts with Cyril and Mrs Honeybun. You see it was too wet outside for us to go anywhere. All the while I kept lookin' at the clock because I'd been told mum would have to catch the 7.15 bus to Haywards Heath so she could catch the London train. I was 6 now and more worldly-wise than most 6 year olds, but I was still a bit tearful when it came time for mum to go. Mr & Mrs Honeybun were kind though and, truth be told, after mum had gone, I soon came round.

By tellin' you about mum's first visit, I'm gettin' ahead of myself. I need to take you back to the early days or you'll not get a proper picture of what it was really like and what went on.

I'd better start by sayin' somethin' about the weather. Well, I am English, so what else would you expect? We'd arrived in Ardingly in late summer – early September to be precise. The weather was lovely – warm and sunny and the days were long. Mind you, as I recall, the nights were startin' to get chilly. Later the days became even longer because they introduced this 'double summer time' durin' the war, so it didn't get dark until really late – perhaps as late as 11pm. That's after they'd decided to put the clocks forward 2 hours instead of one. I'm not really sure when – but I was only 5 goin' on 6 and I wasn't that much into time. I just know they did it.

We'd arrived on a Friday – I think – but anyway, after the weekend, on Monday mornin' it was school as usual – except of course it wasn't our usual school. We all had to go up to the Church School or rather we evacuees went to the Village Hall in the mornin's and to the school in the afternoons when we would swap over with the local village children. To start with – indeed for much of the time, it was very much a case of us and them with village children. As evacuees we had to watch our backs and go around in groups.

The local paper was the Mid Sussex Times and, whilst to be honest I don't recall readin' the article at the time, I have a vague recollection of it bein' talked about, and now I see the paper's archives reveal a degree of alarm at the mass influx of evacuees into the County. For example, in an article dated 5th September 1939, it was stated that, "There are over 250,000 evacuees in Sussex and the population of Mid Sussex nearly doubled in just 3 days by receivin' over 10,000 evacuees. In the first three days, 3,283 detrained at Haywards Heath (Roy and I would have been among those) and were put into the garages of Griffins and Caffyns with their haversacks, bags and gas masks." (They got that last bit wrong because we weren't given our gas masks until after arrivin' in Ardingly, but no matter.)

And on 19th September 1939 a further article included the followin' extract:

"Apart from about 80 mothers and children (some mothers with very young children were evacuated as well), there are, at Ardingly, 121 scholars of Heathbrook LCC School, Wandsworth (includin' Roy and me). Arrangements have been made for these children to share the village C of E School with the village children. Local children will use the school in the mornings and the evacuees will use it in the afternoons." We weren't to be integrated – we were kept separate, segregated from the start. Little wonder we never got on all that well with most of the local kids. In fact, early on, it wasn't just the local kids we weren't all that popular with. I was only a young kid but even

I could sense a feelin' in the village that us evacuees weren't really liked. Thinkin' about it now, perhaps it was only to be expected, given the number of us and the effect we must have had on previously quiet village life. Back then though, if anythin' went wrong it was those Londoners who were to blame.

Mr Kitchener was our headmaster. A stickler for discipline he was and so it wasn't long before our mornin' assembly in the Village Hall would start with a public canin' session for some alleged misdemeanor or other in the village. It was mostly the 'big boys' who copped for it – a stroke on each hand with the cane and one on the backside. I think he thought it would be a deterrent to them and to the rest of us but I don't think it had the desired effect. It seemed like it became a regular, almost daily event.

Another abidin' memory of my early school days in Ardingly is a game we used to play in the urinals. Maybe ladies should skip this bit. They were basic – well very basic and rather smelly, but they served a purpose and the black painted walls we had to wee against were perfect for our game of higher and higher. Bein' small I didn't used to win much, but at least I had a good flow in those days!

It didn't matter how cold it was, come play time we were sent outside. Luckily there was a chimney in the playground and on very cold days we'd all be huddled round it for warmth.

In the beginnin' they didn't have school dinners organised for us, so we'd come 'home' at lunchtime. We'd get a cooked meal in the evenin', but we always had the same thing at lunchtime – bread and home-made apricot jam. Now, it seems a funny thing to have for lunch, especially every day, but then again, it was war time. What was funnier still about it was the sound effects. Mrs Honeybun used to sit next to me. She must have had false teeth because as she was munchin' away on her sandwiches, her teeth would be goin' click, click, click. Luckily, I knew better than to say anythin' or to stare, but it was amusin'. She wasn't an old person, but lots of people had false teeth quite young in those days and I guess hers didn't fit that well.

As I've already told you, the Honeybuns had two daughters. Hazel was about 8 and Jane about 10 or 12. Girls grow up faster than boys at that age and I suppose bein' only 5, I was a bit immature by comparison. Roy, bein' older, probably fitted in a bit better. Mind you, for all children in those days, it was a case of bein' seen but not heard, in the house at any rate. Whilst I learnt a lot by sittin' still and keepin' quiet, if the Honeybuns wanted to talk family business, we'd be asked to go outside and play.

There was a close at the side of the Honeybuns. Listenin' to the grown-ups, which as I say, I did a lot, it wasn't up to much and so everyone said the Germans must have built it. If anythin' was bad, it usually got attributed to the Germans. It was a concrete road runnin' up beside the cornfield – our cornfield you might say – and on the other side were some council houses. Right at the top, where apparently the old brick makin' works used to be years before, there were some big ponds where they'd extracted the clay. As well as that, I think there must have been some saw mills down there at one time. At any rate, when I arrived there were these huge piles of saw dust in the valley.

Goin' back now as John and I did in 2015, the place is barely recognisable. For a start, all the ponds have been drained and filled and the whole of our beloved cornfield where we used to have such fun and games is now all housin'. Of course things change, but in my experience, not always for the better.

We'd often play in the cornfield, especially if, like when we arrived, the corn was stacked – perfect for dens. It didn't do a lot for my asthma, but I wasn't goin' to let that stop me joinin' in the fun. We'd get over where the piles of saw dust were. They were strange, all brown and sort of smoulderin' as if they were on fire. Thinkin' back, I'm surprised we didn't poke about in 'em to see, but I don't remember any of us actually doin' that. They were funny to walk on though – all spongy.

Further up, beyond the piles of saw dust, there was a little wood. Now I'm gallopin' on a bit here, but a little memory has just popped into my head and if I don't tell you now, I might forget. Somebody had given me a packet of seeds, mainly marigolds, and I decided to go and plant them there in the wood to make a little garden. Maybe I was takin' after dad in that respect. This was when I was about 7, so a couple of years on from when I'd first arrived. I couldn't have done too bad a job because they bloomed and although I used to go and look at 'em, I never did tell anybody about my 'secret garden'. When I went, it wasn't just my flowers I used to see. When I was sittin' quiet, I'd often see red squirrels runnin' about and climbin' the trees.

I expect like pretty much everywhere else, they've all been ousted by the greys now, more's the pity. At least I have my memories and can say I saw and enjoyed 'em durin' my time in Ardingly.

Now, back to the early days with the Honeybuns. On school days, Roy and I would walk up the close and through the barbed wire fence as a short cut up to school. That way we could avoid havin' to walk all up through the village. Good idea you might think, but I have a lastin' reminder of that particular short cut. Once, when I was gettin' through in a bit of a hurry, I snagged my knee on it. I made it worse because as I dropped through the fence, I landed on my knee and a stone went in the cut. It didn't half hurt, but I think I was quite a plucky kid – well you had to be, didn't you? I was only 5, or possibly just 6, but it's not like I had a mum to run home to, so I just sat and picked it out with my penknife. That might shock you – havin' a penknife that is – but in those days all the boys took penknives in their pockets to school. The teachers knew. We used to sharpen our pencils with 'em. The thing is, we never thought of 'em as weapons, not like they would today.

As for my knee, it bled like hell for a while, but I was a tough little bugger. I didn't tell anybody. Well, you just didn't, you just put up with it. The only time you told anybody was if you got blood all over your clothes. Then you had to. We thought of ourselves as 'big boys' and big boys don't go cryin' a lot, now do they? If either Roy or I had told, the grown-ups would have most likely put a stop to us goin' through the fence and that would have been the end of our short cut. Believe it or not, I've still got that scar on my knee as a reminder – along with the scar on my leg where they took the vein for my by-pass, but that was later, much, much later.

I made a sort of tin shed to play in at the top of the close near the piles of saw dust. I say I did, but me and this other kid made it together. I can't remember his name, but I think he was a local kid, which was unusual 'cos we didn't generally mix much with the locals. I'm sayin' I can't remember his name, but come to think of it, I reckon it was Andy, Andy Handyside. In any event, I remember he was a bossy type, fond of tryin' to order me about. Then again, he was probably a bit older than me, like practically every kid I knew in Ardingly. Whatever, I was proud of our shelter made of bits of corrugated tin.

One time when the siren went, instead of goin' home like we were supposed to, we went in our makeshift shelter. I should explain that although there were no air raid shelters in the village, from time to time a siren did go off. It was at the Police Station and I think it was triggered by one at Haywards Heath. When the siren went you were supposed to go indoors and sit under the kitchen table! I suppose that might have given some protection from fallin' debris, but not much good if your house happened to get a direct hit. Anyway, this particular day we were feelin' rather brave, rather pleased with ourselves, until we heard this rat tat tat and this kid got nervy and so did I. He said they were firin' bullets. They must know we're here, and with that I lost my bottle altogether and ran for it! Of course they didn't know we were there and nobody was firin' at us, but sometimes when you're kids your imagination runs away with you. I know mine did. Thinkin' about it now, it was most likely that other kid rat tat tattin' on the tin with his fingers and me not noticin'. If it was, he never did let on.

Ardingly wasn't really a target, except maybe the college, but it was on Gerry's flight path up to London, so there was always a chance of a stray bomb or that the odd plane or two out of the hundreds flyin' over would decide to ditch the odd bomb or two they hadn't dropped on London before headin' back. Whilst accordin' to what I heard the grown-ups sayin', the college was thought to be a potential target, it never did get hit, although one or two stray bombs did go in the lake.

Durin' the war, Ardingly had a railway station. It was just beyond the College – about a 1 ½ mile walk from the heart of the village. It was a branch line from Haywards Heath which came over a beautiful big viaduct. Sadly it's gone now – like so many lovely branch lines it suffered under Beechin's axe. Back in the day though, along with the buses, it was a village lifeline. The coalyard was there too – I guess because coal would come in by train.

Dad only ever visited us once in Ardingly. I remember he came by train. Just after Christmas – January 1940 it was. I remember it vividly because there was snow and ice about and there was never any grittin' or anythin'. Some folk threw ashes down on garden paths, but that was it. Anyway, goin' back to the station I remember dad put socks over his boots for grip. I can see him doin' it now. Luckily, Roy and I were still with the Honeybuns at that time, so dad got invited in. In my experience they were the only ones who ever invited evacuees' relatives into their homes. At any rate, none of my other billets ever did.

Readin' about it now, it seems that nothin' much happened for the first few months of the war – in England that is. I can remember grown-ups talkin' about the phoney war, but bein' only five, I didn't know what they meant. I do now, but back then I didn't think or perhaps dare to ask. You see, I was amongst strangers and they might not have appreciated me eavesdroppin'. I'm sayin' 'strangers', but in truth I'd quickly got used to bein' with the Honeybuns. Even so, they weren't family and we never got close like we'd done with Aunt Raithby. It was still very much a time when kids were expected to be 'seen and not heard' when in adult company and really that included the Honeybuns. Don't get me wrong though, we were gettin' on fine with the Honeybuns until the war intervened. Roy and I had been billeted with them for about 7 or 8 months when, about the middle of 1940, Mr Honeybun was called up to the Air Force. His first postin' was at Eastbourne so the decision was taken for the whole family to move down there. They also took Mrs Honeybun's sister's daughter with them. I'm not sure why, but they did. Her sister lived just across the road and, as it turned out, that was to be my next billet. About 6pm one evenin' I was taken across with my little case of belongin's. They couldn't take both of us, so Roy and I were split up and he went to stay with Ken Holmes, a local builder. I was 6 and our Roy was 9.

My new billet was with Mr & Mrs Tummins, although everyone knew them as the "Tummies". When I arrived on that first night at about 6pm, Joan, their daughter aged about 8, was havin' a bath and Mrs T asked if I'd like to get undressed and get in the bath with her. I'd never been in the bath with a girl before and I wasn't brave enough. I don't know what excuse I made, but I didn't do it. The next day Joan went off to Eastbourne with the Honeybuns, leavin' me the only child in the house. They did have another lodger though, a teacher, a rather plain, sad sort of woman who wore glasses. However, she talked to me much more than Mrs T, who never showed me any sort of affection. Thinkin' about it now and tryin' to understand it, she was probably missin' her only daughter and perhaps resentin' havin' to have this strange boy in the house instead. I'm not sure I ever knew the teacher's name, but at any rate I can't remember it. What I do recall though is that quite often she'd sit and talk to me beside the fire in the evenin's - which made the days go better.

As I say, our Roy was with the Holmes and sometimes I'd go round there – not so much to see Roy but to play with Adrian Holmes, who was more my age. Their house had sandstone pillars at the gate. They had deep grooves 'cos all the kids in the village sharpened their penknives on them. We all carried penknives in those days. It wasn't a weapon – it was a tool. Listenin' to adults' conversations, I learnt that Mr Holmes was doin' a job for the government at the time, tryin' to change the course of the River Ouse. Apparently the idea was to try to create a barrier in the event that the Germans invaded the South of England. From what the adults said, it was clear that durin' the war, everybody hated the Germans, even the way they looked. I remember thinkin' their helmets were much better than ours because they covered their ears much better but I didn't let on. I was cute enough to know that it probably wouldn't go down very well.

Somethin' in the garden of the house next to Ken Holmes place in Station Road used to fascinate me and goin' back in 2015 I see it's still there so I think I'll tell you about it - a model of Windsor Castle. It's close to the gate and I think made of painted concrete but I never have touched it to be sure. Whatever it's made of, it's very well modelled and sturdy enough to have stood the test of time - the castle that is but not the soldiers. When I was a boy, there were painted lead soldiers all over it, standin' guard. You know the sort, red tunics and black busby hats. I used to look at it most days on my way to school. I guess that house will have changed hands a few times over the years but, regardless, these days, lead soldiers would more than likely 'walk' before too long. One of the London teachers was billeted at that house. She never taught me and even if I ever knew her name, I can't remember it, but no matter. The thing I do remember about her was she used to drive past us in her car on her way to school but, whatever the weather, never offer to give us a lift. She did stop one day though, to give us a lecture on the dangers of chewin' spearmint! She reckoned it was made of horse manure and we should never buy it or chew it. O' course we took not a blind bit of notice. The thing was we weren't allowed to chew gum in class so we'd often as not 'store it' under the desk lid and some of 'em would get left and cause a mess and so from time to time, the teachers would have purges to discourage us.

Thinkin' about it now, it might have been better if I'd been billeted with the Holmes instead. As it was, every chance I got, I'd pop round there to play with Adrian. He had a lot of dinky toys and, his dad bein' a builder, he always had sand in the garden. We used to make imaginary mountains for the toys to go over. Mrs Holmes would feed their dog in the mornin' at around 11am. Havin' learnt the routine, I used to say to Adrian, "Must be nearly time to feed the dog." His mum would come out with a bowl of Spratts dog biscuits for Prince, but as soon as she'd gone in, Adrian and I would pinch all the black ones for ourselves! Not sure what was in 'em, but they never did us any harm.

We very seldom got any real biscuits durin' the war but, I don't want you to get the wrong impression, we didn't eat dog biscuits because we were starvin'. There was rationin' of course, but as kids I don't think we really felt the impact of rationin' except when it started applyin' to sweets. Well, we were kids and so sweets were important to us. Trouble was, once they were all on ration, even if you had money, you couldn't just go and buy what you felt like. I used to get round that 'cos I liked Victory V's and bein' cough lozenges, they weren't on ration. They weren't in packets, they were kept loose in jars and sold by weight. They'd be alongside the boiled sweets – pear drops and the like.

Smokin' was a 'grown-up' thing to do. Practically everybody's parents smoked, so sweet cigarettes were always popular with us kids – when we could get 'em. Then there'd be wine gums, and black jacks, Mars Bars and Milky Ways, although I seem to remember they were in white wrappers durin' the war. Then there was Rowntrees Chocolate Crisp – that got re-branded as Kit-Kat and re-packaged in the red wrappers you still see today. Amazin' when you think about it how well some sweets have stood the test of time. Bizarrely, it wasn't until post war that milk shortages forced Rowntrees to stop makin' Kit – Kats coated in milk chocolate and substitute plain instead and wrap them in blue rather than the familiar red wrappers. Later, as you'll know, they carried on with both sorts, although milk was much more popular. The red Frys chocolate machines that before the war used to dispense a bar of milk chocolate for tuppence still stood on stations, but throughout the war remained empty. I knew because I tried 'em once on a rare trip back home to London.

Of course it wasn't just sweets, wartime rationin' was applied to a wide variety of foodstuffs, but I think I'm right in sayin' that it didn't happen all at once. As I remember, it came in gradually from about 1940 onwards, but some things like bread, potatoes, offal and sausages, they were exempt, and so we tended to get a lot of that sort of thing. That and whatever was produced at home. Some things were practically impossible to get hold of ration or no ration – like tea – but as kids, we hardly ever drank tea anyway so it didn't make much difference to us.

All this while, there was a real and increasingly devastatin' war goin' on, but as evacuees in Ardingly, we were largely shielded from it. What's more, bein' just a kid, I wasn't aware that, contrary to what government propaganda had led the volunteers to believe, the Germans were no push-over. I didn't really know what northern Europe was, much less that by the middle of 1940 much of it was in Hitler's hands and that was why we kids could see or hear Luftwaffe bombers and fighters, sometimes in broad daylight, swaggerin' in the skies bound for London. In those early days, I had no idea, no real concept of the havoc and destruction they were causin' back home in London. At that stage, to us kids, they were just excitin' to see.

I don't know how much you know about the Battle of Britain, but because it's now regarded as a key turnin' point in the war, I think I should say a bit about it. Not least because since it was fought out in the skies over Sussex and Kent, as an evacuee in Ardingly I witnessed some of it. I didn't realise it was the 'Battle of Britain' at the time. I don't think anybody did. I think the name came later. It was just dog fights in the sky lastin' from a few minutes to maybe as many as twenty. Excitin', frightenin' and spectacular - all at the same time.

Most battles are over in a day or two at most, but this wasn't like that. It was a whole series of skirmishes durin' the summer and autumn of 1940. Quite early in the war, when you come to think of it. The combatants were basically the RAF versus the German Luftwaffe supported by the Italians. Now regarded as a significant turnin' point of the whole war, the Battle of Britain ended when Germany's Luftwaffe failed to gain air supremacy over the Royal Air Force despite months of targetin' Britain's air bases, military posts and, as those left back in London would testify, its civilian population. Contrary to what's often portrayed in the films, most dog fights didn't end with most of the planes bein' shot down. Mostly they'd skirmish for a while, doubtless damagin' and injurin' one another, but then break off and turn for home, leavin' contrails in the sky where they'd been swoopin' and divin' at one another. Whether it was damage, lack of fuel or just loosin' their bottle that prompted them to break off, I've no idea. Now and again though a plane would come spiralin' down out of the sky with smoke billowin' from it, but that was rare. Mostly they'd 'limp' off, but doubtless many would never make it back to base.

Havin' defeated France in June 1940, we now know that Hitler had planned to invade England that same year and that the air assault intended to secure air supremacy was the essential forerunner of a successful invasion. Whilst the Luftwaffe was the largest airforce in the world, the RAF had some of the best fighter aircraft in the world – the Hurricane and the Spitfire – and thanks to radar givin' early warnin' of Luftwaffe raids coupled with a well-organised fighter command, these relatively limited resources were used to devastatin' effect. The battle proper was between July and October 1940.

Up until the first week in September, the Germans targeted mainly air bases and with considerable success but whilst RAF fighter command was badly damaged, it wasn't, as the Germans thought, all but done for. They made the mistake of switchin' the weight of their attacks onto London, which was devastatin' for London's residents, but gave the RAF bases breathin' space to recover. As a result, on 15th September the RAF were able to repel another massive Luftwaffe assault, inflictin' severe losses which history now shows proved to be the turnin' point in the battle for air supremacy. Although the fightin' continued for several more weeks, it had become clear that the Luftwaffe had failed to secure air supremacy and Hitler's invasion plans were postponed indefinitely.

Victory in the Battle of Britain by what Churchill would famously refer to as "The Few" was to prove a decisive turnin' point in the whole war. In truth, losses on both sides were enormous, but by avoidin' defeat, Britain was able to stay in the war – to fight another day and, on the continent, not on home soil. Victory in the Battle of Britain didn't win the war, but it made winnin' a possibility in the longer term. It would be four more long years before the allies would be able to launch their invasion of Nazi occupied Europe and ultimately bring the war to an end. This is fact. This is history, but at the time I was just a kid – Little Jack – an innocent bystander caught up in it all, watchin' the planes sometimes with excitement, sometimes in awe, sometimes in fear, but havin' no real idea of the significance of what I was seein', not until long after the war was over and I could read and learn what I've just told you about the 'Battle of Britain' and it's significance in the war.

Whilst I think it was important to put into context some of what I witnessed, it's all a bit profound and I need to take you back to lookin' through my eyes as a six year old evacuee. My time with the 'Tummies' themselves wasn't especially memorable except that towards the end it was winter time and Mr T had a big toboggan and he took me sledgin' with him. It was all the more memorable because it was my first experience of sledgin' down a snow-covered hillside. The slope went down to the river and the idea was to try to reach the river and then jump off just before the water. As I remember there were about 50 people sledgin' so there was lots of atmosphere and laughter. You'd never know there was a war goin' on.

As it turned out, my second billet was even shorter than my first because after about 5 months I was moved on back across the road. I'd no idea why at the time, but much later I learned it was because their teacher lodger had committed suicide in the house by puttin' her head in the gas oven. Very sad. Much more than Mrs T, she'd taken an interest in me and become a sort of adult companion who'd talk to me, to while away the winter evenin's.

Bein' so young, I'm not sure I was quite so aware of bein' moved from pillar to post as it seems now, lookin' back, which was just as well.

My new and third billet was with an elderly couple, who I later learned were actually Mrs Honeybun's parents – Mr & Mrs Miller. Mrs Miller was really quite ancient – or so it seemed to me – but Mr Miller worked as a plumber with Mullians & Co – a local builder. He was also the local ARP warden whose job it was to make sure everyone observed the lights curfew. All houses had to be properly 'blacked out' and he'd knock on any door where he saw light showin'. If he thought there was a danger of an air raid he'd blow his whistle, which was the signal for everyone to take shelter – which in Ardingly meant to hide under the table! Just as well the Germans didn't consider Ardingly to be a real target worth bombin'. Mr Miller was very distinctive with his big handlebar moustache, but it was his very distinctive car that fascinated me. It had somethin' which looked to me like a great big clock or maybe a thermostat thing on the front. I'd never seen anythin' like it or, come to that, since.

The Millers weren't unkind to me, it's just I don't think they really knew what to do with a six year old boy. I was expected to sit down, keep still and be quiet. They could have invented the phrase, "little boys should be seen and not heard!" I have to say that they made sure I was always well turned out and they fed me well. In fact, Mrs Miller always seemed to be busy preparin' meals. Whenever I got home from school she was slavin' over a hot stove. We always had a hot meal and a puddin' every night – all prepared on a range. The three of us would sit down together at the table to eat it but, do you know, that man never spoke to me, not once. It was as if I wasn't there. Bein' well fed is good but it's not everythin'. It doesn't make you feel welcome or happy inside and, most of the time, I was really rather lonely. Like most of my billets, they had no electricity upstairs so I had to take a candle to bed. It must have been winter time because I remember it bein' very cold up there, but it was the loneliness that really got to me. The other thing I never got used to were the bombs. I know we were in Ardingly, out in the country but that didn't mean there were never any bombs. There weren't many but, occasionally, I'd wake up in the night to hear these screamin' bombs comin' down. I'd just cower under the covers. They used to frighten me to death. Quite a few ended up in Wakehurst lake but the thing was, the screamin' noise carried so far, you couldn't tell where they were comin' down.

A woman named Winnie who turned out to be their daughter and another woman used to call sometimes and occasionally a soldier, who I presume was their son, came home on leave. He always had his rifle with him in readiness for goin' back to the front. He used to come for about two weeks and it seemed to me he was more or less drunk for the whole fortnight. I've already told you I didn't miss much and from overheard conversations I know he thought he wouldn't survive the war – but he did. I used to keep out of his way because he used to frighten me a bit. Speakin' of bein' frightened, I used to try to avoid the man next door as well. He was always sombre. He used to come out of his house dressed in a long black coat and a black top hat. I know now, but I didn't realise then, that he was the village undertaker. He was probably a very nice man, but to a small six year old in a strange place, he just didn't look very friendly.

Winnie worked as a housekeeper on a big farm near the school. One day she took me there. It was a bit like a stately home except that it smelt! You could smell it all the way up the road. The family were away for the weekend and there were only staff there. The reason she took me along was because they had a big rockin' horse which she thought I might like to ride. We had tea there with another lady – another housekeeper – I'm not sure. They were sittin' on chairs at the table and sat me on a sofa covered in brown corduroy material. I'll remember what happened to my dyin' day.

You have to bear in mind that I was very nervous and not used to speakin' up for myself. In fact I was used to "bein' seen and not heard". I desperately wanted to go for a wee but I was too frightened to ask, so I just sat there tryin' to keep it in. If they had spoken to me or sought to include me in their conversation, I might have been able to explain my plight. As it was, I was used to just sittin' quietly, listenin' to adults' conversations, but not to speakin' unless spoken to. It's hard to believe, 'cos I'm so different now, but back then it just wasn't in my psyche. I just couldn't do it. I was too frightened. Then the inevitable happened, a few trickles creepin' down my leg followed by a warm flood. I just couldn't stop. Believe it or not, I can 'feel it now' – the sensation – as if it had just happened. Some experiences you just can't forget even if you want to. All things considered, I suppose they were quite good about it. We just did our best to clean it up. But that was it – visit over. Not surprisingly, I was never taken out visitin' again.

I was only billeted with the Millers for about three months, but durin' that time Winnie decided she wanted to get married. Trouble was, everyone seemed to be against it. I can clearly remember all the conversations tryin' to put her off. It's amazin' what you learn just by bein' in a room and keepin' quiet. I'm not sure if the weddin' did go ahead or not because I rather lost touch when I was moved on again, this time to the Setfords

Before I tell you about my time with the Setfords, there's one thing I haven't mentioned yet, but really I should have done because it was a recurrent problem for me throughout my time in Ardingly. That was my asthma. It made me a bit different to the other kids. I'd had asthma in London, but not so badly. I guess it was triggered and affected by all the pollen in the countryside from the grasses, trees and hedgerows. Mind you, it didn't stop me playin' out, except when it really took hold of me. Then I'd be taken off to see one of Mr Dyer's three daughters. One of them used to walk around the village with a pet lamb on a lead, but that wasn't the one I used to go and see for therapy treatment. Basically she'd massage me and I have to say she was very, very good because by the time she'd finished I'd be as right as rain again. It was like a miracle. I'd be able to run and hop and skip just like the other kids. Mum used to send half crown postal orders to pay for my sessions with her. Before I leave the Dyers, there's a funny incident I should tell you about. Mr Dyer was a very big, very fat butcher and it was said he ate more sausages than he sold. One day everyone in the village went to see Mr Dyer's garden retaining wall lying in the road. Folk said it had collapsed because he'd sneezed!

So on to my fourth billet. This was with another elderly couple, Mr & Mrs Setford. My eavesdroppin' told me that I'd been moved on because havin' an evacuee was just too much for Mrs Miller who, if you remember I've already said was really quite ancient. A thought just occurred to me. Here I am callin' her ancient when it's quite likely she was a good bit younger than I am now – and I'm still a spring chicken really. Well, in my mind anyway.

By this time our Roy had been moved on as well to Mrs Wickens and the Setfords were next door. They were kind to me but I think they thought themselves rather superior to Mrs Wickens and so it was made very clear to me that on no account was I to have anythin' to do with the "Wickens children" – even though one was my brother! When I arrived – I think by now it was 1942 – the Setfords' son Peter had just joined the navy. Mrs Setford was very upset about it and worried about him constantly. It was all the more understandable because he'd joined up with a friend and his friend had already been killed. I know because bein' stuck indoors, I had plenty of opportunity to eavesdrop before somebody noticed me and ushered me into the parlour to sit on my own. Peter came home on leave once, but he didn't take much notice of me. I was just there.

All told, I was with the Setfords for about 9 months. Mr Setford looked after the village sewerage plant and the hedges and ditches and, from my eaves droppin', I knew he liked a pint of beer. Their home was immaculate, very Victorian with nothin' out of place but, as with the Millers', it wasn't really a home for a little boy. I just didn't fit in. In a physical sense they always looked after me very well, makin' sure I was well dressed, clean and tidy and always well fed, but I was very, very lonely there. That's because the Setfords wanted to keep me separate. They didn't want me mixin' with other children and certainly not the Wickens' kids next door. Rather than go out and play, I was forever bein' told to go and sit in the parlour and read my comic. I remember it was Radio Fun with characters like Arthur Askey and George Formby in it. But it would have been much more 'fun' if I'd been allowed out to play with the other kids. I also remember it was often rather cold sittin' in the parlour.

One sunny day I was allowed to go and sit outside on the front lawn with a piece of Madeira cake on a plate. The Wickens' kids were runnin' up and down and some said 'giz a bit'. I didn't in case Mrs Setford was watchin', but in truth keepin' it all to myself wasn't a real pleasure 'cos it was very dry and hard to swallow with no drink to wash it down. I'd gladly have given them the lot to join in their games. I daren't show much interest in what they were doin' in case I was made to go inside.

Of course there were highlights – there always are – and one I especially remember was when Uncle Jack came to visit whilst I was with the Setfords. (If you remember, he was my dad's sister, Auntie Annie's husband). We had taken over their place in Montefiore Street. Uncle Jack worked on the railway and had used one of his 'privilege tickets' to visit me. Originally he'd been a guard with Southern Rail, but just before the war had suffered a rather bad accident. In those days the guard would wave his green flag and the driver would start off slowly and the guard would run and jump back onto the train. Unfortunately Uncle Jack mis-timed his jump and fell between the platform and the train. His legs were always bandaged up after that and whilst he continued to work on the railway, he was transferred to bein' a 'checker' in the goods depot at 9 Elms.

On the day of his visit I was sittin' waitin' patiently on my own as usual and Uncle Jack took me on the bus to Haywards Heath. We went to the 'British Restaurant'. (Similar ones were opened up all over the country durin' the war.) I think it was lunchtime and I can't remember what I had but I can clearly remember that Uncle Jack ordered a bowl of porridge. That sticks in my mind because Uncle Jack did somethin' very strange – or so I thought at the time. He put salt on it! I know now that lots of people do it, especially Scottish people, but back then I could scarcely believe my eyes. Afterwards he took me shoppin' to Woolworths and to Curry's because they also sold toys in those days. He bought me a blue tractor. I can see it now. I'd never seen a blue tractor. It fascinated me. It had caterpillar wheels which I also remember because I kept taking the rubber tracks on and off. Kids do that sort of thing you know.

I had a lovely day out and I think Uncle Jack enjoyed it too – not least because for him it was a day out in the country – away from all the bombin'.

Another highlight should have been the King's visit. It was the talk of the village and we spent a lot of time in school preparin' for it. You hear a lot of good things said about the King and Queen durin' the war, especially the way they put themselves about, and stayed in London, tryin' to boost morale. Unfortunately, my brief experience was a bit different. The school had been told the King was due to drive through the village on his way up to the army camp. We'd spent days makin' and colourin' flags to wave and there we were standin' linin' the street outside Hapstead Hall for ages waitin' for his arrival. When at last he came, the car was there and gone in a flash. There we all were wavin' our flags like mad, but his car didn't even slow down and he never even looked at us, much less gave us a wave. It was very disappointin'.

I should explain that by this time quite a few of the London Schools had re-opened and our teachers and quite a few of the evacuees had gone back to London, includin' of course all those who'd reached 14 years and were now expected to go and get a job. As a result our schoolin' arrangements changed and we were taken by taxi to Haywards Heath. The journey was about 5 miles and I remember they were 'Lavender Taxis'.

As evacuees, we weren't allowed home, not even for Christmas. We may have been away from home, away from mum and dad, but every year mum made sure we got our presents. We never saw her bring them, but she did. Roy and I were lucky. Whilst we were billeted on our own for a couple of Christmases, I'm sure we both had our stockin' and a pillow case. Our stockin's were two of dad's – large woolly things, courtesy of Battersea Borough Council. They'd been issued to him when he worked as an inspector in the sewer department. They'd always be full of little things – nuts, apples, colourin' books, things to cut out and stand up – that sort of thing. As well as that, we'd have a pillow case with a few bigger things in. Every Christmas mornin' there they were at the end of the bed. I don't think any of the billet hosts ever bought us anythin'. I think it all came down from London from mum and maybe Aunt Raithby and Auntie Annie. The trouble is, you know what kids are like. They're not interested in seein' who the present's from. They just want the wrappin' off so they can get at what's inside and I was no different, so I'm not really sure who bought what. I do remember some of the presents though. Like when I was at the Setfords, I had this fire engine. It had a battery with it and I can clearly remember playin' with its searchlight under the covers early on Christmas mornin'. Bein' a kid, of course I'd always wake up early. I couldn't wait, you see. Then I'd play in my bedroom 'till the grown-ups said it was time to get up. Dinky Toys – they were the latest craze durin' the war. I'd have 'em for Christmas and for birthdays. Havin' toys was important to me, especially when I was made to play on my own.

The Setfords had a terrier dog and late one afternoon I remember it had a fit and jumped up on to the range, which was red hot. Harry Setford came home to find the dog and Mrs Setford in a terrible state. The dog was badly burned and had to be put down and Mrs Setford had to be sedated. Very shortly afterwards she died. Worn down by the constant worryin' for her son, perhaps the episode with her dog was the last straw. In case you are wonderin' – Peter survived the war.

At the time I didn't know she'd died. Nobody told me. I guess they didn't want to upset me. I was just ushered off very quietly, and unofficially as it turned out, to Haywards Heath to one of Mrs Setford's relatives. They were a relatively young childless couple in their 40s and right from the start they doted on me. Sadly, try as I might, I just can't remember their names, which is a shame because they were very, very kind to me. They lived in a 1930s style bungalow. I had my own room and was given everythin' a child could possibly want. They also had a terrier dog which I was allowed to play with. They had a biggish garden and that little dog and I played for hours there. The man went off to work in the city every weekday and I would go off to school – which of course was now in Haywards Heath. At weekends they would take me everywhere and often bought me toys. The six weeks I was with them seemed like bein' in paradise, but the billetin' authorities decreed I had to go back to an official billet in Ardingly. I know they tried to keep me, but one evenin' they sat me down and told me I would have to go back to Ardingly. I cried. The next day I had to say goodbye to those very kind people and, sad to say, I never, ever saw them again. When I left, the lady was very upset.

Lookin' back now – when it's too late – I wish I had gone back later in life to thank them for their kindness, but I never did. We all have regrets. I don't have many, but that is one of mine.

One thing I haven't told you – but must tell you now, is that from my very early days in Ardingly I had a perhaps irrational dread of Mrs Wickens. You see we were repeatedly told – "If you don't behave, you'll end up with Mrs Wickens." I didn't know the woman, but my other billets had led me to believe that bein' billeted with her would be terrible, so you can perhaps imagine how I felt when I got back to Ardingly only to find I was bein' ushered into the Wickens household. I'd just come from paradise and it was, to say the least, a bit of a shock and very strange to find myself thrust into this very rough and ready situation. It was only an ordinary council house and rather crowded. She already had twelve kids in there and I made lucky or unlucky No. 13! The Wickens slept downstairs so as to accommodate us all packed in like sardines upstairs.

Up to now I'd played a lot with my toys. I loved my toys. Dinky toys were my favourites. But there comes a point when you have to grow up. My time had come. I was seven.

To be fair, the transition was made much easier because my brother Roy was already billeted there and I already knew some of the other boys. Nevertheless it was still a shock to the system. I'm rather embarrassed to tell you, but one way it manifested itself was, I began to wet the bed. My time with Mrs Wickens was to be by far my longest billet – over 2 years. By the end I was a scruffy little urchin like the others and well initiated into scrumpin' and thievin'! But I'm jumpin' the gun. I need to tell you more about what happened in between.

So, let's get the bed wettin' out of the way. In fairness nobody made a big deal of it. Whenever it happened Eva, Mrs Wickens' daughter – and some of the other girls would strip the bed and put clean linen on. Then it was forgotten about. Well almost – it was forgotten about by everyone except me. When bedtime came round I remembered it again and soon I'd be reminded of it every night because Mrs Wickens sewed cotton reels into the back of my pyjama jacket. At least that's why I thought she did it at the time but lookin' back now I could have been mistaken. She may have done it to stop me sleepin' on my back in an attempt to help with my asthma attacks.

I'm not sure if I always slept in the same bed as our Roy but I think I probably did. It would have seemed normal to me 'cos after all, that's what we'd always had to do back in London when we were younger. I certainly did some of the time because I remember he used to elbow me in the ribs to tell me to stop wheezin'. He wasn't bein' horrible, he just didn't understand that I was fightin' for breath and couldn't help it on account of my asthma.

But for our Roy bein' there, I don't think I could have coped at all for those first few days with the dreaded Ma Wickens, but gradually I got used to it and certainly now, lookin' back, I'd have to say that the reality was far better than the reputation. She wasn't really the pariah she'd been made out to be. Ok, we never felt loved, but we weren't really mistreated either and the thirteen of us – we had each other. I'm not sure I even knew what it was then – but we had camaraderie. Unlike some of my previous billets, I wasn't all alone for hours on end, isolated and expected to just sit with a comic and be good.

Ok, Ma Wickens didn't shower me with love and presents like I'd become accustomed to livin' in my short-lived paradise, but as it turned out, insofar as the real world went, she wasn't a bad old stick really. Lookin' back, she certainly didn't deserve the reputation she had amongst some of the other families billetin' children in the village. She was more misunderstood than anythin'. Now it seems to me that people mistook the freedom she gave us to roam for neglect. At Ma Wickens, life was never borin' – it was colourful and loud. We weren't tied down. We were free to roam and we revelled in it.

Ok, we didn't live in the lap of luxury and Ma Wickens certainly wasn't one to show us any affection, but we didn't really want for anythin'. Yes, she could blow hot and cold sometimes, but then again, you have to remember she had 13 kids billeted with her in her modest 3-bed council house. You could be cynical and say she was only doin' it for the money and the extra rations she got, but when all's said and done, she was doin' it. She was providin' food and shelter for a motley assortment of 13 displaced kids and thinkin' back I have to take my hat off to her.

A lot of the reason I found bein' placed with her so traumatic at the beginnin' was because some of my previous 'hosts' had put the fear of God into me in so far as Ma Wickens was concerned. Fortunately, I had our Roy, already a seasoned Wickens boy, and after a couple of weeks or so, I came to realise that the reality was not nearly as bad as the reputation. More than that, I began to appreciate the benefits of bein' part of a big contingent. The camaraderie that existed and the freedom we were given enabled us to develop both individually and collectively and we revelled in it. We certainly didn't perceive it as neglect – not then, not now – far from it.

Not all the kids brushed their teeth but Roy and I did. Back in London, mum saw to that and now we were in Ardingly, we just carried on. We had tooth paste but it wasn't in a tube like you see today. Gibbs it was, red stuff, rather like stiff ointment in a round tin. You had to rub your brush in it. There was no NHS so even in London, we didn't get regular checks at a dentist but we did get our teeth inspected at school. The LCC were good like that. It wasn't just 'Nitty Nora' who came round, we had a dentist too. That was still the case in Ardingly or at least it was for us evacuees and I well remember one session in the Village Hall when it was decided I needed three teeth takin' out. Not a great experience but it's what happened after that makes me remember it so vividly. My gums just wouldn't stop bleedin'. It went on and on until in the end I was taken to a nurse's house in the village and she packed my mouth with firm cotton wool pads. I was already feelin' queezy from swallowin' blood and havin' my mouth packed didn't feel at all nice but, in fairness, eventually, it did do the trick.

As you know, I suffered a lot with my asthma in Ardingly. I suppose it was aggravated by all the pollen and stuff that I hadn't been used to in the city. Anyway, it was decided that I should have my tonsils and adenoids out. That it would help with the asthma. I don't know how the decision was taken or how it was organised, but one day these two old ladies came in a car to collect me and take me to an annex of Great Ormond Street in Tadworth, just outside Epsom. I don't really know, but I think these women were probably from Women's Voluntary Services (WVS). The car was one of those that could run on gas as well as petrol. It had this balloon on top that I suppose was full of gas. I'll never forget the journey, in part because those women spoke to each other but never once to me and in part because they argued all the time. The one drivin' would cut the engine every time we came to a down gradient because she thought it would save fuel. It was wartime remember. The other disagreed and that's what they were arguin' about, not once or twice, but every time the engine got switched off.

I was in hospital about a fortnight – you were in those days. Mum was very upset when she found out about it. It turns out that no-one had told mum or dad and mum was particularly upset because she would have come to visit me if she had known. As it was, I was in this children's ward for two weeks and never got any visitors, not one, so I got a bit lonely, especially in the first week when I wasn't allowed out of bed. At least there was a window I could see out of. It must have been springtime because I remember I could see daffodils out there. The second week was better because I was able to get up and run about a bit with some of the other kids. There weren't many other kids, but I remember especially this girl who was a bit older than me - about 11 or 12.

When I was ready for discharge, the same two old ladies came to collect me. They didn't take me straight back to Ardingly, they took me to Haywards Heath Hospital first. It was funny really because, as it turned out, it was just so I could have some lunch. Hayward's Heath is only five miles from Ardingly so I really don't know why we stopped for lunch. Maybe it was to comply with some hospital regulation or other or maybe they had the same view of Ma Wickens that most of the village seemed to have. Maybe they thought she might not give me any. Whatever the reason, I'm glad we did because I remember bein' sat on my own at this table on one of these tiny chairs – like infant chairs – and bein' given this beautiful mince and mash. I can honestly say it was the best I'd ever eaten then or since.

It was so memorable, if I shut my eyes I can still taste it. Beautiful it was. I don't know if the two women got any. If they did, it was in another part of the hospital. After lunch, they took me to Ma Wickens' front door and that was it. Ma Wickens wasn't the sort to let anybody in.

For sleepin', we were in the back bedroom at Ma Wickens and from there you could see right across to the Downs. As kids we'd brazenly say, "I'm not goin' to sleep tonight. I'm goin' to stay up and see if Gerry comes flyin' in over the Downs." O'course, when it came to, we always fell asleep and never saw nothin'! Leastways I did, and since I never remember any of the others braggin' about what they'd seen next day, you can be pretty certain we all succumbed. I guess you could say we had big ideas, but not always the stamina to see 'em through.

Normally, we'd go downstairs for breakfast and all sit round a big table. It was covered in American cloth (oil cloth) so it would wipe down easy. We'd each have 3 slices of bread which had already been thinly spread with margarine. You couldn't have any more bread, but you could put either jam or beeftox on your 3 slices. Beeftox was a product they produced durin' the war. It was a bit like Marmite.

After breakfast we'd all go out the front door and the taxi would come for us to take us to Haywards Heath Junior School. It was a makeshift affair in some scout huts. The taxis were paid for by the LCC. The bigger boys, includin' our Roy, would go up the village to catch the bus to Haywards Heath Technical School, which had a very good reputation.

Our Junior School teachers were Mrs Hammond and Mrs Rose. By this time Miss Jones had gone back to London. The scout hut only had one room, so we all had to share it. About half would be facin' one way, bein' taught by Mrs Rose, and the other half facin' the opposite way, bein' taught by Mrs Hammonds. It must have been very difficult for them and it wasn't exactly conducive to learnin' for us either. Mrs Rose was the headmistress and I thought she was lovely. One school day in particular stands out. It was a rather sad day. We all went to our desks as usual, only to find Mrs Hammond absent and Mrs Rose lookin' rather sombre. She told us all to turn our desks to face her and explained as kindly and gently as she could that Mrs Hammond had just received some very sad news. Her son, a bomber pilot, had been killed on a raid over Berlin. Mrs Hammond would be late, but she would be in later and when she came we must all be very quiet and very good. I hope we were.

On a lighter note, I've just remembered about a friend I had at school called Harry. I forget his surname. Anyway, he always used to bring an apple to school, which he'd eat in front of us envious kids at playtime. We never got anythin' like that from Ma Wickens. Me and a few of the others would always say, "Twas up with the core Harry", by which we meant, don't eat that as well – give it to one of us. Beggars couldn't be choosers in those days.

Before I go on to tell you more about my time as a 'Wickens boy', there's somethin' tragic that happened that I should have told you about but haven't, probably because I didn't actually witness it – I wasn't there. A schoolboy drownin' though – as you can imagine, it got announced in assembly and talked about time and again afterwards. It happened before I became a 'Wickens boy' and had the freedom to roam but, from what I was told, it seems a group of lads, includin' Donkey (Derek Viner) and the King brothers, were larkin' around on the banks of the River Ouse and jumpin' in and swimmin'. Donkey got into difficulties and went under for what seemed like too long so Brian, the eldest of the three King brothers, dived in to rescue him. Sadly he banged his head on a boat that was moored there and drowned, whilst Donkey managed to get himself out. How tragic is that – the brave would-be rescuer losin' his life whilst the one in distress somehow manages to save himself anyway.

Mr Wickens, Bill his name was, worked in a munitions factory durin' the war. He used to snare rabbits in the grounds, which he'd bring back to supplement our rations. After our evenin' meal, Ma Wickens would take all the girls into the front parlour and we boys would stay in the back kitchen with Mr Wickens. He'd sit in a chair by the fire. He liked to have his head stroked and we'd do it, not least because it encouraged him to fall asleep, which is what we wanted. As soon as he was off, the fun would start. One of our favourite games was to make cotton wool cigars, which we lit from the fire. Thinkin' about it, the only time Bill Wickens got to go in the front room was to go to bed. To get us all in, the 13 of us plus Eva shared the three bedrooms upstairs and Bill Wickens and his wife shared a put you up bed in the front room.

When the war started, billetin' hosts got four and sixpence per child evacuee per week but at sometime durin' the war that was increased to ten and sixpence. Bein' a bit cynical for a moment, you can perhaps see where some of Ma Wickens' reputation came from in the village because that was 13 times ten and six plus 13 ration books goin' to one 3 bed council house. As far as I know, none of the other houses in the village had more than two child evacuees. Don't get me wrong we had enough to eat but the sharin' lemonade apart, there were never any luxuries. Other billets would sometimes give their charges a few coppers for sweets, but never old Ma Wickens.

Over all though, thinkin' back, as child evacuees in Ardingly, we didn't have too bad a time of it, not really. We were never really abused or used as free child labour, not like some of the stories you hear happened to kids in some remoter parts, reputedly on some farms in Wales. We were expected to help out with some chores, but that was only occasionally. It wasn't an everyday thing. For example, I remember that from time to time Bill Wickens would have his little army of us lads helpin' out in the garden. He had a big garden and made the most of it for growin' stuff to eat. I guess he needed to with all us kids to feed. Fair play to him, he did the really hard work – rough diggin' it. That left great clods and he'd let the rain and weather break them down, but to speed things up he'd get us kids to bash 'em. We'd all have sticks with logs on the end – a bit like mallets – and he'd set us to work bashin' 'em to get a finer tilth.

Old Bill Wickens had a fair sized garden split into plots and each boy was allocated a plot and taught how to grow veg. I suppose it was free labour really, but then again he was teachin' us useful life skills and it meant we had plenty of fresh veg for the table. It was wartime and everybody was encouraged to 'dig for victory'. It's funny though, I liked growin' things, but I was never very happy when the time came to harvest any of it to eat. In particular I grew potatoes and broad beans and I remember feelin' very sad when Ma Wickens announced my potatoes had to be dug up. Silly really because that was the whole point, but havin' put all that effort into growin' 'em, it felt more like bein' made to destroy my garden than harvestin' my produce. I think they must have been 'earlys' I was growin' because when I dug 'em up they were like 'new potatoes'. They probably tasted really good, but I didn't want to eat 'em. It was the growin' I enjoyed. The gardenin' apart, the girls probably did more than we did

– helpin' out with food preparation and a bit of cleanin' and tidyin' up. I suppose you could say Ma Wickens was trainin' em up to be good housewives.

Nearly all the evacuees in Ardingly came from the same part of London, but a few came from elsewhere. Three of Ma Wickens' brood, Doreen, Beryl and Kenny Bowler came from Tooting. Really they should have gone to East Grinstead, but for some reason they ended up in Ardingly. Kenny had been about 11 when he first arrived. He was big for his age and a bit of a rebel. For us he was a natural born leader and about 8 of us used to follow him around – a bit like the pied piper! He got us into a few scrapes, but it was mainly really just harmless fun. Although I'm not so sure all the people who owned the apples and pears would agree 'cos Kenny knew where all the best trees were and the best way to scrump and get away with it.

Kenny was perhaps 'a chip off the old block' because his parents did somethin' no other parents did – they came down to Ardingly for their summer holidays. They'd come for about 3 weeks and stayed in Ma Wickens' shed out the back. They may have only had a shed to live in, but still it must have been nice to get away from the bombin' for a while and be with their kids. Usually the shed was used for storin' potato sacks and stuff and we'd use it on rainy days as a sort of den where we'd do drawin', make pipes and look at our stamp albums and all the other stuff kids do. Anyway we kids would have to clear and clean the shed out in preparation for them comin'. When Ma Wickens told us, we'd make a sort of game of it and chant all the while we worked, "The Bowlers are comin' … The Bowlers are comin' …" I think the Bowlers paid Mrs Wickens and certainly they always brought goodies from London for her.

I remember Doreen Bowler was especially nice and very good friends with Eva, Mrs Wickens' daughter. They remained friends all their lives until Doreen died in 2013. Incidentally, Eva and I are still good friends and we still phone one another for a chat. Like most folk of our age, mainly we like to reminisce about old times.

As for Kenny – well he remained 'the boss' for about my first 14 months with Ma Wickens before he became 14 and had to go back to London to get a job. There were plenty of jobs then because so many of the able-bodied men had been called up to fight in the war. Lots of women worked too, includin' mum, doin' jobs previously done by men, but I'll come to that later. Back in London, Kenny stayed with his parents. They lived behind the Mayfair Cinema in Tootin'. I don't know how he felt about his new status as a workin' man, but I know he missed the camaraderie and the buzz he got from bein' 'the boss' back in Ardingly. He came back several times to be with us, but only for long weekends because he always had to get back to work.

Bein' billeted with Ma Wickens, I had a lot more freedom and, havin' been re-united with Roy, very occasionally he and I would have a weekend back home in London. Mind you, rather than the four or five weeks we'd been expectin' on evacuation day, it was more than two years before Roy and I saw London again. I can't remember how or why it happened, I just know Roy and I went on our own – up on the train. I expect there'd been a lull in the bombin' so we were allowed to go up for the weekend. I'd be seven, but I guess Roy was considered old and responsible enough for us to travel on our own. He would have been ten.

Our visits would always be pre-arranged with mum and, bein' that much older, Roy was in charge really. I suppose you'd say I just tagged along. But that didn't stop me feelin' a bit grown-up when there were just the two of us travellin'.

We'd arrange it so we could do the whole journey by train, rather than takin' a bus to and from Haywards Heath. I told you earlier there was a railway station in Ardingly then. In fact right up until the 1960s when Beeching's axe fell on it. I suppose he was just doin' his job, but if you ask me, he's got a lot to answer for, that man. How it had changed – London, that is. It seemed like there was bomb damage at every turn and the sky – it was alive with barrage balloons. I'd never seen anythin' like it. And there were sand bags stacked on every street corner and on Clapham Common, there were trenches as deep as graves cut out all over it so nothin' could land there. There was no sign of bomb damage in our street, but there were changes and, as time would tell, more significant ones to come. There was sticky tape on all the windows with black-out curtains behind and come night time, everywhere was eerily dark. The London we'd left would have been ablaze with light, but not any more, not with the threat of bombin'. No street lights, no visible light from any of the houses and whilst the trams were still runnin', they'd got shields over their lights so as not to be seen from the air. In the back yard, the authorities had built us a proper brick air raid shelter with a concrete roof. There's a photo of me and Roy on that first visit home standin' on the shelter roof. It's at the end of this chapter. I have to admit, lookin' at it, you can't really tell what we're standin' on, so you'll just have to take my word for it. The other photo with it was taken the same day. It shows mum, Olga, Roy and me standin' at the front of the house and my friend Jonny Gray is sittin' on our wall in the background. As you can see our beautiful railin's are still there but soon, on subsequent visits, we'd find them all gone which I thought was a real shame.

Our weekend trips home were in the school holidays. Not many – perhaps 2 or 3 trips a year – but we were lucky, I don't think many of the other evacuees got trips back home at all. I think even Roy got all excited at the prospect. I know I did. It wasn't just we'd be seein' mum and dad, but we knew we'd be gettin' treats like fish and chips and goin' to the cinema on Saturday afternoon. We never gave a second thought to the danger of the bombin'. The mornin' matinee was cancelled durin' the war, but there was usually a show on Saturday afternoon – leastways there was when we went back in the school holidays. Then there was London itself. It always seemed so excitin' and compared to Ardingly, it was vibrant and colourful, with the noisy red trams and all that sort of thing. Don't get me wrong. I liked the countryside and the opportunities to go fishin' around Ardingly, but London, that had and still has a special place in my heart. Ok, it's not the same place it was as when I was a kid – but in my mind's eye it is.

I've got a couple more photos of Roy and me taken on another of our home visits. They follow on. As you can see, I've grown a bit and my long curls have been cut off, so at least I look like a boy. I'm pictured with my United Dairies milk cart in Kitchener Road, Thornton Heath at Aunt Raithby's sister's, 'Grandma's' to me. I remember Grandma's son Fred bought it for me. I chose it because it reminded me of Jim, our milkman's horse and cart. It was a replica United Dairies cart painted orange with 'United Dairies' in white letterin'. I loved that milk cart.

I expect you think I'm just romancin', but really it was always a lovely sunny day when Roy and I set out for London. I can feel the elation now as we run and skip our way down to that station at

Ardingly to buy our tickets. We were goin' home you see. It was the same feelin' every time, but especially that first time. We were goin' home at last, even if it would only be for the weekend. I don't know, but I suppose mum must have sent the money down beforehand. We changed at Haywards Heath and then had to go over to the other platform to get our train to Clapham Junction.

Whenever we were goin' home, Ma Wickens would make us beetroot sandwiches for the journey. Bein' a bit cynical, I think it was probably more about appearances than desire. She wasn't havin' it said that she was sendin' us on a journey with nothin' to eat. I'll never forget those beetroot sandwiches, not for the way they tasted, but for the 'journey' Roy's took one time when we were on our own in the carriage. Not far out of Hayward's Heath, there's a signal and Roy suddenly jumped up and said, "You know what I'm goin' to do with these, Willie?", and he threw his beetroot sandwiches out of the window at it! After that I could never go past that signal without seein' those beetroot sandwiches flyin' through the air. In case you're wonderin' – I ate mine.

Although Clapham Junction Station would become familiar later, I don't remember much about it then, except that it was big. What I do remember though is the Granada Cinema sign because I used to look out for it. You could see it just before goin' through the tunnel into the station. Whenever I saw it, I'd say to Roy, "We're nearly home." I guess you could say that sign has fond memories for me. It'd be nice to think it's still there, but I expect it's long gone.

From the station it would be the bus or tram, dependin' on what was due. Nobody would be there to meet us, but we knew the drill. That part of the journey was no problem to us. We were veterans at it because before the war we'd go to the pictures on that route. Mind you, if you remember, back then we rarely took a bus or tram home – we 'rode our horses' so as to save the fare to, in my case, buy a lead soldier or two.

Mum was always overjoyed to see us and I expect dad was pleased underneath, although he wasn't the sort to show any emotion. In truth I think he would have preferred us to stay in Ardingly where it was safer, but as it turned out, he needn't have worried because I never once remember the air raid siren goin' off when Roy and me were back home on one of our little trips. Mum missed us terribly and if it weren't for dad I think she would have had us back and risked the bombin'. Dad wouldn't hear of it though and whilst he wasn't a violent man – I never remember him hittin' us as kids – he did have a temper, especially where mum was concerned. I clearly remember some of our trips back bein' marred by rows over whether mum should have arranged for us to come back at all. Sometimes the shoutin' would be accompanied by a token show of violence and dad would throw a quarter pound of tea at mum. It was always loose tea in those days and when all was calm again, mum would do her best to sweep it all up to use. Tea was expensive and on ration, so they couldn't afford to waste it. Sounds a bit comical when you think about it now, but it didn't seem funny then. It was all a bit serious.

Dad never did anythin' with us kids, not then nor ever. I think he loved us though – in his own way. As you know, mum did all sorts with me especially. Maybe because I was the youngest. I've never really thought about it 'till now, but I suppose I was what you might call somethin' of a 'mummy's boy'. When our weekend was over, mum would always pack us up and take us back to Clapham Station and put us on the train. We'd always have our bag packed with goodies – sandwiches, sweets and clothes if we needed any. Dad would never go with us – all he'd say was there was to be no 'pipin' at the station – by which he meant no tears. Mum's eyes would always be a bit glassy and I used to get a bit tearful sometimes. I just couldn't help it. Once – I suppose it must have been the first time – mum put us in the guard's van and asked him to keep an eye on us, but I don't think Roy was best pleased about that. Other times we just rode in the carriage same as on the way up.

Whenever we got back, the other kids would be full of questions about what we'd seen. Things like – Is Heathbrook School still there and what about the fish & chip shop? As for Ma Wickens, there was never a warm welcome back – just a, "Oh, yer back, are yer?" Eva, her daughter, was different again – she was lovely. In fact it was Eva who looked after us most of the time. I'm afraid sometimes when we got back I got a bit tearful. Roy would say, "What's up Willie?" and I'd say, "I wanna go home again," and he'd come up with somethin' to cheer me up, like, "Never mind Willie – we'll go fishin' tomorrow." I used to love fishin'. Still do – leastways I would, if only I could.

Lookin' back, stayin' with Ma Wickens was not just a 'toughenin' up course', I learnt a lot both from her and from the other evacuees. We each had a 'pet' rabbit to look after and forage food for and a vegetable plot to tend. I soon realised that we were growin' vegetables, in my case potatoes and broad beans, for us all to eat, but I had no idea then that I was fattenin' up a rabbit for dinner as well. Mine was a beautiful black rabbit which I'd learnt to look after very well – but one day when I came home from school, Ma Wickens told me I'd been a silly boy and not shut the cage door properly and my rabbit had got out and run off. I was upset, but not half as upset as I would have been if I'd known the truth. Over time we each took a turn to be 'a silly boy' but we never twigged what had really happened. Leastwise, if any of the others knew, they never told me and I'm glad about that. It was Eva who told me, years later.

From the other evacuees I learnt some useful things like how to make bows and arrows and how to fish and how to steal apples without gettin' caught! Ok, scrumpin' was maybe not a good skill to acquire, but in the scheme of things maybe not such a very bad thing. Best of all at Ma Wickens I learnt camaraderie. We were all in the same boat and we looked out for one another and, take it from me, that's a good lesson in how to live your life – and live to tell the tale.

You couldn't afford to upset Ma Wickens. She could be really quite volatile. Friendly one minute, aggressive the next. One day it would be all friends together and the next war would break out. Eva, her daughter, used to make excuses for her and generally broker the peace. But Ma Wickens did have her good points and overall I think she meant well. She used to make us a sort of cake in a big meat dish. It was cut up into squares but she didn't put any sugar in so when it came to eatin' it, it was more like Yorkshire puddin'. We'd have it once a week and to be honest we thought it was 'orrible. It could have done with a bit of jam on it – but we'd had our jam ration on our bread at breakfast. Still, we couldn't look a gift horse in the mouth and we certainly didn't want to offend Ma Wickens, so we ate it anyway. One thing she was good at was do-nuts. When she made them, now that was a real treat. I loved 'em and I wish I had the recipe. Another good thing that would happen was on the first Sunday of every month. Then, instead of goin' down for breakfast, we'd all have a beef sausage sandwich in bed. I don't know why. Maybe the Wickens were havin' a feast on our rations downstairs, but even if they were I don't really care because for me at least that sausage sandwhich in bed was a real treat. I loved 'em and now and again I can still hear me sayin' to our Roy, "Is it that Sunday – the one when we have the sausage sandwiches in bed?"

I just mentioned rations and whilst I'm on the subject there's a little story about our Roy I should tell you. He didn't trust Ma Wickens. He thought she wasn't givin' us our fair share of rations and blow me if he didn't only go and tell her so. None of the rest of us would have dared do that but after Kenny left, our Roy was now our unofficial leader and as much as anythin' I think he was tryin' to impress the rest of us kids. He considered himself as 'top dog' and I think he wanted to show he could even stand up to Ma Wickens. She didn't exactly go spare, but she wasn't best pleased. I think maybe she had the last laugh because ever after that Roy's rations – includin' 2 ozs of butter and 2 ozs sugar – would be kept and brought out separate. As the week wore on, it got smaller and smaller and sometimes the other kids used to snigger when it was brought out. Roy was furious at us for that. He'd be scrapin' the butter on and then practically all off again to make it last out the week. There were no fridges in those days, so goodness knows where perishables were kept through our long, hot summers. On cold stones or in bowls of cold water I suppose.

My brother Roy was always a bit of a rebel and saw himself as somethin' of a natural leader and, as I said, after Kenny left to work in London, he became just that – leader of the Wickens' boys. If Roy declared it was a 'bow and arrow day', then that's what it was and durin' the mornin' we'd all go out and cut suitable material from the hedgerows to make our bows and arrows and in the afternoon we'd be firin' 'em at more or less anythin', includin' each other. We were a bit indiscriminate, so it's a wonder nobody lost an eye, but luckily no-one ever did. Mind you, we came close a time or two.

Ma Wickens had this WVS hat. As far as I could see, she never did anythin' with the WVS but it was noticeable that she'd always put this hat on if anybody official was due to call. I guess it was to impress 'em.

About once a month, she would get us all together and take us out for a walk. It would always be a Sunday, early evenin'. She'd always choose a lovely warm sunny evenin', but then that wasn't that difficult because as I remember the summer days were so often like that. She'd make us all wear our Sunday best and she'd always march us up through the village on the way out and on the way back so everyone would see us. That was part of it I think – lettin' the village see how well we were turned out and how well she was lookin' after us. We all went along with it though – not that she would have given us any choice. Still, we'd always go to this public house and all have a glass of lemonade sittin' outside. We never had one each – she'd make us share a glass between three or four of us. We never went all that far, so it was quite nice really and at that time in the evenin' we'd see all the rabbits out foragin'. I used to like watchin' 'em.

Picturin' us with our glass of sharin' lemonade, it's just occurred to me that Ma Wickens never gave us any at 'home' and yet she must have had some because sometimes, when we were goin' off on a long walk, just us kids I mean, she'd give us an empty lemonade bottle full of water. As I know I keep tellin' you, those summer days in Ardingly were mostly hot and sunny so we'd need a drink with us. I remember those bottles especially because, often as not, on the way back, I'd be knockin' on some stranger's door askin' if they'd mind fillin' our bottle up again. I don't mean in Ardingly but somewhere out in the sticks, maybe several miles away.

Apart from our Sunday walks, Ma Wickens never went out much herself, not even to go shoppin'. She'd make a list and Eva would take it up to Sears and they'd deliver it. Not long after the war started, their delivery van got commandeered by the Government for the war effort so it was back to usin' a boy on a bike for a while but, later, when they got a replacement van, they were allowed to keep that.

Talkin' of shoppin' and Ma Wickens brings to mind somethin' that really upset me at the time. Her birthday was 13th October, or there abouts, and one year I decided to use some of my sweets money to buy her a present. I went to the Post Office and bought her a bottle of ink and a nib pen - the older ones amongst you will remember the type, just a piece of coloured wood with a brass coloured nib on the end that you dipped in the ink for writin'. Ok, not a very special present but I was just a kid and I wanted to get her somethin' and I thought she might like it. When I gave it to her, she didn't just turn her nose up, she took the lid off the ink and, in front of me, poured it down the sink. That was very upsettin' and when I think about it now, even for Ma Wickens, that was a pretty uncarin' thing to do. Ok, maybe she didn't want any ink, but there was no need to do that in front of me. As for the pen, it had a red wooden stem. I'd chosen it 'cos it was bright and I thought she'd like the colour. I didn't hang around to see what became of it, I just turned tail. I didn't cry, not outwardly, but I was cryin' inside.

Rumour had it that after the war old Ma Wickens got summoned to the Palace to receive an award. We assumed it was for havin' so many evacuees durin' the war, but speakin' to Eva, her daughter, the other day it seems that this was just a rumour. (Yes, Eva is still alive, still in Ardingly in her nineties but still with all her marbles and we're still good friends and often chat on the phone. But – don't go phonin' Eva unless you have plenty of time 'cos you're goin' to need it. She's worse than me for goin' on a bit!). Her mum did get some sort of commendation, but that was presented in the village and Eva's not quite sure what it was 'cos her mum just stuck it in a drawer and never said any more about it. She was that sort of woman. To be honest, I never really liked her – I guess because she never once made a fuss of me and generally, she was a bit short on sentiment was old Ma Wicken's. Mind you she did have a house full – twelve other evacuee kids besides me – so it's hardly surprisin', is it? In retrospect, I probably owe her a lot. Whilst in her 'care' I did a lot of growin' up and certainly experienced life and toughened up. That was a given with Ma Wickens. But it's all probably stood me in good stead and really, lookin' back, I have to say now, even if a bit begrudgingly, I have to admire the woman.

Unfortunately, I don't have a picture of Ma Wickens or the Wickens' boys, as we considered ourselves, but I do have a picture of just me standin' outside Ma Wickens' house. It's amongst those at the end of this chapter.

So far I've mostly tried to give you a flavour of some of the things that happened to me in each of my billets and how I felt about them. Now I'm goin' to go off on a bit of a tangent and describe some things generally about Ardingly, the place and some of the characters I encountered there. Being billeted with the Wickens gave me much more freedom to wander and explore and I was that bit older now so much of what I'm about to tell you I probably largely experienced whilst with her, but in a way I think it's more important that I tell you about the experiences than bother too much about when precisely they happened.

I'll start by tryin' to paint you a clearer picture of Ardingly the place. Apparently the village name has been spelt differently over the years, but it is essentially of Anglo-Saxon origin and means "a clearing in the great forest" or weald which had originally occupied all the land between the North and South Downs. As you know, as an evacuee I'd come down by train to Haywards Heath, which compared to Ardingly was quite a sizeable town. It owed its existence to the railway because prior to the buildin' of the London to Brighton railway line in the 19th century, Haywards Heath had scarcely existed.

When I was there, Ardingly was, and to a certain extent still is, dominated by three principal buildin's:

Hapstead Hall, where we first disembarked the coach, had been built in 1902 by the owners of Hapstead house and had subsequently been presented to the village as a thanksgivin' markin' the end of the First World War. The war that it had been thought would surely end all wars, such had been the carnage and loss of life. So much for wishful thinkin'.

John took a photo of me standin' outside Hapstead Hall durin' our visit in 2015. You'll see it at the end of this chapter.

Wakehurst, the largest house in the Parish, had been bought by Sir Henry Price in 1938 – shortly before I arrived. He was the founder of the well-known "Fifty shillin' tailor" chain of stores. You may know it better by its later re-branded name of 'John Collier'. Remember their catchphrase? – "John Collier, John Collier the window to watch!" Sir Henry was a great benefactor to the village and that included us as evacuees. He used to put on really lovely Christmas parties for us kids at the Village Hall – Hapstead Hall, and that included presents for everyone. There's a picture of Wakehurst as it was in my day amongst those at the end of this chapter but, if you'd like to see it for yourself, you can visit Wakehurst because it's now associated with Kew Gardens and run by the National Trust.

Last but not least there was Ardingly College. I've left it 'till last 'cos there are a few more stories to tell you about it. Ardingly College had been built in the 1860s as St Saviour's School – an Anglican boardin' school for what were then termed the lower middle classes.

You have to remember that there was no system of state schools back then and there was a very marked class system. When I was there the institution had been re-invented as a rather well-to-do boardin' school for boys. Mainly Jewish boys I think. You can see it in the arial photo. It was private but I did get to go inside, just the once, one Christmas. That's because, for some reason, one year Hapstead Hall wasn't available for Sir Henry's Christmas party and so he arranged for us to have it in the College refectory instead.

We had lots of scope to go explorin' and do stuff while we were billeted with Ma Wickens. She never bothered where you were so long as you were back for dinner. Sometimes we'd take ourselves off and walk all the way up to the College, which was a good way from our billet – just to spend a halfpenny. In case you're wonderin', that wasn't at all like goin' to spend a penny! Before I explain, I'd better tell you a bit about the College.

First off, the college boys always looked very smart. Always in grey flannel trousers, green jackets and a yellow and green scarf. In summer they wore a thinner grade cloth, but the outfit was the same. Durin' the war at least, one of the pavilions was used as a tuck shop. I don't know how we knew – maybe it was Kenny who found out, but on certain days the college boys could buy a massive rock bun there for a halfpenny. We used to go and queue up with the college boys, spreadin' ourselves out so as to try and blend in. The college boys never gave us away – in fact they never gave us any trouble at any time. I don't know, maybe they felt a bit sorry for us. Anyway, when it came to our turn we'd just stretch out our hand with the halfpenny waitin' for it to be replaced with a big bun, all the time lookin' the other way rather than look the lady in the eye. In truth we must have stood out like sore thumbs, no uniform and all, but it didn't matter because the ladies always gave us our rock bun. It was so big that it took a while to eat, but afterwards we'd always try to go and check out the bins at the back of the college and most times we'd strike lucky. We often found lots of lovely stuff in there – especially paper – half used exercise books and the like, and pencils and rubbers which still had lots of life in 'em. Paper especially, you just couldn't get durin' the War even if you had any money to buy it. Real treasure and it wasn't stealin' 'cos they'd already thrown it away. Whenever we were up near the college we'd take a detour to check out the bins. Proper scavengers we were.

Sometimes, when we were playin' up near the College, you'd suddenly hear this roar in the sky. We knew it was planes, but trouble was we never really knew if they were ours or theirs – Germans that is. Often as not, they'd be College Old Boys and they'd swoop down really low to salute the College. Quite a spectacle I suppose, but I hated it. They frightened me to death, swoopin' that low just over head.

I'm sure Ardingly College boasts lots of famous 'old boys', but I'll just mention three I know of – Terry Thomas, the famous 'old school' English comic actor was a pupil, as was Billy Cotton's son, but then there's one to whom I am personally indebted, a young man who went on to become a heart surgeon and who later in life did a by-pass on me. I was just 58 then and by all accounts they're only supposed to last 10-15 years, but here I am at 82 lookin' forward to my 83rd birthday and the old ticker is still soldierin' on, so I guess he didn't do a bad job, did he? Mind you, I have had 18 stents fitted as well since then and last time I went for a 'check up' they were talkin' about makin' it up to 20. I wonder if that's a full set!?

Most of the children learnt to swim, but unfortunately I didn't. In fact I never have. I did go skinny dippin' with the rest of them though – up at the pool at the college. Trouble was, durin' the war no-one was doin' any maintenance on it so the pool was green and full of tadpoles and newts. Whenever we got near water, Roy was always very protective of me so I just splashed about in the shallow end. We all went – boys and girls. That's where we first learnt about the difference! We'd usually stay 'till we got caught and chased off.

Bein' a village, Ardingly didn't have any big stores like in Haywards Heath, but it did have quite a good range of shops. The biggest, and possibly my favourite, was Sayers – a sort of mini department store. It was strikingly clean. Funny, that a bit of a kid would be impressed by that – but it's how I remember it. Anyway, downstairs on one side they sold bacon, butter, fats and that sort of thing and on the other tea, sugar, tinned food, biscuits and packaged foodstuffs. Butter, they would cut from big blocks and pat it into shape and then parcel it up in greaseproof paper folded very skilfully. Bacon was in 'sides' covered with muslin and they'd cut to it to order and to the customer's preferred thickness on a bacon slicer. I never bought any but I used to like watchin' 'em not least because even raw, it smelt so lovely. Upstairs was haberdashery and, more importantly for me, toys. Mostly, I'd just go in to look.

Fellows was the bakers and maybe the best part about it was the smell. Maybe you have to be as old as me to remember what a proper bakers smells like. They sold wonderful bread which they used to deliver around the village in a big wicker basket. All very traditional and wholesome.

Macey's was a very popular shop sellin' sweets and cigarettes. They had an under the counter service there. No - not what you're thinkin'. I just mean we used to have to duck under the counter to get into the back because Mr Macey was the village barber as well. A haircut was sixpence for a child and it was better to go when there was a bit of a queue. That way you could sit and read from the pile of picture post magazines he had in there whilst waitin' for your turn.

There was also a butcher's shop run by Mr Dyer who, if you remember I've already mentioned on account of his size and the incident with his wall.

The post office was below Hapstead House. As well as stamps they sold writin' pads and newspapers. For Roy and me the post office was very important because it's where we changed the postal orders mum occasionally sent to us. Although it was only a village post office they also had a telegram boy.

We didn't write many letters, but when we did it was almost always to mum and dad at home. It's funny because although we were in Ardingly for about five years, we always thought of ourselves as Londoners. I think we were sort of proud of it and so whenever we wrote a letter we always put our address as: 34 Montefiore Street, London SW8. We never wrote our billet address – not even Ma Wickens, where we were for much of the time – 3 Station Road, Ardingly.

Finally, close to Hapstead Hall, on the island by the crossroads was a shop sellin' stationery and sweets. There was no chemists in the village but, bein' where the bus turned round, medicines from the chemists in Haywards Heath would be dropped off by the bus conductor at the island shop for people to collect. I don't remember his name but the shopkeeper was also a special constable. I do remember he wasn't well liked – not by us kids anyway. That's probably why I've left his shop 'til last. I remember goin' into his shop once to ask if he had any Victory V cough lozenges. I think I've told you that, unlike sweets, they weren't on ration. You could just buy them and I thought they were just as good as sweets. Anyway, the moment I walked in he bellowed at me – "How dare you come into my shop just as the six o'clock news is coming on!" I never went in there again.

Since I've mentioned the news, I ought to explain that throughout the war nearly everyone made a point of listenin' to news broadcasts on the radio, not least to see how the war was goin'. That included us kids. From the various news bulletins we knew all about the likes of Rommel and Montgomery. I know now that much of it was propaganda – lies really – but I suppose well intentioned and designed to bolster morale. I'm sure it did and helped a lot of folk cope and got them through the war. I'm sayin' 'radio', but back then they were known as the 'wireless'. I'm not talkin' transistors – they came much later. No, these were great lumberin' things and they needed accumulators, a type of recharchable glass acid battery to run 'em. Folk would have two batteries. One would always be at the shop bein' charged whilst the other was in use and they didn't last long before needin' to be swapped over. I'm sayin' shop but, in Ardingly, it was Symond's Garage where the rechargin' was done. Folk had a wooden cradle to carry the battery in to make sure it stayed upright and none of the acid got spilt.

Most of my billets had a wireless, includin' Ma Wickens. Her's was on a shelf in the kitchen, just inside the back door. As kids we knew to keep quiet whenever news broadcasts were on. Mind you, we had to – it was hard enough as it was to catch everythin' bein' said over all the cacklin' and cracklin' that was typical of most sets, without any distractions from us. With the outbreak of war, the BBC started the 'Home Service' and in early 1940, 'The Forces Programme' began broadcastin' for a few hours each evenin' but soon became 12 hours a day. I well remember some of the 'forces favourites' like Vera Lynn and some of the songs they used to sing, like 'We'll meet again', except, bein' kids, we'd sing our own version – 'Whale meat again'. My favourite was 'When the lights come on again in London' because for me, home was always London and, although I didn't always pine for it, deep down it's where I wanted to be. At Ma Wickens, when we got the chance, we'd listen to stuff like ITMA. It was supposed to be a comedy and it was Ok and the bigger kids seemed to think it was hillarious but, most of the time, I couldn't make head nor tail of it but I listened anyway. If you've no idea what ITMA is or rather was, I'll explain later.

At Ma Wickens, we might make a bit of noise when stuff like ITMA was on, not least because she'd usually be in the front room, but, whenever the news was on, we'd all keep quiet and we'd listen intently. Back then we took what was broadcast as gospel. It certainly fired our imaginations and provided lots of scope for re-enactment in our various war games. I'll come back to them later, but before I do I ought to finish on the subject of shops.

Sometimes on sunny summer days if the mood took us, some of us kids would take off and walk all the way to Haywards Heath, about 5 miles. We'd go to Woolworth's and Curry's mainly to look at the toys. Generally we wouldn't have money – unless mum had sent us a postal order. Leastways, not enough to splash out on toys. After lookin' we'd play on the swings and roundabout on ground opposite the Paramount Cinema. That was a treat for us because there were none in Ardingly. Then we'd walk across the road to a little tin shack of a shop which sold sweets but it wasn't the sweets we wanted – we could get those in Ardingly – albeit on ration. What we were really after was a glass of lemonade for one penny. Quite good we thought. If we were flush we'd have a glass each. Otherwise we'd share. We needed to save threepence for the bus fare back home to Ardingly. We'd catch it at 5pm and it would have us back by 5.15 in plenty of time for dinner at Ma Wickens. I was only big enough and had the freedom to join in jaunts like this when I was one of Ma Wickens' kids, so that would have been between the ages of 7 and 10 years.

Gettin' back to the village shops for a minute, you remember the one on the island with the grumpy shopkeeper, well that was where Mr Leach, one of our school teachers was billeted. It would be remiss of me not to tell you a bit about Mr Leach and some of our other teachers who'd come down with us from London.

Perhaps I should start with Mr Kitchener, the headmaster of Heathbrook – our school back in London. He was a bit of a stickler for discipline and made it clear to us all that he wasn't goin' to tolerate any disgrace bein' brought on Heathbrook School by pupils misbehavin' in the village. I guess that's why he began canin' boys for what seemed minor misdemeanours practically every day at the start of assembly for everyone to see.

If there was any trouble it was usually between evacuees and local kids. I suppose we were a bit like invaders on local kids' territory and in the beginnin' it was definitely Londoners against Ardingly kids. In those early days at least, as evacuees we had to watch our backs and go around in groups. That was second nature to many of the London kids because back then Londoners were famous for their street gangs and some of the gang leaders were with us as evacuees. I was never in a gang – I was too young and too little. By the end of the evacuation period, bridges had been built and generally all the kids were friends together. In the early years though it wasn't always like that and from time to time hostilities could flare up and village kids would arrange to pick on us, or so it seemed to me. Maybe some of the time they were just retaliatin' for stuff I didn't see. Amongst the locals, there were so many Holmans in the village, they could practically have had a village of their own. One of the Holman lads was a bit strange. He was forever throwin' stones at us evacuees, encitin' us to chase him. 'Poopy' Holman we called him – not very nice I know, but maybe he deserved it, because he tended to try to pick on us younger ones. He'd hide in waitin' so he could pelt us with stones and then run off. He could run like a horse. Sometimes some of the bigger boys helped us out and caught him up and gave him a bit of a pastin', but it never seemed to deter him – a day or two later and we'd be pelted again. He seemed to love bein' chased. I can see him now, runnin' down the road – our lot in pursuit.

I'm sorry, I went off on a bit of a tangent there. I was supposed to be tellin' you about Mr Kitchener. Lookin' back I feel a bit sorry for him 'cos unfortunately he wasn't well liked in the village and grown-ups referred to him just as "Kitchener". In the end they accused him of bein' a German spy! He had a car and where the spare wheel would normally have been on the back he had a black box. Some of the villagers maintained he had a transmitter in it. Along with our other London teachers, after about 18 months he left the village, I think to go back to teach in London because by then some of the London schools were bein' re-opened despite the threat of bombin'. In the village though, rumour had it that the government had taken him back for questionin'.

I think Mr Kitchener had as many as six staff, but I only knew Mr Leech and Miss Jones, so they are the only ones I can tell you about. Mr Leech didn't actually teach me but the thing I remember most about him was he was very tall and he was very keen on boxin'. He used to get the bigger boys to rig up a full-sized ring at Hapstead Hall which he'd found stored away under the stage. Mainly he'd arrange a programme of bigger boys boxin' one another and he'd spend time trainin' them. Sometimes we young ones would be 'volunteered' to have a go. A case of you, you, you and you get yourselves changed. I remember bein' put in the ring with a boy named Handyside. We'd both be about 6 ½ at the time. I don't remember much about the fight but I do remember havin' trouble holdin' up the gloves – they were practically bigger than me! I don't think either of us were very good. It wasn't really my thing and I still hadn't toughened up much by that time.

When I first went to Ardingly I was only 5 – the youngest of all the evacuee children. There were very few of us infants and so before long, rather than have our own class, we were mixed in with the Ardingly infants. I remember their teachers were nice, but I'm afraid I can't remember their names or much about the classes. What stands out is that we did lots of paintin' and makin' things with plasticine. We must have done some sums and ABC and learnin' to read, but it's all a bit hazy. What I remember most are the gas mask practices, which were quite frequent and seemed to take half the day up. We used to have to walk up two by two to the Rectory for our practice and once there we'd be herded into the basement and have to sit down there on the floor with our gas masks on. It was a long narrow basement and I always seemed to be at the end of it, furthest from the door. Nobody could breathe properly down there – least of all me with my asthma. I vividly recall fightin' for breath. I was always havin' to put my finger in down the side to get a bit of air. If there had been any gas down there I would have been gassed!

When I was 7, I went up into the Juniors with the London boys and Miss Jones was my first Junior School teacher. You remember Miss Jones – the teacher who'd come down with us from London – the one who'd come into our carriage halfway down 'cos one or two of the kids were gettin' upset. The one with the hat. I never, ever saw her without that hat. She always wore it even in class. Talkin' of class, I should explain that by this time they'd decided to use the committee rooms at the back of Hapstead Hall as classrooms. Bein' in that classroom also helped me to learn to tell the time because the bus stop and turn around were just outside our window. The bus came more or less on the hour and dependin' on the time of day I quickly learnt that meant either nearly playtime or nearly home time.

Miss Jones was fair, but quite strict. You had to face the board or risk a tellin' off. She wouldn't stand any nonsense. I didn't realise it then, but I know now that the LCC was one of the best education authorities there ever was. War or no war, whatever was required, they sent down from London. Desks, chairs, blackboards, books, paper, pencils – everythin'. Mind you, somebody somewhere must have made a bit of a boo-boo 'cos we had too many desks and so for a while spare ones were stacked at one end of the playground. We were given strict instructions not to go near them – but, well, boys will be boys. We used to position two desks so we could put a hand on each and push ourselves up and swing to and fro – 'till we got told off that is. One particular day at home time I thought, I'll just have another go on those desks while there's no-one around to tell me off. Big mistake. I somehow came off and went crashing into the tarmac chin first. I came up lookin' and feelin' like Desperate Dan.

Just in case you've no idea who Desperate Dan is or was, I'd better enlighten you. He's a comic strip character in the Dandy. More particularly, his most characteristic feature was his large, very flat, square chin. Miraculously, I didn't break any teeth or bones so far as I know. But boy did it hurt. I had a sore chin and jaw for days and days afterwards and for a time at least eatin' was anythin' but a pleasure. Of course I never told anybody – 'till now that is. Who could I tell? – not the other kids. I didn't want to lose face admittin' I'd come a cropper doin' somethin' that should have been easy. And no way was I goin' to tell the teachers or Ma Wickens. All I'd get then would be a tellin' off into the bargain. The grazes probably gave somethin' of it away, but nobody said anythin' and as kids do, I soon got over it. Mind you – the memory lingers.

Miss Jones, as befittin' her very lady-like demeanour, was billeted at Hapstead House. It was owned by a family called the Hetts – very posh. They were the ones who'd had Hapstead Hall built after the First World War. Now, Mr. Hetts was in charge of the local Home Guard. Although she was rather strict, Miss Jones was a good teacher and I felt I learnt a lot in her care. She was very thorough and at pains to make sure we all understood. In those days, as a general rule, children were not allowed to talk in class unless spoken to – by our teacher that is. Perhaps because she was our first junior school teacher, I think you could say she taught us how to behave, how to conduct ourselves. She had a way with her that made it seem the natural and right thing to do. As I said, after a while, some of the teachers who'd come down with us went back to London to teach. I suppose like us, at the beginnin' they'd not expected to be away so long. Anyway, that meant on some days we'd be short of teachers. On such days, whoever was in charge of us might say, "We'll do singing today," or if it was a nice day and blackberries were in season, then we'd just all go off blackberryin'. It was somethin' two or three classes could all do together. If there was an exam in blackberryin', I'd probably have got top marks! Ma Wickens used to like it when we went – she could always find a use for the fruit. Now and again she'd even take us blackberryin' herself. She used to make quite a bit of jam, but her blackberry pies were nothin' to look forward to. They were a bit strange and tasteless. I don't know why because the fruit was lovely when we ate it raw which, bein' kids, we always did whilst pickin'.

When we weren't at school, we'd be out playin' or up to a bit of 'harmless mischief' – well, that's my story and I'm stickin' to it. This is once I was with Ma Wickens, when I had the freedom to go out and play and roam pretty much where I wanted. Before that I never got the opportunity.

We used to have 'fads'. We weren't a gang like the street gangs they had back in London – but we were a group of lads who often went around together – well we were when I was at Ma Wickens'. Now I think of us as 'The Wickens Boys', but back then we were just a group of lads who, by the luck of the draw, had ended up bein' crowded into a three-bed Council house in what was widely regarded as the dubious care of the notorious Ma Wickens. Whether in adversity or not, we were young lads, far from home, and like any young lads, we liked to play games, especially ones that involved a hint of danger, a bit of mischief. One such fad I remember was when we found these lumps of iron and discovered that when we threw 'em down the road, they'd not just make a racket, they'd throw up a shower of sparks as they bounced along. As with any fad, we soon got tired of it, but on and off for a week or two it was a source of darin' and amusement for us.

Bows and arrows was a recurrent fad which, over the years, took up a fair bit of time. Searchin' in the hedgerows and woods to find all the raw materials was a bit of an adventure in itself. Then fashionin' 'em, to get the bows and arrows just so, took time. A learnin' experience you could say, with skills bein' passed from one to another. The only down-side was that bows and arrows fads would nearly always end in tears with first one and then another gettin' injured and then, if we didn't just decide to stop ourselves, the grown-ups findin' out and intervenin' and puttin' a stop to it regardless.

O' course, as kids we all played war games but we had no real concept of what it was really like to be fightin' in a war. To us it was just a game. I remember I used to like runnin' up and down the garden path, arms outstretched, screamin' and hollerin' –'ye-howin' and 'rat, tat, tat, tatin', pretendin' to be hurricanes and spitfires shootin' down the German aircraft over Kent. Those Germans didn't stand a chance!

My personal favourite pastime was fishin'. More of a sport than a game I suppose, but I loved it. We never had any proper fishin' rods, just sticks from the hedgerows, and we'd use button thread for line. It was much stronger than normal cotton. Old Bill Wickens used to let us use his vice and pliers to make hooks by bendin' pins. For floats we'd find a bit of balsa wood or cork and that was it – we were ready to go. All we needed was a bit of stale bread or worms for bait. Over time I became really quite good at it. I guess that's one reason I liked it so much. If you're good at somethin' you generally do. Our Roy, on the other hand, never really got the hang of it. He hardly ever caught anythin'. I don't think he had the patience.

Once we had the idea that we could catch fish and keep 'em in this big cow's trough in the back field. We'd put about 30 of 'em in there. All golden carp they were. Beautiful lookin' things and a good couple of days' work for us to catch 'em. We used to go and check on 'em in the trough. We just liked lookin' at 'em. Sadly though our plan backfired. Apparently the cows wouldn't drink from a trough full of fish. They went dry as a result and there was 'hell to pay' over that. I'm not sure what happened to the fish 'cos we never got 'em back.

Sussex was famous for its bricks and Ardingly had its own brickworks and, at the time we were there, its fair share of brick ponds. Basically these were just holes in the ground where clay had been extracted and which had subsequently filled up with water. Most of the ponds around Ardingly dated from the 1930s when there was a lot of buildin' goin' on, especially in London and hence a big demand for bricks. For us kids, the ponds were a source of adventure and some of them a place to go fishin'. My favourite, 'cos it wasn't too far and was well stocked, was known as 'Gasson's Pond' because it belonged to a brickyard owner called Mr Gasson.

Mr Gasson was an elderly chap who lived in a big Victorian house just up the road next to the row of Council houses that included Ma Wickens' place. He was a bit of an invalid. He had two walkin' sticks. I don't think he went out much. Certainly we never saw much of him and I never remember him speakin' to any of us. Nor his wife either. I think they were a bit aloof. Thought themselves a bit above us evacuees billeted in a Council house. Mind you, as Council houses go, they were quite posh ones and with plenty of space around them. Seein' them now, as I did when John took me back in the summer of 2015, things had changed a bit. By the look of them, we think most if not all the row of Council houses have been bought up under Maggie Thatcher's 'right to buy' policy and made a bit more individual.

Mr Gasson kept bees in his garden and, as bees do, now and again they'd swarm. Then it would be panic stations and you'd hear cries of "Oh my God, Gasson's bees are out!" Havin' said that, those same grown-ups used to tell us never to go killin' any of Mr Gasson's bees. There was a sort of concrete drive comin' off the end of the Council houses and for some reason they'd very often choose to swarm there. If we'd been out in the fields or over to the ponds, that driveway was our quickest route home – back to Ma Wickens'. It was frightenin' walking through a swarm of bees, so instead we'd go back round and take a detour. If that made us late, that would be Ok because we could blame Mr Gasson's bees. Havin' discovered that Ma Wickens was Ok with that excuse, it came in useful a time or two – even when there were no bees!

As far as entertainment went, especially for the bigger kids, there was a wide gulf between what they had been used to in London and what was available in Ardingly. Take the pictures for example. As you know, even I used to go regularly to the matinee on a Saturday. The bigger kids often went to the cinema twice a week. There was nothin' like that in Ardingly, where they only had a 'magic lantern' show and that was of no interest to London kids. I guess the villagers thought we were ungrateful, but I don't think we were. It's just that things had moved on such a lot and we knew it. We'd experienced them, things like the cinema, and to us they were the norm.

As far as playin' out went, as I remember, the weather in Ardingly was kind to us. We had lovely summers with lots of long, warm, sunny days. Of course it did rain sometimes, but not that often and not enough to dampen our spirits. The winters mind, they could be cold, maybe colder than I remember them bein' in London. The winters of 1940 and 1942 were, especially bad. In those years, I remember the ponds, the ones down in the valley, just beyond the Honeybuns, froze over and stayed frozen for weeks on end. The ice must have been very thick because quite a lot of folk from the village went skatin' on 'em. Proper skatin' I mean. I can see 'em now glidin' along with their hands behind their backs. Us evacuees never had any skates, but we had a go at just slidin' along in our normal shoes. Needless to say we spent more time on our backsides than anythin'.

I remember the trouble caused when everythin' froze and some of the bursts when it thawed. Of course there was no central heatin' in those days and although people had coal fires, nobody could afford to keep a fire lit all day. Most houses had electricity downstairs, but most didn't upstairs and we'd have to take a Wee Willie Winkie candle holder up to bed with us. The Honeybuns and the Setfords used to light it for me before I went up. They wouldn't risk me playin' with matches. We had toilets downstairs, usually inside, which was better than we were used to in London. Upstairs we had chamber pots, which was fine until one got knocked over, which inevitably from time to time they would. Boys and girls were always in separate bedrooms.

One of the older evacuees, Doreen Bowler her name was, didn't stay in Ardingly all that long because she became 14 and had to go back up to London. At 14 you were expected to go out to work. Before that though, she'd become very friendly with Eva (Ma Wickens' daughter) and so she still came back down to Ardingly sometimes at weekends. Now and again, Doreen and Eva would take us kids out and if it was a nice warm sunny day, we'd take a picnic up to Balcombe Lakes, which was about three or so miles away. Our route would take us up through the village, past the Church and then the school and then on up towards the caves and then up the Balcombe Road. I was the youngest and by that time I'd usually be laggin' behind a bit, draggin' my feet. The thing was, I didn't see the point and I suppose 'cos my heart wasn't really in it, it seemed to me to be never endin' – like we were never goin' to get there. I remember thinkin', "Why have we got to walk all this way just to eat a cheese sandwich when we get there?" My idea would have been to stop and have our sandwich near the caves and then do somethin' more excitin' and cut out all that walkin'. Lazy logic I suppose.

You might be thinkin', "Why is he botherin' to tell us all this?" Well, the thing is, on one of these jaunts, somethin' more excitin' did happen as we were strollin' along the Balcombe Road. As I recall, we were a big group that day – about 13 of us – so pretty visible. These two planes, I think they were Stuka Bombers, but whatever they were, they suddenly swooped down out of nowhere and started machine gunnin' the road in front of us. We were scared witless and all dived into the hedge bottom. I think that was Doreen's idea to try and hide I suppose. They must have seen us though and a fat lot of protection a hedge would have provided if they wanted to kill us. I think they could probably tell we were just kids and were playin' around, just tryin' to scare us and give us a story to tell. Or they were just practisin', glad to have a little ddddd at anythin' that moved. Whatever, they didn't turn again. They just went on their – I nearly said "merry way"- but that would hardly be appropriate given what they'd really flown over here to do. It could be they just couldn't afford to hang about wastin' fuel on us or they might not make it back across the Channel after their mission.

It's funny how I can clearly remember some things, like Doreen sayin' to us younger ones as we crouched in the hedge bottom, "Don't look up, don't look up." Now I think, as if lookin' up would have made a scrap of difference, but not back then; then I think I was grateful for "the protection". For someone to tell me what to do. After all, to me Doreen was practically a grown-up. As you can imagine, our 'near death' encounter quickly spread around the village and many years later at one of our 'Evacuees Reunions' (I'll tell you about those later), I met up with Doreen again and inevitably our conversation turned to that particular day. Sadly Doreen died a couple of years ago from cancer.

Most of our walks were less eventful, although we'd usually come back with somethin' dependin' on the season. Pickin' wild flowers in the countryside now isn't just frowned on, in many cases it's against the law. Not in our day though. We'd bring Ma Wickens back armfuls of bluebells and primroses from our walks. Sadly, one of our favourite places to go gatherin' was where they've now built a reservoir and all our primrose banks are under water, so law or no law, nobody's goin' to be pickin' any now.

Visualisin' those primroses, somethin's just occurred to me. Earlier, I think I told you dad only ever came to Ardingly once – just after our first Christmas in the village. Thinkin' about it now, I'm wrong. He only came the once on his own, but he did come a couple more times with mum. I can't remember exactly when, but I can remember him comin'. Once must have been late spring because the bluebells and primroses were out. I remember they'd brought a picnic and we went for a walk to the caves – up past the church, on the Balcombe Road. There were lovely bluebells and primroses in the wood and dad had brought a trowel and he dug a few up to take back to London. In those days you could. And the caves – they were littered with ferns. Dad loved them as well and took some back with him to Montefiore Street. I'm digressin' a bit now I know and jumpin' the gun, but when later, as you'll learn, we moved to Gambetta Street, the backs of the air raid shelters in Montefiore Street backed onto our backyard and those ferns dad had brought back from Ardingly had spread themselves into the brickwork all up and down the street.

Over the years, mum came quite a few times on her own and occasionally we did get other visitors too. I've told you about Uncle Jack comin' but I haven't mentioned Olga. You remember, Aunt Raithby's adopted daughter Olga, well she was in the ATS durin' the war. She was probably kept very busy, but she didn't forget us – Roy and me that is. More than once she came all the way to Ardingly with sweets for us. Friends and relatives though, they were never allowed to come in the house, not in any of my billets. The only exception, if you recall, was Mrs Honeybun, who did let mum, and on another occasion dad in once, but none of the others – no way – especially

Ma Wickens – she wouldn't let anybody across her threshold unless, like the Bowlers, they were payin' for the privilege.

I've told you about the shops, but whilst the shops, farms and schools provided some employment, when war broke out the main sources of employment for Ardingly were in the buildin' and brick-makin' industries. The buildin' firm of Mannions employed over 100 men and durin' the war, lorry loads of Ardingly workmen travelled up to London on a daily basis to help with the work of repairin' all the damage done by enemy bombin'. Over time, the able-bodied men of the village not considered to be in employment essential to the war effort were called up for service in either the army, navy or, like Cyril Honeybun, the airforce. Older or medically unfit men joined the Local Defence Volunteer Force (LDVF).

The LDVF was formed shortly after the outbreak of war. Later it would be renamed the Home Guard, a name with which you'll probably be more familiar. In Ardingly, Mr Hetts was in command and at first, in the absence of rifles, the men had to learn their drill usin' broom handles! They probably felt a bit silly, but they did it anyway. It was thought that the valley of the river Ouse could be a likely line of advance for an invadin' army bound for London and so pill boxes were installed on its banks. From what I could see, that was about it, the official village protection, a couple of old codgers in the Home Guard mannin' a pillbox on the edge of the village. Perhaps I'm bein' a bit unfair because they weren't all that old and they were most likely part of a platoon who took it in turns to do the nightly sentry duty. Mind you, how anybody ever thought the two of them could stop or even hinder a German army advance if they had invaded, beggars belief. We were only about 20 miles from the coast at Brighton and about 34 miles from London. Chances are, an invadin' army would have come straight through Ardingly on their way to London. Luckily there never was an invasion, but if you stop to think about it, Sussex wasn't exactly the safest place to stick 250,000 child evacuees.

Searchlights were also positioned on the edge of the village because it lay on the route of some of the bombers bound for London. This was somethin' of a double-edged sword and exposed the village to rather more danger than might have otherwise been the case. However, in practice, whilst dog fights were a fairly regular occurrence in the skies, the village itself suffered little damage. A landmine exploded on "Buster Hill" where the road to Highbrook joins the Linfield Road and a V1 rocket came down not far away on Lywood Common. Fortunately, neither caused casualties. Regrettably the village was not so lucky when what was said to be a stray German bomb destroyed two houses in Street Lane, killin' five people. I'm not so sure it was a stray bomb. It could just as well have been an attempt to take out the nearby searchlight positions.

I'm afraid us kids thought it was excitin' and we couldn't wait to go and see the damage on our way to school. It must have been in the early days when mornin' school for us was still at Hapstead Hall. Before we could get close, we were stopped. They'd got the road barricaded off and wouldn't let us go our normal way to school. We had to take a detour behind the allotments. We tried to see across, but really all we could make out were the skeletons of the houses already in the process of bein' demolished. By the time school turned out, much to our disappointment, the remains of the two houses had all but been cleared away. I'm not sure I ever knew the names of the people who were killed, but I do know they included a blind man and his wife. I'd seen him several times before in the village with his white stick.

In the days after the bomb, I can remember some of the grown-ups talkin' about it. They were sayin' the blind man must have left a light on and Gerry saw it and ditched their bombs. True enough, it was well-known Gerry would ditch any bombs they were still carryin' before goin' back across the Channel, but I can't see why a blind man would have switched the light on in the first place. I suppose it could be that although registered blind, he had a bit of sight and needed a strong light to see anythin' at all. We'll never know for sure because sadly, like his wife and his neighbour, he didn't live to tell the tale.

For me, the most frightenin' bombs were the ones that came down 'screamin'. Terrifyin' they were. I'd heard some in London, but we even got a few in Ardingly. They tried to bomb Wakehurst a few times, but each time the bombs exploded in the grounds. I never lived that close to Wakehurst, but you could hear the bombs screamin' as they fell right across the village. I suppose at night the place was deathly quiet so the sound travelled and when you heard them, you never really knew just where they were goin' to land.

I mentioned the dog fights, but perhaps I should say a bit more about them. Try to imagine a lovely summer's day with just the birds singin', because that's how I remember the days were in Ardingly durin' the war. Then, all of a sudden, planes would arrive as if from nowhere and sometimes a dog fight would ensue. Even in London they wouldn't have seen the dog fights like there were over Kent and Sussex. We'd stand and watch until the rat-tat-tat of machine guns sounded too close for comfort and frightened us into takin' cover – usually under a hedge. Not that a hedge bottom would have given us any real protection. Sometimes a dog fight would last as long as 20 minutes – or so it seemed before the planes would disengage and fly away and the skies become clear again. I was told it was because the pilots had no choice – they'd be runnin' low on fuel and would have to go back or risk a crash landin'.

Whilst quite a few planes got damaged and limped off trailin' smoke, I never actually saw a fighter plane shot down, but on one occasion I did see a German bomber – a Dornier I think – come down very low over the chimney pots. It was bein' pursued and eventually crash landed along the valley to the south-east of the village on land belongin' to Lower Sheriff Farm. Of the crew of 4, only one young German survived the crash. He was just 16. Mr Chatfield, the local policeman, picked him up and I saw him sittin' in the back of Mr Chatfield's car outside the police house. He was wearin' a blue airman's uniform and a 'half hat'. He looked very frightened and I remember feelin' rather sorry for him. Some women were on the pavement and one said, "Should we get him a cup of tea," but another said, "There's no point. He'll only think it's poisoned." Apparently Mr Chatfield had gone in to phone for instructions as to what to do with him. It probably wasn't very clever leavin' him sittin' in the car unattended 'cos I guess he could have tried to 'leg it'. What's more, when he came back Mr Chatfield just got in and drove off, which must have made him pretty vulnerable to an attack from behind. In the event nothin' like that happened and the young man was taken to a German prisoner of war camp on the other side of Turner's Hill, about 5 miles away on the road to East Grinstead. I guess the poor lad was just too traumatised and, havin' seen his senior comrades killed, all the fight had gone out of him. As for Mr Chatfield, I'm afraid he didn't always command the respect perhaps his position warranted. Except when talkin' to him, people in the village used to call him 'Chaplin' after Charlie Chaplin I suppose they were takin' the mickey and thought of him as a bit of a clown, but as far as I could see, he had no sense of humour at all. Maybe that was it – why folk took the mickey.

I did have a near miss myself later on in the fields outside Ardingly – but I'll come to that later. For now I need to finish up tellin' you about the LDVF. As well as watchin' their manoeuvres I used to chat to a 'man' nicknamed Tinker who I guess would have been in his late teens. Tinker's father was Mr Symons, the man who ran the local garage and petrol pumps and Tinker was both a member of the LDVF and the Auxiliary Fire Service (AFS), which I'll come to in a minute. Before I do though, I just want to say somethin' about Mr Symons' petrol pumps because they fascinated me. In fairness, when I think about it now, I wasn't really familiar with petrol pumps of the time because our family didn't own a car and there wasn't a garage near to where we lived in London. Even so, Mr Symons' petrol pumps made a lastin' impression because they were hand pumps, so servin' petrol involved a bit of elbow grease, a bit like pumpin' water up from a well, except the handle had a sort of ratchet arrangement on it.

I can only assume that Tinker had some form of disability that excused him from bein' called up, or maybe he just wasn't quite old enough because towards the end of the war I think he did go in the army. Anyway, I knew him because, like me, he used to fish and, more particularly, because his girlfriend was a friend of June. If you remember June was the eldest daughter of the Honeybuns, so he knew Roy and me right from the start at our first billet.

I'm afraid I've got a rather sad story to tell you about Tinker and I think I'll get it off my chest first. I think it was some time in 1942 that Tinker and his best mate went up to London to see Tommy Trinder at the Palladium. Bein' a bit older, his mate had been called up, and the Palladium trip was a sort of farewell treat. Incidentally, accordin' to what mum told me, Tommy Trinder's father was a tram driver at Clapham Common Garage. Anyway, the show must have gone on late because by the time they got back to Haywards Heath the last bus had gone and they had to walk all the way back – about 5 miles. As they were gettin' close to Ardingly at about midnight, they heard a terrific explosion. It was that land mine explodin' at Lywood on the Haywards Heath road to Ardingly which I mentioned earlier. Fortunately they'd decided to walk up the back road, otherwise they could have been killed.

At the time they thought the explosion had been really close, more or less a couple of fields away. In fact, when daylight came it proved to be a bit further than that - nearly a mile away at Lywood, leavin' this bloomin' great crater. I know because bein' kids we had to go and explore, didn't we, and, as it turned out, it was quite a fruitful trip because the explosion had exposed all this lovely wet clay, some of which we gathered up and took back to use for modellin'. We thought that was a great find. Kids today, pre-occupied with all their electronic gadgets, probably wouldn't bother to get their hands dirty, but to us as evacuees in the early 1940s, it was as good as any toy. We'd mess about with it for hours. Life was much simpler then and by and large us kids made our own entertainment. As for Tinker and his mate, they'd escaped the bomb, but sadly their story still didn't have a happy endin' because on the Monday Tinker's mate went off to the Navy and never returned. He was killed on his first mission and so that walk home with what they'd thought at the time was a near miss, was the last Tinker would ever see of his best friend.

I got talkin' to Tinker in the days just after the bomb, before he heard the sad news about his friend and he showed me this German cap badge. We Wicken's kids had been up to the site and got some clay, but it turns out Tinker, along with some other local lads with bikes had been up there before us huntin' for souvenirs. Apparently, Mr Chatfield, the local bobby had caught them at it and confiscated most of their 'finds' but, as Tinker proudly told me, "He didn't get my cap badge."

As I've said, Tinker wasn't just in the Home Guard, he was in the Fire Brigade (AFS). Durin' the war the National Fire Brigade would give a pump to any village Auxiliary Fire Service provided the village had a suitable vehicle to pull it. There wasn't a suitable vehicle in Ardingly so it was largely down to Tinker to create one. He was a brilliant carpenter as well as a car mechanic. Anyway, he took an old engine out of a boat and put it in an old taxi which he cut up and modified for the purpose. He told me that the engine had a damaged block which he'd had to repair. I'm not sure if the other volunteer firemen knew, but Tinker told me he used to worry that the engine would crack open again every time they took the makeshift fire engine out for practice manoeuvres. In fact it survived the war and never let them down.

I don't recall them ever havin' to put out any real fires in the village, but their practice sessions created quite a spectacle for us kids. Most times they'd practise up at Ardingly College and to get there they'd have to drive down through the village past our billet at Ma Wickens. They'd always be standin' up in the back with their helmets on and they'd ring the big brass bell as they went along, just as if they were on a real emergency. Maybe they wanted everyone to know they were doin' a good job. Anyway, this would alert us to the exercise and then there'd be this makeshift fire engine with a hoard of us kids runnin' on behind. We couldn't keep up but we knew where they were headed – up to the big pond next to the College. They used to practise there because there was a ready water supply and because the College, bein' the biggest buildin' around, was thought to be the most likely to get bombed. Luckily, it never did. Once there they'd set their pump up and run one end of the hose into the lake and start the pump so they could practise their fire drill. Sometimes it was funny 'cos the pressure would cause the hose to curl and twist like a big snake and if they didn't have a good enough grip, it would spiral and send water cascadin' in all directions! Mostly though, they just practised sendin' jets of water onto chosen spots to put out imaginary fires. They took it seriously and would all be wearin' their allotted blue firemen's uniforms and helmets painted black. They weren't issued with the traditional brass helmets that regular firemen used to wear.

I mentioned that one of the reasons I knew Tinker was because we both liked to go fishin' and I'd sometimes see him down at Gasson's pond. Mr Gasson was ancient – he must have been about 90, or so I thought anyway, but in the 1930s he owned a local brickworks. One of the beneficial spin-offs were the ponds created where clay had been dug out. They were good for fishin' in the summer and ice skatin' in the winter. There was one pond in particular which Tinker had stocked with fish and he wanted to see how many were in there now, so he threw some sort of explosive in. I think it was a sort of cordite detonator but, whatever it was, it had more of an impact than he'd bargained for. There was a huge bang, the shock waves killed some of the fish and whether he was summoned or just heard the bang I don't know, but Mr Chatfield, the village bobby, arrived. Fortunately for

Tinker, he'd already decided to beat a hasty retreat. That left Mr Chatfield scratchin' his head.

Tinker was a member of the local football team, so I'd sometimes see him on a Saturday mornin' if we Wickens kids decided to go and watch. Even durin' the war some of the opposin' teams came from quite a distance. To be honest, I wasn't that interested in watchin' the football but I knew there was a chance that one of the local kids with a bike might let me have a go whilst they were watchin.' It might cost me a stick of spearmint or somethin' but it was worth it.

Lookin' back, I'd have to say that the war was an excitin' period in which to spend one's childhood in the village, not least when troops were stationed there. The French Canadians were in the village for about 6 or 7 weeks during the summer of 1942. In addition to the main camp just outside the village, they requisitioned the Rectory, the chapel, the petrol pumps and used Jordans as their officers' mess. They were a friendly bunch and used to give us chewin' gum. Often they'd come down through the village to Hapstead Hall to catch the bus to Haywards Heath for a night out. We'd go and sit with the soldiers on the tank traps that had been put there - The soldiers waitin' for the bus and we waitin' to collect the butt ends they threw down. Sometimes we got quite big ones if they'd not long lit up when the bus came. We'd collect the tobacco to smoke in our makeshift pipes that we'd fashioned out of hollow stems and conker shells. The taste was pretty disgustin', but I suppose it made us feel 'big'.

Some of the older boys, including our Roy, were allowed to go and watch the Thursday night film shows put on for the troops in the army camp across the Klondyke – a big steep field we used to sledge down in the winter. They didn't just go to watch the films. They'd sneak out and try and pinch a tin of biscuits which were sometimes stacked out back. They were great big tins like small oil drums full of Jacob's cracker type biscuits. They were front line rations really, but when the big boys came back with one then all us kids would have biscuits for weeks after. I know it wasn't very honest, but it was every man – or rather kid – for himself durin' the war. You had to grab what you could, when you could.

I told you that I always kept my eyes and ears open and, take it from me, there was quite a bit of romance with the soldiers. Our District Nurse had a house in Ardingly. I knew her because we used to go and see her if we had minor ailments. She married her Canadian sweetheart after the war. Then there was Eva, Ma Wickens' daughter. I might have been only 8, but I was a nosey so and so and I learnt a lot from spyin' on her with her soldier beau in the cornfield out back. He eventually married his girl back in Canada and had three daughters, but he obviously still had a soft spot for Eva because many years later he wrote to her after his wife died. By this time Eva had herself married, so they never got together again.

Although we didn't know they were plannin' to leave, the day before the Canadians left the village, they organised a sports day on the recreation ground. It was also a sort of Open Day to give folks a chance to inspect their equipment. Even their tanks were brought in and parked up under the trees so us kids could clamber over them. It was a real party atmosphere with everyone laughin' and jokin'.

I won the egg and spoon race and they gave me a postal order for two & six – a goodly sum in those days. It was burnin' a hole in my pocket and so on the way 'home' (to Ma Wickens' place) I went into Sears and gave them my postal order for a packet of chocolate biscuits and some change. What had been a brilliant day turned a bit sour after that because when I came out of the shop there were three soldiers carryin' some of the equipment away. It was about 5.45 and they were packin' up. One of them dropped a shot put and it came rollin' down the road towards me. I was only a kid and I didn't realise it was made of solid iron or just how heavy it was. I put my free hand down to stop it for them and my finger was squashed between the ball and the road and my fingernail was ripped clean off. When I saw the blood I was frightened and ran away before the soldiers could see me. It was a few minutes before it really started to hurt, and then boy, did it hurt, but I kept it hidden and Ma Wickens didn't notice for 3 days.

Next day, one of the Wickens' boys said, "Let's go up to the camp to see the soldiers." Of course we were all a bit like sheep and followed on. When we got there we found they'd all gone. Not a trace of them. They must have done a moonlight, but they couldn't have come the usual way through the village or we'd have heard the tanks. Later the grown-ups said the sports and open day must have been a decoy to make the German spy planes think nothin' was happenin' when in fact they were plannin' to leave that very night.

Overnight they'd gone to Sussex – to Newhaven to take part in the assault on Dieppe – the first invasion of the war. It all went horribly wrong. It turned out to be a suicide mission and most of our French Canadians – the ones who'd given us their chewin' gum and been so kind to us – the ones we'd had such fun with – were ripped to pieces by German machine guns lyin' in wait.

As well as with our own troops, us kids cavorted with the enemy, so to speak. Don't worry, it's not as bad as it sounds. To us they became our friends and fun to be with, the 'Iti's' that is. I should explain that towards the end of 1943 they set up a prisoner of war camp for Italian soldiers about half a mile outside the village on the road to Turner's Hill. If you were to go lookin' today, you won't see any sign but it's more or less where the Sussex Showground is now. At the same time they set up a searchlight battery in the field opposite. About half a dozen lights there were, spread out across the field. They'd switch 'em on as soon as they got a message that planes were comin' over.

Whilst all in all, lookin back, I benefited from bein' in Ardingly and for the latter part at least enjoyed my time there, it wasn't exactly the smartest place to put child evacuees – right under the flight path of the German aircraft bound for London. Then installin' searchlight batteries – a bit like a red rag to a bull!

Whilst it's the Sussex Showground now, back then it was known as 'Little London'. Don't ask me why because there were only about two houses in the near vicinity. Most of the prisoners were young chaps – in their early twenties I'd say, and some of 'em only teenagers. They wore a prison uniform which had been dyed dark brown and they had big round patches in the middle of their back and one on each knee. The idea was these were targets to shoot at if they tried to run away. Not that any did. Not that I ever heard of anyway. By all accounts, they weren't the most committed soldiers, the Italians, they didn't much care for Hitler any more than we did.

It wasn't exactly a high security prison camp, just a fence and hedge with wooden huts inside for the prisoners. They were a very friendly bunch and seemed to love children. They spoke broken English but good enough for us to understand and called us their 'bambinos'. More or less from the off, they weren't confined to the prison. They used to leave the camp in work parties of about 30 prisoners and march up through the camp, often past Ma Wickens' place. They'd be goin' doin' hedge trimmin', copicin' or ditch clearin' or somethin' of that sort. Whenever we saw 'em, we kids would jump into their ranks and march along with 'em! Bizarre when you think about it, but they loved it as much as we did – all smiles and laughin'. The two at the back would be carryin' billy cans and provisions 'cos they'd be assigned to cook's duty. We'd tell Ma Wickens that we were goin' with the 'Iti's' and sometimes we'd say, we'll have our lunch with them. We did as well and good it was – rabbit stew and things like that. Lookin' after them and supposedly makin' sure they didn't leg it was just one oldish chap and he didn't even have a gun – just a big stick! Fat lot of good that would have been if they'd decided to turn on him with their shovels and all.

Whilst they were doin' whatever work they'd been brought out to do, we'd be talkin' to the two cooks. Four or five of us there'd be. It was great fun. Sometimes, when we'd eaten the stew or whatever, dependin' on the time, we'd wander off back to Ma Wickens and get another bite to eat, especially if we hadn't bothered to tell her we were goin' to have lunch. We weren't daft.

The more we got to know the Iti's, the more friendly they became. I think they looked forward to us joinin' in with them as much as we did doin' it. At any rate, they encouraged us to tag along and pretty soon we were joinin' in not just watchin' them or kickin' a ball around. They used to let us make up the fire. Stokin' a fire up when we were only eight or nine years old was somethin' we knew we'd never normally be allowed to do. It felt great. Responsibility, excitement, darin' – all rolled into one. I never remember any of the local kids joinin' in with us – just us Wickens' kids. The kids with freedom to roam. Sometimes we must have stank of smoke, from stokin' the fire I mean, but I never remember Ma Wickens sayin' anythin'. So long as we were back for meal times or had excused ourselves and she wasn't gettin' any complaints about our behaviour in the village, she was happy to let us be.

Like I say, the more the prisoners got to know us, the more they seemed to like us hangin' around and because they could talk to us in broken English, we could have quite a friendly chat. Before long it wasn't just their food they were handin' out. Now and again they'd give us a cigarette to share. That was probably quite a big deal for them because I wouldn't think they had that many. For us that was luxury because normally we'd have to make do with dog ends we picked up round the bus stop.

I should explain that it was mainly in the holidays we got to tag along with our Iti's because they were generally confined to camp at weekends and of course we were at school on a normal weekday. When I say they were confined to camp, I think it's just there were no work parties arranged at weekends and they were told to stay put and they did. If they'd wanted to escape, I think it would have been easy. There didn't seem to be much in the way of security, but in any event, I don't think they wanted to. They were content to sit out the war with us. Everybody got so used to them bein' around and I guess nobody saw them as a threat because by the middle of 1944 they were let out to wander around the village on their own especially at weekends, goin' in the shops and even goin' to village dances. After the war one of them married a village girl and settled down.

There were two big holly trees near the P.O.W. camp and, comin' up to Christmas, Ma Wickens would send us up there to collect some berried sprigs and sprays. As well as that, we'd go up to the camp to barter. The prisoners made some lovely things – I guess from stuff they could forage. I remember the baskets in particular. Us kids would go up to the hedge surroundin' the camp and go psst psst and wave our half crowns in the air. The prisoners knew what we wanted and would bring baskets and pass them over in exchange. We wanted them as Christmas presents for our mums.

Talkin' of mums, mum continually worried that I wasn't gettin' a proper education in Ardingly. Roy was at a good technical school in Haywards Heath and doin' well. She was pleased about that and happy to leave him there, but she thought my education was haphazard and she worried for my future. By this time it was 1944 and all our London teachers had long since returned to teach back in London and most of the Ardingly evacuees had also gone back. Some because they couldn't cope with bein' evacuees, some to start work and some just to go back to their old schools. Mum was still worried about the bombin', but there seemed to be a bit of a lull. It had been a long time since the main 'blitz' on London and although there was still bombin', it wasn't nearly so frequent or intense as it had been and so in June 1944 she took the difficult decision to bring me back home to Montefiore Street and to Heathbrook – my old school. I'm sayin' my 'old school', but in truth I'd only ever been an infant there for a relatively short while before bein' evacuated.

Some things had changed dramatically whilst I'd been away. In Montefiore Street all the beautiful wrought-iron railin's had been cut off and taken away. Our street, like countless others, would never be the same again. I'm not sure that so much scrap iron was really all that useful to the war effort, but someone high up somewhere had decreed it and on the back of that, what the Germans couldn't do to wreck our heritage, the authorities did or so it seems to me.

Another big blow – for me at least – was that our beloved milkman Jim had lost our round as a result of the war. Apparently when rationin' came in they divided the rounds up differently and we got a Mr Jones & Son. In fact he had two sons, both very overweight. They were Welsh people and I dare say they did a good job, but to me they were no substitute for Jim and his horse and cart. They didn't even have a horse – they had a hand cart which they pushed along themselves. Thinkin' about it now, it's a wonder the sons were so fat with all the exercise they got. They also had a dairy shop on Silverthorn Road run by Mr Jones' wife, Lottie. If mum was makin' custard or somethin', she'd ask me to 'pop over to Lotties' for an extra pint. There was usually a queue, but that woman never stopped talkin'. It took ages to get served. It seemed to me that most women went in there for a chat and to catch up on the scandal. You could learn a lot just 'poppin' out' for a pint of milk.

One thing I forgot to mention was that when I was told I'd be leavin' Ardingly I went fishin' to Gasson's Pond. There were other ponds, but we'd found Gasson's Pond was good for fishin'. In fact it was so full of fish I don't remember tryin' anywhere else. Mostly we'd catch golden carp. They were a beautiful colour. Sometimes Roy would make a sort of oven out of clay and we'd cook 'em. I suppose we knew they weren't really ours and that we'd poached 'em, but there were loads in there and I don't think anybody minded all that much. I loved it – the fishin' and the cookin' and the eatin'. They tasted lovely. I thought so anyway. To me it was all a big adventure and with that little element of risk – well, you know what kids are like – I suppose it made us feel sort of 'big'. We used a rod and line to catch 'em. Not a proper one. One we'd made ourselves. We'd get a hazel rod out of the hedge. They were good 'cos they were a bit springy. We didn't have any reels, so we'd just tie button thread round the top and fashion a hook from a bent pin. All a bit Heath Robinson, but with a worm on the end or a bit of bread made into a paste, or a bit of cheese, they worked well enough. I'm gettin' a bit side-tracked again. I expect you're used to it by now. It's just that sometimes I get these really vivid pictures of how it used to be and I just can't help tellin' you – while they're still fresh in my mind. I love re-livin' 'em, my memories. Well, the good ones at least.

All this talk of fishin' though isn't really relevant to what I was startin' to tell you before I got side-tracked. The thing was, I knew I couldn't take live fish back with me to London, but I'd decided I wanted to take a big jar with pond weed and tadpoles in it. I suppose I wanted to take a bit of the countryside back with me.

Anyway, havin' travelled up to London on the train by myself, I was home and it was now Sunday 4th June 1944. I'd only been home a day with a view to startin' back at Heathbrook School on Monday. I didn't know it then, but it was the weekend before D-Day – the start of the Normandy landin's, which, if you know your history, was Tuesday 6th June 1944. Somethin' else I didn't know, somethin' mum didn't, couldn't know, was that the Germans had developed a new weapon designed mainly to attack London and that they were about to start usin' it. I'm sayin' nobody knew. The military intelligence services might have known, but they didn't alert the general public to any impendin' danger. They never did, not until it was blindingly obvious. Records now reveal their thinkin' was they didn't want to cause mass panic or 'unnecessary' alarm! The Germans' new weapon? Well, it was the V1 rocket bomb with which all too soon Londoners would become familiar, except they didn't call 'em V1 rockets, they called 'em doodlebugs.

Bein' a Sunday, Dad was busy cookin' Sunday lunch ready for when mum got home from work. I think I may have told you that durin' the war mum worked on the railway, originally as a cleaner, but by this time she'd been promoted to the stores. Amongst other things she'd give out oily rags to engine drivers and so wore overalls at work. She kept them at home so she'd always be wearin' em when she got back. On a Sunday she finished work at one o'clock and then it was about a twenty minute walk back home. As I say, dad was busy cookin' Sunday lunch as usual. The only thing out of the ordinary was it wasn't a roast he was doin, it was some sort of stew. Anyway, dad realised he was runnin' low on tobacco so he asked me to nip up to Maceys to buy some, but told me not to dawdle because he was ready to dish the dinner up as soon as mum got back. It wasn't like it is today, tobacco wasn't considered harmful and as kids we could go and buy tobacco or cigarettes. It was just accepted that it would be for mum or dad. Maybe the shopkeepers knew we wouldn't have had the money to go buyin' tobacco for ourselves anyway.

Macey's was one of those shops I never minded goin' to. A real old fashioned London shop it was. I suppose the 'shop' was really a front parlour converted. The doorbell would tinkle as you opened it and this old woman would come out from the back to serve you. She was always very nice. Nice with everyone. Never barked at us kids, not like some shopkeepers did. Remember that one in Ardingly? Talkin' of Ardingly, the sharp ones amongst you will remember there was also a Macey's in Ardingly but I doubt they were related. I got dad's tobacco and was back home again at about a quarter past one. Just as I was comin' in the door, the air raid siren went. I can't just remember it, I can hear it as if it was yesterday. You'll understand why in a minute. I gave dad his tobacco and he told me although he didn't think it would be much, I'd best go out into the shelter.

Our back garden was mainly concrete with a washing line and such and soon after war broke out, we got this brick-built air-raid shelter. Everybody in Montefiore Street had one. There was a sort of trap door with a chopper so you could get into nextdoor's shelter in the event that a bomb blast blocked your own entrance.

Mum must have heard the siren as she was walkin' up our street. In any case dad sent her into the shelter after me and told her he'd be in in a minute after he'd finished up. As it happened, he was in quicker than he'd thought. As we learnt later, one of the guns on Clapham Common had shot this 'doodlebug' down. I'm sayin' shot it down but I suppose it would be more correct to say 'deflected' it. At this stage 'doodlebugs' were very new. Nobody really knew what they were. Later of course we got to know that they were flyin' bombs that came over with no pilots or anythin'. I don't know why they came to be nick-named 'doodlebugs'. They were particularly lethal and universally feared because they were designed to come down silent after the engines had cut out so the hapless victims would have no audible warnin' of the impendin' doom.

'Doodlebug' seems such an innocuous name for somethin' so destructive. This one had been tipped by a 'lucky shot'. Lucky for some I guess, but not for us in Montefiore Street. Once they became better known, you knew to run like hell if you heard one go silent 'cos then they'd pretty soon be down to earth and explodin'. This one, havin' been hit, came down with its engines on, which is just as well, 'cos that's what alerted dad to it and almost certainly saved his life. Hearin' it, dad didn't hesitate. He had the presence of mind to just dive out of our scullery. Our shelter had an iron door on it which was left open 'till the last one was in. Dad threw himself on top of us just as the thing went off.

There'd been no time to shut the door, so the dust was all over us. We were covered in the stuff. For a split second though, before all that, as dad was divin' in, out of the corner of my eye I saw this enormous sheet of flame as the thing blew up. An enormous bright red flame, gone in a flash. It's funny, because I can remember that vividly, as if it had just happened, but I can't, don't remember any noise, any explosion. Just this huge flash of flame.

The explosion had covered us in dirt, but we weren't hurt. Badly shaken but not hurt. The bomb had struck the house across the street, but the explosion had wrecked our house too. All the windows were out and there was glass and debris everywhere, although we couldn't see it at first for all the dust. The air was blindin' thick with it. You couldn't hardly see. It took a long, long time to settle. As it did, the damage became more and more apparent.

When the dust had settled, dad told mum and me to stay put in the shelter whilst he went to inspect the damage. Somehow he managed to salvage the dinner. I guess the pan bein' heavy had stayed put on the stove. He brought plates and the pan out and proceeded to dish it up, but none of us could really eat it. I think we were sufferin' from shock.

The all clear had long since gone, but dad made us stay in the shelter for the best part of an hour or maybe more. I think it was because the ARP were clearin' up in the street and dealin' with casualties. We'd survived unhurt but, as I was to learn later, our neighbours across the road weren't so lucky. A brother and sister they were. I guess like dad they thought it would be 'nothin much' and hadn't bothered to go to their shelter. It seems that he'd been playin' his saxophone and she the piano when the bomb dropped just behind their house, destroyin' it. Most of it collapsed and both were killed.

As for our house, I clearly remember dad sayin', in a matter of fact sort of way, "Well of course, the house has gone." Thinkin' back, you'd think mum at least would have been cryin' seein' her home destroyed. But she wasn't. None of us were, not even me. Maybe we were all just too much in shock for cryin'. Mum decided the only thing to do was to take me over to Auntie Annie's. If you recall, she was my father's sister. Along with Uncle Jack, she'd lived in our house, 34 Montefiore Street, before us – before movin' out to Tootin'.

Miraculously, my tadpoles – the ones I'd brought from Ardingly - had survived the blast but dad decided the best thing to do with them was to pour them down the drain. I just hope they made it to the river and survived.

Eventually, mum took me through what was left of the house. It was still standin' but that's about all you could say. The lath and plaster walls were now just broken laths and you could see straight through and there was dust and plaster everywhere. Bizarrely, and when I think about it now, rather sadly, mum got this yellow duster and started to try to clear some of the dust 'till dad intervened. Walkin' through our house was bad enough with plaster and dust everywhere and all the walls reduced to see-through skeletons, but outside, in the street, the devastation was much worse. The houses opposite were all but gone and the street was full of bricks and rubble and, most memorable, these great big roofin' timbers criss-crossed everywhere and this smell – cordite I suppose it was – still hangin' in the air.

Until then I'd had no real concept of just how much damage just one bomb could do. Back in Ardingly I'd been protected from it – the stark reality. It was hard to take in and I'd probably have stood starin' for ages but mum had me firmly by the hand and we marched off, hand in hand, down the street over all the rubble up to the bus stop in Wandsworth Road to catch the 77 bus to Tootin' to Auntie Annie's.

I'm sure we were both still in shock – mum included. She couldn't have been thinkin' straight or she wouldn't have tried to clear some of the mess back at the house with a yellow duster. What's more, she wouldn't have still been clutchin' it in her hand as she rushed me off to catch the bus to Auntie Annie's. I can see her now as clear as anythin' in her now dusty work overalls – you see she'd not had time to change with the siren goin' and then the bomb droppin' – clutchin' hold of me in one hand and this yellow duster in the other with her fist clenched. Some images never leave you – never. To help you picture her, I've included a photo of mum durin' the war in her overalls and headscarf with her workmates on the railway. It's at the end of Chapter Three.

Just digressin' for a second, that was typical of mum, duster or no duster, walkin' with her fist clenched. Not in anger, it was just her way. My Sandy walks like that. In lots of ways she is the spittin' image of my mother. Mum never got to see her grow up, but I know she would have so loved our Sand. You'll get to know Sandy later, but I just had to mention her now as the image of the pair of them flashed through my mind.

Dad stayed back, I guess to salvage what he could and to safeguard against the looters. It's sad to say that all the carnage and destruction caused by all the bombin' in London and doubtless everywhere else as well didn't just bring out the best in folk, the pullin' together, the sharin', the camaraderie, it also provided opportunities for the low lives in society to get in quick and try to profit from misfortune, even tragedy, by lootin'.

Mum didn't stay with me at Auntie Annie's, she went back to dad and, as I learned later, spent the next few nights in a shelter. Not an air raid shelter – a sort of hostel for bombed out families. I'm not certain, because we never talked about it, but that would most likely have been in Tennyson Street School, which was only at the end of our street. I do know that durin' the war, the main hall on the ground floor had all its windows bricked up against possible bomb damage because it was used as a rest centre for overnight bomb evacuees. Apparently, part of the school was also used as a temporary mortuary for those killed in the bombin'.

Whilst on the subject of Tennyson Street School and its role durin' the war, somethin' else I should tell you is that dad was in the Civil Defence Corps and did fire watchin' on the school roof. It's a very high buildin' with views all over London. They had a rota and he'd do so many nights a month. The idea was to alert the emergency services to any fires that started breakin' out. The quicker they could get there, the more chance they had of rescuin' folk and limitin' the damage. Sadly, even towards the end of the War when I was back in London, I wasn't allowed up there. I did see the ARP givin' lessons on how to use stirrup pumps in the school playground though, but that was months away and for now, I need to get back to the day of the Bomb.

As for me, later that same afternoon, Auntie Annie took me over to Cleve's house, or rather I should say her son's, where Cleve was stayin'. If you remember, Cleve was the lady who lived at No. 34A, the flat above us in Montefiore Street. We had to take her the sad news that she'd been bombed out. That must have been upsettin' for her on top of everythin' else she was goin' through. The reason she was stayin' with her son was to look after his new-born son. Tragically his wife had died in childbirth. In all the circumstances you can't call it lucky, but in a sense it was, because apparently Cleve was the sort to often stay put rather than comin' down into the air raid shelter. If she'd done that, she'd more than likely have been killed. That would have been tragic for her and her son, who, with his new-born child had turned to his mum for help as he struggled to cope with the loss of his wife.

Thinkin' about it now, that was the last time I saw Cleve. I guess she stayed livin' with her son and grandchild and hopefully they survived the war and things worked out well for them after, but in truth I really don't know what became of them.

I stayed with Auntie Annie for about ten days whilst arrangements were made for me to go back to Ardingly, back to Ma Wickens. Mum had brought me back to London to what she was convinced was better schoolin' but I'd never got that far, it bein' the weekend when the bomb dropped and now I missed another couple of weeks altogether because there wasn't time to organise a new school in Tootin' just for those few days. Meanwhile, mum and dad got re-housed in a flat in Prairie Street. Mum didn't really like it, but it was better than hostel-style livin'. It was a roof over their heads and you had to be grateful for what you could get in war-damaged London. They had to count themselves lucky. They'd lost their home and some of their possessions, but none of us had been killed or even injured – not physically anyway. There were many worse victims of a terrible war that was destroyin' so may lives indiscriminately.

Like many before it, that bomb didn't just destroy property. It killed people – ordinary people who were just tryin' to get on with their lives in the most difficult of circumstances. The fatalities included our neighbours across the road. They were musicians and rather than go to their shelter, they'd carried on playin' their instruments and paid the ultimate price. Saddest of all, although no-one told me at the time, my friend Jonny Gray was killed too. Apparently he'd been sittin' on the pillar outside our house waitin' for me as he'd done so many times before. He must have arrived just after I'd got back from Maceys and decided to sit and wait for me. I never saw him. I learned about it later from mum on a visit to Ardingly. If you look at the picture of mum, Olga, Roy and me taken outside our house in Montefiore Street on my first visit home durin' the war, at the end of this chapter, you'll see my friend Jonny Gray in the background, sittin' on that pillar.

In the short time I was with Auntie Annie, even as far out as Tootin', I didn't really feel safe. Even out there we had a few more air raid sirens go off and had to retire to the shelter. Auntie Annie's shelter was rather flashy because it had a slidin' door and an electric light inside. That wasn't standard. Her son David had put it in. Flashy or not, I still didn't feel safe. Now that I knew what damage just one bomb could do, I have to admit, I was frightened. Auntie Annie was good with me though – she was a school teacher and I guess used to calmin' children. I remember she used to try and make light of the situation and with a smile on her face tell me not to worry because "They drop most of the bombs in the bone yard!" By that she meant the nearby graveyard. Sadly the reality was different. On the very next Saturday afternoon a stray bomb dropped on Woolworths in Tooting Broadway when the place was packed. I think as many as 200 people were killed by that one bomb.

I didn't know then, but I know now that our bomb was one of the very first of its type to hit London. That it was a V1 rocket bomb, a winged, pilot-less, fuel propelled flyin' bomb that had been launched from ramps near the French or Dutch coast. It was only later they became known as 'Doodlebugs'. Why, I don't know, because they were big and deadly things. Records now show they were about 25 feet long with a 16 foot wing span and when loaded with fuel they weighed a staggerin' two tons and carried 2000 lbs of explosives. They were noisy, very noisy, which was just as well because Dad heard the thing and knew somethin' wasn't right. Their engines sounded like a lorry engine goin' really fast. Normally they would keep flyin' until they ran out of fuel. Then their engine would cut out and they'd go silent. Once people got to know what they were, whenever they heard a doodlebug, everyone would look up and follow its path until it had gone well past and with it the danger to them at least. If the engine stopped whilst the thing was still overhead, then it was panic stations and you'd have to run like hell away from the thing. Sometimes, it would already be too late because sometimes it would just drop like a stone. Other times they'd continue to glide silently down, gradually losin' height until they came into contact with buildin's and then it was mayhem. It wasn't publicised at the time, but now records show that by early July an estimated 2,500 Londoners had been killed by Doodlebugs, includin' the 200 killed in Tootin' Broadway whilst I was stayin' with Auntie Annie.

Mum and dad must have gone back to our bombed out house in Montefiore Street to salvage what possessions they could, but I never did go back there, not even after the war when eventually it was repaired. John and I visited it in 2015 and I have to say it looks rather nice now. They never did rebuild the houses opposite though. As you can see, in the photo at the end of this chapter, there's a small park there now.

I couldn't just go back to Ardingly – it had to be cleared with the authorities. Eventually, after about two weeks, I was dispatched back to Ma Wickens. There was no air raid shelter at Ma Wickens'. In fact I don't think there were any at all in Ardingly. Now, whenever the sirens went, I'd have to admit to bein' a bit scared. I'd been traumatised by my experience of the bombin' and seein' just what a single bomb could do.

I'd just been saved by an air raid shelter and I knew for sure that hidin' under a table wouldn't be much use. Those doodlebugs were comin' over regularly now and a few weeks after I got back, they put artillery guns in the big field at the back of Ma Wickens' place to try to stop 'em. They wanted to shoot 'em down in the open where they'd do no real damage – before they got near London. That was all very well, but now I knew just how much damage they could cause if one happened to come down in the village.

As a result, for a while I became a bit of a home bird. Not goin' out much except to school. Not joinin' in much with the others when they went off up to the College or wherever. But I was missin' out and I suppose I felt it. Part of me – an increasingly big part of me – wanted to be one of the Wickens boys again. I missed the camaraderie and wanted to be part of it. Gradually I started venturin' out, but ever after I was never quite so keen to watch dog fights any more and even friendly planes flyin' low scared me to death. This was a regular thing up near the College. Old boys who'd become pilots used to come back to salute the place by divin' low over it. The noise was deafenin' and I hated it. The College was always thought to be a target and when the planes dived down from the sky, you could never be quite sure they were friendly.

The planes apart, I gradually got my bravado back and started joinin' in the fun again. It was now the summer holidays, so we had lots of time, lots of freedom. We Wickens kids would even go and sit with the soldiers and their guns in the back field. They were right on our doorstep. All we had to do was squeeze through the hedge at the bottom of the garden. They were mostly from London, so we had somethin' in common. One of 'em even knew my turnin' (my street) and knew about 'my bomb'. Mostly we'd just chat and mess about, but when it was gettin' serious, one of them would blow a whistle as a signal that they were goin' to start firin' and then we were supposed to go off back 'home'. To begin with we did, but over time I guess we got braver and you know what kids are like – they egg each other on.

The guns were out in the open field, but fairly close by, more towards the edge, the soldiers had tents. When they started firin' the guns, instead of goin' back to Ma Wickens' place, we'd sneak into their tents. For us it was excitin' and bizarrely, I actually felt quite safe in their tent. Barmy when you think about it – hidin' in a tent from a bomb! The other kids hadn't experienced what a doodlebug could do like I had and I should have known better, but by then I was one of the lads again and I'd got my bravado back and it was excitin'. It was fun. We never felt we were in real danger. We'd just be sittin' there sayin', "It's good, init? They won't hit nothin'."

The soldiers were too pre-occupied to bother with us, but try as they might I never remember them hittin' a single one. You could clearly see flames comin' out of the back of the flyin' bombs as they came over. Tryin' to shoot them down though was a bit futile really.

They went over so fast that by the time the shells got up there, they'd already gone by on their way up to London. Perhaps because they were havin' no success, after a few weeks they packed up their gear and went off to the coast because they thought they'd have more chance of hittin' them as they came in over the sea and less chance of them doin' any damage if they did. It was common sense when you think about it – they should never have been in the village in the first place. I'm glad they were though, because we had fun with them.

It's bizarre when you think about it. These were men fightin' a war – a real war – and we were just kids, larkin' around. Why they bothered with us I don't really know. Maybe we were a distraction for them, provided somethin' more like normality in their lives. Just like the Iti's, we used to have dinner with them and everythin'. Sometimes we'd be eatin' our dinner and they'd have to break off and start firin' their guns. We'd sit 'safe' in their tents munchin' away and jokin', "It's OK, they won't hit nuffin'." Thinkin' back, I'm sure it was the time we spent with those soldiers from London and their friendly attitude towards us that helped me a lot in gettin' over my nervousness after the bomb – in gettin' my bravado back. For a while, the other kids probably thought I was a bit of a 'wuss', but they hadn't seen what I'd seen. Not even our Roy had experienced anythin' like it. He never did. Right through the war he stayed in Ardingly because mum was happy with how well he was doin' at the technical school in Haywards Heath. It was just me and my education she was worried about, enough to risk tryin' to have me back. For now though, it was the summer holidays and mum was happy to leave me be in Ardingly.

It was about five weeks after first arrivin' that the soldiers announced they were bein' redeployed to the coast. We were gutted. We'd had some fun and some excitin' times with them. Mind you, it wasn't over, not quite yet. Come the day we 'helped' them clear up and I was especially lucky gettin' to have a ride around the field in one of their 'lorries'. Not a normal lorry. It had a round hole like a gun turret in it and there I was bein' driven round and round this field with my head pokin' out of the top, just like a tank commander, or so I thought. Great fun that was, especially on a bumpy field. But next day they were gone, gone without a trace, and we all felt a bit down because that was the end of our fun.

A week or so after the soldiers left our back field, I'd got enough confidence back to take off on my own on a fishin' trip. Somethin' I'd done loads of times before the bomb – no problem. Anyway, as usual I went out of the back of Ma Wickens place down the garden and squeezed through the gap in the hedge that us kids had made and started off across the cow field, my home made fishin' rod in hand. It was a very big field with loads of hollows deep enough so you couldn't see if there were cows in there. Not that they would have bothered me. Today you hear of folk bein' attacked by cows, but I never remember cows bein' anythin' but big docile creatures. We'd just shove 'em out of the way if they didn't move to let us pass and at times, when there were no grown-ups around, we'd even try to lasso 'em like on the films.

Anyway, towards the middle of the field there were two trees – oak trees I think they were. As I was walkin' towards them, but still a good way off, suddenly out of the sky this thing came glidin' down and got stuck between them. I thought, "Oh my god – is that a doodlebug!?" I couldn't be sure but fortunately we'd been lectured time and again at school, "If you ever see anythin' come down out of the sky, always dive onto the ground." So I did and a good job too 'cos just as I hit the ground this thing exploded and I can still feel the force of that blast goin' through my hair like a strong wind. I wasn't hurt, but it's somethin' I'll never forget. Just tellin' you about it gives me the shivers – like it had just happened.

This had been my second close encounter with a bomb and I was scared. My first instinct was to run back to Ma Wickens' place, but then I thought, "Blow it. I'm not goin' to go cryin' back there. I'm goin' to go fishin'." So I got up and legged it the other way, puttin' more distance between me and what was left of those trees. It was a bit of a detour, but I could still pick up the path which led over to Gasson's pond. The police and all came to investigate the bomb. I could see them in the distance, but I didn't get involved. I just carried on. Whilst fishin' I remember thinkin', "That's the second time the Germans tried to blow me up, but they didn't get me." I don't remember catchin' anythin', but that wasn't really the point. I'd had another pretty narrow escape and lived to tell the tale. I hadn't let it beat me and again I had the braggin' rights which, as you can imagine, I milked for all they were worth.

Durin' the summer, I remember mum came to visit and although it was the summer holidays, it was clear she was still concerned about my education. Hearin' what I had to say about the blackberryin' we'd be doin' when school resumed didn't help much. Although nothin' much was said that I recall, I think she left all the more determined to get me back to London. What I do remember is askin' after my friend Jonny Gray and mum goin' quiet before lookin' at me and takin' my hand and sayin', "I'm sorry, but it's better I tell you now. He died. He was killed outside our house when the bomb dropped." It seems the ARP people would have taken him away before mum and I came out into the street on our way to Auntie Annie's. I didn't know what to say. I suppose you could say I was 'shell shocked' – long after the event itself, but still shell-shocked.

When I think about it now, I never even saw his parents. In fact I'm not sure even which house he lived in. We'd played together a lot, but he'd always come to call for me. We liked eachother and I felt an empty space inside. I think he was the first person close to me who'd died. I felt the loss. It's difficult to describe and perhaps I don't really want to recall it. I just know I felt it. Then again, I was a kid, so thankfully I don't think I dwelt on it for long.

Now it's different. Now I have time to reflect without the distractions of youth. Perhaps for the first time I can empathize with Jonny because reflectin' back, maybe in those early years in Ardingly I'd walked for a while in his shoes. When I arrived in the village, I was young and streetwise for my age, but I can't really say I was carefree. After Roy and I were split up and I was billeted on my own with elderly and doubtless well-meanin' strangers in first one billet and then another, I experienced loneliness like never before. Even if there was no-one else I could play with, I used to try to stop out because bein' outside was better than havin' to go and sit in a room on my own. Even when it rained, I'd got a place under a hedge where I'd shelter 'till it stopped, but if it persisted and started drippin' in on me, I'd have to go in. I didn't want to get too wet and get a good tellin' off into the bargain. Then it would be back to sittin' quiet in a room on my own with a comic I'd already read, feelin' lonely and a bit miserable. I don't really like to recall, but there were times when a terrible loneliness descended on me that it's difficult to describe even now, with a lifetime of experience to draw on. All I can say is that sometimes I was surrounded by it, enveloped in it, drowning in it.

Thankfully not very often, but there were times when it got the better of me – overwhelmed me. If you've ever been really, really lonely, you'll probably know what I mean. If you haven't, then think yourself lucky. I don't know, because he's not here to ask, but I think Jonny Gray may have felt like that at times. Just thinkin' about him now, I can't help feelin' that if he hadn't been an only child, he might never have been killed by that bomb. Poor Jonny paid the ultimate price for bein' lonely, sittin' waitin' patiently on our wall for me. Sometimes life's just not fair.

Back then, I'm afraid I didn't even consider his mum and how she must have felt. I'm not even sure he knew his dad. But his mum, she must have been devastated. Her only child so cruelly killed by an unseen foe launchin' missiles from the continent without knowin' or it seems really carin' who their victims might be. What they did know, what they must have known, is that they would be civilians, a fair number of them women and children, because all the fightin' men would be away at war. What was the point? What was the point of killin' women and children?

Talkin' to you about this is makin' me feel depressed and that's not goin' to change anythin', not goin' to bring Jonny back so I'd best get back to recountin' my life as it unfolded.

Mum, Olga, Roy and Me standin' at the front of our house in Montefiore Street. I can't be sure, but I think this was probably taken on our first visit home. In the background, just behind mum, sittin' on our wall, is my friend Jonny Gray. As you can see, I've grown a bit and at least now I look like a boy. Look carefully and you'll see part of Tennyson Street School in the background and wartime tape on our windows. Our lovely railin's are still there at that stage and dad's hollyhocks are in flower. He loved his bit of garden and people used to top and admire it.

Roy and me on a home visit standin' on the roof of our air raid shelter in the back yard of 34 Montefiore Street. I'd be about 7 then.

Me on a weekend visit to London playin' with my United Dairies milk cart at 'Grandma's', 46 Kitchener Road, Thornton Heath.

Roy with his cap gun and me with my beloved milk cart.

Me outside Ma Wickens' house, Ardingly, aged about 8. I seem to be growin' out of my jacket – but then again, we had to make our clothes last. The windows behind me were to her front room.

Ardingly College.

Aerial photo of Ardingly College

Wakehurst Place.

Wakehurst as it looked durin' the War

Me outside Hapstead Hall in 2015.

Me outside Hapstead Hall in 2015 showing the wall plaque.

CHAPTER 3

Back In War-Torn London

So it was that I spent the summer with Ma Wickens back in Ardingly, but come September – the start of the new school year – Mum was 'back on her old horse again', worryin' about my education and thinkin' on balance it would be best to have me back in London gettin' what she thought would be a proper education. So that's what she did. Despite dad's misgivin's she took me back. She'd secured a place for the two of us in an underground shelter so we wouldn't be exposed to the continued threat of nightly raids either from doodlebugs or planes. What's more, the allies were pushin' the Germans back in Europe now so there was optimism the war would soon be over. What mum didn't know, couldn't have known, was that the Germans had somethin' else up their sleeve – a new and even deadlier weapon to launch on London – the V2 rocket.

If you ask me, I don't think the Government covered themselves in glory as far as we evacuees were concerned. We were just expected to go back to London and get on with it – as if nothin' had happened. In some ways I was pleased that we had moved from Montefiore Street, not just because of the lucky escape mum, dad and I had had, but because I now knew my friend in the street, Jonny Gray, had been killed sittin' on our wall. I didn't like the thought of havin' to pass it every day. Mum felt differently and made it clear she didn't like livin' in Prairie Street. I was still only a kid but I knew mum and how determined she could be, so I knew it was only a matter of time before we'd be movin' on.

Talkin' of movin', I should tell you that Aunt Raithby had also moved whilst I was in Ardingly – to a council house at 123 Norbury Avenue, Norbury, South West London. As you can imagine, I was anxious to see her and tell her all my news and listen to hers. I was part of the family – at least that's the way she always made me feel. I often used to cycle over to cut her grass and trim her hedge, but the back garden was more or less left, except for the vegetable patch. I'll tell you more about Aunt Raithby later, but for now I need to carry on tellin' you more about my life now that I was back in London.

Mum had taken me back for the sake of my education and so straight away, I found myself back at Heathbrook except now I was in the Juniors. My school was pretty much as I'd remembered it except Mr Kitchener had retired and been replaced by a new headmistress. There were familiar faces though, not least my 'new' teacher Mr Leach. If you remember, I'd got to know Mr Leach from the boxin' matches in Ardingly. I'd not noticed before but now I saw he smoked Gold Flake cigarettes – but never in class. They were the same cigarettes which it was said killed the King. Sadly, a few years later Mr Leach died in service, but I'm not sure if it was through smokin'.

Our place in Prairie Street was next door to the Co-op so I was often sent there for bits of shoppin'. One particular day towards the end of September 1944, when I was standin' on the Co-op steps, I saw this great flash in the sky. The doodle bugs had more or less run out by then and, although I didn't know it at the time, this was one of the first of the V2 rockets they began sendin' over. Trust me, I'd nearly been on the end of one of the first V1 'doodlebugs' and now I was witnessin' one of the first of the Germans' next generation rocket bombs. Later, much later, I learned that these V2's were the first 'true' rockets and as it turned out, the forerunner of the American space rockets. It was their German inventor who, long after the war, would enable the Americans to put a man on the moon. But that was all in the future. Back in 1944/45, the V2 rockets were the latest and most terrifyin' weapon yet to be launched by the Germans. In truth, they were way ahead of anythin' the allies had in their armoury. If they'd managed to produce them earlier, then I'm convinced London would have been done for and the outcome of the war might have been different.

Back then, in September 1944, ordinary Londoners, adults, not just kids like me, had no real idea what the V2's were. Now we know they were powered by a liquid ethanol fuel which pushed them to the edge of space and that they took just 5 minutes from bein' launched from mobile launchers in Europe to reachin' their target in London. They even had an inbuilt automated guidance system which could adjust itself in flight to ensure they reached their intended target. They were so fast, there was no air raid warnin' – nothin'. No chance to take cover or get out of the way. They just arrived and in the same instant – boom, that was it. Barrage balloons, anti-aircraft fire, fighter planes – they were all useless against them. Fortunately that one and only sightin' was as near as they got to me. Even that wasn't a clear sightin' because the things moved so fast, it was more of a streak across the sky. That was the thing with the V2's, normally you didn't see the actual rocket – all you saw was a big flash and if you saw the flash you knew you were safe because it had already gone by you. That particular rocket fell about 5 miles from where I was standin' – on a church in Princess Head, Battersea.

In Prairie Street we had no air raid shelter, but to get me back from Ardingly, somehow mum had managed to get tickets for the two of us to go to the communal shelter at Clapham Common Underground Station. You could only get tickets if you'd been bombed out or had no shelter in your street. Dad wouldn't go – he always stayed at home, but mum took me there every night between September 1944 and when the war was finally over in May 1945. It was like a huge underground dormitory stretchin' for as much as maybe a mile. We always had the same bunks, Nos 612 and 613. It was deep underground, stretchin' from Clapham North to Clapham South, beneath the normal underground tube line tunnels, so you could hear the trains runnin' above your head. They ran 'till about 1 am and started up again about 4 am. The shelter had been excavated just before the war and it was said that it was built to billet troops overnight before bein' sent abroad, but I don't know if it was ever actually used by troops. You can imagine the amount of earth they dug out. It was piled in a huge mound on Clapham Common which stayed there right through the war. Eventually they did shift it.

There was a canteen down there which sold hot food and drinks. It stayed open 'till about 10 pm. From our bunks it would have been about a quarter mile walk to the canteen. Like most people, we always ate our food at our bunks. Mum used to send me 'cos it was very safe down there – everyone looked out for one another and there was no risk of bein' abducted or anythin' like that. We'd take billy cans along and they'd fill 'em with tea or coffee. That way we had somethin' to drink in the mornin' as well – although of course by that time it was cold.

When we arrived we'd always wait and go down in a lift but when we came out we'd have to walk up lots of steps. We needed to be out by 6am because mum had to go to work on the railway. With so many men away fightin' in the war, lots of women did jobs which before the war would have been exclusively men's jobs. Mum worked at Stewarts Lane, Battersea. In the beginnin' she used to clean and fire up the steam engines in the mornin's, gettin' them ready for the drivers to take them up to Victoria where they'd hook up to the carriages. There's a picture of mum with some of her railway workmates at the end of this chapter.

When we came up out of the deep shelter – which incidentally is still there today – we didn't catch the bus. We'd always walk across Clapham Common. I don't know why but we did – maybe mum wanted us to have some fresh air after bein' in an underground shelter with hundreds of other people all night. It would only just be becomin' light and normally quite foggy. Fog borderin' on smog was normal for early mornin' London in those days in Autumn and Winter. Fog or no fog, emergin' into the light of day, we never knew quite what we'd find. What havoc last night's bombs might have wrought. What changes there might be to familiar streets. Whether some of the buildin's would still be smoulderin', whether there'd be houses with their sides blown away exposin' interiors to anyone passin' by – a kitchen, a bedroom or a bathroom with a mirror miraculously unscathed on the wall and winkin' in the beams of the mornin' sun. I know I've said this before, but it's funny the things you remember. The images that stick in your mind. As a kid I don't recall bein' especially troubled by them – fascinated, but not especially troubled. If I'd had a more mature perspective, I'm sure the impact would have been much worse. Lookin' through the eyes of a kid, I guess, to some extent, cushioned me from the stark reality.

As well as normal bombs from planes and the V1 and V2 rockets, the most common bombs the Germans dropped were 'incendiary bombs'. Not very big – like thin tin cans about 18 inches long, but they'd drop 'em in their hundreds. They were really nasty things 'cos they caused a mess when they landed and then when people went to inspect the damage, they'd go off properly, injurin' or killin' anybody close by and causin' a big fire. What kind of sick mind dreams up a thing like that? They were never intended for use on enemy soldiers. They were designed to kill, maim and burn ordinary folk, women and children included. Most of the damage we were seein' was more than likely caused by incendiary bombs.

Havin' crossed the common, mum and I would catch the 137 to take us back to St Philips Church in Queenstown Road. From there it was only a few minutes walk home. That gave mum time to freshen up and have a bit of breakfast before headin' off out for work.

We'd always try to get to the shelter early on a Thursday because as a morale booster they used to put on a concert down there every Thursday startin' at about 7 pm. I loved it. They created a real concert party atmosphere with a purpose-built temporary theatre with curtains and everythin'. They'd put lots of chairs out, but you still had to be early to be sure of a seat. I especially loved the music. I'm a bit musical myself, you know – but I'll tell you about that later. Most of the theatre people had been called up to entertain the troops, but our entertainers were certainly very talented professionals and very versatile. It was the first time I'd heard a pianist play the Warsaw Concerto. It made a big impression on me – a big impression. All these years later I still get goose pimples whenever I hear it and the memory of that concert comes floodin' back and my eyes well up. The shows lasted about an hour and a half. I looked forward to them – I loved them. Over 70 years on – if I close my eyes I can still re-live them. I really can. That's how big an impression they made on me.

That's me, lookin' on the bright side, but as ever there were some darker moments. One time mum and me were lucky not to get killed tryin' to be early for that theatre. We used to leave Prairie Street at about 6.15 pm and walk up to Queenstown Road to catch a bus – the 137 to Clapham Common, and change there for the tram to Clapham South, which is where the entrance to our part of the underground shelter was. The stop on Queenstown Road was a request stop and when we got there we put our arm out, but the bus didn't stop – it just sailed on by. We were a bit miffed, but maybe we weren't standin' in quite the right spot and it didn't really matter 'cos another would be along in a couple of minutes. It was a very frequent service. When we eventually got the second bus a strange thing happened. It was detoured to get us to Clapham Common. It was only later that we learnt that a rocket had fallen on the bus before – the one that didn't stop – destroyin' it, killin' everyone on board. Not for the first time I'd had a very narrow escape.

On a much lighter note, the next really excitin' thing that happened was in early April 1945. When I'd left Ardingly in September 1944 for what would prove to be the last time as an evacuee, as I've told you, mum and dad were livin' in a first floor flat in Prairie Street, but mum didn't like livin' there. Dad wasn't bothered. I think so long as he had a roof over his head, a bed to sleep in and somewhere to read his newspaper and smoke his tobacco, he was happy. Mum though, she was determined, and whenever mum set her mind to somethin', she'd usually find a way, and so it wasn't all that long before mum found us a place to rent in Gambetta Street, just over the garden wall, so to speak, from where we used to live in Montefiore Street. In those days, Gambetta Street was considered posh. All the front doors were French polished and everyone used to put a screen out in summer to protect the finish from the sun. I'd never seen that done anywhere else before and come to that I've never seen it anywhere since. I mentioned earlier that many London Streets had a gang, but not Gambetta Street. It was a cut above and gangs were not allowed. The move was fine by me because it was nearer to Heathbrook School where I continued to go until 1948 when I transferred to Tennyson Street for bigger boys, and that was even nearer, just at the end of our road.

We moved in early April – the 4th I think it was. One thing I am sure about – the day was very cold. There weren't many removal people around in those days and those that were tended to be pricey, but mum, bein' on the railway, knew a few people. She arranged for 'Clarky' the coalman to move us! I was flabbergasted when she told me because 'Clarky' paraded the streets with coal on a horse and cart. As a result the cart was covered in coal dust and besides, I couldn't see how all our furniture was goin' to fit on unless piled really high and then how on earth it was goin' to stay on all the way to Gambetta Street. I just had to ask, "When Clarky comes tomorrow will he be bringin' his horse and cart to move us?" Mum laughed, "No, he's got a van as well." I seem to have had a thing about makin' mistakes where horses and carts were concerned. You'll see what I mean in a bit when I tell you about a certain royal procession!

As you've doubtless twigged by now, I'm a fount of useless knowledge. So in case you didn't know – at that time, 1945, you were only allowed to buy coal from the merchant you were registered with. Leastways, that's how it was supposed to be, but in reality there was a black market for everythin' and if you ran out and needed a bag or two you could always get one for a couple of bob extra, which was Ok if you could afford it.

Anyway, back to movin' day. Dad didn't like any fuss or upset and so he wasn't exactly thrilled to be movin'. He wasn't very keen on or good at DIY either. Already not in the best of spirits, I remember he got very upset when, durin' the move, somebody sat on his Anthony Eden hat! Luckily, it wasn't me. You know how he'd never go anywhere unless he was wearin' that hat.

Now, in those days the first job you had to do when movin' in was to put the lino down – the lino you'd taken up from the last place just before you left. Quite what you did if the place you were goin' to was much bigger, I don't know, but I do know you had to be sure you had a box of tin tacks and a hammer handy for when you arrived to tack it down. Dad hated such jobs, so it was lucky nobody bothered much how well it fitted. Give him his due though, when it came to decoratin', he was pretty diligent. Havin' reconciled himself to the job, with a pot of paint he'd paint away for hours – and I do mean hours. He wasn't the quickest and it had to be cream – always cream.

Our new address was No. 15A Gambetta Street. It was an upstairs flat, but unlike Montefiore Street, we didn't have to share the same front door with No. 15, the downstairs flat. We each had our own front door, side by side. A bit posher and it felt like we had gone up in the world. Mum thought so anyway. We still had an outside toilet, but at least in Gambetta Street it wasn't shared like it had been in Montefiore Street. It had a wooden seat which stretched the whole length of the lavvy. That was useful because there was space at the side of where you were sittin' to put a wee willy winkie. If it was dark, you needed that to see because there was no electric light. I don't think anybody had toilet paper. We didn't anyway. We'd use newspaper cut into squares and threaded on a wire and hung on a nail. As kids, whenever it was wet, one of our jobs would be to sit cuttin' up old newspapers into squares and threadin' 'em on a wire ready for the lavvy. A trip to the toilet in the pourin' rain or worse still on a cold winter's mornin' or night was a far from pleasant experience.

When we arrived there was a range in the kitchen, but soon after we had it taken out and a brick fireplace built for the coal fire. It would be considered sacrilege now, but brick built fireplaces were all the rage then. How times change. Bein' an upstairs property, Clarky, our coalman had to carry our bags of coal through the front door, up the stairs, along the passage, through the kitchen and out onto what we called 'the flat.' That was really an outside rooftop veranda where the coal bunker stood. We didn't have best lump coal, we'd always have two bags of 'nutty slack' which was small lumps down to more or less dust. It was popular because it was cheaper and, once you got it goin, it burnt for longer provided you didn't go pokin' it too much. Leastways, that was my understandin'. As a kid, I wasn't allowed to go pokin' the fire.

For the first few years we rented, but in 1948 mum managed to buy both flats – 15 and 15A. I don't know how she did it or where the money came from, but she did. Then we really had gone up in the world, no doubt about it – but there I go again, jumpin' the gun. Back to April 1945.

Mum was much happier livin' in Gambetta Street and to be honest it suited me better too, not least because, as I told you, it was much nearer to Heathbrook, my school. I was eleven now and beginnin' to think of myself as one of the 'big boys'. Now that mum was workin' as well, the house would be empty when I got home from school but, no matter, I had my own key. Ok, I was 11 not 21 – key of the door and all that – but needs must. My key wasn't on a string hangin' round my neck like the so called 'latch key kids' it was on a key ring with my bike lock key in my pocket. As I say, I was beginnin' to think of myself as one of the big boys and as such I'd put the stew on or whatever for mum so that it would be well on its way to cookin' when she got home. I knew what to do 'cos she'd shown me but she'd still make a point of remindin' me the night before : "Tomorrow, when you come home, don't go straight out to play. I want you to put the stew on. You know what to do – wait 'till it comes to the boil, then turn it down" and so on. I reckon it all stood me in good stead and is the reason I know how to cook for myself, which is just as well, 'cos there's nobody else to now.

We hadn't been livin' in Gambetta Street very long – only about a month – when it finally happened – the war ended. Time for rejoicin', time for big celebrations, you might think? And you'd be right, there were, and I'll tell you about them in a minute, but before I do, there's a couple of things I need to tell you.

Firstly, with the end of the war, the blackouts finished and in some ways it was strange to see London lit up again. Lookin' back, you'd imagine people would have been rejoicin' about the fact, but that's not what happened. Not in my experience anyway. I suppose Londoners were quite 'matter of fact' and took things in their stride, the good and the bad. I was pleased mind you, because there was a lamp post just outside my bedroom window and that was nice because it gave a bit of light inside.

The other thing I'm goin' to tell you might surprise, even shock you. Durin' the course of the war we'd had some hard times, of course we had, and there'd been times when I'd been scared witless, but you have to remember that even as the war ended, I was still just a kid. And kids don't necessarily think like adults – they don't necessarily see things in the same way. Yes, I was pretty streetwise and I'd seen and experienced a lot which thankfully most kids, certainly kids today, will never have to experience, but despite all that, to me as a kid, the war had been an excitin' time. On balance, livin' with Ma Wickens had been excitin'. I'd had friends and the freedom to roam. There had always been somethin' happenin'. Always somethin' new. Bein' back in London, I'd actually enjoyed goin' down the air raid shelter with mum and I'd looked forward to the next underground concert. Walkin' the streets next mornin' and seein' them sometimes smoulderin', sometimes transformed by the previous night's bombin' was, to a kid, more excitin' than anythin'. I hadn't been hurt. Those close to me hadn't been hurt and as a kid I'm afraid I didn't really feel the horror or the loss that undoubtedly was happenin' all around me, but not **to** me. I wasn't a mum or a dad. I didn't have responsibilities. I'm not sayin' I thought of it as some sort of game, but when it ended I can't say my first reaction was relief. You may be shocked to learn that it was more like disappointment.

As a responsible adult now lookin' back, I'm almost ashamed to tell you, but I will because it's true; in a strange sort of way, as a wartime kid, I felt almost let down. The source of all the excitement that I'd become accustomed to, it was over and I felt a sense of loss. What's more, it wasn't just me. My friends at school, we all felt pretty much the same way except perhaps those who'd lost loved ones. For them it must have been different – but we were kids and we never really spoke about it, so I can't tell you for sure.

Havin' got that off my chest, I'll tell you about some of the celebrations, because some of them at least were excitin', but alas, they were also short-lived.

Wartime photo of mum with some of her workmates on the railway. Mum is on the front right. As was typical for the time, many of the women are wearing headscarves. For many families, including ours, the war brought an unexpected bonus, with women being able to get paid work, many for the first time. I think mum was paid about four pounds a week.

CHAPTER 4

Life As A Kid In Post-War London

The war in Europe officially ended on 7th May 1945, when Germany's surrender was formally accepted in Berlin. The next day celebrations broke out all over the world to mark Victory in Europe – VE Day as we called it. Mr Churchill declared the day, the 8th May, a public holiday, but to be honest I don't remember anythin' significant happenin', not in my life anyway. People hung flags out of windows and there was a bit of 'hoo-ha' in the streets, but nothin' really memorable. It seems crowds massed in Trafalgar Square and up the Mall to the Palace where apparently the King and Queen and Prime Minister, Mr Churchill, waved to the crowds from the balcony, but I suppose because this wasn't pre-announced, on this occasion mum didn't take us and we just heard about it on the wireless. The war had only just ended, so I guess it was too early and it took a while before there were any more organised celebrations. One thing that was bein' talked about were street parties, but even they took a few weeks to organise.

Somehow things never ran quite smooth. We had a street party, but it was a street party with a difference. We were newcomers to Gambetta Street, but when it came to organisin' a celebration street party, it looked like we were goin' to miss out because none of the 'old timers' seemed interested in doin' anythin'. Mum didn't want us to miss out. This was somethin' worth celebratin', that should be celebrated, and so, newcomer or not, if no-one else was goin' to do it, then she'd organise a street party herself. Except there was a

133

problem. The air raid shelters for Gambetta Street were still there – 2 great long brick things, right in the middle of the street. So mum came up with a plan. We'd have our street party, but we'd have it up in the Church Hall. Ok, it wouldn't be quite the same as havin' it in the street, but needs must and it would still be our street party because everyone in our street would be invited and encouraged to participate. A very resourceful and determined woman was my mum. There'd be an up-side as well, because if it turned out to be a wet day, then we'd be in clover compared to all the others takin' place out in the streets.

Mum went door knockin', drummin' up support and gettin' folk to pledge to contribute provisions. After all, you couldn't have a party without food and we couldn't supply it all. For a start, we didn't have the money. So it was a case of sandwiches here, cakes there, tins of fruit, jelly, you name it and mum made sure somebody would be bringin' it along.

As well as the food, Mum organised a fancy dress for us kids – and for group photos to be taken outside our house. That's why there are pictures of us kids both before and after dressin' up. Our Roy wouldn't take part – but then I can't blame him. He was now 14 – old enough to leave school and go out to work, so he rightly considered himself a young man now and dressin' up with a bunch of kids was probably beneath him.

Uncle Vic and Aunt Maisie came to our 'street party' and brought along their daughter, Margaret, then about 6 yrs old. I'll tell you about what happened in a minute but before I do I think I'll just take you back a bit to tell you somethin' unusual about Uncle Vic and his relationship with his daughter Margaret.

As you know, Dad and Uncle Vic were marched down to the recruitin' office in Sidmouth in 1916 by granddad and more or less co-erced into signin' on. They both made it through the last two years of the Great War and after it was over, dad came out, but Uncle Vic signed on and in the end served 40 years with the signals, finishin' up as a Major. That meant he served through two World Wars plus other conflicts, but that didn't dent his sense of humour. In that respect, Uncle Vic and dad were like chalk and cheese, whereas the two of us, me and Uncle Vic, we shared a similar sense of humour and I always found him good company. Easy to chat to and interestin' with it.

For many years, Uncle Vic and Auntie Maisie lived in a bungalow on Hayling Island. Her mum had a council house there, which was just as well because accordin' to what I was told, Aunt Maisie was on that island with their baby daughter all through the War and, for whatever reason, Uncle Vic never got back to see her once. Margaret, the baby's name was, and the story goes that she was 5 years old before Uncle Vic even saw her. At times I think he had it tough durin' the War, but he must have had some leave, so I can't understand why he never managed to get back. Mind you, it was said he was lucky to be alive. On one occasion he'd been on a troop ship which sank in the channel – torpedoed I think and Uncle Vic was adrift in a life raft for days before bein' picked up.

Anyway, that's enough of me digressin' when I'm supposed to be tellin' you about our 'street party'. Uncle Vic, bein' Major Wattley, was a bit of a celebrity and so mum roped him in for givin' out the prizes. There were prizes for fancy dress and prizes for various games. I was a Scotsman in a kilt, but needless to say, I didn't win. That accolade went to Betty Lilley. She won first prize for bein' a doll in a box. You can see her in the photo at the end of the chapter. I have to admit she was probably a worthy winner. Just dressin' up as a doll wouldn't have cut it, but quite a novel idea, puttin' her in a box and yet still enablin' her to walk around. As for me, if you look at the photo you'll see that by this time I'd shot up. I was no longer 'Little Jack'. OK, I was a bit rakish, but no matter, I'd caught up with my peers.

We even had a three-piece band for the dancin' in the evenin'. Most of the kids were still in fancy dress and doin' their best to dance along with the grown-ups. You have to remember it was proper ballroom dancin' – waltzes, quick steps, fox trots and so on. None of this just jigglin' about like they do today. Betty had ditched her box by this time, but I was still resplendent in my kilt. At least I was until Auntie Maisie took a shine to it. Apparently they were hard to come by and mum took the hint and in a flash whisked it off me and gave it to her for Margaret. Now, in case you're wonderin' what a Scotsman wears under his kilt – well, in my case the answer was nothin'! Well, nothin' but a pair of blue gym shorts, which was just as well. I felt awkward enough havin' to carry on dancin' in a pair of gym shorts, but dance on I did. I wasn't goin' to miss out.

I'm digressin' again and jumpin' the gun a bit now, but whilst I've got Uncle Vic and Aunt Maisie in mind, I'll tell you a bit more about them before movin' on. I remember just after the war, mum took me down to Hayling Island to see Aunt Maisie. There was no Uncle Vic. At that time he was a captain and he was posted away somewhere. I remember thinkin' she was a bit unusual. Now I suppose I'd say eccentric. All the time we were there she was nursin' this duck in front of the fire and lettin' it be known she wanted to get off the island. I suppose the isolation through the War Years had taken their toll and she wanted out. Not long after she got her wish 'cos Uncle Vic got a postin' to Canterbury and was given officers' quarters there. A beautiful place that was.

We were invited down to see it and for once, dad came too. I remember the three of us goin' on the train. I think it was the spring of 1946. I would have been twelve. I was pleased to go because Uncle Vic was goin' to be there. Aunt Maisie was alright, but Uncle Vic and I got on like a house on fire. He and dad might have been twins, but looks apart, were they different. For a start, just like me, Uncle Vic had a sense of humour. Mind you, the moment they got together, dad changed. Not his sense of humour, but the way he spoke. The Devon twang came out. It was really funny to listen to because dad never normally spoke like that at all.

It was a really big impressive place. Before the army bought it, it had been 'a gentleman's house'. All the rooms had bells in them and in the kitchen there was this big board to indicate which bell in which room had been rung, so the servants knew where to go. What's more, it had beautiful gardens too and whilst I think mum was taken with the house, it was the gardens that really interested dad. That was one thing dad and his twin brother did have in common – a love of gardens. It was really well stocked and full of late spring flowers. A real picture.

As we sat down to lunch, Uncle Vic announced that was he glad we liked the place and glad we'd all gone down to see them there, but he'd got some news for us and, judging by her reaction, by us I think he meant all of us – Aunt Maisie included. "I've been posted to Hong Kong." I think everyone was stunned, especially Aunt Maisie, but she soon recovered her composure and put her foot down. I suppose she'd been used to Uncle Vic goin' off here, there and everywhere, but she made it pretty clear that if he was goin', then this time, she'd be goin' too. "You left me on my own on Haylin' Island all through the War and I'm not bein' left again."

And so it was that they only lived in that posh house in Canterbury for 6 weeks. Just 3 or 4 weeks after our visit, they had all their things packed up for despatch and the three of them came up to stay with us in Gambetta Street. I'm not sure why they came, but they stayed about a week. They had mum and dad's room – our front room. I don't know how we all managed, but we did.

As you know, on Sundays dad would always cook the dinner and, as you can imagine, he'd want to put on a special spread when we'd got visitors. There wasn't a lot of room and generally it was best to be out of dad's way when he was cookin'. Uncle Vic knew that too and so he said to me, "Come on Jack. We'll take a wander up to the Palace" and off we went – Aunt Maisie, Margaret, Uncle Vic and me. Mum stayed behind – not so much to help dad, because she knew to keep out of his way too - but to see to the table makin' it just so. Knowin' mum, she wanted to let Uncle Vic and Aunt Maisie see that she could put on a show too. Anyway, the rest of us went off and if you can picture it, Uncle Vic was wearin' this long army trench coat and bowler hat. As we came to the sentry boxes outside Buckingham Palace, the guards stood to attention and sloped arms. That was an army salute when on sentry duty. They couldn't do a normal salute with a rifle. They must have recognised his rank from that trench coat, but they certainly took us all by surprise, not least Uncle Vic. I can hear him sayin' it now as we walked away, "Oh my God. I didn't expect that!"

The war in Europe had ended, but the war in the Far East with Japan carried on for another year, so it wasn't until the 8th June 1946 that big Victory Parade celebrations took place in London, accompanied by fly-pasts, fireworks and everythin'. Bein' so much later, there's a few more things I need to tell you about first. Not momentous things, just stuff to help you get a picture of what life – my life – was like in post war London.

The war had ended, but the aftermath was everywhere, the bomb sites, the rubble, the devastation. Gambetta Street had survived more or less unscathed. Blasts from bombs that had caused carnage a street or two away had smashed windows but, in Gambetta Street, that was about it really. Less than a hundred yards away at the top of our turnin', in Robertson Street, the picture was very different. There were great gapin' holes where houses had once stood and over the back, in Montefiore Street – well you know all about the damage that one doodlebug did. All across London, especially in the East End towards the docks, there was so much damage everywhere, that it would be years and years before the scars were healed. In some parts, open areas in streets created by the bombin' remain open to this day. There's a photograph of one such which is now a children's playground. Read the caption and you'll see that's the space where houses once stood across from our house in Montefiore Street. If I didn't know, lookin' at it now, I'd find it hard to believe that such a great big gap could have been created by just that one bomb. Seein' it brings home just how lucky we were that the doodlebug didn't come down on our side of the street. No way would that air raid shelter have saved us from a direct hit.

Whenever we came across a bomb site, as kids we didn't think about the horror of it all, rather we revelled in the excitin' opportunities the bomb sites represented. They were new places to play where you could hunt for bits of 'treasure'. That's why durin' the war and for a good time after we kids went searchin' in the rubble for bits of wartime memorabilia. We weren't supposed to, but we were kids, so we'd often go rummagin' around. It was excitin'. You never knew what you might find. Luckily I never came across any live incendiaries, but I knew what to look out for and not to touch 'em. It had been drilled into me often enough. Other kids weren't so lucky, especially after the war, when folk became a bit complacent, feelin' the danger was over. I can understand it because we'd often find spent incendiaries. We'd often see them just lyin' in the gutter – the burnt out cases. They weren't all that big, just metal canisters, only about a foot long. They had a distinctive smell and bein' kids we'd sniff 'em. I don't know why I did it really 'cos I didn't like the smell. There were loads of 'em about because the Germans had dropped 'em by the thousand – well, maybe not by the thousand, but a lot anyway. We collected stuff. Most kids thought it was marvellous to have a bit of German somethin' or other. Even dad understood that. When we'd been bombed out of Montefiore Street, dad had collected some of the shrapnel and given it to me when we were livin' in Prairie Street. I had it in a box, but to be honest I didn't really like it because of the smell. I expect it was cordite, but whatever it was, I didn't like the smell.

One by one the bomb sites were gradually cleared and levelled, some for redevelopment, but many became emergency re-housin' sites with temporary prefab bungalows bein' erected in a matter of hours. Don't underestimate the task though. There was no quick fix. There were so many of 'em that many bomb sites remained virtually untouched for years and years as you'll see later.

Even the air raid shelters in the middle of Gambetta Street stayed for over a year after the war. If you remember, in Montefiore Street, we'd all had individual ones in back yards and I expect many of those were kept as 'garden stores', but in Gambetta Street they just had these two long communal ones in the street itself. Long narrow things they were. As you know, mum and I had never used 'em. We'd always gone to the underground shelter at Clapham Common but apparently they hadn't been popular even durin' the war. In particular, they'd been very cold in winter because there was no heatin' in 'em. Now the war was over, nobody liked 'em because they blocked the street and they smelled. I suspect they'd been used as impromptu toilets from time to time. There was a light on the end of each which was on all night. Somebody must have pinched one of the bulbs and I remember thinkin', "I wonder if that's still workin'?" Fool that I was at that age, about 11 years, I put my hand inside and got a shock! You learn – you only do that once. I never told anyone and especially not mum and dad. Well, I wouldn't, would I? I'd only have got a tellin' off to go with the shock.

Somethin' else I never told mum and dad about was where I sometimes 'misspent' my school dinner money. Pie & Mash shops were somethin' of an institution in London so I think I should tell you about 'em even though they were somewhat frowned upon in my family. You see, unlike me, mum and dad weren't really Londoners. Dad was from Sidmouth and mum from Wales, so they hadn't grown up with pie & mash, which was very much a London thing, particularly in the East End.

Pie and Mash shops were very basic establishments providin' cheap, fillin' food and as a result were mostly patronized by the lower echelons of society – includin', on occasions, me and my school friends. In those days, the London schools used to carry on servin' school dinners right through the holidays so kids like us who had workin' parents could still get a meal at lunchtime. I'm talkin' here about the couple of years after the war when mum still had her job on the railway. Anyway, if instead of goin' for my school dinner like I was supposed to, I made do with nippin' home for a couple of slices of bread and butter, then the next day the money I'd saved would enable me to go up the Wandsworth Road to the Pie & Mash Shop. The thing was, a couple of the lads I used to knock around with, playin' football up on Clapham Common, were more into Pie & Mash than me. If truth be told, I didn't really enjoy traditional pie & mash that much. For me it was more about the adventure and bravado of goin' and doin' somethin' I knew I shouldn't really be doin'. But then, that's kids for you, isn't it?

I can still see all the real old Cockney Sparra's sittin' there with their characteristic scarves, a bit like cravats, tied round their necks, chattin' away on those bench-type seats. The pie & mash itself I don't remember with that much affection. To me they were always a bit anaemic lookin' and they'd flop right down 'cos there wasn't much in 'em in the way of mince. On top they'd pile loads of mashed 'potato' and on top of that they'd pour all this liquor, not gravy like you might get in other parts of the country, but a green liquor. That was the liquor off the stewed eels. I think it had parsley in it as well, which is perhaps why it was green. A lot of the regulars would have stewed eels to start wiv' followed by the pie & mash. We only ever had enough money for the pie and mash.

You may not have known about the importance of pie and mash shops to cockney folk, but everybody must have heard about 'Cockney rhymin' slang', so it would be remiss of me not to tell you a bit about it. I'm a 'cockney sparra', no doubt about that, but in truth I've never been one for usin' much rhymin' slang myself, but that doesn't mean I don't understand it or acknowledge it as an important part of Cockney heritage. Anyone can tell you that 'apples and pears' means 'stairs', and even if you don't know you'll guess what somebody means when they they tell you they're goin' for 'a Jimmy Riddle' or 'a you and me' but did you know that 'on your tod' is rhymin' slang as well? Ok, you probably know that it means 'on your own' or, more correctly, 'alone' but how come it's rhymin' slang? Tod doesn't rhyme with alone. Well that's because it's a bit more mysterious. A bit more lost in the mists of time. A proper Cockney –

well, an old one like me – might well be able to tell you that there was once a famous jockey called Tod Sloane. He was so good that he was always comin' home first and well ahead of the pack – alone. So there you have it …. Sloane …. alone. Over time it got shortened to just Tod and then the capital letter got dropped. Not a lot of people know that, but you do – now.

Durin' the summer holidays especially, we kids would spend a lot of time playin' out whilst, in my case at least, mum and dad were out at work. Mostly we'd just play in the street but often we'd take ourselves off to somewhere like Clapham Common for much of the day where there were swings and more space to kick a ball. Usually, three or four of us would go up together – kids from the street like Derek Green, Betty Lilley, Sheila Green and me. We'd walk there and back which was quite a trek but nobody bothered us. Kids on their own were quite safe in those days.

Now and again, we'd have a sort of 'committee' meetin' and decide to take ourselves off to somewhere special like London Zoo. Then we would tell our parents first, not least because we'd need a bit of money for the trip. We weren't daft. We knew if we said we wanted to go to the zoo our parents would most likely let us go. It wasn't like a theme park, it was all animals so they'd see it as educational but we saw it as more of an adventure. It was way too far to walk so we'd need a few coppers for the Underground as well as entrance money. We'd get the bus from St Peter's Church to Clapham Common and then take the Underground from there. We may have only been 11 but as I've said, we were street- wise, we knew how to use the Underground. Our mums would have made us some sandwiches so we'd be all set for the day.

Another trip our parents were likely to approve of was if we said we wanted to go up to the West End. I can hear you thinkin' "Why on earth would they do that ?" The thing is, what we'd actually be askin' was to go up to the West End to the Science Museum. The Museum was free but again we'd need money for the journey with hopefully a bit more besides because for us it was more the adventure of the trip that appealed – well, that and the ice cream they used to sell outside. For the West End, we'd go up to Lavender Hill for the bus. Like I say, we were street- wise, we knew our way around and we knew how to behave. There was never any raucous behaviour on the bus. It wasn't like today, any of that and you'd expect to get a clip round the ear.

Before, durin' and for a while after the war, as streetwise kids we'd stop any 'likely characters' in the street and ask 'em if they'd got any fag cards and silver paper. Sounds a bit cheeky, but most of 'em didn't mind. Most of 'em only really wanted the cigarettes and even if they were collectin' the cards, few could be bothered to keep the silver paper once they'd opened the packet. We weren't daft. We knew the best spots to hang around for askin' was outside a tobacconists, and busy bus stops usually yielded rich pickin's as well. The cards we collected, swapped or played with. I'll explain what I mean by 'playin' with' in a minute. The silver paper, that was money to us. We got to recognize the most likely ones. Young men would most often give 'em to you. Some of the older ones wanted to keep 'em for their own children or grandchildren even but, by and large, no matter who we were askin', so long as we were polite, we wouldn't get into any bother.

We'd roll the silver paper into a tight ball and once we'd got enough we'd exchange it for cash accordin' to its weight at one of the rag and bone man shops. There were a few of them in those days, but we'd usually go to Clarky's in Silverthorne Road, Clarky would take more or less anythin' – old clothes, jam jars, silver paper, but contrary to what you might be thinkin', it wasn't a smelly junk shop. In case you're wonderin', no he wasn't the same Clarky who brought the coal. In fact they couldn't have been more different in looks, physique and demeanour. Really they were both Mr Clark, but everybody called 'em both Clarky. Very upright was Clarky. He wasn't at all like your regular rag & bone man, not at all rough and ready. His speech was very proper and he was always polite, even to us kids. Whenever we went in his shop he'd be standin' behind his counter in a brown coat. Never sittin', always standin'. I don't suppose what we took him was all that interestin' but he would always buy it with good grace. We'd collect anythin' we could to take to Clarky. For jam jars I remember he'd give us a ha'penny each. Two other things I remember about Clarky. Although he was gettin' on a bit, he had perfect skin, so perfect that you couldn't help noticin' and, I was told, he was a very good dancer – practically a professional. Not your average rag & bone man at all wasn't Clarky.

Both Roy and I had really good collections of cigarette cards. There were lots to collect. Film and radio stars, footballers, cricketers, wildlife. Each brand had its own collections. As well as beggin' 'em, we used to try and swap 'em. After the war that would be mainly at school, the idea bein' to try and get the set before the cigarette company switched to another series. We had albums and tins for keepin' 'em in. We had separate tins for 'keepers' and for swaps and cards for playin' with. When I say playin' I mean 'fag cards' – it was a game. Expensive brands had silk cards in 'em and we had loads of 'em. Funnily enough though, we didn't really like 'em as much, mainly because they were no use for playin' 'fag cards' because they had no substance to 'em. You couldn't' flick 'em. I'd better try to explain how the game worked. Basically, we'd flick 'em against a wall and if you got one to fall on top of another already on the ground, then those two were yours. That's why we weren't so keen on the silk cards – pretty as they were, they were no use for flickin'.

Money was always tight, but Roy and I, we never went without. Havin' said that, we didn't have much either – in the way of possessions. So havin' a good collection of fag cards and alleys (marbles to you) was important because your popularity amongst other kids was in part 'what you had'. Kids would want to play with you more if you had a good collection.

As kids we'd make our own entertainment and I can remember in particular playin' football with a tennis ball in Gambetta Street. All the kids in the street would join in – boys and girls. Not Roy because by this time Roy was already 14, a young man and out at work. We played this other game with a tennis ball, which I think was called 'tin can copper'. I suppose you'd say it was a form of cricket except there was no bat. We'd divide into two teams and one team would have to set up the 'wicket' and the other would be bowlin'. Somebody would have to prop three bits of firewood up against a wall and balance a tin can on top and the other side would try and knock 'em down with the ball. When they fell, somebody on the wicket keepin' side had to run and try to set 'em up again but if the bowlin' side could hit 'em with the ball before they'd done it, the kid that is, not the wicket, they were out. There was a lot of runnin' back and forth in that game, dodgin' this way and that, tryin' not to get hit.

Talkin' of runnin', sometimes we'd have to make ourselves scarce when gangs of lads from the slum houses near the railway came round to play havoc for a while and then move on their way. For some reason though, they never went into Gambetta Street itself. In fact nobody ever did unless they lived there or they were collectin' rent or sellin' somethin'. That was one of the good things about Gambetta Street, it was safe.

Another game we used to play, usually in each other's doorways, was jacks or five stones. 'Gobbo's' we used to call 'em, maybe because we'd often make do with usin' cherry stones which we'd have cleaned up in our mouths first. Then of course there was marbles. Mum would make us a bag to keep 'em in. We'd buy the odd few, but most of 'em I'd get by winnin' 'em. Mind you, we didn't call 'em marbles, we called 'em 'alleys'. I'm really not sure why, but maybe just because we used to play with 'em in the alleyways.

Another game we thought was darin' was 'Knock down Ginger' and yet again from the name you probably wouldn't guess what it was. Basically, we'd just dare each other to knock on doors and then run away and hide, but somewhere we could still see the person comin' to the door. Better still, we'd get a length of fishin' line and tie it to a few knockers at once so when we pulled the other end, all the knockers would go at once.. Then we'd get a few irate folk all out at the same time. It doesn't seem funny now, but as kids we thought it was hilarious. Unless of course we got caught because then we'd be for it if mum or dad got told.

On nice summer evenin's I'd often be sittin' out on the front step. I especially remember playin' draughts with Doreen Fag who lived downstairs. We'd sit out there playin' for hours sometimes 'till eventually mum would shout down, "Come on you. It's about time you packed up now. It's bed time." I know these are only ordinary, simple things, but I hope they're helpin' you to see what life for kids like me was like.

Bonfire night is always an excitin' time when you're a kid and it may surprise you to know that when I was a kid, there were loads of street bonfires all over London. We weren't allowed to build a bonfire in Gambetta Street, but that didn't matter because there was always one in Robertson Street, which as you know, was only at the end of our turnin' and an especially big one in Tennyson Street, which wasn't much further but in the opposite direction. Everythin' would be goin' swimmingly until the fire brigade came to put it out. Then we'd scarper. Mind you, no sooner had they gone than the kids would set to buildin' it back up and gettin' it alight again. The fire brigade would come from near Clapham Common and long before they arrived we'd hear the bells ringin'. Then we knew they were on their way and we'd best get ready to make ourselves scarce. It was all part of the fun. Next day there'd be a big burnt patch on the road where the fire had been. Eventually the Council would come and repair it, but the same would happen again the followin' year.

As well as doin' stuff with other kids, somethin' I did a lot and mostly on my own was fishin'. I was fishin' mad. I guess I'd caught the bug as an evacuee back in Ardingly. Anyway, I got myself a permit so I could fish legitimately in Hyde Park and Bushy Park (Hampton Court) without havin' to leg it every time the Park Wardens came along. Funny thing is, havin' got myself a permit, try as I might, I never did catch anythin' in either of 'em! I had better luck in Battersea Park. Dad would never go with me, but he would take me to buy bait. I'd finish fishin' about 4.30pm to get home in time for tea, but I was mad on it, fishin' that is, so sometimes in the summer I'd head back again after and I'd even take the bus to get there quick. They were all freshwater coarse fish I was catchin', so mostly I'd just put 'em back, but sometimes I'd bring home a roach or bream for the cat, but even I could see our Dinky wasn't all that keen on freshwater fish. Mind you, that didn't dampen my enthusiasm any.

Fishin' wasn't the only attraction for me in Battersea Park. At weekends, afternoon and evenin', there'd be dance bands playin'. They'd usually be a 12-piece band and I remember especially the Nat Allen and Arthur Copperfield Bands. They were much more my cup of tea than all the Fairground rides and I'd spend hours and hours listenin' to 'em, mostly on my own because my school mates weren't that keen. I was only a kid, but I was developin' a taste for big band music.

Sometimes I'd be a bit more adventurous and go a bit further afield, but still usually on my own. Fishin' that is. This particular Saturday I decided to take a bus out to Richmond and try my luck on the river. I suppose I'd be about 12. As usual, mum made me a pack-up lunch so I wouldn't be goin' hungry. I'd set up on the St

145

Margaret's side of Richmond Bridge, opposite the Ice Skatin' Rink – leastways it was then; it's probably long gone now.

I was mindin' my own business, in a bit of a world of my own, when this bloke on the path at the top of the bank shouts down to me wantin' to take my photo. I thought, I'll just turn a bit so he can get a good profile shot. As I did, I'm lookin' up at him, smilin'. Big mistake! I lost my footin' and fell backwards into the river. Now the Thames is still tidal at Richmond and at that particular time it was pretty deep, I can tell you. I've already told you I can't swim, so there's me startin' to be swept away, flounderin' and splutterin', tryin' to get upright and out of there without losin' my precious rod. Although I didn't see the funny side, I must have looked a comical sight strugglin' to retrieve my rod and get back up the bank. Whether that chap was takin' shots of all this, I don't know. All I know is, havin' made dry land and looked around, he'd gone, scarpered. I thought, charmin'. I'd fallen in the river 'cos of him and not only had he not tried to fish me out, he'd not even stopped to see if I was Ok. He'd just legged it.

Fortunately there are nicer people in the world and, as luck would have it, there was one on the opposite bank. I guess he'd seen what had happened and he shouted me over. So I sloshed over the bridge, drippin' water in my wake, and he took me in and sat me down in the Ice Rink's boiler room. Lovely and warm in there it was. Just as well, 'cos I was well and truly soaked. I was in there for ages before decidin' I'd better head for home. The 37 bus took about an hour to get me back to Clapham Junction. Not the most pleasant bus ride I've ever had. I'd dried out quite a lot, but my trousers and underpants were still pretty wet – no mistakin' that. I had to change at Clapham to get back to Queenstown Road and home. All a bit embarassin', not helped by folk starin' as they do. I wouldn't have minded so much, but the only thing I caught that day was the makin's of a cold!

That particular fishin' trip was on a Saturday and the next day bein' Sunday, somethin's just occurred to me that I didn't notice quite so much at the time. Roy and me, post war, apart from goin' to CLB, we didn't do so much together. I guess it was the age gap showin' more, Roy bein' 14 and me bein' 11 and especially now he was at work whilst I was still a school kid. Most Sundays though, we still did go our walks to Chelsea Bridge the same as we'd done before the war.

Sundays would start with us gettin' up a bit later than usual — about 8 am for breakfast. We'd all have to get washed in the scullery before dad took it over for preparin' Sunday dinner. He was a good chef, was dad, but very particular and he liked the space to himself. He did a proper job, mind you, tyin' up the meat with string and everythin' before it went in the oven, but preparation took hours, so it was best to get out of his way. Roy and I would get despatched to walk to Chelsea Bridge, just the two of us, Roy proudly sportin' his longs and me taggin' along in my shorts. I don't really know why we always went to Chelsea Bridge, but we did. Thinkin' about it now, I bet we were packed off every Sunday afternoon so mum and dad could have a bit of 'quality time' together. Even at 14, Roy took a pride in his appearance and always had to be in his Sunday best. I guess that came of bein' that much older but, best clothes or not, when we got to the embankment he'd be itchin' to get down there and do a bit of explorin'. I guess a part of him was still a kid at heart. Often as not he'd find a likely spot and, tellin' me to 'Stand there Willy" where he could see me, he'd be off down and into the mud, jumpin' from one piece of wood to another, treasure huntin'.

Trouble was, sometimes he'd slip and get all muddy, his shoes, socks and even his best trousers. Then he'd be up and out of there and it would be, "Quick Willy, help me get this mud off." Of course we couldn't, leastways not properly. Roy would come up with this elaborate story as to how it had happened but half the time I'd forget what I was supposed to say, so I don't think I was ever much help. Sometimes he'd be lucky. Dad would still be out back in the scullery still busy with the dinner and mum, whilst not best pleased, would just tell him to "go and get changed quick — before your father sees 'em." He never learnt. Next week would be just the same, although the outcome might be worse. Whenever dad found out he'd have a real go at him and he had a bit of a temper did dad, although I never remember him hittin' us. Instead he'd fester and happen he'd end up takin' it out on mum. I remember more than once dad throwin' a quarter pound of tea at mum. I can see her now tryin' to sweep it all up again when things had calmed down. It was loose tea and for mum, too expensive to waste.

I remember one time, after the war, when Roy was in long trousers, he'd gone down treasure trovin' and got well and truly stuck in the mud. It wasn't long after he'd had this operation on his knee and it was still a bit weak. He shouted up to me for help, which wasn't like Roy at all, and I asked a passer-by, "Mister, can you help my brother? He's stuck in the mud." Luckily he was a sport and went down and pulled him out. Mind you, you can imagine the state Roy's best long trousers were in and the reception we'd be gettin' when he got home. As usual, Roy made up this elaborate cover story, but, it didn't wash, it never did. The thing was, once a rebel, always a rebel, and Roy was used to bein' in trouble with dad for one reason or another and so when next Sunday came, often as not it would be the same old story.

These days, even young kids wear long trousers, especially in winter, but not in my day. Back then they were a sort of symbol of maturity. You only got to wear 'em when you were more or less ready to go out to work for your livin'. When, around the age of 14 years, you went into long trousers, you were the 'kiddy' then. Leastways you thought you were. You could walk with a swagger – you were 'Jack the Lad'.

Whilst dad would never take me out, not even fishin', mum was different. I had loads of outin's with mum. Mum would never miss a spectacle and in days before TV, if you wanted to see somethin', you had to be there and more often than not, mum made sure she was. Dad would never go. If it was a big occasion, sometimes Roy would be persuaded to go, but always mum would take me. If mum got wind of somethin', we'd be there – front of house, so to speak.

The first 'spectacle' I can clearly remember mum takin' me to post war was the official openin' ceremony of Waterloo Bridge. In truth, the ceremony itself wasn't all that interestin' or memorable for me as a school kid who'd just turned 12 but I'm tellin' you about it because the bridge itself is a bit special. I think so anyway. As you could doubtless guess, the original Waterloo Bridge was named after the famous victory over Napoleon at Waterloo in 1815. It spans the Thames between Blackfriars and Hungerford. Apparently the first bridge was opened as early as 1817, fittingly by the Prince Regent and the Duke of Wellington. The bridge I remember though was the replacement which they started buildin' in 1938. Somethin' you may not know and what in my eyes makes it special is that to many Londoners, it's affectionately known as the 'Ladies' Bridge'. Why? Because much of the work was undertaken durin' the War and with so many able-bodied men away fightin', women were recruited as stone masons, welders and labourers. The bridge was finished and in use durin' the War, but not officially opened until December 1945. I know because, as I say, I was there. Mum made a point of takin' me. She wanted to show me everythin' major that was goin' on in London. You could hear about it on the radio or read about it in the newspaper, but if you wanted to see it, you had to be there because there was no TV back then. The openin' ceremony took place at the northern (Strand) end and whilst I can't remember much about the ceremony itself except that Herbert Morrison, the Deputy Prime Minister, was there givin' a speech, I remember thinkin' how clean, white and modern the bridge looked. OK, it's not intricate and historic like Tower Bridge, but bein' the Ladies' Bridge and knowin' the reason why, that makes it special.

If the King and Queen were doin' a commemorative service at St Paul's, the event would be publicised in advance and folk would line the streets all along the route. St Paul's is at the top of Ludgate Circus and I remember one time mum got us a good frontage spot at the bottom of Ludgate. We generally took a collapsible stool and it was OK, but sometimes it seemed like we'd be standin' or sittin' for hours before anythin' happened – apart from the crowds gettin' bigger and bigger and the pavements gettin' thronged 'till they were nearly blocked. I have a feelin' that on one such occasion I hadn't been long back from Ardingly, but I suppose it must have been post war. Mind you, the King and Queen did stay in London durin' the war to help keep up morale so the war could have still been on but I don't think so. Those overcrowded pavements would have been too big a target.

It's even possible that this particular time that sticks in my memory could have been as late as 1948 – April 26th to be precise because John recently showed me a photo of the King and Queen's Silver Weddin' Day procession, as it happens, taken in Ludgate. It's at the end of this chapter and shows just how crowded the pavements were – almost unbelievably crowded. One thing's for certain, a big event like that and mum and I would have been there, no question. Anyway, the main reason I remember this particular occasion, whether it was 1948 or an earlier one, is because I made a bit of a 'faux pas'. There we were, in the front, standin' in Ludgate Circus near St Pauls and I made a comment which caused a fair bit of hilarity round abouts. The crowd was hushed with anticipation and in a pretty loud voice I asked mum, "Will they be comin' in a horse and cart?" I meant carriage and horses, of course I did, it just came out wrong. Some faux-pas you just never forget, particularly if, as you can imagine, it gets recounted time and time again after.

Southend, bein' only about 45 miles from London, has long been a favourite seaside destination for Londoners. Now the war was over, people started flockin' back and I remember two trips in particular.

One was an evenin' railway trip which mum took Roy and me on. It would have been whilst she was still workin' on the railway and able to get concessionary tickets. We went because mum had heard they were puttin' lights on but whilst the train trip was nice, when we got there, to be honest, we were disappointed because all we saw was one ship lit up out at sea.

The other was a daytime coach trip, but I don't think that day could have been all that special either because all I remember is the food and the journey back. We had a plate of sausage and mash, which was quite nice, but it wasn't very 'sea-sidey' and as I've said before, mum liked her food, so along with lots of others, she sought out and ate the jellied eels and liquor, which in case you don't know, looks like a sea of green gravy. As you've probably guessed, the way back was most memorable because the coach had to keep stoppin' so people could get off and be sick!

Fairs and circuses used to tour the City and doubtless further afield. They'd go from one common to another. If we were lucky, we'd get to see them when they came to Clapham Common. Both pre and post war, Grays Fair would come from Mitcham Common to Clapham Common, as would Sangers Circus. Neither was really big, but they were colourful, lively and excitin' nonetheless.

Post war, Billy Smarts Circus started comin' to the Common. Now they really were somethin' to behold. They'd arrive with loads of pomp and ceremony all designed to drum up trade I guess. The afternoon parade from Clapham Junction to the Common was a spectacle in itself and free to all comers. And come they did. The streets were buzzin'. Everybody turned out to watch. The horseback riders, clowns, acrobats and so on were a sight to behold for us youngsters, but the really big attraction was the elephants. They'd arrive by train, which is why the parade started at the station, and they'd walk in line nose to tail. By that I mean the one behind would hold the tail of the elephant in front with its trunk. There'd be about six of 'em in line. There'd be celebrities too. I remember one time mum pointin' out Freddy Mills, the famous boxer.

Another outin' with mum that springs to mind was when we went to Olympia. They used to have shows at Olympia. I remember mum took me and Roy to one near Christmas. I'm not sure what year, but it was post war, so probably 1945 or 1946. It was a sort of indoor fair with jugglers, acrobats and the like, but the star turn and the main reason I'm tellin' you this was Johnny Weismuller, of Tarzan fame, was performin' a high dive. I have to say it was pretty spectacular. When I say the divin' platform was high, I mean it was really, really high. Once he'd climbed all the way up this ladder, you could barely see him up there. Then to a drum roll, he did this fancy dive into this big round tub. I'm sayin' big, but considerin' the height he was divin' from, it wasn't very big at all and not that deep either. It's a wonder he didn't do himself an injury.

Havin' seen Tarzan doin' a high dive gave me a few braggin' rights at school, but do you know, years later I met this chap who lived in Suffolk who looked a lot like Johnny Weismuller. Talkin' to him, it transpired he used to do all Johnny's stunts, includin' the high dive, so it wasn't Tarzan I'd seen at all. It was still a spectacular dive though, Tarzan or no Tarzan.

That same Christmastime, somethin' else happened which I thought was rather funny so I'll tell you about it before I forget. On Christmas Day dad would always wear his chef's hat and take special pride in preparin' Christmas Dinner. Mum would always make Christmas puddin' and put 'silver' joeys in (silver threepenny pieces). She would dish up the puddin' and somehow she'd always make sure both Roy and I got a joey in our portion. Thinkin' about it now, she probably slipped them in as she was servin' up, but at the time I thought they were cooked in there and it was just pot luck if you got one. It added to the excitement. If we had guests, then they'd be sure to get a 'silver surprise' too. That always went down well except this particular year when Len Bedcock stayed with us for a couple of days. He was an old school friend of dad's back in Sidmouth. He worked for a removal firm – perhaps he ran it, I'm not sure, but anyway the firm sometimes did trips up to, or from, London. When they did, he'd stay for a night or two. Dad enjoyed catchin' up and as they chatted, very soon dad's voice would change and the 'Devon twang' would come out just like when Uncle Vic was with us.

Anyway, Len (Mr Bedcock to me) was all smiles and compliments as he munched through his puddin' but mum couldn't believe her eyes when the last mouthful went down and still no joey to be seen. It seems that year the 'silver surprise' went down a bit too well – he'd only gone and swallowed it!

Christmas Day was one of the few times our front room would be used for anythin' other than our bedroom. At such times there'd be a fire lit and our put-me-up bed would be folded away. After dinner, Roy and I would be ushered in there to play while mum got on with clearin' away and tidyin' up and dad would sit and, bein' Christmas, smoke a cigar with his friend. Mum came into us in the front room all of a fluster tellin' us how she was sure he'd had a joey so he must have swallowed it. Roy, bein' that bit older, calmed her down but she daren't tell dad 'cos he'd have gone mad and she never said anythin' to Mr Bedcock. Over tea, mum kept lookin' him over, but he seemed none the worse for wear so nothin' more was ever said about it – leastways not to Mr Bedcock.

The followin' year, 1947, mum took me off to Chessington Zoo. Mum was still workin' on the railway then, so she got special concessionary travel. On this occasion she got a combined ticket which took us from Clapham Junction to Chessington Station. Clapham Junction is or was the busiest rail transport hub in the country. It was said that 4,000 trains a day passed through it. I always liked travellin' on the train (I still do), but our 'combined ticket' made this journey extra special because we were met at Chessington Station by a coach and four to take us on to the zoo. It was a bit chilly, but no matter, it felt like we were really 'lordin' it' up there. In those days Chessington was still mainly a zoo with a small circus and a few swings, not the Theme Park it is today but we enjoyed it – mum and I. Talkin' of swings, there are photos of me and mum taken that day at the end of the chapter. It wasn't the warmest of days, in fact at one point it actually started snowin'! As you can see, though, whilst both mum and I have thick coats on, I'm still in short trousers. Kids were hardy in those days, we had to be because, as I've told you, we didn't get to wear long trousers until we were 14.

In what's come to be known as the 'post war era', an annual event for us lads was a trip to the Boat Race. Thinkin' back, it was a bit of a waste of time, but I always went along. I suppose as well as the trip it was the spectacle I enjoyed. I must have, because I even went on my own once – to Hammersmith – and that day it was rainin' and not just a few drops, it was pourin' o' rain. No wonder I was the only one – I must have been mad.

Usually there'd be four or five of us and we'd go to either Hammersmith or Mortlake. In case you don't know, the race starts at Putney – just the other side of Putney Bridge. As it happens, only about a 100 yards from the Star & Garter, which as you'll see later would become a very important venue for me, but as kids we weren't really interested in goin' to the start. It would always be either Hammersmith or Mortlake for the finish. We always supported Cambridge. I still do, but if you were to ask me why, I'm not sure I could tell you. Maybe it's because, often as not, they'd be the underdog.

We'd go for the day and be standin' around on the banks for hours and hours and then in two minutes they'd flash by and that would be that. Time to get on a bus and go home. I'm bein' a bit unfair because there was more to it than that. People flocked to any live event in those days because, as I've said before, there was no television, so if you wanted to see somethin' you had to be there. That's why the banks were always buzzin' and that created atmosphere and wherever there were crowds, there were the chancers –well opportunists might be a better word. I'm not talkin' about pickpockets, though doubtless there'd be a fair scatterin' of them as well, but what I mean is folk sellin' flags, souvenirs, sweets and the like. Most spectators had a flag to wave – light or dark blue dependin' on their allegiance. We'd usually just get a paper one that they gave away with sweets. They sold metal badges and all sorts. Probably quite collectable now, but we never bought one. We never had much money and you couldn't eat a badge, could you?

Somethin' I should have mentioned because it was important to me and somethin' I did quite regularly, havin' got back from Ardingly, was go to visit Aunt Raithby. I'd go on the train. Sometimes I'd get off at Norbury Station rather than payin' to go up to Thornton Heath. Then I'd have about a twenty minute walk up to

Aunt Raithby's at No. 123 Norbury Avenue. The street name doesn't really conjure up an image of what the street was really like except, bein' called an avenue, you'd imagine it bein' lined with trees and it was. But it was also very straight and very, very long – about a mile and a half altogether. Because it was so long and straight, the police used to use it for motorbike trainin' and I'd often see 'em goin' up and down as I was walkin' up. Goin' back home I'd invariably walk up to the other end of Norbury Avenue into County Road to get the bus to Thornton Heath Station. It wasn't all that far – only about three stops.

The train line ran at the back of Aunt Raithby's back garden. I've been sayin' "I this" and "I that", but in the early days at least, usually Roy and I would go visitin' Aunt Raithby together. It would be somewhere between half and threequarters of an hour after leavin' that we'd be goin' past her back garden and without fail Aunt Raithby would be standin' in her back doorway wavin' her handkerchief and Roy and I would be hangin' out the train window wavin' our handkerchiefs back. Nice really when you think about it. I always knew when Aunt Raithby's house was comin' up because just back from her's there was a big group of sheds and garages visible from the train. Incidentally, the line we were on was the Brighton Line run by Southern Rail – the same line we'd travelled on when we were evacuated to Ardingly. Sometimes in the summer, Roy and I would go to stay with Aunt Raithby for about a week as a sort of holiday. Mum would give us some money for our keep because Aunt Raithby never had any money and dad would pack us up a box of vegetables from his allotment. He'd pick out the best ones and wash 'em and tie 'em and arrange 'em just so.

Durin' our stay we'd always go to the 'Flea Pit' at Thornton Heath (That's what we used to call the smaller cinemas because compared to the bigger newer ones, they were a bit basic and rather 'tired'.) We'd go and see films like Laurel & Hardy and Old Mother Riley, but it appears none other than Roy Hudd used to frequent the same cinema as a boy and accordin' to a story he was fond of tellin', one time the 'entertainment' was off screen. Apparently he was sittin' two rows back and durin' the film the side doors opened. This in itself was a bit odd, but then these two blokes waltzed in and unscrewed the front row of seats. I'm sayin' the front row, but I guess it would have been about half of 'em, up to the aisle. Then they just picked 'em up, one at each end, and calm as you like, walked back out the door. Where the usherettes were, he didn't know, but nobody moved or said a dickie bird. Talk about brazen – walkin' into a cinema whilst the film was on and pinchin' a row of seats!

When I was older – from about 13 onwards – I'd almost always go over to Aunt Raithby's on my own, usually on my bike. I'd go to see her but to do little jobs as well. Dad had an allotment by this time and he'd usually want to load up my saddlebag with parsnips, carrots and the like. That was all very well, in fact really good of him, except there I was, itchin' to get goin' and dad would always make such a drama of it. Loadin' me up would take ages. It was like tiein' up the Sunday roast half a dozen times. Every bunch had to be just so, tied up and knotted in a particular way. On top of that, I'd have dad's shears strapped to my back. I needed them for Aunt Raithby's garden hedge and front lawn.

To avoid as much of the heavy traffic as possible, over time I learnt which back roads and rat runs were best, but there was no avoidin' some of the main roads. Then I had to really keep my wits about me because it wasn't just the heavy traffic, but all the tram lines I had to watch out for. What I don't think dad really understood was that cuttin' Aunt Raithby's privet hedge and front lawn with a pair of shears was a full day's job, which is why I was always anxious to get goin'.

One thing you need to appreciate is that in those days – the mid 1940s, very few people owned a lawnmower, leastways not ordinary folk like we were. Aunt Raithby didn't even own any shears and, believe it or not, if the grass was gettin' long, Aunt Raithby would spend hours tryin' to cut it with a bread knife! She was a very proud woman and didn't want her front to look uncared for. In truth it never came near bowlin' green standard, but at least it looked tidy when I'd finished. For most folk, just clippin' round the edges of a lawn with shears is plenty and pretty time-consumin'. It wasn't a big lawn, but clippin' the whole lot with shears, especially when you've already cut the hedge, doesn't just take a while, it takes it out of you and Aunt Raithby understood this and so now and again she'd pop out and with genuine concern in her voice would say, 'Are you alright duckie?' You see, although she'd long since adopted London as her home, and she spoke the Queen's English very well, now and again she'd use expressions which harped back to her Lincolnshire roots.

To me it was a small part of what made her so special. I don't mind tellin' you that by the time I'd done all that clippin', my arms would feel like they didn't belong to me any more and then ridin' back was a whole new experience.

One time, I rode over to find Aunt Raithby had a family of relatives livin' in her front room. I'm not sure what relatives they were or where they'd come from, but they were waitin' to be re-housed by Croydon Council. I can't remember the parents' names, but the man was interestin' because he'd lost a leg durin' the war and now, to make a livin' he used to make plaster figures and paint them to hang on a wall – three flyin' ducks, that sort of thing. Quite popular, they were. The thing was, despite his obvious disability, he was resourceful. People didn't, couldn't, just rely on bein' able to claim benefits in those days, not even disabled people. He had 3 kids and I can remember their names – Joan, Sonny and David. When the kids were lookin' for work, it was Katie, one of 'grandma's' daughters, who came to their rescue, gettin' David a job on the Times and Sonny with the Sportin' Life. I knew Sonny best because he used to take Roy and me out sometimes. He was Sonny by name and 'sunny' by nature.

Whilst I'm on the subject of Aunt Raithby's relatives, there's somethin' more I want to tell you about Fred. Remember him, Grandma's son who worked at Croydon Airport. I'm goin' back in time to durin' the war because some of this I only found out about havin' got back from Ardingly. Fred had a job to write a letter, but with anythin' technical he was brilliant. It seems that when the war came, Fred was sent to a place in Wales. I don't know where exactly, but I think it was a 'secret location'. He was sent there as a civilian, but workin' for the government. Whenever a German plane was captured or just parts recovered, they'd be sent to this place in Wales for Fred to take apart and analyse – the idea bein' to see what the Germans had that we didn't that might be worth copyin' or to look for weaknesses that could be exploited.

Now, bear in mind that I was an evacuee in Ardingly at this time, miles away from dear Aunt Raithby and no means of keepin' in contact except via news mainly from mum. And we didn't see mum very often. Regular contact was discouraged because it was thought to be unsettlin' for us as child evacuees which, thinkin' about it, I suppose in fairness it probably would have been. But as a child livin' alone with strangers sittin' in a room on my own, 'bein' good', there were times when I would have given anythin' to be back home with mum or Aunt Raithby or just to know that I'd be seein' 'em soon. Rememberin' is makin' me well up so I'd better snap out of this or I'll be goin' all emotional on you when it's Fred I'm supposed to be tellin' you about.

It would have been about 2 years into my time as an evacuee when I learnt that Fred wasn't doin' the secret work in Wales any more. He'd been called up into the army and sent out to Burma of all places, to fight the Japanese. Talk about drawin' the short straw. I don't know how long he'd been out there, but I think it could have been some while, but the next news I got was that he'd been brought back and sent back to Wales to carry on with the 'secret stuff'. I'll tell you how that came about in a minute, but first I need to tell you somethin' of the terrible time Fred had out in Burma at the hands of the Japanese that I only got told sometime after the war. In particular, there was one time, when the outfit Fred was with were lyin' low in the jungle, hidin' from a much larger Japanese force. Fred and his mate were hidin' close by one another. The thing was, Fred must have been better at hidin' than his mate, or just lucky – who knows? The point is, his mate was discovered and the Japanese weren't for takin' prisoners and just hacked him to bits with machetes more or less before Fred's eyes. In truth, Fred had no choice. After the first blow, it was too late to save his friend and if Fred had broken cover he'd have been dead too, no question. So he just kept still 'till they'd all gone by. In some ways, you could say Fred's friend, havin' been discovered, was better off bein' killed because you hear such terrible stories of what the Japanese in Burma did to prisoners. Even so, what he'd witnessed had a marked and lastin' effect on Fred and I remember hearin' it said that he was never quite the same again. Fortunately Fred never did get captured, but he was wounded before bein' called back to Wales and ever after he wore this sort of leather brace support on his right forearm.

It wasn't bein' wounded that got Fred brought back from Burma, it was his expertise. Apparently, some big wig in the War Ministry in London had a job he wanted Fred to look at and the story goes that when he was told Danaby had been called up and dispatched to Burma, he blew his top and immediately sent orders out for him to be brought back to Wales to carry on as before. And so it was that Fred spent the rest of the war in Wales extractin' what secrets, weaknesses and technological advances he could from captured German planes and, most often, wreckage. Orders or no orders though, Fred didn't go straight to Wales. The first thing he did, felt he had to do, was go and tell the parents of his dead friend what had happened. I think he spared them the gory details, makin' it sound quick and painless, but havin' witnessed 'the real horror if it', for Fred those images were to haunt him for the rest of his life. There was nothin' he could have done, but I think he still felt a sense of guilt for not havin' tried and by all accounts, the experience changed him, which was a real shame.

Post war, Fred worked at London Airport, mainly in charge of the radio side of things for BOAC. He was still in aviation, but the damage to his arm prevented him from doin' the sort of work he'd done pre-war.

It would have been about 1947 when Fred's sister Gracie got married and 'the lady that did' for his mother (grandma to me) and her daughter, were invited. Later on, you'll see a photo of Gracie on her weddin' day. I was still a kid at this time – well 13 – but, as I heard later, up 'till then Fred had never seemed to take much interest in or have the time for women. That all changed at this weddin' because Fred got friendly, very friendly, with this daughter of 'the lady that did' and they had a bit of a fling which unfortunately resulted in her gettin' pregnant. I don't know why, but the two of 'em never got together, but she had the child, a baby boy, Stephen. What became of the girl I don't know. All I know is Fred never did marry or it seems get together with another lady, but baby Stephen came to live with 'grandma' who, together with Fred and his sisters, brought the child up.

Fred's sister Dolly in particular was a real family stalwart. The others worked in the City, but Dolly was head 'Nippy' (waitress) at an Express Dairies place in Streatham High Street which was very posh in those days – a bit like Lyons. For Dolly, work was just a 159 bus ride away, so she'd always be home before the others and so would be most help in the house and would always help her mother prepare the evenin' meal for everyone. They were a lovely family and the only problem I ever had when visitin' 'grandma's' as a kid was they all smoked like troopers, so it was usually a bit 'foggy' indoors which isn't much good when you suffer from asthma.

Before I move on to somethin' else, I just want to say somethin' about 'Raithby', their family name because as you know dear Aunt Raithby was special, very special to me. In the old days people often took their name from the place where they lived or even, as often happened when people went out to the colonies, gave their name to the place where they lived. Aunt Raithby had come from Lincolnshire and when Roy and I checked, we found two small places called Raithby either side of Louth. When he's got time, I might get John to do a bit more research on that, but right now I think he's got enough on writin' my book!

Although the war was over, mum continued to work on the railway at the Stewarts Lane Rail Depot, which was only about an eight minute walk from our house. I remember there was a door in the brick wall alongside Dickens Street. It was just an ordinary wooden door and it wasn't locked – you could just open it and walk through. There in front of you were the railway lines – quite a few of them as I remember. After checkin' for trains, you could just walk across 'em to the depot where mum worked. I often used to go across on my own to see mum to take messages or whatever. You couldn't do it now. If you didn't get electrocuted, you'd probably get arrested and prosecuted. Back then they were steam trains mum was workin' on – the ones that worked out of Victoria. The Golden Arrow was probably the most famous train she worked on. In its day it was regarded as the pinnacle of steam locomotion. I can't remember when exactly it was, but mum got a promotion and with it a welcome rise in pay. Instead of cleanin' and maintenance work, she was now in the stores where the drivers and firemen used to go for things like sand for the sandbox, oil and green liners, which were a sort of cloth. As I remember, a driver was allowed two a day to wipe his hands on. To my mind train drivers of today don't know they're born. They don't even have to get off their backsides – much less get their hands dirty. Mind you, I think it was the firemen who had to do all the stokin' who did most of the really hard work.

I mentioned early on that there was a big age gap between mum and dad and I think that was part of the problem. Moreover, dad had come through the First World War, but he would never talk about it.

I know he'd marched across Mesopotamia, but that's about the top and bottom of my knowledge. Whatever had happened, I think it had a profound effect on the rest of his life and his relationships with other people, particularly those closest to him. Whatever the cause, theirs wasn't a very presentable marriage – they never – or almost never – did anythin' together. I never remember them goin' out together except to the very occasional whist drive.

Dad never went anywhere or did anythin' – apart from goin' to work or the occasional political meetin'. He just stayed at home. Money never meant anythin' to him. He never spent anythin' except on his weekly tobacco – an ounce of A1 and an ounce of Gold Leaf. Every Sunday afternoon he'd put a newspaper on his lap and mix them together. Then he'd keep it in a tobacco jar and roll his own from that durin' the week.

I've told you dad loved his newspaper – the telegraph to be precise, but that wasn't the only paper he read. He had the 'local paper' sent up from Sidmouth, the town of his birth. He had it sent up once a fortnight. It would come in the post in a paper sleeve. When dad had read it, and he'd do so cover to cover, I'd have to take it down to Mrs Barron on my bike. She lived with her mother in Robertson Street. Now, the reason I'd have to take it there was because Mrs Barron had been married to an old school friend of dad's – back in Sidmouth that is. I don't know what his real name was – maybe it was Nicholas Barron, but anyway, his nick name was 'Nick Nore' – Nick Nore the Barber. His shop was in Queenstown Road, so we'd go and have our hair cut there sometimes. I'm sayin' only sometimes, because there was one a lot nearer to where we lived. Sadly Nick Nore died quite young and that's when I started havin' to take this paper round to his wife. That went on for years after.

Dad wasn't interested in anythin' to do with the house. He was content just to sit in it and read his paper. Havin' said that, he did do the paintin' from time to time, but everythin' always had to be cream. Two things he was good at though – cookin' and lookin' after the family pets. He always did the Sunday dinner and Christmas dinner come to that. They took an age because everythin' had to be just so and it didn't do to get in his way. The kitchen was definitely 'out of bounds'. At Christmas he'd even wear a chef's hat. Not for any comic effect – he was very serious about it. In fact you'd probably say he was a miserable old sod with no real sense of fun. It was all we could do to get him to pull a cracker. Life and soul of the party? Definitely not. A good cook though, you'd have to give him that, and thanks to mum, there were always 'threepenny joeys' in the Christmas puddin'.

Like chalk and cheese though, mum and dad. She revelled in the festivities and she loved her food did mum. That was her downfall really. Always room for an extra helpin'. What's more, as soon as dinner was over she couldn't wait to get cleared away and the table laid for 'high tea'. She'd have it all set out by 3pm – in time for the King's speech. This is Christmas Day I'm talkin' about. Sittin' down together to listen to the King's speech on the wireless was somethin' of a ritual in our house. I thought he was interestin' to listen to 'cos he stuttered. He had a real job to get his words out. Don't get me wrong. Nobody 'took the Mickey'. Everybody sympathised. We were willin' him to have improved from the previous year. Afterwards, that's what all the talk was about rather than discussin' what he'd actually been tellin' us.

He was popular – the King, so, before I move on, I'll just say a bit more about him because I think he deserves that. I'm not sure if it was his own idea, but durin' the war the George Cross and George Medal were created to recognise acts of bravery by citizens. Whatever the case, it seems his popularity grew durin' the war. Rather than retreatin' to some safer place in the countryside, the King and Queen saw out most of the war in the Palace and regularly visited bombed areas in the capital in an effort to show solidarity with the people and help boost morale. I didn't witness any of this myself, but I remember hearin' about it and I'm told the Palace was bombed no less than nine times. He struggled to make his speeches right through the War. Even in Ardingly, I got to hear some of the King's wartime radio broadcasts. On the downside, as you know, I and the other kids were disappointed to say the least when he whizzed through the village without so much as a wave.

I've already touched on the impromptu celebrations that took place on VE Day, 8th May 1945, but now I want to tell you about the big organised celebrations that took place the followin' year on 8th June 1946 after the war in the Far East with Germany's ally, Japan, had finally ended. As you know, mum was one for pomp and ceremony and takin' part in celebrations, but dad wasn't the least bit interested. Mum and dad, like chalk and cheese.

Whilst especially as he got older, Roy might refuse to go to some spectacles, the Victory Parade was another matter. He was just as keen as mum or me because he knew all the Services would be represented, all in their various uniforms. To make sure we got a good place, mum packed up provisions and off we went the night before. When I say we, I mean mum, Roy and me. Roy was into uniforms and that was the attraction for him. They'd erected a big white podium in the Mall close to the Palace. Aluminium I think it was. Very grand lookin' – I thought so anyway. I remember callin' it a 'salutin' base' because it's where all the dignitaries were to take the salute as wave after wave of troops marched by. Anyway, we got a front row position near Admiralty Arch, more or less opposite this stage cum salutin' base – about as close as you could get and from where we could still see the Palace. Only trouble was, it was nowhere near any toilets, so we had to keep goin' there in shifts all the way to Green Park – one at a time so as not to lose our place. Luckily it was a lovely warm summer's evenin' because we were goin' to have to be out there all night. As the night wore on, more and more people arrived so, in the end, there must have been thousands of us spread out on the pavements, all willin' to be out all night so as to be sure of a good view of the parade the next day. By early mornin' the pavements were packed behind us, but it was no problem. All we had to do was keep sayin' excuse me and they let us through back to our place at the front. From there we could look right to the Palace and left to Admiralty Arch, so we could see pretty much everythin' that was goin' on.

Once the march past got under way, we were definitely in the pound seats – right there opposite the King and Queen, Churchill and all the other dignitaries perched up on their podium takin' the salute. All the forces were represented in the march past – the Army, the Navy, the Air Force and Civilian Services and weaponry too and of course there were my particular favourites, all the marchin' bands, lots and lots of 'em. All sorts of troops marched by, includin' from Australia, New Zealand, Canada – all the Commonwealth countries and others that had been our allies in the war. A real spectacle it was and for us kids quite an eye-opener, especially when the coloured regiments went by. Back then we'd hardly ever seen coloured people.

To say the parade that day was memorable is an understatement. Ok, I was only 12 and no, I can't tell you every regiment, every band that marched past us that day. Nobody could. There were far too many of 'em, but that's the point. It was the sheer scale of it that was so memorable. Like nothin' before or, I'll wager, since. I'll just try to give you a bit of a flavour of the spectacle, the pageantry on parade that day. For starters there was the Household Cavalry and lots and lots of marchin' bands, includin' the Royal Horse Guards, the Grenadier Guards, the Coldstream Guards, Scots, Irish and Welsh Guards. There were regimental bands from every county in the country and bands representin' the various army corps, includin' the Royal Army Ordnance Corps which, unbeknown to me at the time, would leave a lastin' impression on me in later life.

I think I had an ear for music. Certainly I enjoyed it, but for me, aged 12 years, I suppose that was about the extent of it. But it would come; it would blossom, and when it did, it would take centre stage and, for a time at least, it would become the most important thing in my life. But that's all in the future; for now I'm just standin' there enjoyin' it without fully appreciatin' its qualities.

There was even a detachment of the Home Guard and contingents representin' key wartime industries, which to be honest seemed a bit dull by comparison at the time. Interestingly though, they included the so-called 'Bevin Boys', who I later learned, on call-up, were selected by random ballot to go down the mines rather than serve in the armed forces.

Knowin' now somethin' of what it was like to work down a coal mine, the conditions and the dangers they faced, you can't say they had it easy by comparison, but I'm digressin' again.

The parade just went on and on and it wasn't just on the ground. In the air there were fly-pasts by lots of planes that had helped to win the war, includin' the famous Hurricanes, Lancasters and every schoolboy's favourite, the Spitfires.

The celebrations went on for hours, but mum had packed enough provisions to keep us well fed and watered. Only trouble was, mum was a generous soul and fond of givin' our sandwiches away to all and sundry around us who hadn't thought to bring their own. We had some of course, but by the time we really wanted one – they'd all gone! I'd like to say I didn't mind, but I'm not sure that would be true. The spectacle though – I wouldn't have missed that and especially the marchin' bands, lots of 'em, maybe thirty or more – they were well worth goin' without a few sandwiches. Livin' in London, we were lucky. We could be there. Remember there was no television in those days. If you wanted to see somethin', you had to be there. They did have Pathe newsreels at the cinema, but nothin' could replace the excitement of actually bein' there wavin' flags and cheerin' along with all the rest, especially when you were at the front with nothin' to obstruct your view. At some point- I think it was towards the end – this Lancaster bomber flew down the Mall, over us and up to the Palace, sprayin' poppies onto the crowds below.

When all the marchin' past was over, most of the crowd headed for the Palace where all the Royals came out onto the balcony to wave to the cheerin' crowds. As for us, mum needed us to get a move on. We had to walk down all the 'back doubles'(side streets to you) at the back of the Palace goin' towards Victoria to catch a No 28 tram to Clapham Junction. Mum wanted us home quick because we'd hardly had any sleep. We'd seen all the best bits and havin' been up all night, now she wanted us to get some sleep before takin' us off out again to see the aquatic display and fireworks on the embankment in the evenin'. She was good was our mum. She always knew the best spots to stand and made sure she got us there that evenin' by about 7 pm in time to grab 'em. Our spot was on the embankment against the wall overlookin' the river close to Lambeth Bridge – more or less where the Eye is today.

There was stuff happenin' before but the displays proper really kicked off at around 10pm with the arrival of the King on the river bein' saluted by masses of searchlights and the national anthem blarin' out from hundreds of loud speakers. After that, the rousin' music just kept playin' as the surface of the river got lit up and Westminster and Lambeth Bridges too and there were coloured jets from specially equipped barges and from beside the bridges. Although I don't specifically remember it, apparently the music included excerpts from Handel's Water and Firework Music. Mind you, back then you have to remember I was only a kid and wouldn't have recognised it anyway. To me it was just a rousin' sound addin' to the atmosphere of celebration and I loved it.

Various firework and searchlight displays started at around half past ten. In truth I suppose all the rockets were a bit tame by modern standards, but certainly not in their day. I for one thought they were brilliant and in between displays the RAF flew planes through the beams of searchlights playin' in the sky. All very excitin' and dramatic, especially to a twelve year old. Then there were more set piece firework displays from barges on the river, all endin' with what was for me perhaps the best bit, maybe because of the surprise of it – Lambeth Bridge all lit up with fireworks spellin' out a message which bizarrely I can't for the life of me remember, but if I had to guess I'd say it was probably a message declarin' 'VICTORY'.

It was gettin' late – about 11.30 pm – and mum started to take us home after that. All the buses and trams were packed and the queues went on forever so, like it or not, we'd got a long three mile trek ahead of us, but it had been worth it. When it came to spectacles, she was a glutton for punishment was our mum. Readin' up on it now, apparently the water displays went on a bit longer, endin' with a final firin' of 50 magnesium shells and the playin' of the National Anthem at around midnight. We might have missed a bit, but even now I'd say we definitely witnessed all the best bits and thanks to mum we had a 'ringside seat'. Well, actually we were standin' same as everybody else, but you know what I mean.

Before I got on to the victory celebrations, I was tellin' you about the King and I suppose I got a bit side-tracked, as I'm wont to do. Anyway – the King. He was what mum would call 'a bag of nerves'. That terrible stammer must have made life very stressful for him, havin' to be forever meetin' officials and foreign dignitaries and makin' speeches and radio broadcasts. Very sad really. It's probably why he was a chain smoker. I remember it was always said, "It was the smokin' that killed the King." It likely was too, because he died young of lung cancer aged 56 on 6th February 1952. He was at Sandringham, where the Royals went – and still do – at that time of year. But there I go again, gettin' ahead of myself when I haven't finished with the 1940s.

So now – back to dad – which if you remember was where all this about the King and VE Day, the King's Speech and stuff started. I'd told you he was good at two things: cookin', includin' the Christmas dinner, and at lookin' after the family pets. Notice the plural. So far I think I've only told you about Dinky, I guess 'cos he was such a character and lived with us the longest – survivin' the bomb and keepin' me warm at night! You'll see a photo of Dinky at the end of the chapter. Anyway, the thing is, we also had a guinea pig called 'spot' and a white budgie which must have had a name, but I can't for the life of me think what it was. Spot lived a pretty grand life for a guinea pig. He lasted 8 or 9 years with us and I'm not sure how old he was when we got him. I'd swapped him for two white mice with a lad at school. Dad made a hutch for him – a bit like a rabbit hutch on legs, out on the balcony.

Spot was my pet really but dad took to him and did a lot of the 'lookin' after' but it was down to me to make sure he always had clean beddin'. Once a month, on a Saturday mornin', I'd take a big sack and the coal shovel and head off down to Broughton Street. It wasn't that far, about a third of a mile or so. I'd be headed for this timber yard – Cayless's it was called, where I noticed they made ladders. That bit of information was to come in handy, as you'll discover later. Where I was headed wasn't all that obvious – behind a little recess between the houses, backin' on to the main Victoria – Waterloo rail line. All the shavin's were in a huge pile on the ground and I used to just help myself. I didn't need to ask and no-one ever challenged me.

In the winter Spot came indoors for the night 'cos dad always said it would be too cold for him outside. There was a cupboard at the side of the fireplace in the scullery and inside a box for sticks that were used to make the fire. The guinea pig used to sleep in that – 'snug as a bug in a rug'. It was fairly high up off the ground so Spot never offered to jump out. He was white with a big spot of black fur over one eye – hence his name.

Most nights, after tea, this guinea pig would be scurryin' round the outside of the room, the kitchen, that is. I suppose he felt safer keepin' to the edge, especially with Dinky sittin' eyein' him up all the while. Sometimes the budgie would be flyin' about as well, but Dinky seemed to know better than to touch either of 'em. Once dad had read his paper, which was itself a nightly ritual, he'd sit there with Dinky the cat on one knee and this guinea pig on the other. They'd both be content to lie still, but I can't help wonderin' if Dinky wasn't lyin' there thinkin', "Enjoy it while you can matie, 'cos I'm goin' to eat you one day." Cats are fairly easy to house-train – but guinea pigs

– I'm not so sure. Our 'Spot' was though. Never made a mess anywhere he shouldn't.

One year – about 1948 ish, dad made Spot into a bit of a celebrity at the Church fete – St Philips on Tennyson Street. The parishioners were asked to come up with ideas for stalls to raise money for the church. All the usual stalls were there like roll a penny and coconut shy and dad decided he could charge threepence a go to come and see and hold Spot. It was amazin' really, 'cos whilst mum was one for church fetes and helpin' out, it wasn't the sort of thing dad would normally have gone to, much less have his own stall. But fair play to him, he painted Spot's cage up and had it lookin' very smart and he did quite well, made quite a few bob for the church. I guess not many kids had seen or handled a guinea pig – leastways not one as tame as Spot. I'm not sure he really enjoyed it though. He was a bit too serious was dad and in his blue serge suit and Anthony Eden hat he looked a bit like a fish out of water surrounded by all that buntin' and carnival atmosphere. Come to think of it, I can't remember ever seein' dad out and about in casual clothes. If I had, I probably wouldn't have recognised him!

Don't get me wrong, dad did do stuff to help the church, it's just that fetes weren't really his thing. In fact he was treasurer at the church and got very friendly with Rev Hopkins who ran this debatin' class at Tennyson Street School once a week. Now debatin' was much more up dad's street, so he'd go to that. I suppose you could say he was 'a man's man' and about the only thing I can remember him takin' mum to was the occasional whist drive. So, whilst dad did go to this one fete to raise money with 'Spot', he still wouldn't take mum to the ballroom dancin' in the evenin'. St Philips fete always finished with ballroom dancin' in the Church Hall. Everyone, includin' teenagers and mums and dads, went to that, but not our dad. Mum would take me instead. I remember bein' a bit embarrassed at that particular one because I only had boots to wear. I didn't have any shoes to dance in. I didn't let it stop me though, but I didn't get to dance with the beauty queen. Not that shoes would have changed that. Earlier in the day, she'd been paradin' around the streets in a coach and four. I say coach. It was actually a coal cart and four horses but, dressed up, it still looked the part. For that day at least it was regal – in our little corner of London anyway.

Whilst dad wasn't exactly what you could call 'a family man', it was a recognised thing that once a year – on Boxin' Day – we would all go to the cinema as a family. As far as I know they were the only times dad ever went to the cinema and as I recall, mum would always have to talk him round to goin' and even then, he'd always insist on it bein' an 'adult' type film – the sort of thing James Mason would be in. Films would run continuously from 12 midday until 10 o'clock at night. Usually there'd be 2 films plus a newsreel plus a cartoon and people could walk in and out whenever they wanted. As a result there was quite a bit of comin' and goin' with people stayin' until they got to the bit in the film where they'd come in. The gettin' up and down to let people by really annoyed dad and he rarely made the second film. Even I could sense he was there on sufferance and in some ways it was a relief when he announced he was goin' home to lay the table for tea.

Now and again, mum would take me to the cinema on my own, but more often it would be Roy and me goin' on a Saturday with some friends, leastways until Roy left school and then I suppose I was too young for him. Seats would be 9 pence, a shillin', one and nine, two and three or two and ninepence – gettin' pricier and a bit more plush as you went back. An usherette would show you to your seat with a torch. Particularly as we got a bit older, for a bit of bravado, we'd go in for a shillin' and then gradually sneak our way further and further back, makin' our way up to the two and threepences whilst the usherette was otherwise engaged.

The Granada Theatre at Clapham Junction, as its name suggests, wasn't just a cinema, it was a theatre with a beautiful stage. Where we sat depended on what we were there to see. If it was a film, we'd try to sit near the back. If there was goin' to be a talent show as well, then we'd try and sit at the front. A chap called Brian Mickey would act as compere introducin' the acts. He might be in Clapham for a week before movin' on, takin' the show to another Granada Theatre in the circuit. If he wanted to watch a particular act, he'd come round the front and stand near us. A big fat bloke he was. The reason I'm makin' a point of tellin' you about him is because you'll meet him again a good few years from now havin' an altercation with a London Bus!

The children's matinees apart, cinemas in those days were always full of cigarette smoke. Not great if like me you suffered from asthma, but the thing was, smokin' was synonymous with growin' up. Practically every grown-up smoked, includin' all the role models of the day – film stars and the like. As soon as you got into long trousers, you wanted to be seen with a cigarette. It was all part of the image. Cinemas always had smoke, lots of it. It would be streamin' up through the projector beams. It was part of the atmosphere. All the seat backs had ashtrays and directly we got seated we'd be lookin' to light up – me included once I became 15. Here I go again, racin' ahead of myself because I'm not even 13 yet!

Sometimes on a Sunday, mum and me would go off to Brighton, or Margate or wherever, but dad would never come with us. We'd always have dinner out – fish and chips or whatever (we didn't call it lunch then). When we got home – maybe as late as 9 pm, dad would have another roast dinner waitin' for mum and she'd eat every potato. You could say mum liked her food and as a result, as she got older, she put on a lot of weight.

Dad was somehow more old-fashioned than mum and very set in his ways. Whenever he went out – which as I've said was pretty much only to work, he'd be very Edwardian in his dress. You can see that from the photos of dad on my Weddin' Day later on. I'm mentionin' it now because they're the only photos I've got of dad. Dad's twin brother, Uncle Vic, was different in lots of ways. Whenever the brothers got together – which would pretty much only be when Uncle Vic and Aunt Maisie came to visit – their speech would immediately change dramatically to the Devon twang they spoke as youngsters. I've already told you that Uncle Vic was in the army. He'd survived both world wars, but that hadn't dented his spirits.

Occasionally, Uncle Vic and Auntie Maisie would come for the weekend. Then after tea on Sunday we'd usually all go for a walk to Battersea Park. Even dad would come. I've not been back for years, but in those days it was very well kept. The flower beds and the rose garden were especially beautiful and it was said to be Queen Mary's favourite park. The Royal car would often be seen there.

I suppose dad was rather old-fashioned and set in his ways. He wanted us to walk gracefully and more or less "be seen and not heard". I was young enough to pretty much 'tow the line' but Roy was that much older and a bit of a rebel. He'd be forever gettin' told off for draggin' his feet, throwin' sticks or whatever. There was always a bit of friction between Roy and dad.

As kids we'd often go down to Battersea Park on our own just to mess about and go see the deer in their enclosure. They were very tame and used to bein' fed. They'd eat anythin' – even rubbish. We'd give 'em all sorts – includin' ice cream wrappers. I suppose we just thought it was funny testin' what they would and wouldn't gobble up. We didn't mean 'em any harm – as kids I suppose we just didn't know any better. I'm sayin' that but then again, we knew not to do it with dad around. I don't know why, but durin' the war the deer were taken away and replaced with wallabies. With meat bein' rationed, maybe they thought the deer would get poached.

I'm gettin' side-tracked again – back to walkin' round with Uncle Vic, Aunt Maisie, mum and dad. There was this round, art deco type café buildin' in the park. A beautiful, rather elegant buildin'. We'd go in for tea and ice cream for us kids – and mum. She was a devil for ice cream was mum. Sometimes we'd get taken out on the lake in rowin' boats or we'd queue for a trip on the motor launch. A beautiful white thing it was. A shillin' a go – for a trip right round the lake.

Uncle Vic and Auntie Maisie would usually come to stay with us for maybe two weeks at a time just before a new postin'. Two weeks was probably long enough because there'd always be some friction between the two brothers. Dad was a Labour man and his brother a Conservative. They'd argue a lot about politics. Uncle Vic had a terrific sense of humour – very unlike dad, who was somewhat dour. In temperament and outlook I was, and still am, more like Uncle Vic.

Dad's other brother, Uncle Dick, was a submariner in the Navy. He used to visit about once a fortnight, generally on a Thursday. I think you might find one particular visit interestin', so I'll tell you about it. For a start it was a Sunday, which I'd already thought was a bit odd. I don't remember the date, but I was still at school, so I think it was probably some time in 1946 or 47. To give you an idea of what I looked like then, there's a school photo taken around this time in the group at the end of this chapter. In those days on a Sunday night our family, like many others, would listen to the radio. From 8.30 'till 9.00 there was always a play and 9.00 'till 10.00 pm was my favourite show of the week, Variety Bandbox. I often didn't listen to the play, but this particular night dad said he wanted me to listen to the play with them. I did, but to be honest my mind wasn't really on it and I was just waitin' for what I really wanted – Variety Bandbox – to come on.

Anyway, it was about this submarine which had got stranded. Somethin' had gone wrong and they couldn't surface. It was stranded submerged and eventually the air began to go sour. They tried everythin', but all to no avail – and about 100 men were killed. In the end divers did manage to gain access and were able to rescue four men from an air pocket. They were the padre, a cook and two seamen. As I say, I was about 12 or 13 at the time and I don't remember all the details not least 'cos I hadn't been listenin' all that intently. Had dad told me why he was keen for me to listen beforehand I would have paid more attention. Anyway, when it had finished dad said, "Did you enjoy that?", to which I replied somethin' like, "Oh yes, it was good tonight." Well, I couldn't say any other could I? But then dad dropped somethin' of a bombshell when he said, "The fourth man who got out alive is sittin' next to you – it was your Uncle Dick!"

Mum had two brothers – Uncle Bob and Uncle Jack. Uncle Bob was a miner like his dad and, like his dad, he died relatively young – probably as a result of all the coal dust he'd had to breathe in. I remember mum took me to see him once to his home in Wakefield. He worked down one of the pits there. I'm not sure which one. I do know that it was a very big minin' area then, but like most pits, I doubt if it's producin' coal any more. If you are interested though, one of the Wakefield pits has been turned into a museum. The windin' gear has been restored and you can go down as part of a tour. Compared to the old days, I suppose it's rather sanitised, but at least it gives some idea of what it must have been like to work underground.

Mum's other brother, Jack, stayed in the army after the war and served in India. She had a picture of him hangin' in the parlour and she often used to tell me, "Uncle Jack will take you fishin' on the River Dee when he comes home." Sadly we never did go fishin' on the River Dee. In fact I never even got to see Uncle Jack because he never did come home. He was killed out in India. Mum was very, very upset and she never really got over losin' him without ever seein' him again. Thinkin' back, the trauma could have been one of the factors that triggered mum's illness. But I'm jumpin' the gun again.

I'll come to that later.

The winter of 1946 was particularly harsh. When I'd got the money, sometimes on the way to school I'd call in the baker's on the corner and buy a small four-penny loaf of crusty bread. They were a sort of oval shape and hot out of the oven. To us they were a double treat – we'd stuff them up our jumpers where they'd keep us warm, and keep us fed. It wasn't that I was hungry, it was more of a status thing – a big boys' thing to do. We'd eat the inside first, sneakin' bits in class, and still have the crust for playtime.

Truth be told, I was never a dedicated student, but even so, lookin' back mum was right – my education in Ardingly was a bit too hit and miss and not really a patch on what I would have had back in London had there been no war. Sometimes they just didn't have the staff and the classes were often too mixed up. I'd have got top marks for blackberryin' but I don't suppose many employers would be too impressed by that. Even in London, everythin' was a bit behind because of the war and so I didn't exactly make big strides bein' back at Heathbrook. I was always kitted out well though. Mum saw to that. The only problem was that bein' kitted out well for school in those days meant wearin' short trousers. Come rain or shine, summer or winter, frost or snow, it was always short trousers until you became 14 years old. Then it was a bit like gettin' the key of the door at 21.

It was a really big thing to start wearin' long trousers. At first though, it was only on a Sunday – not for school. I suppose it was akin to the start of manhood, preparin' you for your workin' life, which in those days started at 14. Once you became 14, you were expected to get a job and start payin' your way. Before all that though, it was always short trousers and always grey, the only difference bein' they were thicker for winter. Grey flannel in summer and a sort of woolly serge in winter. The winter weight might have been a bit warmer, but the rather coarse, unyieldin' material chafed between your legs. Mind you, not as bad as wellies chafed your bare legs if you had to wear 'em for any length of time, especially if the tops got a bit wet, as they would in the rain. We wore long socks, but the wellies chafed above 'em. Perhaps the short trousers and wellies we kids had to wear was all to do with the "British Bulldog Spirit", the "stiff upper lip", bein' "hardy." Whatever it was, I'm tellin' you, it was bleedin' perishin' cold and jolly uncomfortable sometimes havin' to go around in short trousers, long socks or no long socks.

It was at Heathbrook School that you got a chance to have a dip in the sweetie jar if you got your sums right. It was a proper big glass sweet jar like they had in the shops, or at least they used to in our day. The only thing was there were only ever a few in the bottom so you had to dip your arm right in and there wasn't much choice when you got there. It was better than a borin' old star though.

All the lady teachers were addressed as 'Miss' – never as 'Mrs'. I'm not sure if it's true, but I was told there were no married lady teachers – that they had to leave the profession if they wanted to get married.

Despite the setbacks that I'd had personally and that the education system had suffered generally even in London, now that I was back at Heathbrook, mum still had high hopes and big ideas for me. I never took an eleven plus exam. With all the disruption of the war I'm not sure anyone did. In any event, in mum's eyes my big chance would come with the scholarship exam when I was 13. Before I get to that, somethin' really momentous happened in my life that I need to tell you about.

When the snow did eventually begin to thaw in the early spring of 1947, the air was damp. Everywhere was damp and still felt cold – the sort of damp cold that penetrates. Bein' asthmatic I guess I was more susceptible than most, but anyway I caught bronchial pneumonia. It turned pretty nasty and I had to be admitted to St Thomas' Hospital in Westminster, opposite the Houses of Parliament. It was, and still is, a renowned chest hospital. I was in a general ward, Nightingale Ward, with a load of men, not a children's ward. We all had big iron frame beds on wheels, very Victorian lookin'. I know I was the only child and I don't remember talkin' to any of the other patients. Maybe we were all too ill for conversation. What I do remember though is that they could all cough and spit much better than me. I was never a good 'cougher upper' even when I needed to be. I think I was rather quiet and maybe a bit over-awed. One thing I do remember clearly is that all the beds were centred twice a day for cleanin' – not the beds, the floors. In those days it was parquee floorin' and they'd put this oily sawdust down for cleanin'.

The other thing that sticks in my mind is the nursin' care. I wasn't allowed out of bed. I suppose to start with I was just too weak and so everythin,' and I do mean everythin,' was done in bed. Every day the nurses would sort me out with bed baths, bed pans and bottles. A bit embarrassin' but it was all part of the care. At night there were no screens around the beds and nurses would take it in turns to sit at this table that had been placed in the middle of the ward. There was a single ceilin' light on a very long lead with a shade over it so it cast light just on the table and not on the patients. I think the nurses did about two hour stints, but it could have been longer. If anybody stirred, the nurse would get up with a torch and go and see what was goin' on.

Durin' the first week, despite hospital care, I took a turn for the worse, a big turn, and at one point I actually died. I was 13. I guess if I was goin' to die, I couldn't have been in a better place, because they managed to bring me back. Havin' said that, they obviously thought my problems were far from over because a few days later I overheard the doctors tellin' mum that she should understand that I'd never be able to work. They thought my asthmatic condition was so bad that I'd not be able to hold down a normal job. Well, that just goes to show that doctors don't know everythin', or maybe it was just that I was determined to prove 'em wrong. But we'll come to all that later.

Lucky for me, my bed was in a nice location on the end, near the window. That became my 'window on the world'. When I became well enough to sit up, my spy hole to the river was in itself a bit of a life saver. Rather than lyin' there bored and feelin' sorry for myself, it gave me somethin' to do, somethin' to focus on. I remember especially watchin' all the steam boats goin' up and down the river and from my bed I could see 'em lowerin' their funnels to get under Westminster Bridge. They'd lower 'em down and haul 'em back up on cables, clever really. There was always somethin' happenin' because the Thames was very busy in those days. It was more of a workin' river then - more freight than there is now. All the coal used to go up to the power stations by boat and those boats would be runnin' day and night. They'd have come down from Newcastle, bringin' coal from the collieries in the North East. Big boats they were, all feedin' the power stations alongside the river at Battersea, Wandsworth and Fulham. Just like today, there'd be quite a bit of recreational traffic as well with passenger boats comin' out from Westminster Pier.

These days you hear people complainin' about hospital food, but back then I never remember anybody complainin'. At 13, I suppose I would have just eaten what I was given anyway, but the thing is I liked the food. In fact, I looked forward to it. It wasn't what you could call fancy, but it was wholesome and plentiful and I think that was the idea – to build patients up. Almost as much as the surgery and the medicine, it was all part of the care and once you were well enough, it was off to convalescin' for more rest, recuperation and buildin' up before they sent you home. For me, and I dare say for most, if not all patients, it was more hot meals a day than they'd been used to gettin' at home. We'd get a hot breakfast with bacon and egg and I remember with that gettin' somethin' I'd never seen before – 'flapjacks'- savoury, not sweet like I've seen since in America. Then it would be meat and two veg and a puddin' for lunch and another hot meal at supper time which might be somethin' like bubble and squeak, I guess to use up any left-overs.

Although I had my window, sometimes the days seemed long, but mum would come visitin' me every night after supper and, when I was gettin' better, I remember dad came once too, but only the once. That was dad, never one for sentiment.

Once I was 'out of the woods' so to speak, they sent me to Hydestile, a convalescent facility near Guildford. To transfer patients they used Greenline buses converted to take about six stretcher beds. Before the war, Greenline buses used to run right across London, from suburbia to suburbia and durin' the war, some of 'em were commandeered as ambulances. As I discovered, even two years after the war had ended, some were still bein' used. You couldn't see out of the windows because they were blacked out – just like war time blackouts. When I was there, I wasn't allowed to just get up and wander around. In fact half the place was like a sanitorium cordoned off for TB patients. Bein' more or less confined to bed the staff used to push patients' beds onto the veranda so we could get some fresh air. It was springtime and I remember there were beautiful daffodils in the woods in the grounds. I was supposed to be out there gettin' my lungs full of fresh air, but the man they usually pushed out there with me smoked a pipe and I don't need to tell you where the smoke kept driftin'. To make matters worse he also chewed tobacco and spent all day spittin'! Revoltin'!

I'd been there about two weeks when mum came visitin' and

announced that if I could get better soon I'd still be able to take the scholarship exams back at Holbrook School. Apparently there were special arrangements bein' made for those who'd been unable to take it at the proper time. Mum wanted to take me home there and then, on the train but that wasn't allowed. Before I could be discharged, I first had to be taken back to St Thomas's. Undaunted, mum had another word with the staff and managed to get me discharged about a week early. First, though, I still had to be taken back to St Thomas's by ambulance and be discharged from there. I arrived to find mum already there, but before we could leave she had to see the Lady Almoner. It was somethin' about an outstandin' payment. I don't know what I was expectin', but when I saw the Lady Almoner I remember thinkin', "She's just an ordinary woman." I didn't know it then, but apparently the Almoner's Department was a pre-NHS forerunner of the Social Work Departments found in modern hospitals today. The Lady Almoner's job was mainly to organise after-care for patients, includin' stays in convalescent homes like I'd just come from. It was also the Almoner's job to identify families with the ability to make some contribution towards the cost of treatment. I don't know how much mum had to pay or how it was assessed.

I'd been cosseted for a month in hospital and then two weeks convalescin'. Now it was back to reality. I hadn't had much exercise for quite a while and my legs didn't really want to know me. Even so, we just walked across the road and queued for a No 26 tram to take us home. Goin' down with bronchial pneumonia had been a further setback for me, missin' weeks and weeks of school but, undeterred, mum seemed to think that if she bought me a new Parker pen, then I'd be sure to pass my exams and become a solicitor or somethin'. Of course in reality I'd got no real chance of passin' any exams. I'd not been at school for any tuition and so, it wasn't surprisin',' that I didn't even understand half the questions!

Despite mum's hopes, an expensive pen with a gold nib didn't make a scrap of difference. Just as I'd feared, blackberryin' wasn't on the paper. I didn't pass and that's how I ended up goin to Tennyson Street School and not the Grammar School. What's more, havin' been transferred, my new Parker pen barely lasted a week. It got stolen at school. I knew the boy who'd got it, but he never admitted it or gave it back. Mum and the teachers made a big fuss about it and the real pain and embarrassment for me was bein' forced to go into every class in my new school, and bizarrely, back at Heathbrook School as well, askin' if anybody had seen or found it. I knew it was pointless, but I was made to do it. Mum didn't want any stone left unturned. Thinkin' a Parker pen would make me a successful scholar was mum all over and it's a shame mine got pinched because they were expensive in those days and it's not like mum had money to throw away. Endin' up at Tennyson Street School, along with all the other waifs and strays, was fine by me though and handy too, bein' just at the end of our street. Now, lookin' back, and seein' how my life's turned out, I think it was for the best really – but I'll let you be the judge of that, as you read on.

So, for most people 1947 was memorable for the harsh winter and the big snow which was and still is one of the most severe on record. For me it was the year I died, but lots of other much nicer things happened too, so I'd better tell you about at least one of them – my return to Ardingly, in August, it was. It happened on the back of one of our Roy's daredevil brainwaves. If you remember, Roy's best friend was Donkey (Derek). He'd been with us in Ardingly. They were also friends with a lad more or less the same age called Fegeant. I'm really not sure if that was his surname, his Christian name or what or how to spell it come to that, but it was the only name I ever heard anyone call him. I knew him because we were all members of CLB. That's somethin' else I must tell you about. First off though, Roy's brainwave.

Roy planned to cycle with his two friends all the way to Ardingly and back on August Bank Holiday Sunday. In those days that was the first week in August – not the last like it is now. I wasn't supposed to go, but you know what kid brothers can be like – a right pain at times – pesterin' and pesterin' 'till they get their own way. That's how it was with me sometimes. It's not that he didn't want me along. He was a carin' brother was Roy. I can hear him now, "Look Willy – it's too far – it'll be too much for you – with your asthma and all." But, in the end, against his better judgement, he agreed, which if you think about it was really good of him and doubtless mum and dad left him in no doubt he was responsible for me.

Mum made sandwiches the night before and we left early – about 7.30 am. It bein' a Bank Holiday, we were out of London before most folk were up. Our route took us through Stretton, Thornton

Heath, Red Hill and on the Brighton road to Gatwick, Balcombe and on to Ardingly. I guess it would have been about 50 miles all told and I think we got there before midday so you can tell we didn't hang about. We had our picnic and we went to see some of our old haunts like the caves and the Clondyke, where if you remember we used to go sledgin'. Roy wanted to go and see Ma Wickens. I'm not sure why. Maybe he just wanted her to know we'd ridden down all the way from London. I didn't go. I stopped with the bikes on the crossroads by the War Memorial. It seems that he didn't get asked in and only Eva, Ma Wickens' daughter, came out to talk to him. I think he was a bit upset about that, but thinkin' about it now, I guess Roy wouldn't have been one of Ma Wickens' favourites, would he? Challengin' her the way he had over the rationin'. Remember?

Around 3.30 pm Roy decided we'd better set off back. If you've ever ridden a bike in those parts, you'll know that it was a bit more uphill goin' back. We were goin' Ok though – even me – until we got to Red Hill where Fegeant's chain snapped. Mum had made sure we had 'emergency money' with us and Roy, who everyone recognised as bein' in charge, decreed that I'd go with Fegeant and catch the train from Red Hill Station. O'course I protested, but this time Roy was havin' none of it. He'd always felt I'd been pushin' my luck. I'd done well to get that far, but, as Roy saw it, I was an asthma attack waitin' to happen. I admit I was tired, so maybe I didn't protest all that much. So in the end only Roy and Donkey made it all the way, arrivin' back about an hour after us. It had been a good day though and still quite an achievement, don't you think?

A little while back I mentioned CLB, Church Lads Brigade, to give it its full title. Well, as it turned out, CLB played quite a big part in our lives – Roy's and mine – so before I go any further I think I should enlighten you a bit.

Roy, bein' that much older, was already a member of CLB when I joined as a 'choir boy' no less. Imagine that – me a choir boy! Whilst it was 'Church Lads' Brigade', in truth I don't think any of us joined 'cos we were religious – not at all. It's just that it was somethin' goin' on "round the hall". Somethin' to get involved with locally. Think of choir boys and you think of 'angelic' and I was never that. I could sing, mind you, but it was never really my thing. Music though, now that's a different matter. I'd got used to bein' part of a group as one of the Wickens' boys back in Ardingly, and I think it was that – bein' part of a sort of boys' club, that attracted me. That and the chance to be part of a band.

Bein' that much older and I guess with aspirations to be a leader, my brother Roy was the band sergeant Major. He'd strut along in front, tossin' the mace. I'd started growin', but I was still more or less the youngest, so I was given the cymbals and marched along pretty much at the back. It was primarily a bugle and drum band and at 12 yrs old I had no musical ability, but I enjoyed bein' part of the band. As for musical ability, well that would come later, as you'll see. For now it was the cymbals for me and I even had trouble with them. I remember Jim gave me a good tellin' off once for breakin' 'em. Jim Rogers was in charge of CLB and, when we were out marchin' the streets and playin', he'd march at the very back – I guess where he could keep an eye on us and keep us all in order.

It was Church Lads Brigade and, whilst we took part in the church bit – the services, really for us they were incidental and in truth we didn't take 'em very seriously. I've told you that Donkey was Roy's best mate, and that he'd also been an Ardingly evacuee – in fact that's where he got his nickname. I never did know why. Not an especially nice nickname really, but for some reason it stuck. Even Roy called him Donkey and he didn't seem to mind. Anyway, on a Sunday we'd have a service, but Donkey was nearly always late and an abidin' image I have of Donkey and one I want to share with you, is of him runnin' up the road behind us with this blue satchel on his back as we were marchin' in formation off to church. As I picture him, it brings a smile to my face because that satchel of his was stuffed with all the comics he'd always bring for us to read in church.

We were choir boys and dressed for the part, but we weren't interested in the service at all – especially not the sermon – it was all above our heads. We only went because it was expected of us as members of CLB and because we liked the marchin' and playin' in the band after. Picture us all, passin' comics along the minute the Vicar moved towards the pulpit. We didn't mind, in fact we really rather liked a long sermon because we never listened to a word of it. We'd be sittin' with our heads bowed for all the world lookin' like we were prayin' when all the while we were actually readin' comics! We'd hide 'em again as the Vicar came out of the pulpit.

Before the war, Jim had been a boxer – quite well known I think – and he was a part-time policeman. Sometimes you'd see him when the traffic lights were out in Queenstown Road with those white 'oversleeves' on directin' traffic. On Sundays though, Jim used to take communion and he'd get ribbed rotten – not by me, I was too young for that. Besides, he'd have given me a clip round the ear. That was par for the course in those days. Teachers, policemen, they'd all give you a clip if you got cheeky or out of line. It never did us any harm. It helped us learn the rules, know our place, have proper respect for property and our elders. Our 'mamby pamby' society of today has outlawed all that and just look where that's got us. Ask anybody of my generation and they'll tell you straight, but I'm digressin' again. I was tellin' you that folk used to rib Jim over the way he took communion. They'd say, "He always makes sure he gets a proper swig of that wine, 'dun' he!"

I'm sayin' we knew our place, and by and large we did, but we were lads together and lads have to bend the rules a bit – show a bit of bravado, like when we'd be lookin' all angelic like butter wouldn't melt in our mouths, whereas all the while, when we weren't singin,' we'd be readin' comics. We must have been good at it because we never did get rumbled.

After the service was over, we'd all form up outside with our instruments ready to march off in formation. We'd go a good big circuit which took in Queenstown Road and even our Street, Gambetta Street. People would come out into the street or lean out of upstairs windows to watch and listen to us, marchin' and playin' as we passed by. It was rather nice really and made me feel quite proud to be part of it – even if I was only on the cymbals. I should explain that we'd all be in our uniform – blue it was, a bit like the marines, with chrome buttons and a broad white belt and a peak cap – Jim included. He was Captain of our Division, the Greenwich Division. I can't remember seein' her, but I know he had a wife and three children, one of whom was disabled.

We weren't all youngsters – leastways not as young as me. At one point we had a chap join from the Marines. He was allowed to keep his rank – Sergeant Major Page. A very snappy dresser. I'd say he was in his late '30s. Roy was very impressed by him and, you could see, wanted to be like him. I'd say his arrival and his influence were key reasons why Roy decided to join up – that and gettin' away from dad and showin' him he'd got what it takes. I'll tell you about Roy joinin' up later.

For me, one of the best bits about CLB was the summer camp. Jim would take us and we'd join up with other battalions there. The first one I went on was at Bosham Bay near Chichester. It was for just a week in the summer holidays, but for me it was the best week. I loved it.

It's not that anythin' really momentous happened, I just loved bein' with a big group of lads – the camaraderie of it – like I'd experienced as a 'Wickens' boy, but 'writ large' and without any of the downsides. It never occurred to me at the time, but now I can see even more of the benefits. It wasn't just that we were havin' a good time, I can see now that it wasn't a bad trainin' ground for how to live your life – gettin' on with others, workin' as a team.

As I say, nothin' much momentous happened, but I'll just tell you about one little incident that's just sprung to mind. On one of our 'free time' afternoons, a group of us lads decided to hop on a train and go into Chichester. . Chichester wasn't far – only a couple of stops on the train – and bein' CLB, the idea was that we'd go and look around the Cathedral. Leastwise that's the impression we gave, but in reality we were off to the Gaumont Cinema to see a film. It couldn't have been that special 'cos I can't remember what it was, but what I do remember is that after we all decided to go upstairs to the restaurant for somethin' to eat. You have to bear in mind that I was about 12, one of the youngest ones, and eatin' out in restaurants wasn't exactly an everyday occurrence for me. Even with mum and dad, it wasn't even an annual event. Anyway, I looked at this menu and the waitress was hoverin', but I didn't know what to have, so I asked her for advice. Why not try our 'Welsh Rabbit' she says. Like most of the things on the menu, I didn't know what it was. I just assumed it was some sort of rabbit – like we'd had in Ardingly durin' the war. You can imagine my surprise when it came. I didn't like to say anythin'. I just ate it, but I was disappointed to say the least and I remember thinkin'; "The Welsh must be a funny lot if that's their idea of rabbit!"

The followin' year I managed to get in on the 'advance party'. This time it was to Bentbridge on the Isle of Wight and a small group of us went with Jim to help set up camp. Puttin' up all the bell tents and generally layin' the place out in readiness for the rest of 'em. We went by train from Waterloo Station, but a lorry took all the tents and stuff.

As luck would have it, one of the parents had a furniture business and so took the lot of us includin' our gear in the back of this van from the Church Hall to the station. With our gear in the goods van, the train took us to Southsea Harbour via Portsmouth. From there we got the ferry to Ryde on the Isle of Wight. In those days, Southern Railways ran little steam trains from the pier along the coast to Bradin' Station. Lovely they were; a smaller gauge than regular service trains. A farmer was waitin' with his tractor and trailer at Bradin' to pick us up – the advance guard - and take us to the camp site.

When we arrived, it was just a big field and the first job was to set up tents for sleepin' in that night. There were no toilets, showers or anythin' like that. Whatever we needed, we had to bring it along and set it up, includin' diggin' latrines. The advance parties would arrive on a Thursday afternoon followed by the main Brigades on the Saturday. I'm sayin' brigades because it wasn't just our brigade. For summer camp we'd join up with other brigades from around London. We were part of the Greenwich diocese and there'd be lads from the London and Southwark Dioceses too. There'd be as many as 150 lads altogether. Each Brigade has its own Major, in our case Jim Rogers, but at camp there was a Major in overall charge and funnily enough his name was Major, so you'd hear someone say, "Best check with Major Major!" Yet again, 'you just couldn't make it up'!

By Saturday, the field would be transformed. As well as tents for sleepin' – about a dozen to a tent – there'd be Marquees – one for a sick bay, one for a cookhouse and a really big one set up with trestle tables and benches for dinin'. I'd loved it at Bosham Bay but goin' to the Isle of Wight, which we did year on year after, well that was even better, not least because it lasted a fortnight and on top of that I got an extra few days at the beginnin' and again at the end to help clear and pack up.

The train bringin' the main party would arrive at around 2pm on Saturday afternoon and those of us that were in the band as well had to be down at the station in full uniform with our instruments. Me with my cymbals, Roy with his mace. We were a drum and bugle band and all three platoon bands would amalgamate into one and march all the others up to camp – drums and bugles blazin' and cymbals crashin'. Quite a spectacle we were.

I suppose you could say the whole thing was run sort of army style. It had to be to make it work. Otherwise it would have been chaos. Bein' CLB, at about 7pm each evenin' there'd be a service in the main tent. Just a few hymns with a chaplain presidin'. You might like to know that in the First World War CLB Battallions were sent out with the regular troops. Luckily for me, my time with CLB was all in peace time, all focussed on games, sports and havin' fun and a sense of adventure with lads from all walks of life. As well as sports like athletics and football, there'd be games like volleyball and skittles. Games and fun, but also designed to develop skills and teamwork.

From the camp, there were just a couple of fields to walk over and then we were on White Cliffe Bay. A beautiful swimmin' bay it was. After breakfast we'd all line up with our rolled up towels and be marched down across the fields. We'd generally go swimmin' every mornin', although if truth be told I didn't actually swim. I'd never learnt. In fact I still can't and maybe at 83 it's a bit late to start now. Mind you that didn't stop me enjoyin' myself. I'd always be straight in there, splashin' about with the rest of 'em. As well as exercise, I guess it was our ablutions as well. We did have an ablutions tent, but we only had a bowl of water to wash in there. Often we'd be down there playin' organised games the whole mornin' and then be lined up and marched back for lunch.

Every afternoon we'd have 'free time' from about 2.30 pm 'till 'tea time', which was 5.30 pm. Sometimes, we'd go in to Sandown – the local seaside resort. Sandown was about 2 miles away and to get there, we'd walk down the road to Bradin' Station and, followin' the signpost, we'd turn left more or less along the coast road 'till we came to the Grand Hotel. We'd usually make that our first stop because it had an icecream parlour where we'd buy a cornet and eat it on the way into town – about a quarter of a mile further on. In Sandown, as well as buyin' sweets or stuff for ourselves, we'd get presents for our mums. One year I bought mum a sand picture – a photo frame filled with sand from Alum Bay. It's not just ordinary sand, it's all in layers of pretty colours. Mum's gone now of course, but that's one thing I've kept to this day. It's only a small, cheap souvenir really, but it's survived this long so I hope one of my own kids will treasure it as much as I have when I'm gone.

Generally, we'd make sure we were back from Sandown in time for tea, not least because by then our sixpences would be spent up. I should mention that we had a sort of bank on camp. We'd pay in all our money when we arrived and then take out a bit each day. That way we could make it last the whole time and I suppose part of the idea was to give us the experience of how to manage our money.

We didn't have to prepare our own meals. We had cooks with us to do that. Sleepin' arrangements were about 10 to a large tent. We had to keep that 'tidy', but that was about it as far as duties were concerned, for me anyway. Some of the older boys were given more duties. In particular they had to dig trenches and place wooden seats straddlin' 'em. Rather like wartime latrines I suppose. Then parts would be filled in each day after use. Fortunately for me I was never asked to help dig or fill 'em in and I wasn't goin' to volunteer!

I was the only one with a camp bed. I wasn't allowed to sleep on the ground because of my asthma. To and from camp I'd be marchin' along with the band with this camp bed strapped to my back and playin' the cymbals as well. Luckily nobody ever ribbed me about it, but I must have made it look like Fred Carno's Army comin'. Whatever, clearly it must have left an impression because many years later when I had kids of my own, Arthur and Grace, who lived at No 23 Gambetta Street, asked me if I could remember the days when I went marchin' off to CLB with a camp bed strapped to my back. Grace said she never knew how I ever managed to march along and play with that thing on my back and then, with the glint of a tear in her eye, "but they were good times, just after the war, weren't they Jack?" To them, I'd been Jack as a kid and Jack I stayed.

Grace and Arthur's son, Derek, bein' that bit older, was a friend of Roy's and he was in the CLB too. Remember his name because you'll be meeting him again later. In fact all the boys I knew from roundabouts were in CLB. It wasn't just a Sunday thing. We'd go two or three times a week, up to the Church Hall. There'd be table tennis and games one night and PT and keep fit another. Jim, bein' an ex boxer, was keen on keep fit and he'd get this wood and leather horse out and have us jumpin' over that. Once, he even had us doin' a display in Tennyson Street School for all the parents. I don't know why we held it there. Maybe he thought the church hall wouldn't be big enough. We'd jump on this springboard and vault over this horse and Jim would catch us. I suppose we were a motley crew really, but the parents thought we were great gymnasts. It's amazin' I was there at all really. Only a few months before that I'd been layin' in a hospital bed – dead!

When I first joined CLB I was in the juniors, but later I had to go to Portland Place off Baker Street to get issued with my official uniform. A proud day that was. I even had long trousers to go with my blazer, peak cap and badges. We even had CLB cufflinks. Roy especially loved dressin' up in his uniform and for him it had to be just so. He would never put his white blanco belt on 'till he was in the Church Hall for fear it got a mark on it. It had to be pristine for our Roy. As you'll see in the photo at the end of the chapter, the band wore dark leather belts, but bein' the mace bearer, marchin' at the front, Roy had a white blanco belt, I suppose to set him apart from the rest of us.

As I recall, before the war, the Church Hall had been used by Sea Cadets. I know it seems odd in the middle of London, but it's true. I've no idea what happened to them. Maybe they went the same way as CLB because that just seemed to fold about the same time I left school. That was in December 1948 when I was 15. I suppose there weren't many new recruits comin' along and the 'old timers', me included, were gettin' a bit too pre-occupied with girls. By this time Roy hadn't just left CLB, he'd left home and gone into the army. I'll tell you about that in a bit.

Although CLB had folded, Jim didn't just disappear off the scene. He started organisin' dances, still usin' St Philip's Church Hall as the venue. They were good as well and some good bands too. It's where I first learnt to dance – well, properly that is. As you know I'd been havin' a go before that. I'd saunter round on a Saturday afternoon to help set up for the evenin'. We'd chalk the floor to make it better for dancin' and set out all the chairs and, if it was winter, lay the open fire in readiness for lightin' in the evenin'. I'm sayin' 'chalk the floor' because I'm pretty sure it must have been powdered chalk we were scatterin' over the parquee to make it easier to glide across the floor once the dancin' got underway. Whatever it was, it was a fine white powder in a big tin. The chairs would be arranged down the sides and in those days it was one side for the boys and men and the other for the girls and ladies. As soon as the music started, it was up to the boys to walk across and ask a girl to dance. It was a big achievement if she said yes and a long walk back if she didn't.

Jim's friend, Mr Smythe, would come and help set up and run the dances. I think he was an ex copper, but the really notable thing about him was his feet. When I tell you they were big, I mean really big. I'd never seen feet like 'em. The dances were once a month, sometimes twice, and by helpin' to set them up I'd get in for free! I'd go home for tea and then get back again in time to watch the band settin' up. Mr Smythe would be on the door and he'd always let me in for nothin'! I'd be about 14 when I first started goin', so still at school, so gettin' in for free was important. It meant I never missed a one. It became my local regular dance venue, very handy, it was only just up the road and round the corner from where we lived. What's more, it was lucky 'cos it came at a time when I was just gettin' interested in girls.

Jim, bein' an ex boxer, could handle himself and everybody knew and respected that. When the pubs turned out sometimes men would try to get in through a side door, but Jim was wise to it. He'd be on to 'em in a flash. He'd never tolerate any trouble and because of his reputation, there never was any. I guess a little drunk or not, they still knew not to mess with Jim.

Thinkin' back, I've got a lot to thank Jim for. St Philip's Hall, and the events Jim ran there, had been the focus of my social life for years. First with CLB, which, as I've told you, wasn't just a Sunday thing or a band thing, but a youth club we'd go to 2 or 3 times a week, and then there were the dances and last, but not least, there were the drums - my first drums, they came from Jim as I'll tell you later.

A little while back I mentioned that by the time CLB folded, Roy had already left, swappin' his beloved CLB uniform for a regular army uniform and before I go any further, I need to explain how that came about. When Roy left school, Katie, Grandma's daughter, had helped him get a job as a trainee electrician. The problem was, it wasn't really his thing and there was always friction at home with dad. I'm sorry to say that dad and Roy never really got on, especially when Roy was growin' up, seekin' to assert himself a bit, seekin' a bit of stature and independence. When I think about the pair of them, it seems that maybe they were just too alike. Maybe that's why there was always this atmosphere of mutual misunderstandin'. Maybe both were just too stubborn to give credit to the other. Maybe one wanted to say more and didn't, whilst the other tended to imagine the worst and did. With a lifetime of experience to draw on, now I can see that, but back then I was just a kid unable to be of any real help in gettin' 'em to see eye to eye.

I think it was the combination of all those things goin' on in Roy's life and his love of uniform and pomp and ceremony that made him decide to join the Army. He was 17 and a half so they took him as a 'boy soldier' until he was 18. He'd planned to join the Guards and whilst Roy never regretted joinin' the army, he deeply regretted not stickin' to his guns and joinin' the guards. He would have fitted in so much better there. As it was, because of his success at technical school and his background in electronics in civvy street, the recruitin' office steered him into joinin' the REME. Plus, there was his height. Roy was tallish, but in those days they wanted guards recruits to be six foot plus and Roy was just shy of six foot. Havin' joined up, Roy was determined to make the best of it. He certainly wasn't goin' to let dad see he couldn't hack it, but once his initial trainin' was over, for much of the time I fear Roy was a bit like a square peg in a round hole, never really fittin' in, never really comfortable with his lot. I'll come back to Roy and more about his army career later.

I've got to admit that at home, Roy goin' in the army did have a bit of an upside for me. I got my own room. Ok it was only the box room and as its name suggests, it was small. To start with I had the put-you-up bed that Roy and I had shared as kids in the front room, but eventually that got replaced by a second-hand single divan bed. Most of our stuff was second-hand and doubtless mum had picked it up cheap somewhere. She was always on the lookout for a bargain. With just the 3 of us in the house (Roy bein' away in the army), the front room reverted to its proper function as our main reception room. Not that it was ever used very much, but mum was proud of it and really that was the main thing.

I don't want to keep goin' back and harpin' on about the war, but havin' read this far, I guess you'll understand that it was a really big thing in my life – in everyone's life who'd lived through it. It changed lives. There is no doubt about that. In many ways our family had been lucky. Yes, we'd been bombed out and I in particular had had a few near misses, but we'd all survived and none of us had suffered serious injury, at least none that showed. Mum hadn't liked livin' in the flat in Prairie Street, but once she got us into Gambetta Street, things seemed to be lookin' up for us at least. Other families didn't fare so well. Many had lost loved ones and with the war ended and the celebrations over it wasn't long before disillusionment spread and before the year was out, strikes, marches and protests began to hit the streets of London. The workin' classes in particular felt let down Discontent showed itself at the ballot box and Churchill was booted out and Clement Attlee's Labour Government came in.

The discontent didn't just end there. There was no quick fix. About 3 years after the war ended, there were still lots of men out of work. As a result, mum and the other women on the railway were obliged to stand down and their jobs were given back to men. That really upset mum.

Mum was a worker though and soon got a job back in the hotel business – this time at the Army & Navy Club in Piccadilly. It was where the Army and Navy officers used to stay. The entrance had 'in' and 'out' signs on it and so it was generally known as the 'In and Out Club'. Mum worked on the caterin' side. She was a good worker and well regarded, but somethin' wasn't right. I don't think it had anythin' to do with the job, but mum's mental health deteriorated and eventually she admitted herself into Epsom Mental Hospital. That was a very worryin' time and a big milestone in all our lives, but a lot happened before that I need to tell you about first.

In any case, I think it's time I lightened the mood a bit. You remember those concerts I so enjoyed in the underground Air Raid Shelter? Well, in the summer of 1947 they started havin' concerts again, but this time in and around the Bandstand on Clapham Common. It was still on Thursday evenin's and ran I think from May 'till September. One week it would be a band with ballroom dancin' on the smooth tarmac surroundin' the bandstand. The next it would be a show with music and singin' and so on, alternately.

They were free concerts run by the LCC and lasted from about 7.30 pm – 9.30 pm. I'd be about 13 ½ when I started goin' – about the same time I started takin' a bit more of an interest in girls. The acoustics were quite good and I went mainly to listen to the music.

Particularly as I got a bit older I became very keen on big band music, although I didn't really let on to my school friends at the time because none of them were so keen.

Talkin' of school friends, you know before I'd told you kids left school at 14 to start work, well in 1948 all that changed. They decided to reform the Education System and put the school leavin' age up to 15, so those of us who thought we were goin' to be leavin' soon had to do another year.

Now I'm tellin' you the school leavin' age was raised in 1948 because that's certainly the perception I had at the time. However, I now know that the legislation which brought about the changes was the Education Act, 1944. Dubbed the 'Butler Act,' after the Conservative Education Minister, R. A. Butler, it introduced the tripartite system of secondary education and made all schoolin' free for all pupils. It raised the school leavin' age from 14 to 15 but kept Primary School age 11 as the decision point for sendin' children to secondary education. Why I thought the system was only changed in 1948, I'm not sure, but it's possible the new leavin' age of 15 wasn't actually implemented until 1948. Certainly the Act's stated intention of further raisin' it to 16 wasn't implemented until as late as 1972!

The new tripartite system consisted of 3 types of secondary school: grammar schools, secondary technical schools and secondary modern schools. It allowed for the creation of comprehensive schools which would combine these strands but initially only a few were founded. To assess which pupils should attend which school, the idea was they'd take an exam before leavin' Primary School known as the 11-Plus. The system was intended to allocate pupils to the schools best suited to "their abilities and aptitudes" but, in practice, the number of grammar schools for the academically inclined remained unchanged and few technical schools or comprehensive schools were established. As a result most pupils went to secondary modern schools whether they were suitable or not. On the plus side, at least the majority of education fundin' went to secondary modern schools. Maybe that's why, when I was at Tennyson Street, we got to go to 'summer camp' in the autumn term.

With all the disruption of war, I don't think the 11-Plus was introduced straight away either. Certainly I never took one. As you know, I did take and fail the 13+ scholarship exam. That's how I ended up at Tennyson Street, my last school. I didn't mind at all, not least because as I've told you, it was handy, very handy – just at the bottom of our street and, at Tennyson Street, we got to go to 'summer camp'. It wasn't as good as CLB Camp, but I still enjoyed it and it was a whole lot better than bein' stuck in a classroom. Sadly, I don't have any photos of CLB Camp, but I've included a few taken at school summer camp, which I'd say were taken in September 1948 in my last year of school.

Perhaps the main thing I want to get across to you about Tennyson Street School is that there was discipline back then. Discipline and respect. None of this answerin' back or messin' about in class like you get today. And the Prefects system – that was there mainly to reinforce the sense of order and discipline. We were expected to file into class in an orderly manner and there were prefects on each landin' to tell you to keep in line and generally maintain decorum and order. Bein' late just wasn't acceptable without a really good excuse, so if I was ever late back at lunchtime, I'd try and sneak in the girls' gate and up their steps to our floor. I should mention that girls and boys always had separate entrances.

For the record, my last ever teacher was Miss Philips and our classroom was up on the top floor on the far right-hand end of the buildin'. I'm told it's part of a penthouse apartment now – belongin' to some pop star or other – Roland Keating I think his name is. Nice for him, but to me it seems rather sad really and somehow not quite right. I never remember the term bein' used, but I suppose you could say it was a 'community school' with all sorts of out of hours activities bein' held there. Mum went to sewin' classes in the evenin'. It got her out of the house for a bit. She was good with her hands was mum. Best of all, for me, it was also another dance venue with various bands takin' over the ballroom on the ground floor some Saturdays.

As I say, my very last teacher was Miss Philips. I liked Miss Philips. In fact I don't recall really dislikin' any of my teachers. Mind you, I wasn't too keen on the deputy head, Miss Leary, but then again, I was never in her class. I think it was her appearance as much as anythin'. You'd think she was half woman and half man the way she looked – that short back and sides type hair cut and the way she dressed. Like a man, not at all feminine or lady-like.

As it turned out, 1948 would be momentous in our house for two more very different reasons. As you know, we'd always lived in rented accommodation of one sort or another. Pretty much everyone I knew did, but, unbeknown to me, mum had aspirations to own her own home. I don't remember the actual date, but it was towards the end of '48, I came home from school one day and mum announces, "I'm goin' to buy the house!" She was full of it. Dad didn't exactly put a damper on mum's excitement. I don't think anythin' could have done that, but he wasn't exactly enthusiastic either. He would have been quite content to carry on rentin'. He was much older than mum and very set in his ways. He hated change of any sort. He was content just to come home from work, sit in a chair and read his paper. He wasn't one for DIY and he hated anyone else comin' in to do any work. The prospect of ownin' property and havin' the responsibility for maintenance and upkeep just didn't appeal. He wasn't interested in money at all, so mum had always taken care of the finances and paid all the bills. She was pretty shrewd was mum. She liked a bargain and at 400 pounds for both our place, 15A, and the downstairs flat, No 15, she was convinced she'd got one. It's amazin' when you think about it considerin' what property costs now in that part of London. Mum had gone from tenant to owner occupier and landlord in one fell swoop. No wonder she was full of it. Where she'd got the money from though, I don't know. She must have been savin' up over the years, I guess mainly when she'd had that job on the railway.

There was one other major change in our household in 1948, but before I go on to that I'll just tell you a bit about Mr & Mrs Fagg who lived in the downstairs flat and were now our tenants. They weren't new – they'd been tenants in No 15 for a long time – right through the war. They were a bit snooty, so I don't think they were best pleased at mum becomin' their landlord. One thing you might find interestin' about them is they kept chickens in the back yard. They weren't alone in that. In fact, in those days, lots of households in central London kept chickens. So much so that there were quite a few seed chandlers shops in the city. That was lucky for me because later on it's where I would buy my fishin' bait – hemp seed to go with the elderberry which, take it from me works a treat. As for Mr & Mrs Fagg, they stayed put until 1951 when they bought somethin' in Devon to retire to.

So, that other momentous happenin' in 1948? – our Roy joined the army. He'd always liked uniforms and pomp and ceremony and he really missed his role as mace bearer with the CLB band. He was in his element then – marchin' up front, tossin' the mace with a bit of a swagger – leader of the pack. No doubt about it, for Roy Sunday had been the best day of the week and he'd always made sure he'd been immaculately turned out, shoes and buttons polished and shinin'. For reasons I never quite understood, our CLB platoon got disbanded and Roy felt the loss even more than I did. What's more, as I've already mentioned, there was constant friction between Roy and dad at home. I think Roy was growin' up and wanted to assert himself a bit and somehow he and dad used to rub each other up the wrong way. There'd often be flare-ups, especially on Sundays. The scullery was pretty much out of bounds when dad was preparin' dinner and he used to take an age over it. We had no bathroom in those days, so any washin' had to be done in the sink. Roy wanted to get himself spruced up for goin' out and dad wasn't havin' any of it 'till he'd finished with the dinner. So, if you ask me, it was in part the lure of the uniform and in part to get away and maybe prove himself to dad that Roy decided to join up.

If Roy had been happy at work, maybe things would have been different, but he never really took to his job as a trainee electrician with Shell Mex. He used to come home pretty grubby after work and that just wasn't Roy at all. Given the choice, he'd always be immaculate. Whenever he went out for the evenin' he'd be dressed as if he was goin' off to a weddin'. He was good lookin' too. Very much like dad in his younger days. In a strange sort of way that might have been part of the problem between them. Maybe dad saw too much of himself in Roy. Lookin' back, one thing I can't understand is that Roy never once brought a girl back home. It's too late to ask why now – but he never did.

Anyway, for whatever reasons, the fact is that Roy joined the army in May 1948 as a boy soldier. He was 17 ½ and whilst he was allowed to join early, he wouldn't become a fully-fledged recruit until he turned 18. With his background as a trainee electrician, the recruitin' office persuaded him to join the REME section rather than the Grenadier Guards, which he'd really set his sights on. Sadly, that was to prove a big mistake and a lifelong regret, as you'll find out later.

Havin' said that, it seems Roy enjoyed his initial trainin' which was at Arborfield Camp just outside Readin', Berkshire. The only dampener on that was in the first week somebody pinched his knife and fork. As I was to find out later, that was a common occurrence in the army and normally meant you had to resort to pinchin' somebody else's. Roy didn't do that. He wrote home and as a result mum took me up on the train with a replacement set. It was a Saturday and we assumed Roy would spend the afternoon with us. He didn't though. He just said, "Thanks very much. Sorry I can't stop," and off he went again.

This left us at a bit of a loose end waitin' for the train back, so mum decided to turn it into an opportunity to see if there were any bargains goin' in the second-hand shops. As you know, she'd not long bought our house and the 'bargain' she spotted was this bloomin' great copper. In case you don't know what one is – you might think of it as a geyser or water heater. In those days people installed them in the scullery to provide hot water direct to the sink. Before that there was only the kettle. I'm not sure when immersion heaters came in. Maybe posher people had them already. Anyway, I suppose this copper was quite a nice-lookin' thing but more than that, it was big and heavy and took two of us to carry it. Even then we had to keep stoppin' before we reached the railway station. Mum's idea was to take it to Carter & Patterson and get them to deliver it. They were a sort of forerunner of companies like DHL. Only trouble was, when we got there, their offices were closed, so we had no alternative but to take it on the train with us.

We were on Southern Railways bound for Clapham Junction and bein' a Saturday afternoon, luckily the train was pretty quiet so our 'luggage' didn't cause that much of a stir. Our next and rather bigger problem though was gettin' it on the tram up to Queenstown Road, but mum was pretty brazen about it and nobody challenged us. Once on, we kept our heads down and still nobody said anythin'. Then there was just the walk home. I say 'just', but it was the longest quarter of a mile I've ever walked, or rather staggered – in between all the stoppin' for a rest. Fair play to mum though, once she'd got a gas fitter to install it, that copper made the world of difference to us. Much better than havin' to keep waitin' for the kettle to boil. Roy would have really noticed the difference, except of course it had come that bit too late. He'd just left home.

After his initial trainin', which I think lasted six or seven weeks,

Roy was transferred to the REME camp at Derby. He was there about a year. Plenty long enough to get himself a girlfriend, but we never saw her. He never brought her home and I think they lost touch when Roy was transferred to Kenya. It would have been late 1949 or early 1950 – I'm not quite sure. Before leavin' Derby though, there was this incident with a Tilley – a type of army van. It got turned over and I think it must have caught fire as well because Roy injured his arm badly and I'm pretty sure it was burnt. I'm not quite sure because he kept it covered up and would never show me. All I know is, it was very painful and he had to keep changin' the dressin' and puttin' talcum powder on it. It was bad enough for the army to give him six weeks sick leave. Far from bein' sympathetic, I remember dad havin' a real go at him about it. Years later I was told it was all to do with drink – or rather too much of it. Certainly it seems Roy got a real taste for it in the army and that, it seems in part, was to be his downfall – stoppin' him progressin' up the ranks as fast or as far as he might otherwise have done. I don't know, but maybe he just didn't 'hold it' as well as the rest of 'em because, as you'll learn later, in my experience, officers in particular put plenty of it away.

Apart from a compassionate flight home, two things stick in my memory about Roy's time in Kenya. Firstly – he learnt the local language – Swahili, I think it was. I thought that was pretty impressive, but there's a funny little incident I want to recount. One time when Roy was on leave, he and I were out together. I can't recall why, but it would have been because either we were goin' to the cinema in Chelsea or he wanted to buy clothes. Roy was a real film buff and he would go to the West End to see a film rather than wait to see it come round. If he bought any clothes, he'd take me along to see if he looked alright. He'd never buy clothes on his own. Anyway, on this particular day – I'd be about 16 at the time, we were standin' at a No 34 tram stop in Cedars Road waitin' for the tram and these three dark-skinned men came and stood beside us. Without any warnin', Roy suddenly starts jabberin' away to them in Swahili, but he gets no response – nothin'. I should say that at that time it was still quite unusual to see three black men, even in London. I think Roy had wanted to impress me by engagin' these three chaps in conversation in their own language. Still gettin' no response, Roy resorted to askin' 'em in English, "Where do you come from then?" – to which they replied, "Brixton"! Now, that was a conversation stopper.

The other interestin' thing I wanted to tell you about Roy's time in Africa is that he was still stationed in Kenya in 1952 when Princess Elizabeth and the Duke of Edinburgh were out there on honeymoon. Roy had been promoted to corporal by then and his company were responsible for supplyin' and maintainin' the generators for the Royals' stay at Tree Tops. As you probably know, that visit was cut short when news came that her father, the King, had died, but there I go again, gettin' way ahead of myself. I'll come back to Roy, but for now I need to take you back to 1948 and to what was happenin' to me.

I was 15 on 4th October 1948 and so I was able to leave school at the end of term, which was Christmas, and potentially could start work on 1st January 1949. Before that though – I needed to get a job.

You were allowed time off to go for interviews whilst still at school and it was normal in those days for a parent to go with you. I guess for moral support, or maybe to make sure they were happy with the workin' environment you'd be goin' into. Anyway, I wanted to go into the newspaper business and mum took me to the interview at the offices of the Evenin' News in Blackfriars – just off Fleet Street. The man who interviewed me was quite an old chap, but I can't recall his name. I do remember thinkin' he had a strange sense of humour though, because after I'd said I was willin' to start at the bottom and work my way up, he said, "I've got some good news for you, son – if you come to work here, that's where you will start, at the bottom." He then went on to explain what that would entail – basically doin' odd jobs, but that if I did well, in time I could progress to become a reporter. Unfortunately, the whole while we were there, the man kept takin' snuff, which mum thought was revoltin'. It really put her off.

Given the level of detail for other things I can remember, it seems strange that I'm not really sure whether I was offered that job or not. Maybe he just didn't make it clear. Irrespective, when we came out mum was adamant I wasn't goin' to work with that man so, whether I was offered a job or not was immaterial. Somethin' I do clearly recall is that as we were leavin' the buildin' mum was still goin' on about how disgustin' he was and that she needed to find a toilet. There were toilets across the street – one of the below ground ones – and the funny thing was, mum was so distracted by the snuff takin' episode that she went down the steps into the gents by mistake! She came up quite happy though 'cos she'd gone to spend a penny, but instead she'd found a penny! - on the steps outside the gents' toilets. What's more, she also came up with the idea that she was goin' to speak to Katie (Aunt Raithby's older sister's daughter) at Thornton Heath because "Katie knows everybody and she'll get you a job". So that was it – as far as mum was concerned, my Fleet Street career had ended by 2 pm in a trip down into the wrong toilets! You couldn't make it up!

Katie was one of the 'big secretaries' at Shell Mex House on the embankment and, as mum said, she did seem to know anybody who was anybody in the city. I suppose now you would say she was a career woman – she never married. Mum did have a word with Katie, who had a soft spot for me anyway from my visits to Gran's (her mother's) when I was a kid bein' fostered by Aunt Raithby. Katie arranged an interview with Newson Smith & Co, a firm of city stockbrokers. The only trouble was, I didn't even know what stockbrokers did. It didn't seem to matter though because, thanks to her introduction, I think my interview with Mr Over, the Office Manager, was pretty much a formality and I got the job – very well paid too as it turned out.

My interview was just before Christmas 1948, so bein' offered the job was a great Christmas present. Frank Newson-Smith, the founder of the firm, was still alive. Just before I joined the firm he had become Lord Mayor of London and so he resided in The Mansion House that year. He always wore a top hat and, befittin' his station as head of the firm, he had a very impressive office in our buildin'. It had a sumptuous air about it with a beautiful red Persian type carpet and all around the walls were cabinets full of cigars in rolls. The cigars alone must have cost thousands. He smoked cigars – rather like Mr Churchill – and was known as Sir Frank, havin' been knighted at some stage earlier in his career. His son, John Newson-Smith, was one of three partners with the firm together with Mr Wigan (who had been a tank officer durin' the war) and Mr Boddington (who unfortunately died whilst I was there).

My last few days at school, Tennyson Street School, were pretty uneventful. I suppose I'd have to say, much like the rest of my school career. I don't recall any of the teachers askin' what I'd be doin' when I left or even if I'd got a job. On the last day it was a sort of tradition that those who were leavin' would bring in goodies to eat and we were allowed to have a bit of a party in the afternoon. I took a box of cakes that mum had made. It was all rather low key though and, when it was time to go, we all just went our separate ways, just like any other day. None of the teachers said goodbye or wished me well or anythin' like that. I just walked out of school for the last time and that was it. All a bit of an anti-climax really.

Gambetta Street kids taken on the day of the Street Party in the summer of 1945. We're outside mum's house, 15 and 15A. I was 11 going on 12 and I'm standin' at the back, second from the left. Roy bein' nearly 15 wouldn't get involved. He thought he was too big for it – especially the fancy dress.

Gambetta Street kids in fancy dress on the day of the Street Party, summer 1945. We're standin' outside St Philip's Church Hall. I'm on the left dressed as 'Scots Porridge Oats'. Betty Lilley as 'a doll in a box' was awarded first prize.

Mum on the swings at Chessington Zoo, 1947.

Me on the swings at Chessington Zoo, 1947. Although it was a very cold day, I am still in short trousers as all boys were under 14 years in those days.

Gracie with husband Bob on their wedding day, 1947.

My school photo aged 13 or 14 years. We didn't have an official school uniform, but I always wore a jacket and tie for school.

The King & Queen's Silver Wedding Day Procession, Ludgate,
April 26th 1948.

Roy in his CLB uniform, possibly taken just before I joined.

Our CLB band marchin' through the streets after the service on a Sunday. Unfortunately neither Roy nor I are in the shot. Roy would have been up front with his mace and I'd have been at the back with my cymbals.

My CLB Badge.

A 'railway do' at the Lyceum Theatre in the West End around 1948. I'm in the centre with the stripy tie. The boy behind me to the left is Billy King. Like me, he was one of the 'Wickens Boys'. It was one of his brothers, Brian, who was drowned tryin' to save Roy's best friend, Donkey. Mum is sittin' right behind me on the same table as Billy.

Tennyson Street School 'summer camp', either Boxmoor, Hemel Hempstead or Hindhead near Guildford, possibly September 1948. I'm third from the right on the back row.

Tennyson Street School 'summer camp'. Again I'm third from the right on the back row. Mr Allen, our maths teacher, is seated. The girls look more 'grown up' than the boys, don't you think?

A number of schools would go to summer camp and we'd have competitions and games like cricket and football.

Filin' into and past one of the dormitories at summer camp. Notice how orderly we all are, marchin' more or less army style.

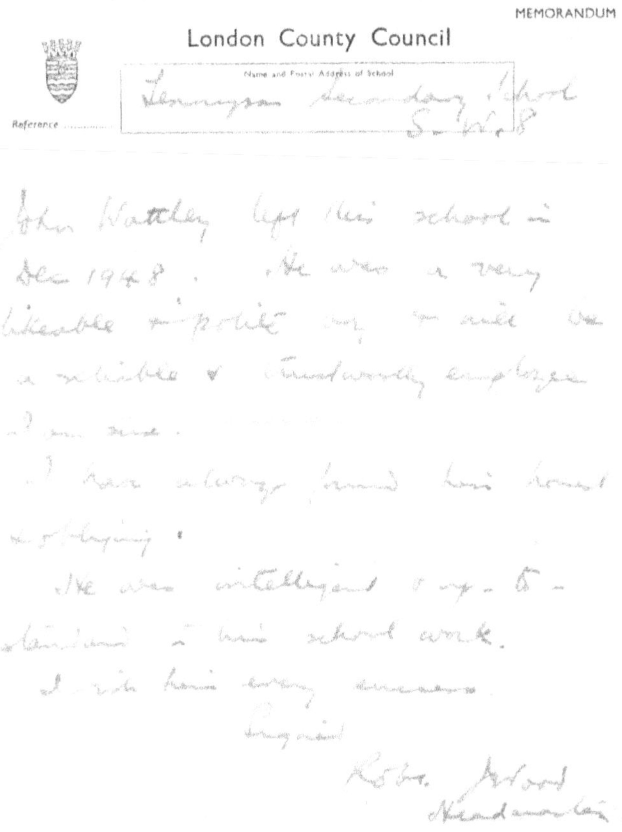

MEMORANDUM

London County Council

Name and Postal Address of School

Tennyson Secondary School
S.W.8

Reference ....

John Wattley left this school in
Dec 1948. He was a very
likeable & polite boy & will be
a reliable & trustworthy employee
I am sure.
I have always found him honest
& obliging.
He was intelligent & up-to-
standard in his school work.
I wish him every success.
Signed
Robt. Wood
Headmaster.

Copy of my School Leavin' Report intended as a sort of reference to help in gettin' a job.

JOHN DEARNLEY COLLINS

London County Council   DO 15

SCHOOL LEAVING CERTIFICATE

This is to certify that

John Wembley

of   15ᴬ   Gambetta Street, S.W.8

is exempt from the obligation to attend school within the

Administrative County of London from 17ᵗʰ December 1948

E. G. Savage
FK

Education Officer

NOTE. Further education for those over compulsory school age is provided in the Council's voluntary day continuation schools and evening institutes. Your head teacher will be pleased to give you the addresses of the schools and institutes in the neighbourhood, and to put you in touch with them.

School Leavin' Certificate dated 17ᵗʰ December 1948 statin' that I'm now exempt from havin' to attend school.

CHAPTER 5

Now I'm A Workin' Man

I started work on 1ˢᵗ January 1949. It wasn't a public holiday in those days. I was 15. I'd left school with no qualifications to speak of, but thanks to my connections with dear Aunt Raithby, via her sister's daughter Katie, I'd landed a job. Not just any job – a good, well-paid job in the City with a well respected firm of stockbrokers no less. To be honest, I still didn't even know what a stockbroker did, so I guess I was lucky to have been offered the job at all. Mind you, I had to start at the bottom as a sort of runner. I did that for about a year – all over the city between the Stock Exchange and all the various banks. The current incumbent showed me the ropes, includin' all the short-cuts. I soon got to know my way around all the back streets and alleys and, just as important, all the bus routes to take when it was rainin' so I wouldn't get wet.

I guess you could say I was proud to be workin' in the city. It felt good. The only problem was, I'd only got one suit and workin' in the city, that wasn't goin' to be enough. You needed at least 2, so that every six weeks or so one could be sent to the dry cleaners. Any old suit wasn't goin' to cut it. The name of the game for a 'city gent' was to get one tailor made. There was quite a big shoppin' centre down at Clapham Junction and I went to a tailor's there to get measured up. But that wasn't the end of it. This was my first made to measure suit and the process seemed to go on and on. I had to go back twice for a fittin', with pins bein' stuck here, there and everywhere, so fine adjustments could be made.

Usually I'd take the bus when goin' up as far as Clapham, but this particular time I rode my bike down to Clapham Junction and found a convenient spot near the tailor's to park it up. I just stood it with one pedal on the kerb at the roadside, same as I would anywhere. Except in Clapham there was a lot of traffic. Still, it seemed to stand just fine even with the buses goin' by.

I was in the tailor's a little while before bein' attended to and I suppose my mind was wanderin'. When eventually I came out after what I hoped would be my last fittin', I could see my bus comin' and just managed to dash across the road in time to catch it.

Several hours later I was sittin' havin' my tea and there was somethin' I wanted out of the bedroom. I can't remember what. The point is though, as I walked across the landin', to my horror, I suddenly realised, no bike! You have to remember we lived in an upstairs flat and I used to have to carry my bike up the stairs and keep it on the landin'. I stood and thought for a second – "Where is it?" Then of course it hit me – I'd only gone and left it hours ago, 5 miles down the road at Clapham Junction. It had been about half past one – two o'clock time when I'd put that bike on the kerb. Now it was after 5pm.

I didn't stop to finish my tea. I dashed up the road to get the bus back. It must have been about half past five when I got there – to the shops at Clapham Junction that is- and do you know, there it was, my bike, still standin' on its pedal at the kerbside, with all that busy rush-hour traffic whizzin' past and the pavement still buzzin' with folk. It was just as I'd left it all those hours ago – no lock, no nothin'. You can imagine my relief – bloomin' marvellous. I could have jumped for joy, but all I actually did was hop back on and ride it home. Try leavin' your bike like that today. I bet in five minutes it'd be gone – that's if it lasted that long.

So, I got my bike back and about a week later I had my made-to-measure suit, which I have to say looked the business, but I still had to alternate it with my old blue serge suit, which was Ok, but I suppose it had already seen better days. You were expected to look smart and I did my best with it. I'd press the trousers every Saturday. I'd do them myself with a damp tea cloth. Fortunately we'd got an electric iron, but not quite like you get today. In those days it was a case of pluggin' the lead into a light fittin' in the ceilin'. We had electric lights you see, but power points came later.

Havin' only just started work, Sunday nights I'd usually be in listenin' to the radio. I'm sayin' radio, but durin' the war and for a good time after, it was referred to as the 'wireless'. Now I think about it, that was a strange name for somethin' with wires stickin' out all over it. More bizarre still, it wasn't until advances enabled us to get rid of most of the wires that we started callin' it a radio. For me, Sunday was the best night on the radio. At half past five, as we were finishin' tea, there was ITMA and later in the evenin', at 9 o'clock, my favourite, Variety Bandbox, famed for showcasin' a wide variety of talent.

ITMA, starrin' Tommy Handley, is hard to describe, but it was a sort of 'mad hatter's tea party' of eccentric voices, jokes and musical interludes. Born in the dark days of the war, it became an institution – a weekly rallyin' point for civilian and service personnel. "It's that man again", originally referrin' to Hitler, later became synonymous with Handley himself and became possibly the most recognised catchphrase of the day. Each show would start with what you might call the "It's that man again" theme tune and once that had died down, this old dear would pipe up, "Can I do you now Sir?" The innuendo was quite risqué for the time. Each show would feature more or less the same characters who became household favourites, like 'Colonel Chin Strap' who would always be portrayed as somethin' of a drunkard. To give you an idea, this is typical of Handley's brand of humour:

"Do you know, I'm feelin' a bit down. But for a quirk of fate it seems I could have been brought up in an ancestral pile. Rumour has it that in 1885, great grandpa built an east wing and the followin' year added a west wing. But that was his big mistake because the year after, the whole thing up and flew away!"

Don't get me wrong, I liked ITMA, it's just that sometimes it was, as they say, "a bit too daft to laugh at". Mind you, I was as shocked and saddened as anybody when early in 1949, the ITMA show was followed by a special BBC news broadcast announcin' that Tommy Handley, radio's Mr Comedy, was dead. I don't think the show died with him, not straight away, but its days were numbered.

Fortunately, my favourite, Variety Bandbox, didn't rely on one man for its popularity. Its strength, as its name suggests, was its variety, its mixture of music, song and comedy that kept the mass audience tunin' in, me included. For sure there was variety, but there were rousin' favourites too, like Colonel Bogey, which featured regularly, played by the resident band, Billy Turnnant and his Orchestra. Now that was a band worth tunin' in for. Many famous names were showcased by Variety Bandbox includin' Beryl Reid and it's where risin' stars like Frankie Howerd first made himself popular.

A condition of my employment was that I learnt to type, so durin' my first year I had to attend night school. Because I was considered 'under age', night school classes were only sixpence per term, which I thought was very cheap. Mind you, that's because, as I told you, I was well paid. Very well paid in fact. By gettin' a job with a successful firm of Stockbrokers, I'd really fallen on my feet. At the age of 15, I was gettin' four pounds and five shillin's a week. To put that in perspective for you, this was at a time when a policeman's pay was just two pounds ten shillin's a week. As well as typin' and English, I went to a recreational night class to do woodwork. The typin' classes were held at a school in Wickes Lane, which ran parallel to Lavender Hill up to Clapham Common and woodwork was at Basnet Road Recreational Night School. I hated the typin' and never did get the hang of touch typin'. Fortunately, I did become very good at one finger typin', which seemed to satisfy Mr Over. I met some good mates at Basnet Road night school and amongst the things I made was a wooden 'suitcase' which you might think sounds odd, but, as you'll learn, it was to come in very handy later on.

The classes all finished at 9 pm, but then they laid on ballroom dancin' for half an hour. A pianist used to come and play the piano for us. Bein' especially interested in music, I got friendly with him. Bill Worrel his name was – he lived in Princess Head and had a wife and loads of kids – six I think it was. He was an engineer by trade, but the piano playin' brought in a bit of extra cash. He used to do nightly spots at two venues, Basnet Road Rec and Wickes Lane School. As I got to know him, it came out that at weekends he also ran a very good dance band called the Melody 4. They did lots of gigs, includin' high society stuff in the West End. He was a brilliant pianist, dedicated to his music, and, as I soon discovered, he was always in demand, always workin'. When he wasn't bein' an engineer, he was playin' – Friday, Saturday and Sunday. I don't know when he found time for his wife and family – or to produce so many kids!

Before long he invited me to go along and listen to the Melody 4 and to cut a long story short I became what today they'd call a 'groupie' – in the end they hardly went anywhere without me. I got especially interested in the drummer. Charlie, his name was. I used to watch him intently. Charlie became the catalyst I needed to launch my own music career. He was a good drummer and back home I learnt to copy his every move. Charlie was my inspiration in everythin' but demeanour. He was no showman. In fact he was a bit 'po faced'. His expression never changed no matter what he was playin'. After each gig I used to help him with his kit. No-one much had a car in those days and all his gear had to go with him on the bus. Like me, he used to go via Clapham Common so that was handy. One particular night sticks in my mind. The Melody 4 had been playin' at Latchmere Baths. On dance nights they used to cover the pool area to produce a dance floor literally over the water. Trams ran quite late on a Saturday and we'd wait to catch the No 34 which ran from Princess Head round to Clapham Common. When the tram came as usual we had to put all the gear round the front where the driver was. This particular night was different though 'cos when we got to Clapham Common and came to unload, Charlie's gear was there – minus his bass drum. It had rolled off! – somewhere along the way.

We found a policeman, which wasn't difficult because they actually used to walk their beat in those days, and reported the loss. He was very good and made a report in his notebook about it. And, what do you know, that bass drum was recovered from Clapham Common the very next day – Sunday mornin'. Fat chance you'd have of gettin' your drum returned if you lost one today. By today's standards most folk were poor – but then again most folk were honest too. They had more respect for other people's property in those days. Most everyone had an inbuilt sense of right and wrong, handed down, drilled into 'em if necessary. I'm not sayin' that today that's gone altogether, but I do feel it's been heavily diluted by a 'mamby pamby' society that has banned any form of meaningful punishment in schools, that has made policemen largely impotent and that has sent out all the wrong messages and taught wrong doers that if they are brazen enough, by and large they'll get away with it. It's blurred the lines between right and wrong.

My first set of drums were 'antique' wooden ones I'd got from Jim Rogers, the chap who ran the Church Lads' Brigade. Mum bought them for me whilst I was still at school. I used to have them set up in the front room and practised there. I think I told you that our front room was only ever used on high days and holidays, so mum didn't mind. Doubtless today those drums would be considered collectors' items and quite valuable, but back then I wanted to bring 'em a bit more up to date. All the fittin's were brass, so I took 'em round to Halfords in Clapham Junction and they chromed 'em for me. Today Halfords is a much bigger enterprise, but you'd never get that kind of service.

Charlie, the Melody 4 drummer, was married and, as it turned out, that was lucky for me. The thing was, havin' worked on a Saturday, he didn't always want to do a Sunday night spot as well. This particular Sunday Bill had a bookin' at the Ravenscourt Public House in Kings Street, Hammersmith (part of the Chef & Brewer Group). The other three band members either didn't want to or couldn't make it and Bill, knowin' I was keen, asked me if I thought I could do it. I jumped at the chance.

So it was that my first ever paid job as a musician was with the pianist Bill Worrell. No rehearsals – just straight in at the deep end. He was takin' a chance with me 'cos just the two of us were playin' and it was a big venue where the audience didn't dance, they just sat and listened, so they were a discernin' lot and the music had to be good. Occasionally someone would get up and sing, but most of the audience had come to listen to the music. I should say that by this time I'd bought myself a slightly more up-to-date second-hand set of drums. I don't know what happened to the old ones, but mum had a way of gettin' rid of things that were "in the way".

I was 'green', but I couldn't have been too bad 'cos I did that Sunday night spot with Bill for about 12 months. It gave me quite a buzz seein' the concert room packed every week with folk come to listen to us. I don't know what Bill got paid for the gig, but at the start he used to give me thirty bob and after a while increased it to two pounds and ten shillin's. Together with my stock exchange money that meant I was really quite well off, especially for a young chap.

After about a year workin' at the stockbrokers, I was promoted to the office, but part of my job still entailed goin' to the 'House', which is what we called the Stock Exchange. Our offices were at No 9 Basinghall Street, just beside the Guild Hall. I don't have a picture of our offices but there is a photo of me standin' on the roof of No 9 that you'll see later. We occupied the first floor and there were other businesses in the buildin', includin' Lever Bros. My firm of stockbrokers hadn't started out life in Basinghall Street. Like so many old London firms, they'd been a victim of the war. Havin' been bombed out, they'd had to move from the London Wall, more or less where the Barbican is now. In those early post-war years, with so much bomb damage, businesses were lucky to secure premises in the city and generally had to take whatever they could get. The managers' offices were laid out at the back, but my desk was in the general office at the front, close to the reception area.

I've already mentioned that Mr Over was the Office Manager. He was in his 50s and always came to work in a bowler hat. He was doubtless good at his job, but ran the office in a very formal, rather strict way. I guess he was one of those chaps who didn't need any friends. Certainly in the office he was very much a loner who didn't fraternise with anyone. If I say so myself, I was very popular with everyone in the office except, maybe not Mr Over, but then, as I say, Mr Over kept himself distant from everybody. He was in charge and took his role very seriously, but behind that bold exterior, I think there dwelt a lonely man. Mr Over sat at one end of the office and I sat or stood at the other near to Mr Lee, the cashier. He was a lovely old chap, but then again, you had to be careful what Mr Lee saw because, as I quickly learned, it would go straight back to Mr Over.

I had my own desk, typewriter and so on, but it was a bench type situation. We had stools, but many of the workers preferred to stand to type - two to a bench. My main job was to send out share certificates to clients. Companies would send me their share certificate and it was my job to make sure they all went to the people who'd bought them. They used to have lovely embossed share certificates in those days. Most of that has stopped now with shares generally bein' held electronically on behalf of clients. We had a mailin' room and because certificates were sent by registered post, it was important that I got to know our regular clients in order to put certificates together and save postage.

Because my desk was near to the reception area, I'd see all the comin's and goin's and part of my job was to greet clients and find out why they'd come. Politeness and courtesy were essential and because we were givin' a very personal service, it was important that I quickly got to know our regular clients so as to be able to greet them by name – then instead of good morning or good afternoon, Sir or Madam, it would be, "Mr so and so, how nice to see you again" (even if it wasn't!) Many of our clients were business people and people of substance and often people who'd come into money – perhaps an inheritance – and wanted to invest it. Some were celebrities. In particular I remember Jack Warner (of Dixon of Dock Green fame) who came in occasionally – always on his own – and his two sisters, Elsie and Doris Walters, who always came in together. Perhaps less well known now, back then the two sisters were celebrities in their own right – comediennes who appeared on radio a lot with the likes of Arthur Askey and Jimmy Edwards. They were regulars on Variety Bandbox on a Sunday Night which, as you know, was my favourite show of the week. They had a really good banter, quite unique to themselves, with phrases like, "Oh, lovely duckie." Just readin' it now, it sounds a bit lame, but you'll just have to take my word for it - in context and the way they said it made it sound hilarious. Why the three siblings had different names, I don't know – maybe 'Warner' was a given stage name.

I used to get the bus, then the tube into the city every day and get off at Bank Station. In the mornin's I wouldn't go into the office. I'd go straight from Bank Station to 'the House'. I'd walk down Princess Street alongside the Bank of England and left at the bottom into Gresham Street and then into Throgmorton Street, where the Stock Exchange was. Don't go lookin' for it there now though because it's been relocated to new, up to date premises in Paternoster Square, close by St Paul's Cathedral.

I was never 'before time', so I'd always be in a hurry. On Fridays I'd always buy a Melody Maker from a stall on the corner of Princess Street opposite the Bank. I was such a regular that the lady would hold out my copy of the Melody Maker so I didn't even have to break my stride as I was walkin' past. Most people would be buyin' the FT, but it was the Melody Maker for me! If I close my eyes I can see that lady now – especially in winter when her hands would be in knitted fingerless gloves and you could hardly see her face for her woolly balaclava. It must have been very cold standin' on that street corner from the early hours. Folk were trustin' in those days. She only expected me to stop and pay about once a month.

Whilst workin' for the stockbrokers, I practically wore a hole in the pavement between our offices at No 9 Basinghall Street and the Stock Exchange – I was up and down that often. My route would take me down past the back of the Bank of England and what I'm goin' to tell you now – well, you'll think I'm makin' it up, but I'm not. It happened. I saw it time and again. This lorry would pull up at the back of the bank. Pretty ordinary-lookin' – no obvious armour-platin' or anythin' – and these two blokes would get out, no guns, no nothin' and start loadin' bars of gold onto a pallet. Then they'd put a trolley under and wheel it into the back of the Bank. It was a frequent sight and as far as I could tell there was no real security to speak of and all that gold there for all to see, glistenin' in the sun when it was shinin' or else splashed with rain when it wasn't. Amazin'.

I was called a 'blue button' – because I wore a blue badge in my lapel which allowed me access to the Stock Exchange. I worked for 3 dealers. My job was to check all the dealin's from the previous day. There was a real atmosphere in the 'House', not least because some of the brokers wore top hats, keepin' up the tradition of the 'Old Days'. As well as 'stockbrokers', there were 'jobbers' – I never did fathom the real difference! Inside the Stock Exchange they had an early type of internal 'telephone' system. In the foyer there were 'phones' on the wall and if you needed to contact a particular dealer, this chap in a red uniform would pick up a 'phone' off the wall and literally blow down it. One of the porters would then pick up the 'phone' on the floor of the House and they could have a conversation down this tube. That's where the expression, "I'll give you a tinkle on the blower" comes from. I've not been back, but it's possible they've retained the same system – just to keep up the tradition. Whilst I was there, a new central distribution system was introduced beneath the Stock Exchange. In effect it was a series of about 200 or so pigeon holes and that's how messages were delivered to the brokers. Each would have a runner pickin' up messages for them. Tradition or no tradition, doubtless they'll have a much more sophisticated electronic system now because speed is of the essence even more so these days.

At lunchtimes the pubs and restaurants in Throgmorton Street would be packed with folk from the 'House', many still resplendent in their top hats. Quite a sight. Some of them looked a bit funny – especially the little chaps with these great big tall hats on. It was only their ears that saved 'em!

I always did a bit of duckin' and divin'. My timekeepin' in the mornin's wasn't the best, especially if I'd had a late night gig, but because I was goin' straight to the House I got away with it. I always got the job done and that's what really mattered to Mr Over. The House didn't open for actual tradin' until 10.00 am, but I'd usually manage to be there before then and, havin' picked up my work, I'd be back in the office by the time tradin' got properly under way. Tradin' would cease at 3 pm and then our dealers would come back to the office. By then I'd have checked everythin' from the previous day and made a note of any discrepancies. For example, their paperwork might indicate they'd bought 2000 of a particular share whereas it was only 1000. To be on the safe side, I often did somethin' I wasn't supposed to do – I'd go into the Dealers' Room and check their pads from the previous day to make sure there were no discrepancies I'd missed. Havin' reported to the Dealers, that was that part of my job done – they'd sort it out from there.

As a kid in London before bein' evacuated to Ardingly and as a young man workin' at the Stockbrokers, I remember seein' the lamplighter. Battersea BC was one of the first to have electric street lights, but when I was workin' at the Stockbrokers, they still had the traditional gas lights. Dependin' on the time of year as I was leavin' No 9 Basinghall Street at just gone 5pm, there he'd be, gettin' the lamps on ready for it goin' dark at about half past five. He'd ride along on his bike steerin' with just one hand and usin' the other to balance this long pole on the other shoulder. It must have been quite heavy because it was metal – steel I suppose, with a brass cover. It always struck me how he'd ride very upright with his lightin' pole on his shoulder. When he reached a lamp he'd use this pole to pull the chains and start the gas flowin' and then to create a spark to ignite the gas at the mantle, which would fairly quickly be givin' off quite a bright light, but more than that, it was a sort of comfortin' glow in the street. To someone who never saw them, that might sound an odd description of a street light but, take it from me, it was. On he'd go, lightin' up the city streets, lamp by lamp. Okay, they weren't as efficient as modern lights, but they were very atmospheric and if you ask me, for those of us lucky enough to have witnessed him, the lamplighter was a welcome sight goin' about his job literally lightin' up people's lives. I know the electric lights are much brighter and more efficient now, but lookin' back, I can't help feelin' somethin' precious has been lost in the name of progress.

I never knew one personally, but I guess bein' a lamplighter would have been a full time job because I'd often see him goin' round durin' the day still on his bike but with a ladder, climbin' up and polishin' the glass with a cloth and, although I can't recall seein' him doin' it, I know he'd change the mantles when necessary as well. It was all part of his job, both lightin' and maintenance.

You may also be surprised to hear, that another common sight in the city, even as late as the 1950s, were horses and carts. Coal, especially, was still quite literally bein' 'carted about'. When I was workin' at the stockbrokers I'd often see carts piled high with coal and I remember thinkin' I don't know how they did it – especially when it was peltin' down with rain and I'd ponder on what could happen if the horse suddenly got spooked and bolted. Now that is, or rather was, a frightenin' sight. I only ever saw one, but once was enough. I was doin' some shoppin' for mum in Queenstown Road. I suppose I'd be about twelve. The first thing you're aware of is this terrible noise and then this horse comes thunderin' out of Cedars Road across the tram tracks and boltin' down past me down Queenstown Road draggin' this cart, or what was left of it, on its side and all the contents long gone. The noise was incredible and sparks flyin' everywhere. I don't know, but I guess somethin' must have spooked it and it had just reared up and bolted.

Somethin' else I just want to mention that I witnessed, albeit only a couple of times on my way home. I've told you that despite all the effort bein' put in by the LCC and numerous developers, there were still loads and loads of more or less untouched bomb sites scattered across the city. What I want to explain now is that gradually, many were bein' cleared, flattened and used as sites for 'temporary' prefabs to re-house the homeless and overcrowded. It must have been as late as 1949 when I was walkin' home I witnessed them erectin' prefabs, first in Robertson Street and then in Montefiore Street, the site left by 'our' bomb. Havin' got off the tube, I'd get the bus up to Lavender Hill and then I'd walk up Robertson Street to get to mum's house in Gambetta Street. Goin' back now with John (2015), I see the prefabricated bungalows in Robertson Street have been replaced with permanent buildin's whereas in Montefiore Street there's now a public park cum children's playground. As I've mentioned already, you can see that in the photos at the end of the chapter.

Movin' on from work for a minute, in my spare time, goin' to the pictures was still a regular event. You have to remember that the pictures was still the main source of entertainment for the masses and would remain so for a good number of years to come. There's a photo of me in Wixes Lane, off Lavender hill with Pat, a friend. We're outside another friend's house – Jonny's place. I guess Jonny must have taken the photograph. I'm the one standin', in my tweed suit which was fine for the weekend whereas for work I'd alternate between blue serge and grey. The three of us would often go off to the pictures together, usually the Granada at Clapham Junction. As I recall, Jonny was always lucky with the girls. He'd hardly ever come back with us, he'd be with his girl on Clapham Common. As time went on though, I saw less and less of Pat and Jonny because, as you'll learn, my music took up more and more of my time.

Word got around that I was playin' with Bill on Sundays and after maybe a couple of months, one night when I came home from the stockbrokers mum said, "Stan's been over – he wants you to pop across and see him." He was a married chap who lived over the road. Although he was fairly young – maybe about 25, bein' that bit older, I didn't really know him, but I did know he played with a band called the Debonaires – quite a big outfit who had a regular spot at Battersea Town Hall. Anyway, it turns out that their drummer had left at short notice and Stan asked me if I could help them out.

The Debonaires were a slick outfit and all wore formal dress. Trouble was, whilst I did have a dress suit, I'd no black shoes – so I had to wear my brown brogues. I hoped no-one would notice with my feet obscured behind my drum kit. Whilst by this time I'd played a few times as a duo with Bill, I'd never played with a big band set up and to be honest, come the night, I was as nervous as hell. Maybe that's why I remember it so clearly. It was a Thursday night gig and not that easy to get to with my kit. We had to take the train to Clapham Junction, then the train to Raynes Park and change again there for Wimbledon.

It was an 18-piece band and we played the first half, which seemed to go quite well. We had a front man cum conductor who also played the violin on some numbers. He was a class act in his own right. I was last off the stage and still self-conscious about wearin' brown brogues. At the front of the stage there was this huge basket of fruit. It was the raffle prize.

I was still just 15 comin' on 16 and this was my first major gig. It was all goin' so well, but things were about to turn sour. Those brogues were determined to get in on the act – if nobody had noticed them before, they sure did now, 'cos as I came off the stage somehow I missed my footin', caught the basket of fruit with my foot and sent the whole lot flyin' down the hall. This woman came out furious with me. I said I was very sorry and tried to help gather it all up – but I think I just put my foot in it further by tryin' to explain it had happened because I'd been tryin' to keep my feet hidden because I was embarrassed about my shoes!

Afterwards the band were all very nice and told me I'd done really well. I was only supposed to be standin' in whilst they got a permanent replacement, but in the end I continued doin' gigs with them for the best part of a year. Mind you, they never did let me forget my tangle with the basket of fruit 'cos ever after they all called me 'pineapple John'. Notice John, not Jack. At home I remained Jack, but in my workin' world I was John. And my workin' world, it wasn't just the stockbrokers and playin' with the Debonaires, largely because of word of mouth, I was doin' my own private work as well. I'd usually make up a four-piece, mostly usin' the same musicians who I knew were good and reliable. Dorothy on piano, Douggie on tenor sax and George on piano accordion and of course me on the drums runnin' the show, even though I was the youngest by a distance.

The war hadn't long been over and war-time songs were still very popular, so we'd generally throw in some of those – like Tipperary and Lily Marlene. Sometimes we'd play 'quiet background stuff' whilst guests enjoyed a sit down meal, but mostly it was after the meal when, dependin' on the venue, there'd often be dancin' too. Most of us would bring along our own instruments, but for the pianist, the venue would have to have its own piano. There were none of those lightweight keyboards you get today. Just traditional heavy-weight pianos which hopefully were kept in tune. Often we'd be playin' somewhere in the West End. It could be just pub rooms or somewhere like the London Rooms in Charing Cross Road.

And so it was that by the time Olga, Aunt Raithby's adopted

daughter, got married towards the end of 1949, I was already puttin' myself about as a part-time musician and promoter. I'd already played a few weddin's with my three or four piece band and so I was really pleased and yes, proud, to be able to play at Olga's weddin' reception. As I recall it was held in the rooms above the Prince of Wales at Thornton Heath. There's a picture taken at Olga's weddin' amongst those at the end of this chapter. The groom, Vic Griffiths, looks a bit chubby. There's a reason for that. He'd been a prisoner of war with the Japanese and havin' been nearly starved to death, well let's just say he appreciated his food. He did well for himself, did Vic, endin' up as pro Vice Chancellor of Surrey University. Olga's adopted mum, dear Aunt Raithby is on the far right.

As you know, I was always doin' stuff with mum, especially as a kid, but I was never really close to dad – not like I was to mum. Maybe it's a 'man thing' or maybe we just didn't have that much in common – I don't really know. When we were little, I suppose you could say he'd been really rather old to be a dad – much older than mum – and I guess rather dour and set in his ways. He liked his paper and serious stuff like politics. We didn't do that much together – not just the two of us – not like me and mum.

As I say, dad liked serious stuff and one of the few things I do remember us doin' together was when I was growin' up a bit and he took me to see Herbert Morrison at the Albert Hall. He was a little bloke; little in stature that is – nothin' of him – but a big noise on the political scene. I wasn't into politics, but even I knew that. He was a labour politician, and dad was staunch Labour and even I could see Herbert Morrison was a good orator - he had pedigree. He'd been leader of the LCC in the 1930s, served as Home Secretary in the Wartime Coalition and now he was Deputy Prime Minister in the Attlee post-war government. Mind you, it was widely known that Attlee didn't like him. Maybe that explains why dad did. Good speaker as he was, he still didn't do much for me and I remember thinkin', "What on earth am I doin' here?"

About the only other 'jaunt' I remember goin' on with dad was a coach trip from the church. I was on holiday from the Stock Exchange so I'd be 16 or 17. It was a trip to Cambridge to look round the universities. Again it wasn't exactly me, but I didn't like to say no when dad asked if I'd like to go with him not least because, as

I say, an outin' with dad was such a rare event. I think dad quite enjoyed it, but the best and only really memorable bit for me was the carp ponds around some of the colleges. Me and my fishin'! I tell a lie, the other thing I clearly remember was the lunch we had in the Gaumont Cinema's Restaurant before tourin' the colleges. It's not the lunch itself I remember. It's the little incident that dad was at pains to point out to me. There was this American soldier at a nearby table and dad wanted me to take note of the way he ate - spendin' a while cuttin' up all his food and then proceedin' to use just his fork. Not dad's idea of good table manners at all.

1949 rolled over into 1950 and work was already well under way in London in preparation for the Festival of Britain the followin' year. The main focus of the Festival was to be on the embankment, but they also built beautiful gardens in Battersea Park. At this time part of dad's job with the Council involved him goin' down sewers occasionally to do inspections, or at least it did in connection with the construction works for the gardens in Battersea Park, because everythin' had to be just so. He'd long since been promoted from sweepin' the streets and was now mainly workin' in the offices, but occasionally his job still involved site inspections. On his way out of this sewer, dad grazed his arm on the side wall of the manhole. No big deal – just a bit of a scratch really, except, as we were to discover, a bit of a scratch can become life threatenin'.

Not long after, dad started to feel ill, became feverish and went rapidly downhill, but nobody connected it to the scratch. We'd had the same doctor, Mr Livingstone-Smith, for years – since well before the war. He took one look at dad and immediately got him admitted to the South Western Fever Hospital, Landor Road, Clapham. His fever had worsened and he was yellow – just like a Chinaman. Nobody at the hospital could figure out what was wrong, but they put dad in isolation in an oxygen tent – a scary plastic thing in those days. His symptoms weren't wholly consistent, but they thought he might have polio and arrangements were made to fumigate our house as a precaution.

Mum and I would go up to the hospital every night to see him, but it was obvious he wasn't gettin' any better. It was serious – so serious that our Roy was put on compassionate leave and flown back specially from Kenya to be with him. Everyone, includin' the doctors, thought his chances of survival weren't good. Flyin' Roy back was such a big event that the newspapers printed a story about it. In the event though, Roy only ever went to see dad just the once. Mum and I would go up every day, but Roy declared that he didn't like hospitals and after the one visit never went back. I think part of the trouble was that dad and Roy had never really hit it off and even in adversity, they just couldn't seem to be able to build bridges.

Mum was beside herself with worry and at such times she needed to keep busy – even more than usual. A good job, as it turned out, because when I came home from work one day, mum announced that she'd been tidyin' up dad's bureau and found this card. It was a card issued to dad by Battersea Borough Council and said words to the effect of, "If this man goes into hospital, present this card to the doctors." When mum and I visited that night, we did just that. Within minutes of them seein' it, all hell broke loose. Doctors were runnin' around like 2-year olds. Now they had a good idea of what the problem was. They organised tests to confirm it, but they were right. Dad had contracted leptospiral jaundice – the plague! That bit of a graze from the manhole wall had given dad an infection from a rat. If mum hadn't tidied out his bureau and found that card, the chances are the doctors would never have made the right diagnosis and dad would probably have died. As it was, with the right treatment he started to pull through.

He'd been really low, so it took a few weeks before he was well enough to be discharged from hospital. In those days though, we had a proper health service. They didn't just send you home to get on with it, they sent you to a convalescent home first so you were properly recovered by the time you were sent home. Back then, I was always 'duckin' and divin'' and so come the day of his discharge, I sloped off work to be at the station to make sure he got on the train Ok. I knew an ambulance would take him to Liverpool Street Station, but when I got there, I was a bit concerned because he was nowhere to be seen on the platform. I needn't have worried because when I checked the train, he was already sittin' on it. The ambulance people had taken him directly to his seat. As I say – we had a proper health 'service' back then. I waved him off, then walked back to work with no-one the wiser – or maybe they just turned 'a blind eye'.

Later we learned that dad's case of 'the plague' had been the first in London for 20 years. He was 52, but by today's standards he looked and acted much older and that was even before he'd contracted the plague. Such a serious illness took its toll, but the main thing was that thanks to mum needin' to 'keep busy', in the nick of time he'd got the right treatment and survived. He enjoyed his two weeks convalescin' by the sea in Clacton and often talked about it. On his return he was and looked so much better, but still there was an ambulance at the station to meet him and take him home and it would be another month or so before he was deemed well enough to return to work.

Dad had somehow come back from the dead. Not quite literally like me, but he had been pretty close to it. Close enough for us all to feel the anxiety and then the relief when, with the right treatment, he started gettin' better. He was staunch Labour but very conservative and serious about his newspaper. He read the Daily Telegraph and to be sure of his copy, he'd have it delivered every day. Whilst in hospital he had been much too ill for newspapers, so it had been cancelled. When he was just back home after convalescin', it hadn't been re-ordered. It was a Saturday so he asked me to pop down to the corner shop and get him a copy. The Sketch and Mirror were much more popular papers and they didn't have any Telegraphs left so, rather than come back empty-handed, I bought him a Mirror instead. That went down like a lead balloon. To say he wasn't best pleased would be an understatement. I got a right tellin' off endin' with, "….. and don't you ever bring that comic into this house again!" That was tellin' me. That was dad – back to his old self. I may have been 'a workin' man,' at the Stock Exchange no less, but I wasn't too old for a tellin' off from dad.

That little newspaper incident was evidence that dad was on the mend, but it had been touch and go and a worryin' time for us all, especially mum, for whom I fear it would have lastin' and as yet unforeseen consequences. I'll come back to that later, but for now I think I need to lighten the mood again – so back to my music.

After about a year the Debonaires started breakin' up, but I had no intention of packin' away my drumsticks. I was hooked and wanted more. Fortunately I saw an ad in the Melody Maker for a drummer at the Star & Garter. The Star and Garter was, is at Putney on the banks of the Thames. You'll see a photo of it later. I went there on the followin' Saturday night to enquire. The joint promoter was there and he looked me up and down. I was 16 goin' on 17. "You're a bit young, aren't you lad?" he said, to which I replied, "Well, yes, maybe – but I'll soon be very old if I don't get a job." Maybe we shared a sense of humour. In any event he must've taken a bit of a shine to me 'cos he just said, "Can you start next week" – no audition – nothin'. Back out into the hustle and bustle, the noise and the clatter of the street, there was a strange upliftin' harmony. I couldn't so much hear it as feel it. I was borne along by it. I couldn't believe my luck. How easy it had been. Like never before, I was walkin' with a spring in my step. I was ten feet tall and risin'. I'd been given a regular Saturday and Sunday night spot and in the end I did that job for the best part of 4 years. The Saturday spot I did even right through my 'army career' – but my 'army career', well that's another story. I'll come to it in a bit.

It was a very professional set-up at the Star & Garter and a good payer. The stage wasn't especially big, but usually there'd be 8 or 9 of us playin'. As with all bands in those days, and generally still today, some 'seats' were paid more than others. But it was always done on a very 'gentlemanly' basis so no-one ever asked what the others were gettin'. You couldn't help wonderin', but if you'd asked me, I'd have told you I was more than happy – bein' paid pretty well for somethin' I loved doin'. Unless of course you were the promoter doin' the askin', in which case I'd probably have made out that I thought I wasn't gettin' paid enough – a man with my talent for bringin' in the punters! You see, life had already taught me that you get no prizes for bein' modest. If you want to get on, you have to put yourself about a bit.

Our singer compere was a chap called Joe West. He was also the joint promoter along with the chap who'd interviewed me. He was probably a bit before his time – rather like Matt Monroe. I thought he was very good, but unfairly, or so I thought, the rest of the band took the mickey out of him a bit.

I started out doin' Saturday and Sunday nights, but before long I became what they called 'resident' and often did Thursday and Fridays as well. They even did a photo shoot of me for publicity purposes. It was stuck out front for all to see. I thought it made me look quite dapper but you can judge that for yourself when you get to the photos. Notice the cigarette. It was considered 'cool' to smoke in those days. All the film stars did. I was no film star, but I was in demand – and not just at the Star & Garter. I'd often get bookin's elsewhere as well and of course there were specials around Christmas and New Year when things got really hectic. But then I was young – I had the stamina – plus, if I were honest, I had a pretty cushy daytime job at the stockbrokers.

Hardly anybody had a private phone in those days so people used to just call in home and leave messages for me. I got a lot of private gigs that way – especially weddin's. Do a good job and word soon gets around. I may have only been 17, but I'd grown in confidence and I was already quite experienced in the entertainment game. I'd put small bands together – three or four pieces – dependin' on the job. I had a little gimmick – I'd say, "What do you want, a 3 piece or a 4 piece?" and they'd say, "What's the difference?" and I'd say, "Two pounds ten!" (That's like two pounds fifty pence today – except of course it's not 'cos a pound was actually worth somethin' in those days.)

I guess you could say I was on a real high. No drugs – nothin' like that – it's just that things were goin' so well. I was earnin' very good money at the stockbrokers and a good deal more besides from indulgin' my passion for music. I'd got a lot of good mates – many of 'em from night school. Life could hardly be better – or so it seemed. Mind you – I'd seen enough of life to know that it has a way of takin' you down a peg or two. It's a bit like a game of snakes and ladders and I was about to step on a snake – or, to be more correct, I suppose I should say mum was, but in a very real sense, it would take me down too.

It started with mum actin' a bit funny now and again. Nothin' much really, or so we thought. She'd probably been overdoin' things a bit – that's all. Nothin' to worry about, especially since she seemed to be right as rain again in between. Except snakes can be deceptive. You start by thinkin' it's just a little thing. Somethin' to take you down a rung or two. No big deal really. Nothin' much to get over. You'll soon be up and movin' forward again. That's the way it is with snakes and ladders and that's the way we thought it would be with mum. Except this wasn't a game it was real life and mum didn't just bounce back. As time would tell, she'd been well and truly bitten and there wasn't goin' to be a quick fix.

I've already told you that in my day London kids were pretty street-wise and I reckon with all my experiences of bein' moved from pillar to post, I was more street-wise than most and pretty perceptive with it. I never missed much. But I didn't see it comin'. Maybe I was livin' too busy a life – dashin' here, dashin' there. All my life, mum had been there for me. Ok, I know, not always there physically next to me or even near to me, but deep down I always knew that when push came to shove, she'd be there for me. She was my rock. She was dad's rock too. Yes, dad was nominally head of the household, but really it was mum who ran the show. Now suddenly, things had changed. Mum was ill. Not physically ill – mentally. Now mum needed me. I was 17. Physically quite a big lad now – but emotionally, I still had some more growin' up to do. I had to become mum's rock and, as it turned out, in many ways dad's rock too.

They say hindsight is a wonderful thing – but it's not, is it? It's useless 'cos you can never change what's happened. You can never make it right. I don't know. I'll never really know – but, lookin' back maybe the start of the slippery slope for mum was when they told her she would have to give up her job on the railway. She loved that job. Perhaps more than that, she loved the camaraderie that came with it. She loved her mates. By comparison her marriage was – always had been – a rather lonely affair. Ok, it was only a job, but I don't think it seemed so much like hard work as the dull routine and drudgery that was her life outside of it. Havin' her workmates and, thinkin' about it, havin' me to look out for, were maybe the things that helped her get through the rigours of the war and the constant fear of all the bombin'. Yes, it was only a job – work – but she had put her heart and soul into it and now that had been ripped out.

At the time, at first, she seemed to bounce back. She was mum. She always had. She had soon got herself another job – back in hotels – but somehow I don't think things would ever be the same. She'd lost the camaraderie. And that wasn't the only change. There was me – that little kid who'd needed lookin' out for and takin' to the shelter every night. The war was over and I wasn't that little kid any more, a kid at school who needed lookin' after, takin' out to places. I was a man. I was workin' for a livin'. I was goin' my own way, playin' my music. Mum was proud of me but now I see that maybe she was feelin' the loss.

Now mum didn't need to be so strong any more and maybe she

just 'let go' that bit too much. Maybe psychologically, it all became too much – too many changin' circumstances – too many adjustments to make, too much emotional turmoil. Who knows. Even so, maybe she would still have been alright if it hadn't been for dad's illness. He'd pulled through but it had had a marked effect and not just on dad. Lookin' back I think that was the tippin' point. All the worry of it – thinkin' he was goin' to die and, maybe even the relief after he pulled through. All that emotional turmoil. Maybe that was the final straw, the thing that tipped the balance of her mind, pushed her beyond that fine line, over the edge. The ups and downs, the highs and lows were maybe just too much for mum to cope with this time. We'll never really know, but I've gone over and over it in my mind, tryin' to figure it out.

I'm told that stress and worry can trigger bouts of mental instability and illness. Some folk are more susceptible than others, but mum had never struck me as havin' any sort of weakness in that department – far from it. So why did mum succumb to her illness? Even lookin' back, goin' over and over it, I can't detect any increase in pressure or anxiety at the time it actually started to show itself so perhaps in her case it was the reverse – a release – which somehow tipped the balance of her mind. Or maybe somethin' did happen in her life that I simply didn't know about – that now I'll never know about.

Whatever the cause, mum knew herself she wasn't right – knew she just couldn't carry on regardless. She needed help. So mum quit her job at the Army & Navy Club and on Dr Livingstone-Smith's advice, she admitted herself into the Epsom Mental Hospital. She was goin' to take 'a little break away'. That would sort her out. She was a voluntary patient and in theory she could walk out any time she wanted to.

At first dad and I thought she'd be gone a couple of weeks and then she'd be back right as rain again. Mum was mum. She'd always been the strong one. Dad was nominally head of the household, but it was mum who had always run the show. She'd always looked after the money side of things, made sure the bills were paid, carried the burden of responsibility. Mum wasn't physically ill so a little break away would do the trick, or so we thought. Nothin' much to worry about. Except, in real life, snakes can be deceptive and this wasn't a little thing. What seemed minor was to become major. The snake she'd stepped on turned out to be a particularly big, long and venomous creature capable of takin' mum down, and, to an extent, dad and me with her. I had youth on my side and I suppose you could say that I was to emerge a stronger and wiser man from the experience, but as for mum, she was to undergo years of hospital treatment. This was goin' to be a very, very long drop from which mum would never fully recover. She'd never be the same again, never. But we didn't know, couldn't even begin to imagine it, not then. Much as I'd like to, I can't just leave it at that. I need to tell you more about what happened – painful though it is for me to recall.

I'd been workin' at the stockbrokers for about 14 months when mum announced she was goin' to admit herself to hospital. We knew things weren't right, but it was still a big shock. We hadn't expected mum to need treatment in a mental hospital.

Then there was just dad and me at home because, if you remember, our Roy was in the army stationed overseas. Dad, as you know, worked for Battersea Borough Council in their offices now at Clapham Junction. That meant he'd always get home from work before me. I told you he used to be a chef in service and I must say that now with mum away, he rose to the challenge and he cooked me some wonderful meals. He really did.

On a Sunday we'd have an early lunch at about 11.30 am and then we'd catch a train down to Epsom. Dad always wanted me to go with him to the hospital. I would've anyway, but somehow he needed me to. It was more than just a wish. Around the time I was given a lift up by bein' promoted into the offices at the stockbrokers, mum went the other way - really downhill. She didn't seem to know us – we couldn't get any response from her at all. It was worryin', very worryin'. I know now – but I didn't know then, that it was almost certainly due to the electric shock treatment they had started givin' her. Whether they were tryin' to erase the bad memories which they thought were troublin' mum and causin' her mental breakdown, I just don't know. Nobody ever explained to us. Maybe they didn't really know themselves. Maybe voluntary patients were a bit like guinea pigs. It was all very experimental back then. More recently I've been able to read reports about it – about how after treatment patients just lie there starin' into space or straight at visitors with empty eyes, no hint of recognition even. That was mum. It upset dad and it upset me

I can tell you – but I couldn't let it show. Now I had to be strong for both of them.

I hadn't been long promoted into the offices, but I stuck my neck out. I went and did the unthinkable. I went and asked Mr Over if I could have time out on a Tuesday, every Tuesday, to go and see mum. I've already said that he ran the office with a rod of iron. He didn't care whether he was popular or not. All that mattered to him was that the office ran efficiently and that everybody knuckled down and did their job. But he wasn't made of stone and he could see how concerned I was about mum. He agreed – so long as my work didn't suffer, I could go. And so it was that for the next couple of years I went to see mum on my own every Tuesday afternoon as well as Sundays with Dad. I did that 'till I was called up for National Service – then it was back to just Sundays because even I couldn't get away from the army in the week.

Every Tuesday I'd take a late lunch and grab a quick bite to eat in the ABC (Aerated Bread Company) who occupied the ground floor of our buildin'. Instead of goin' back up to the office, I'd go and catch the underground to Waterloo and then the train to Epsom and a bus up to the hospital. I can't say it was an enjoyable experience or a journey I relished, but I never missed a week and outwardly I was always up-beat and all smiles. I had to be for mum's sake. I had to try to lift her spirits. As you can imagine – the times she didn't recognise me, didn't acknowledge my presence at all – they were the really low points – for me as well as mum. It was devastatin' to see her like that. Re-countin' it now, the pain comes floodin' back. Not a physical pain – a mental anguish and a hollow feelin' deep in the pit of my stomach.

When mum was first admitted to that hospital we all thought she'd be there for two or three weeks at most. In reality the weeks were to turn into months and then years – five whole years between 1951 and 1955. Even now it's difficult to comprehend. How she survived it, I don't know. All I know is, she seemed to want to be there. She was a voluntary patient and free to leave at any time, so we just had to go along with it. But it was hard – very hard seein' her in that place with so many, to me so much more obviously mentally ill patients. I used to wonder how many of those patients were voluntary like mum. At the time most seemed much worse than her. We didn't think she was like them. We worried she was in the right ward, but mum, she didn't seem concerned. She seemed strangely content. I wonder, did she find the hospital atmosphere somehow amenable and beguilin'? Did she somehow form a dependence? Is that why she stayed so long?

Lookin' back I'm not sure what real care the patients actually got. Don't misunderstand me, they were fed and looked after in that way and there was always a big teapot and urn and cheap cakes to buy at visitin' times, but in all my visits I don't recall ever seein' anybody actually attendin' to any of the patients. Lots would just be sittin' there starin' blankly and rockin'. For me it was disturbin', but mum didn't seem to notice them. They all seemed to be in their own separate world, mum included. She never once mentioned any other patient and I never saw her speak to any of them. The place was packed, but it must have been lonely and thinkin' about it now, bein' shut in there with so many strange strangers, seemingly none of 'em communicatin', must have affected her in some way, unless somehow she could shut it all out. I know I couldn't have, no way, not for a few weeks never mind all those months, not for all those years.

I was always pleased if it was a nice day, or at least not too cold, and then we'd walk out in the garden. I thought it would do mum good to get her out in the fresh air, but in truth it was probably as much for my benefit as for mum's because it helped to pass the time and I found it difficult to stomach bein' in that place even for the short periods I was there. Even as the years went by, it never really got any better. I suppose I got used to it, but I never got comfortable with it, not at all.

Visitin' time was about two hours, but it seemed longer, and I'm ashamed to say that although I never missed goin' to see mum, I was always glad when it was time to go. It was always difficult to keep the conversation goin' because mum didn't really have much conversation. Small wonder, bein' stuck in that place with pretty much the same four walls and the same routine day in, day out. What she did say tended to be a repetition of whatever had been said to her, by way of agreement I suppose. Other than that, time and again, she'd look at me and say, "I'll be Ok when this sound goes out of my head." Even years later after she'd finally come out of hospital, from time to time she'd still be sayin' that. I wanted to make it right for mum but I couldn't, nobody could. The best I could do was to carry on lovin' her and learn to cope with no fuss, with the way things were, the things I couldn't change.

I guess everyone has a bond with their mum but, we'd been close, really close, my mum and me. Seein' her so low, so changed, did more than just tug at my heart strings. Bein' a percussionist, I suppose I should better liken it to an irregular beat but, whatever way you try to describe it, it was a strange kind of music that I didn't like and didn't want to hear but I had no choice. I had to keep goin' even when, time and again, visitin' seemed futile. I had to try to show her that I was there for her, that I cared, even if sometimes I couldn't be sure she even knew I'd been visitin' at all.

I'm sorry, there's lots more I still need to tell you about mum, but I just need to take a little break – talk about somethin' else, anythin' really, just for a minute or two. Somethin' to lighten the mood – a trip to the dentists!

As a kid and even after startin' work, I never went for regular check-ups to the dentist. I don't think anybody did. Not ordinary workin' folk anyway. You have to remember, there was no National Health in those days. Now and again though, ravaged by toothache, we had no choice.

I hadn't been long workin' at the Stock Exchange when I had to visit the dentists and I went to the nearest - in Queenstown Road. I should have known better really because he didn't have the best of reputations. As it turned out though, I thought my shillin' was well spent because after I came out, the toothache was gone. Next day, well that was a different story. My face had swelled right up, so much so that I couldn't go to work. Rumour had it that he didn't sterilize his instruments properly. I guess I must have picked up some sort of infection. Another day went by and no sign of improvement, so I thought, "I'll take myself off to the pictures to cheer myself up." In the interval the usherettes used to sell choc ices and other treats from a tray hung round their neck. I'd not had a choc ice in ages and really fancied one. By the time I came out my face was a picture – of health that is. Believe it or not, all the swellin' had gone! So there's a little tip for you – if your face is swollen up, get yourself a choc ice. It'll work wonders. Well, it did for me.

There's more than one mental hospital in Epsom – or at least there was in those days, so I should explain that the one mum was admitted to was St Ebbas. It was originally built in 1903 as part of the 'Epsom Cluster' – a development of 5 mental hospitals around the Surrey town. Originally it had been a home for epileptic patients, but in 1927 it had been handed back to the LCC as a mental hospital. In 1930 the Mental Treatment Act made provision for voluntary patients to be admitted and treated in public mental hospitals. Prior to that, all patients had been 'sectioned' and incarcerated, often for life, irrespective of their wishes. St Ebbas had been enlarged twice in the 1930s to cope with the increased demand. Accordin' to hospital archives, St Ebbas achieved good results with a large number of voluntary patients by retainin' them for a maximum period of two years before dischargin' them or transferrin' them elsewhere if necessary. Sadly, time would show that this was not to be the case with mum.

On Tuesdays I'd take the bus from the station both ways but on Sundays, weather permittin', dad liked us to walk up to the Hospital, ostensibly because he liked to look at all the gardens of all the various houses along the way. It was about a 25-minute walk and as well as a chance to see how the gardens were comin' along, it gave dad time to prepare himself. We were always a bit apprehensive because we never knew what we would find – how mum would be.

St Ebbas had pretty extensive grounds, so it was still a fair walk from the main gate to the hospital buildin' itself. Whilst the outer door was generally open, the inner doors were always locked to prevent patients from wanderin' or, to put it more bluntly – from escapin'. No doubt some would have been a danger to others as well as to themselves. Visitin' time was 2 'till 4 pm and a member of staff would always be on hand to let us in. Other than that though, none of the staff or doctors ever communicated with patients' relatives at all. There was never any progress report or opportunity to ask questions – never. Not once in all the 5 years mum was a patient there. Nearly a tenth of her life, as it turned out.

When mum was physically sick, we would visit at her bedside, but mostly she'd be sittin' in a chair in a big communal room along with maybe 30 other patients. It pains me to recall it, but I think I need you to understand what 'bed' meant for mum. It wasn't so much a bedroom as a dormitory and my abidin' memory is of an impersonal, not very wide room with what seemed like too many beds packed in very close together. There was nothin' personal or homely about it. Nothin' welcomin' or comfortin'- just functional, institutionalised, cold. I don't mean the temperature. It was plenty warm enough – too warm really. I mean the atmosphere – cold and impersonal and enveloped by an all-pervadin' 'hospital air' which seemed to all but embalm my very presence. Lukewarm 'used air' often flavoured with disinfectant to disguise the body odours inevitable with so many ill and often elderly people confined in such an enclosed space. Air that has been breathed and breathed again without ever havin' been allowed out to be refreshed from outside. And then there was the uneasiness, a growin' sense of anxiety that comes with bein' surrounded by people – strangers – who have troubled minds and act strangely.

It was the sort of place you feel you want to leave whilst you still can and, as I've admitted already, I'm ashamed to say that I was always glad to get out of there. But that atmosphere – it always took time to shake off. It seemed to surround me like a vapour. A lingerin' presence I could feel, but which thankfully began to dissolve as I walked out through the grounds and dissipate by the time I reached the main gate. I didn't like to think of mum trapped in there, but what was the alternative? She was in the best place, wasn't she? Dad and I convinced ourselves of it. I think we had to, in order just to cope.

Havin' said that, in truth, dad and I were never comfortable with the place, not even from the start. It came as somethin' of a shock to us that followin' admission, mum seemed to get worse rather than better, and dad and I weren't at all sure it was the right place for her, but whenever she was lucid, or as near lucid as she ever was in there, she was insistent she wanted to stay, so I guess we just went along with it. I remember she had this expression, "I'll be Ok when my head lifts." It doesn't sound much to achieve, but it is. It really is, and when it never seems to happen, you start to wonder if it ever will.

When she was well enough, mum would speak to us and sometimes she'd seem quite normal. They would be the good times and we'd grasp at 'em and we'd ask if she was comin' home, but invariably she'd say, "Oh no – I don't think I'm ready yet" – or words to that effect. Even in the good times, it was noticeable though, that she didn't speak to other patients. In fact, I don't remember any of the other patients communicatin' with one-another

- never. Those that didn't have visitors – which was most of 'em – just sat starin' into space or rocked backwards and forwards, not unlike caged animals in a zoo. Was it symptomatic of their illness – their mental state or, like animals in a zoo, somethin' brought on by the conditions in which they lived – unnatural and lackin' in stimulation – a combination of restricted freedom and sheer boredom? It was pitiful and disturbin' to see. I don't know, but I suspect most of 'em – particularly the 'more difficult patients' – were on various levels of medication to keep them quiet and manageable. Whatever the case, it was far from a pleasant or upliftin' atmosphere – quite the reverse.

Whilst they didn't seem to speak to one another, not all of the patients just sat quiet all the time. Some seemed to 'jibber' and jerk their heads and, on occasions, even yell out loud. After years of visits, I came to learn or at least accept that such behaviour passed for normality there – nothin' to be alarmed at. But, early on, it most certainly was a source of worry borderin' on anguish that mum wasn't in the right ward, bein' put with such people. As for mum herself? – I have to say that she didn't seem alarmed or disturbed by the other patients at all and sensin' this, I never broached the subject lest my concerns be transmitted to her. In all those years of visitin', mum never spoke of them, but then you have to understand that for most of the time it wasn't really mum I was visitin'. Not the mum I'd known. Week after week, month after month, year after year, I always went to see mum. I never let her down. She'd never let me down, but I have to say that it was never easy and rarely pleasant. Even for me, two hours was a long time to keep a one-sided conversation goin' with mum hardly speakin' at all. She had no conversation of her own. The contrast with my mum of old was hard to take.

For me, the atmosphere in there was soul-destroyin' – it really was, and I don't know how mum coped with it. I can only guess that the medication helped and that in her mental state mum just didn't perceive it the way I did. It's hard to admit it, even now, but, as I've told you, truth be told, it was almost always a relief when visitin' time was over and it was time to go. I think I keep tellin' you because even now I'm still tryin' to shed the guilt of feelin' that relief. I'm sure dad was the same. We both felt terrible leavin' mum in there, but it seemed it was where she wanted to be. For me at least though, especially on the days when I'd been visitin' on my own, walkin' out through that door felt like bein' released from prison. The world outside wasn't always easy, but it seemed like paradise compared to that place. The bus back to the railway station went from the main gate at ten past 4, so there was never any time to hang about – not that I felt like doin'.

You have to put your faith in doctors. Mum had by admittin' herself. By givin' mum electric shock treatment I'm sure they thought they were doin' their best. But it was all very experimental – trial and error – and we'll never know whether it did more harm than good. Whatever the case, some time after the course of shock treatment was over and done with, mum seemed to get a bit better. But then again, maybe it's just that the effects of the 'treatment' had worn off. By visitin' I was supposed to be liftin' her spirits, but I have to say that when she started recognisin' me again and started chattin' with me – almost like normal – she probably did more to lift my spirits than the other way around. I was choked, but hopefully I never let it show.

When she was feelin' better, mum started doin' evenin' classes at the hospital. I well remember she made an ironin' board and one Tuesday she asked me to take it back home with me. By the time I got to Epsom it was rush-hour and Clapham Junction was very, very busy. My train was late leavin' but fortunately I did manage to get a seat and stack the ironin' board in the overhead rack above me. It was a big heavy thing and I remember havin' a bit of a struggle gettin' it up there. Anyway, it was noticeable the train was goin' at 'a bit of a lick' and the carriages were swayin' about a lot. I guess the driver was tryin' to make up time. We hadn't gone all that far when, without warnin', this great heavy wooden thing came hurtlin' out of the rack and crashin' onto my nose. It was a hell of a shock I can tell you for me and for the other passengers, who were wrestlin' with its legs which had somehow splayed themselves out. To a fly on the wall it must've seemed hilarious - reminiscent of a Charlie Chaplin film, but neither I nor the other passengers saw the funny side of it at the time. What's more, they were the innocents – it was me who should've made sure it was secure up there. As for my nose – it was split across the bridge and the scar and dent it made is still visible to this day.

It was indestructible – that ironin' board – mum and dad never wore it out. Even after they died we had it and used it for years and years. It was a sturdy old thing.

Mum had always had a tendency to be somewhat on the large side, but she put on a good deal more weight whilst she was at St Ebbas. I guess all the long periods of prolonged inactivity, just sittin' about waitin' for meal times, didn't help. When she was feelin' up to it and weather permittin', we did try to get her up and about when we were there. Mum was a voluntary patient, so I'm not sure if it applied to all patients, but we were allowed to take her out into the grounds durin' visitin' times. She seemed to enjoy that and, as I know I've already told you, to be honest, it was a relief for us not to have to sit in that communal room for two hours. I'm sorry if I seem to keep harpin' on about it, but how mum coped with it, I don't know, because she wasn't just there for a couple of hours, she was there 24/7 for the best part of 5 years. It doesn't bear thinkin' about. It really doesn't.

Throughout all this, I still made time for my music – my regular weekend spots at the Star & Garter and the other jobs that came my way mainly by word of mouth. By puttin' a small band together to suit the occasion and people's pockets, I could undercut the regular bands and still give folk a really good time. Good for me – good for them. I had a burgeonin' reputation and I think even dad was proud of me for bein' able to go out and entertain folk and make a few bob into the bargain. If I say so myself, I'd become a polished performer and a pretty successful small time promoter. I was confident, assured. I had an extensive and expandin' repertoire and I could improvise. I had, as they say, 'savoir faire'.

When I went out to the Star & Garter or wherever, dad would go off to bed at about 9 pm. As usual he'd read his Telegraph from cover to cover, but he never went to sleep 'till he heard me comin' up the stairs at about midnight or even 1 am – dependin' on which band I'd been playin' with and the type of venue. He'd always say, "Is that you then?", to which I'd reply somethin' a bit flippant like, "Yeah, I hope it is." He'd then feel Ok about goin' to sleep while I'd make a cuppa and a cheese sandwich or somethin'. I was tired, but even more than that, I was always starvin'. No matter what the hour, I'd always need that sandwich before turnin' in.

I was earnin' good money so rather than lug all my gear on trams and buses, I started usin' taxis quite a bit. I really had gone up in the world. This one time I'd got home pretty late and I was whacked and probably a bit bleary-eyed. It had been a long night – enjoyable but long. I couldn't get all my kit out of the taxi in one go so the taxi door was open whilst I was tooin' and froin' to our house.

Anyway I got in the house and dad shouted, "Is that you?" as usual and I made my cuppa and cheese sandwich. It was only then I realised that Dinky wasn't around. I don't think I've told you much about our Dinky so I'd better put that right now. Dinky was a massive tabby cat. He only had one eye. He'd lost the other one when the bomb dropped – you know, the one that nearly did for mum, dad and me back in Montefiore Street. Anyway, dad would always put Dinky out around 9 pm as he was goin' off to bed to read his paper and Dinky would always be waitin' for me to come home – sittin' on the wall outside where the railin's had been cut off durin' the war. He'd always slip in past me whilst I was gettin' my drum kit into the house. Now the reason I'm botherin' to tell you this is that our Dinky was no ordinary cat. He always used to get in bed with me and he'd sleep straight up and down with his head on a pillow – just like a human bein'. Quirky or what?

This particular night was different – no Dinky. But I was wrecked and just droppin' off to sleep when I heard a car pull up outside. I knew it must be a taxi 'cos it was about a quarter to 2 in the mornin'. Nothin' much else ever came down our street and certainly not at that hour. Next thing there was this tap, tap, tap on our door. As you can imagine, my first thought was of mum. I dragged myself out of bed and opened the door to find the taxi driver who'd brought me home earlier with our Dinky. Apparently he'd just taken another fare in Piccadilly only to be told that he'd got a cat in the back. Dinky was an inquisitive cat and must've jumped in for a nosey and not seein' I must've slammed the door shut on him. I think it says a lot for London taxi drivers – or at least this one in particular. He didn't just toss our Dinky out – he drove him all the way back home.

As for Dinky – he wasn't bothered – he just clambered into bed beside me like nothin' had happened. Got himself comfy – lyin' straight up and down, head on the pillow as usual and slept there all night not stirrin' till he heard dad gettin' his breakfast at around 7 am. If you're interested, there's a photo of Dinky at the end of this chapter.

Back at the Stockbrokers things were pretty much the same except that the firm was gettin' more and more business as the effects of the war receded. To cope with the increased volume, they had to take on more and more staff. As for me, I did everythin' that was asked of me and I think I was pretty well regarded, but to be honest I never really learned a lot about how the Stock Exchange actually works. I still don't know the difference between a trader and a jobber! What I did learn and what has stood me in good stead throughout my life was the importance of punctuality when it matters, that first impressions and hence dress and appearance count and, most of all, it taught me how to deal with people in a proper manner. And that's important.

Another thing I should mention at this point – because it was a big problem, not just for Newson-Smith & Co, but for any company takin' on school leavers, was that just as they'd trained them up to be really useful employees, they'd be called up for National Service. That's what had happened to Tommy, the lad who'd taken me under his wing and showed me the ropes when I first joined the firm. He'd joined the Royal Army Pay Corps at Devizes. Maybe that's why when I was promoted up into the office, instead of takin' on another school leaver they took on a man in his 50s to do my old job. Bein' the office junior and startin' at the bottom as a 'runner' must have been a bit difficult for him. I don't know – maybe he'd been a bit down on his luck and, as I told you, the money was good. Fair play to him though - he stuck to it and in the end he was to do quite well with Newson-Smith.

I've told you about my music because, well, aside from work and visitin' mum, it took up most of my spare time. It was my passion in life – so much so that although 1951 was Festival of Britain year, I barely made time for any of it. Mind you, as you'll learn later, some of the facilities, especially those in Battersea Park, do hold special memories for me. For now though I ought to at least give you some idea of what was provided.

For those of you who don't know London well like I do, Battersea Park is big – about a 200 acre green space on the south bank of the Thames. Mostly reclaimed marshland, apparently it was first opened to the public in 1858, but in 1951, as part of the Festival of Britain celebrations, the northern parts of the park were transformed into the "Pleasure Gardens". As well as beautiful floral displays, there was a new water garden with fountains and a tree walk and highlights like the Guinness Clock and the 'Far Totterin' and 'Oyster Creek Branch Railway'. For us youngsters – because, despite all that had happened in my life I was still a teenager – for us youngsters, the biggest transformation was the addition of the Fun Fair and in particular its spectacular 'Big Dipper' rollercoaster. At the time it was probably the scariest ride on the planet. In truth though, even back then, it wasn't really the Fair that attracted me, it was the Bands. I used to love listenin' to the bands whenever I got chance.

I well remember posters at the time proclaimin, "Come to the Fair in lovely Battersea Park". They showed steam boats and sailin' boats on the river and the marquees and new fairground attractions in the Park. They invited folk to 'Come to the Festival Pleasure Gardens – to experience all its delights includin' the bands and the illuminations and the dancin'; the theatres and the fireworks!' There were admission charges. I think it was 2/- on weekdays and 1/- on Sundays, children half price.

No doubt about it, the Funfair and the gardens were amazin', but one of the biggest attractions for me was the 'Riverside Theatre', constructed and decorated in the Victorian style but equipped with electric lightin'. There were as many as six different shows a day includin' Musical Hall, dancin' and Festival Follies.

Whilst I never got to see inside at the time, I well remember them buildin' the Royal Festival Hall on the Thames beside Waterloo Bridge. It had its own landin' stage and everythin' and was completed in time to house the Great Exhibition. Mind you, it was controversial because of the cost, but unlike most of the facilities provided for Festival year, at least it's still standin' and functionin' on the Embankment just beyond County Hall and where the 'Big Eye' now stands. I'm sayin' County Hall because in my day that's what it was – the headquarters of the LCC. Now it's a hotel – part of the Marriot Group I think.

Somethin' amusin' has just popped into my head that happened in the summer of 1951 and so before I forget, I think I'll just tell you about it before movin' on. So, I'm seventeen and I've been workin' for Newson-Smith for a couple of years. I'm also playin' with the Debonaires. I mention that because two of my friends – Ted and Elsie Mallings, I met through the Debonaires. Ted was a travellin' salesman for Frosto, a well-known grocery chain – well, it was in the early '50s – and Elsie worked in the city. I guess they were in their forties, but what I would call 'with it'! Ted was a brilliant guitar player. I suppose a bit before his time, because guitars hadn't become popular instruments back then. As we know, a decade later and they would dominate popular music. Ted played occasional spots with the Debonaires, but more often with a five-piece at a big pub called the French Horn in Wandsworth. When I didn't have a gig myself, I'd go along and listen sometimes. There was a good atmosphere and a lot of musicians frequented the place. I remember there was great excitement and many congratulations the day I came in with the news that I'd got the job at the Star & Garter. The Star & Garter is still there, but the French Horn is one venue I can't tell you to go and see for yourself 'cos the place was pulled down for road improvements in the sixties. It's a pity – you'd have liked the French Horn. It was a lovely buildin' and a great venue.

Anyway, about this little trip. Ted and Elsie wanted to try out this restaurant they'd heard about out in the country – on the A3 Portsmouth road, the other side of Guildford. I'd never been, but in time I would come to know that road well because it would be my regular hitch-hikin' route from Portsmouth to London, as you'll learn later. For now, the thing that first struck me about the place were these two big lakes on the opposite side of the road. Whenever I saw a likely stretch of water, I always fancied tryin' my luck, but as it turned out, I never did – I never went back to fish there and it's a bit late now. Mind you, I never say never, so if you're local and you see this old codger reelin' one in, it could just be me.

I'll have to stop this digressin' and get back to my little story. Ted picked me up in Gambetta Street in his three-wheeler Morgan. Nippy little thing, but a bit tight on space and Ted had to be careful drivin' round the city because it wasn't the most stable of vehicles and you have to remember there were still a lot of tram lines about in those days. Anyway, Ted got us there, no problem, and despite bein' a bit cramped, it was a warm, summer's day and a lovely trip out into the countryside. So far so good. We were greeted at the door by this waiter in a 'penguin suit', white napkin over his arm. Very formal, very posh. I remember feelin' a bit uncomfortable. I was a teenager. I'd never been in a place like this before. I was a bit out of my depth. I hadn't been expectin' anythin' this posh, this formal, but I needn't have worried. Elsie was about to lighten the mood and take the focus well and truly off me.

Havin' established Ted had booked a table for three, this waiter led us along a corridor to one of several dinin' rooms. It would have been memorable for the plush red carpet if Elsie hadn't suddenly stopped in her tracks, puttin' her hand to her mouth with a gasp. There was a look of horror on her face and I thought, "Oh dear, has she forgotten to put her teeth in," but as it turned out I was lookin' at the wrong end. She'd forgotten to put her shoes on. She was wearin' her carpet slippers! That would have been bad enough in a place like this, but you should have seen 'em. They were those plush furry type – at least they had been once. To say they were rather grubby and had seen better days wouldn't do them justice in a perverse kind of way. They were rank – positively rank – and I'd bet they could have walked out on their own if she'd taken 'em off. You couldn't make it up, you really couldn't, and it was all I could do not to laugh.

I can't really remember the meal. Maybe if I tried hard enough I would, but, whatever it was, I doubt very much Elsie enjoyed the experience. She kept her feet firmly under the table and couldn't get out of there fast enough when we'd finished. The poor woman wasn't just embarrassed – she was mortified. I never saw those slippers again either when I went visitin' Ted and Elsie at home. They were the first people I knew to have a TV and I'd go round to watch with them sometimes. Before our little trip I'd taken no notice, but next time I went round there I couldn't help checkin' Elsie's feet. My guess is those slippers had gone straight in the bin. I never asked. I didn't want to rub it in.

I'd been workin' at the stockbrokers for just over 3 years and on top of that I had my regular spot at the Star & Garter. I thought I had it made. Come to think of it, I had. I'd landed on my feet, earnin' good money at the stockbrokers and more besides, just for doin' what I loved best, pursuin' my passion as a drummer. I loved bein' on stage and in the limelight and by word of mouth, I was gettin' loads of extra gigs, playin' at weddin's, functions and various celebrations. I was in demand and lovin' it.

Everythin' was goin' so well until one day this brown envelope drops through the letterbox. No big deal – except it was. Inside were my call-up papers. It wasn't an invitation, it was a requirement – a summons. It didn't matter what your circumstances were, it was National Service, you were goin' and that was it. I'd been expectin' 'em, but even so, come the day it began to feel like my perfect world was collapsin' in around me.

I doubt most kids of 18 could cope with it today. They're all thinkin' about goin' off to 'uni' or takin' a year out to go travellin' first.

Talkin' of travellin', there's somethin' else I ought to at least mention before movin' on – the demise of the trams in London. They'd been good to me, the trams. I'd used 'em a lot both as a kid and now as a young man workin' in the city and, early on at least, as a musician. I know it's only nostalgia but they held, no they hold, a special place in my heart. To me, they weren't just a means of transport, a way of gettin' from A to B. I always felt they were so colourful and, the noise they made, to me it was all part of the atmosphere – the colour and the noise, that made London special. I knew that the 'writin' had been on the wall' for a long time. London transport had long since made their intentions clear, to replace all tram services with buses which they saw as a more modern, attractive and flexible form of transport. Because they ran on fixed rails, the trams were blamed for bein' the main cause of increasin' traffic congestion but I think gettin' rid of 'em had more to do with money. Even I'd have to admit that the tram network and infrastructure was gettin' old and probably needed some updatin' and London Transport weren't prepared to spend the money. Buyin' extra buses would be cheaper. 'Last Tram Week' was actually in July 1952, but, as I recall, many of London's tram services had ceased even before I went in the army.

Fortunately, under the terms of National Service they'd have to keep my job open at the stockbrokers and, because I was popular, even the Star & Garter agreed to keep my spot open provided I could wangle gettin' back to London to play every Saturday. As luck would have it, Joe West, who if you remember was our 'front man' and normally did the singin', was also a bit of a drummer himself, so he agreed to stand in on the odd occasions I just couldn't get back. When he wasn't performin', Joe would be dancin'. He was a real character was Joe and a bit of a showman. Mind you, whether he wanted to or not, Joe didn't get much chance to stray because his wife made a point of bein' there, keepin' a watchful eye.

Like it or not, now for me it was the army – I just wasn't lookin' forward to it at all. The soldierin', the discipline, the square bashin', it just wasn't me and I'd got two years of it to get through, and that's if I was lucky, and didn't end up bein' sent out to fight in Korea! As it turned out, lady luck and my musical ability would save me from all that, as you'll find out as my story unfolds.

At this point, I should explain that in the post war years all young men were obliged to do National Service unless medically unfit. In view of my medical history, I had high hopes of bein' excused and on the day of my medical I did rather get the violins out. I had to go to Blackheath (East London) and my medical was goin' surprisingly well – too well for my likin', until I was asked if I had ever had any broken bones. That was my cue. I started off by tellin' him the story of 'Billy Bunter' and my arm and seized the opportunity to follow that up with my asthma and bronchial pneumonia and actually dyin' in hospital. I was doin' a good job 'cos I could see concern written all over the young doctor's face and I can well recall him sayin, "I'm afraid this isn't lookin' good. I just need to have a word with my colleagues about you." Now I had three white coats standin' starin' at me. Maybe I shouldn't have smiled 'cos the most senior of them – by age anyway – suddenly pipes up, "What a remarkable recovery you've made," and without another word stamped my papers A1! And that was it. Like it or not, I was in.

I was a bit shell-shocked, but it was no good protestin'. To lessen the blow, I'd actually asked if I could go into the Royal Artillery Band to do my National Service, but I was told no, that was only for regulars. If I wanted to join an army band, I'd have to join up and I wasn't goin' to do that. If I'd known what it could have been like, I might have done. If I'd had the benefit of Victor's experience – but that's all in the future. You'll come to know Victor later.

For now there was nothin' for it but to go home and carry on as normal at work until the date came through for my call up. They gave you a couple of weeks' notice to tidy up your affairs and the day before my start date I went to work as usual to say goodbye and to have lunch with a few friends. The weather didn't do much to lift my spirits – it was pourin' with rain.

Me on the roof of No 9 Basinghall Street, the offices of Newson-Smith, Stockbrokers. Notice the dome of St Paul's behind me and the 'obligatory cigarette' in my hand. Probably taken in 1952, just before I left to go in the army.

Me aged about 16 standin' with friend Pat in Wix's Lane, off Lavender Hill. I've got my 'weekend' tweed suit on. For work I'd wear blue serge and grey alternately.

I was fishin' mad. Here I'm tryin' my luck on the Wey Navigation Canal near Weighbridge. I've still got that rod!

The Star & Garter on the banks of the Thames at Putney.

My publicity 'photo shoot' taken for the Star & Garter. It was considered 'cool' and grown-up to smoke. I was 18.

Olga's wedding group photo. The groom, Vic Griffiths, became Pro Vice Chancellor of Surrey University. Aunt Raithby is on the extreme right. Joan and Gracie were bridesmaids.

Dinky, our beloved cat, lyin' on the 'coal box' on the upstairs balcony of 15A Gambetta Street.

CHAPTER 6

I'm In The Army Now!

Originally, I'd thought, if I've got to do military service, I might as well make the best of it and apply for the artillery band, but as I've told you, that turned out to be a forlorn hope. I was turned down flat because they only took regular soldiers. Instead I was bein' sent to Deepcut Camp – part of Blackdown Base. It was, and still is, renowned for bein' 'a hard camp'. To say the least, I wasn't lookin' forward to it.

Come the day, the 4th March 1952, dad was pretty cut up about me goin' in the Army, which was a bit odd bearin' in mind it seemed to me that he'd practically forced our Roy to join up as a regular. Maybe he thought I was different and not cut out for it. Anyway, he pushed a ten bob note into my pocket – which again was very out of character. I protested 'cos, as you know, I'd got money of my own, but he said, "You never know when you might need it, son" and gave me a hug and sent me on my way. Gettin' a hug from dad – that was practically another first. Mum of course was still in hospital, so now I was leavin' him on his own. It wasn't like dad to show me emotion, but maybe with me goin' as well, he was feelin' the loss a bit himself.

I set off with my wooden case – if you remember it was the one I'd made at night school – and took the train from Bank Street direct to Waterloo – no stops. At Waterloo there were quite a few youngsters gatherin', all around 18 – like me. Some very tired, some a bit tearful even. Some had travelled all night and for some who'd come from backwater country locations, even the city was a bit dauntin', never mind the prospect of the barracks themselves. Trepidation or no trepidation, we all piled onto the train which took us to Brookwood Station (best known for its race track) where an army lorry was waitin' for us. As we walked up to it a voice came from the passenger side, "Hello Jack," and I thought, "Blimey – somebody knows my name." It was a bloke from Battersea – one of the greengrocer's sons. As it turned out though, it was what you might call a 'brief encounter' because despite presumably bein' based at the same camp, our paths never crossed again.

The back of this lorry was open and we all had to pile in like cattle and sit squashed up on benches facin' one another. We were all white as sheets and nervous and nobody spoke on the way to the barracks. On arrival the day that greeted us reflected how we felt – awful – cold and wet. Once inside the camp, our misgivin's started to be confirmed. From then on, we were never asked to do anythin' – we were told, and in no uncertain terms. We were in the army now and we were goin' to have to get used to bein' yelled at. They didn't waste any time gettin' us kitted out, lined up and marchin'. At 5.30pm, we were given a meal in the cookhouse. It was truly disgustin'. My worst meal ever! Cold bubble and squeak with a cold shop-bought excuse for a meat pie. As I was to discover, army food wasn't all that great but it was never nearly as bad as that first meal. I can't fathom why they made it so bad. Maybe it was the way they liked to 'welcome' conscripts and things would have been different if we'd signed on. Mind you, on that first night, nobody was all that hungry anyway – we were all too traumatised to eat.

After, we were marched off to our barracks – about 40 to a block. Our first introduction to what accommodation army style was goin' to be like – another real eye opener. They were two storey brick built blocks, but very austere, very impersonal and cold, in every sense of the word. We each had a bed, a locker and a small piece of carpet. Collectively they were your bed space and, as we were quickly to discover, woe betide you if you didn't keep it clean, neat and tidy. When I say 'neat and tidy' I don't just mean any 'neat and tidy,' I mean neat and tidy army style which meant every bed had to be done the same – exactly the same. We had inspections every mornin' and so every mornin' your bed had to be 'squared up' just so. Blankets and sheets had to be folded perfectly square with pillows on top. It took ages to get it 'just so' but, woe betide you if it wasn't.

We were each given the rank of Private and a nominal role generally dependent on what we'd been doin' in civvy street. I was put down as a clerk. We were given a load of kit and, seein' it on the bed I remember thinkin', "What am I goin' to do with this lot when I want to go to sleep?" As it turned out, the locker was more spacious than it looked. On that first day, it was made very clear to us that we had to make our beds up in that very particular way, with our blankets 'boxed', and our beret placed on top. Throughout my two years' service I never did get the hang of it properly – but always just good enough to get away with it. The beret on top bit did prove useful though – for hidin' stuff you didn't want the officers to see.

Along with about twenty others, my bedspace was on the top floor. They say heat rises but then again, there has to be some heat to rise and on that cold wet day there was none. There was a fireplace at one end, but on that first day, nothin' to make a fire with. I remember that first night seemed particularly cold, damp and miserable. Later we were issued one bucket of coal per floor, but that one bucket had to last all week, so most of the time, bein' March, it was freezin' in those barrack blocks. As I was sayin', on that first night it seemed especially cold and miserable and this one young chap wanted to phone his mum, but I guess he'd got more chance of flyin' to the moon! Bein' our first night, we weren't even allowed to go up to the NAAFI for a drink to drown our sorrows. I guess they didn't want any abscondin', but it made us feel like prisoners in a concentration camp. In case you don't know, NAAFI stands for Navy, Army, Airforce Institution. It's the one thing that every service camp has in common. We did get entertainment though! Ok, I'm just jokin'. This chap arrived and proceeded to demonstrate how precisely we were expected to iron our shirts and trousers. 'Entertainment' over, it was lights out at 10 pm and some of the blokes went out like a light – mind you the Scottish lads had been up for over 24 hours. Despite the cold, the less than comfy bed and no Dinky to keep me company, I did eventually get to sleep.

At 6 am we were woken by the Sergeant's shouts of "Wakey, wakey". It was still darn cold. With barely enough time to drag some clothes on, it was down to the toilet block for a shave. One bloke said, "But I don't shave, sergeant", to which he got a dirty look and a, "Well, you do now!" Razors were provided, but you had to buy blades. The first six to the basins were the lucky ones – they got a bit of hot water. The rest of us had to make do with cold. Once a month – and really, I'm not kiddin' – once a month, we were marched down to the ablutions block for a shower. We were herded in like prisoners – all together. Luke warm they were. But I'm gettin' ahead of myself again 'cos I need to tell you what happened on the mornin' of day two. Bed space inspections over, we were all given a sheet of brown paper and some string and told to parcel up all our civvy clothes so they could be sent back home. We were in the army now and not allowed any civvies. Fortunately I had the presence of mind to keep back my wooden 'suitcase' – you know, the one I'd made at night school – 'cos that was goin' to come in handy later.

After a few days, some of us at least were beginnin' to get used to the routine, well some of it, and not let all the shoutin' and bawlin' of 'orders' get to us. For many more – in the beginnin' it was difficult to say the least. A rude awakenin' so different to anythin' they'd ever experienced before. Compared to most of 'em, I suppose you could say I had it easy, because in some ways I was already 'an old soldier'. A lot of 'em had never been away from home, ever, and they were really feelin' it, especially the normally quiet, shy retirin' types. Me, on the other hand, I'd been fostered out, passed from pillar to post as an evacuee, endin' up with Ma Wickens where, as one of 13, I'd learnt the value of camaraderie, of stickin' together, of lookin' out for one-another and then of course I'd been a member of the CLB, used to goin' away with the lads on camp, used to havin' a uniform to take care of. Ok, the army was different – 'course it was, but maybe not so very different for me as for many of my fellow conscripts.

I didn't have really long hair, but as you can see from my 'poster photo' at the Star & Garter, it was long by army standards. I'd heard that if you turned up as a conscript with long hair, then they made a point of cuttin' it really short and I didn't want that, so I thought I'd outwit 'em and took myself off to the barbers the week before D Day. Not the Normandy Landin'. For me, my D Day was the day I was due at the barracks. Sure enough, on about the fourth day we were all marched down to the camp barbers. Thinkin' about it now, I'm surprised it wasn't sooner, but anyway, we get there and I pipes up, "I don't think I need mine doin'sir. I only had it done last week", to which I got a sharp reply, "Well, you're a very lucky lad then, aren't you? 'cos you're goin' to have it done this week as well." And I did, but I was shorn no more nor no less than everybody else. We all had the same, more or less crew cut – less chance of lice I suppose, but at least it was easy to manage, which, as well as enforced conformity, was probably the point. Discipline, conformity, obedience, routine – that would be more or less it really – my assessment of army life in those early days.

Speakin' of routine, as well as lookin' after our bed space, another part of our daily routine was boot polishin'. Every night we'd have to polish our boots 'till they shone. It really was a case of spit and polish to get the – I nearly said 'desired effect' but 'required effect' would be a truer description. As with everthin' else, like it or not, we soon learned to toe the line. We were conscripts, we weren't regulars who'd chosen the army as a career, but that made no difference. They made no allowances for whether we were cut out for it or not. Step out of line and you'd be a marked man. They'd make a point of breakin' you. The idea wasn't to think for yourself but to do exactly what you were told, when you were told, no questions asked. It wasn't just boots we had to polish. We had a thing called a 'bumper' to polish the wooden floor with. It was a weighty metal thing with a pad on the bottom and a broomstick type handle. If the officers decided it wasn't good enough, they might make us spruce it up with our boot brushes as a form of punishment.

In case you're wonderin', Deepcut is 'near' Wokin', but in truth the camp itself is miles from anywhere. My band job at the Star & Garter was bein' kept open for me on Saturday nights, so I needed to work out a way of bein' sure to get there. As you know, I've always kept my eyes and ears wide open. I knew I needed to get to Brookwood Station for the train to London and I quickly sussed out that the bus turned round at the camp more or less on the hour. Trouble was, when the first weekend came they said – no passes for us new recruits and even I hadn't had time to work a way around that. But I had sussed that anybody who was anybody disappeared on a Friday night and I realised we new recruits were left pretty much to our own devices with just a skeleton staff of officers.

That first week was pretty miserable for all of us new recruits – even me. We were like fish out of water, but at least we were all in the same boat – or at least most of us were. For some conscripts though, it was worse and it never really got any better – the so-called deferred conscripts. Most of us were 18 with no ties, but they were older, 21, some married and some with kids. Usually they'd have been deferred to allow them to complete apprenticeships and that kind of thing, but somehow, bein' that much older and often with ties and responsibilities, they just didn't fit in. They never really gelled with the rest of us. For us youngsters there was the makin's of camaraderie. We could make the best of a difficult situation. For the married chaps, especially those with kids, their lives were on hold and with the enforced separation, relations with home often became strained. For them, those two years must have seemed like an eternity. But there I go again, gettin' way ahead of myself. We're only just into our second week, havin' endured that first enforced weekend on camp.

One afternoon durin' our second week, we all had to go and queue outside this hut. When I say all, I don't just mean our lot from our hut, there were loads of us. Bakin' hot it was. Once inside we were ordered to strip to the waist, still formin' an orderly line for the medics. It was 'inoculation day', eight or nine injections we got, all in the same arm and all while we were standin' up straight. Some of the blokes fainted, one or two even before they'd had any jabs. Just havin' to watch the blokes in front gettin' theirs was enough for them. One of the blokes just in front of me was one of 'em, and I and one of the other lads were told to "pick him up". No sympathy mind you, no givin' him chance to sit down for a minute to regain composure. I've no idea what they were all for. Nobody bothered to tell us. But then again, it's not like we were goin' to be given a choice. We were havin' em – all of 'em and that was that. I suppose it was considered to be part of our trainin'. You have to remember that the Korean War was on and once initial trainin' was over, you could be posted anywhere, even as conscripts – Korea included. It was just the luck of the draw.

Come the evenin' a lot of the blokes were moanin'. They wanted to have some aspirin for the pain, but there was none of that. All we got was floor polishin' duty. We had to get our boot brushes out and get on our hands and knees polishin' the whole bleedin' floor, with the 'officers' lordin' over us with their canes. When I say officers, I mean our two corporals. It was evenin' time and the real officers had long gone. I suppose the idea was to keep our arms active – to keep the circulation goin', stop the muscle seizin' up. I'm not sure it did any good and some of the lads who weren't feelin' that well practically conked out while we were doin' it.

The corporals got fed up after a bit and the minute they'd cleared off, despite 'orders' to the contrary, some of us thought, "blow this for a game of soldiers" and I for one got into bed. I knew I'd got a bar of chocolate stashed and I ate it under the sheets. I suppose you could say I was 'comfort eatin'. Pretty soon all of us opted for an early night and, as far as I know, the corporals left us alone.

Over the followin' few days that arm got really sore. Some suffered more than others, but one of those blessed injections caused trouble for nearly everyone – me included. I never did find out what it was for.

A while back, I mentioned the NAAFI and how we weren't allowed to go for the first few days. After that though, unless we were out on the range or some other exercise, we'd get a half hour break mornin' and afternoon and usually we'd go over to the NAAFI for a cuppa. NAAFI sandwiches we called 'wads' because they were thick slices of bread with nothin' much in em' but the sausage rolls were good. About 9 inches long and always very tasty so most days I'd have one. Army meals were free but anythin' we had in the NAAFI had to be paid for but the prices were Ok. Tea was tuppence a mug and the sausage rolls were five pence.

Somethin' else I mentioned was the cold. Ok, it was March so you wouldn't expect it to be warm, especially not at night, but it seemed un-naturally cold in that place. Yes, there was a fireplace at one end of our barrack room and yes we did get a bucket of coal a week but that was nowhere near enough. Even when it was lit, it only warmed one end and we quickly learnt it was more trouble than it was worth because it had to be cleaned out again ready for Officer's inspection in the mornin'.

When Saturday came around again – our second weekend at the camp – pass or no pass – I'd already made up my mind I was goin'. I couldn't expect them to keep my Saturday night spot open if I didn't show up again. And then there was dad. I was worried about how he'd be copin' all on his own. And then there was mum. After visitin' her twice a week for so long, now it was a fortnight since I'd seen her. I wasn't sure if she'd really understand why or how she'd be takin' it. Just after lunch we normally had some free time and most of us were in our barracks – sittin' on beds chattin'. I was already thinkin' about takin' myself off for the bus when there were these loud footsteps at the door and our duty sergeant shouts out, "Ok you lot. Grab yer knives and forks. You're all on cookhouse duty this weekend." I thought, "No way," and I jumped backwards into my locker and pulled the door to. Some of the lads must've seen me, but thankfully the sergeant didn't and nobody gave me away.

I waited 5, maybe 10 minutes 'till they'd all gone and I was pretty sure the coast was clear. Now all I had to do was get myself onto that bloomin' bus. It would be the first time I'd be outside the barracks with my army uniform on and I was pretty nervous – not least of bein' picked up by the red caps (military police), who I knew were always on the lookout for absconders. I'd seen them loads of times when back in civvy street, but this would be the first time I'd be a potential target. I figured if I carried my wooden case it would make me look more credible. Whether it did or not I've no idea, but it gave me somethin' to do with my hands and made me feel more confident, which was important, I can tell you. So, the first hurdle - to get myself onto that bus. Trouble was to get there I had to walk right past the cookhouse. It was a hot day so the windows were open and I could hear the banter from inside. Needless to say, some of the lads saw me …. "Bloody hell, Jack's only goin' to get that bus!" I just kept my head down and somebody up there must've been watchin' over me 'cos I caught that bus. I was sweatin' like a pig as it pulled out, I can tell you, and not just 'cos it was such a hot day.

From Brookwood Station I caught the train to take me up to Waterloo. Whilst I was growin' in confidence, I didn't want to risk runnin' the gauntlet of the red caps at Waterloo. I knew it would be crawlin' with 'em. I'd seen them there loads of times. I didn't want them stoppin' me and askin' to see my pass – 'cos of course I was AWOL! So I was crafty. I got off at Surbiton and then caught the slow train direct to Clapham Junction. No red caps – no problem. Just the bus home now and a nice surprise for dad.

That evenin' I had a meal with dad then got washed and changed into my dress suit and went off to the Star & Garter to earn myself a few quid. After two weeks in the army, it felt great to be in my posh civvies again and doin' what I loved best. For me it was never really so much about the money – not that it didn't come in handy – rather it was about indulgin' my passion for music and the buzz of bein' on stage entertainin' folk. I was never more alive than when up there on that stage. We were always busy, but bein' just down the road from the Hammersmith Palais we'd often get their overspill on top and then we'd be really heavin'. It was a boy meets girl sort of place. Right by the Thames – where the boat race starts. Lovely buildin'. If you remember, there was a picture of it at the end of Chapter 5. It's still there if you want to go and see it.

Next day, Sunday, dad and I had an early lunch as usual and went off to the hospital together to see mum – somethin' we would do every Sunday whilst I was in the army, except for the odd occasions when I was on tour and just too far away to get back. My bein' away sometimes will become clear later. The lads back at camp knew about my job at the Star & Garter. If I were honest, I suppose I bragged a bit about that, but I kept mum's plight and the weekly visits I made with dad to see her to myself. All through my army career dad coped pretty well on his own, but I know he valued my weekly visits and especially that I always went with him to see mum. If truth be known, I think we needed each other's support, especially when mum was really low and didn't even seem to recognise us or acknowledge our presence. They were the really bad times.

That second weekend I got back to camp on Sunday without a hitch and fortunately I didn't need to keep goin' AWOL after that 'cos we could usually get weekend passes. As for the camp itself though – it was a pretty horrible place, I can tell you – full of thieves and rogues, mostly from Peckham in London. They were supposed to be trainers, but if you ask me, really most of 'em were just bullies and low lives.

You know the sayin', "It takes all sorts ...." well it was no different in the army, and particularly in those first few weeks. There was pressure. You could feel it. You have to remember we were a real mixture, a motley assortment of unwillin' youth, wary of one another, there by Government decree, not by choice. We weren't volunteers. We hadn't joined up – we were conscripts and at first it seemed a bit like prisoners, held against our will. We were a cocktail of disgruntled young men, some undoubtedly frightened, some puttin' on a show at least of bravado and, as in life I guess, in every barrack block, there were a few bully boys waitin' to emerge and, given half chance, seekin' to dominate the rest. Some were quick to temper – always burnin' on a short fuse, you might say. They were the ones to be wary of.

I'm tryin' to give you a flavour of the atmosphere I encountered in those early days and, recognisin' it, I quickly realised it didn't do to make enemies in that isolated world of disgruntled young men. It was no good thinkin' of relyin' on the officers to help you out. The lower ranks, the NCO's who more or less ran our daily lives, were the biggest bully boys of all. In that environment it was much better to rub along with whoever rather than rub against the grain. They wouldn't all be your type, but as I say, better to go with the flow or even better still, create the flow as I learned to do, usually with a bit of humour. Nothin' like a laugh and a joke, especially when the atmosphere needed calmin' down a bit or when some of the blokes were really down and needed a bit of cheerin' up. You had to have a positive outlook, put a positive spin on things. That's how you got by. It was no good bein' miserable and feelin' sorry for yourself. That way, you'd go to Hell and back long before your 2 years were up.

Some of 'em had sweethearts. Some of 'em were married, some had kids even and responsibilities they felt they were bein' forced to neglect. For them it was the worst. By comparison I was footloose and fancy-free. I had my music. Back then, that was my love affair. I was lucky and I knew it. What's more, as I've told you, my Saturday night spot at the Star & Garter was bein' kept open for me so long as I could get there. Was that important to me, you bet it was, but in between, I wasn't pinin' for it all the while. It wasn't quite that kind of love affair but I was determined not to lose it. And that stroke of luck, that bit of guile, presence of mind, intuition – call it what you will – that got me away that first time whilst everybody else was stuck at camp doin' kitchen duties. That gave me a bit of a reputation, a bit of kudos to build on and I wasn't goin' to let that slip. From then on you could say I never looked back. I had it made. I wasn't 'Little Jack', the youngest and probably most vulnerable evacuee forced by circumstance to be away from home amongst strangers in Ardingly. Like it or not, I was in the army now, but compared to most, I was Ok. I was 'Jack the Lad'.

You often hear it said – leastways you used to – that "the army will make a man of him" and doubtless for some at least that was probably true. But for some conscripts, those first few weeks were just a portent of what was to come. For them those two years must have been pure hell. They just weren't cut out for army life at all and to make matters worse, they were the ones who usually got picked on.

In our intake, as I suppose you might expect, we had 'em all – from the would-be 'hard nuts' to the real softees who wouldn't say 'boo to a goose'. Scots, now they can be hard drinkin' hard nuts, but we had two from the other end of the spectrum. Right from the off they were very homesick and you could hear 'em cryin' in the night. Then there was another young chap, Rose I think his name was – from Kensington – very well to do, spoke with a plum in his mouth, but a bit backward. Sadly, it was the likes of those three that got picked on right from the start – sometimes by the other recruits, but more pointedly by our so-called officers in charge. NCO's they were – a corporal and a lance corporal who lived in our hut, but in separate quarters at one end, separate from the rabble they might say. In reality, most of the time just a pair of bully boys, abusin' their so-called rank. We'd have regular kit inspections and those three never seemed to get it right. Not to the satisfaction of our so-called officers at any rate. They carried these canes and they wrought havoc with 'em. Kit had to be folded and displayed on our beds in a certain way. One tiny thing out of place or folded or facin' the wrong way and that was their cue to send the whole lot flyin' in all directions, includin' out of the window if they felt like it, underpants and all.

Our rifles too, they had to be cleaned and positioned just so. I did that. You were in trouble otherwise, but I had no interest at all in firin' the thing. We had these 'pull-throughs' to clear and keep the barrel clean, but there were never enough of 'em to go round. Rose, bein' a bit simple, was an easy target. They'd pick his rifle up, look down the barrel and give him what for for havin' a bird's nest down it. The poor bloke took them literally and takin' it back off 'em and lookin' down it would declare he couldn't see any bird's nest. Now for starters, the rest of us knew better than to take your gun back without it bein' offered to you, so all round he was for the high jump, which was a shame because he never really understood what was what.

Another time we were all lined up by our beds waitin' for the officers to walk in and start their inspection and Rose decides he needs the toilet. As you know, we had a toilet block where we washed and shaved in a mornin' but there were also toilets in the barrack block, one on each floor. In all the silence and with the officers now present you could hear him in there and then the toilet flushin'. Only Rose would be daft enough to come out with his braces hangin' down, all dishevelled, lookin' like he'd just got out of bed, when an inspection was under way. They just took one look at him and told him to get back in there out of their sight and lock himself in and stay there. Meanwhile his kit got flung everywhere as per usual. You couldn't help but feel sorry for him. Havin' said that, I'm sorry to say that we left him in there for ages after inspection was over before eventually we went and let him out. I'm afraid that, to some extent, it was a case of, if it was him gettin' picked on, it wasn't you, and most of us were content to keep our heads down. Stickin' your head up above the parapet too often to stand up for the likes of Rose might pretty soon make you the next target.

In the army your most prized possessions are your knife and fork and your mug. Not a tin mug as you might think, but a china one. I'm sayin' China, but it was more 'pot' really, but the point is it was breakable. If ever anybody dropped theirs, everybody always cheered! That happened right through my army career. If for any reason you lost your knife or fork, it was generally a case of pinchin' somebody else's. Not very nice, I know, but everybody did it. A case of 'dog eat dog' I guess.

Our initial trainin' at Blackdown lasted about 12 weeks – twice as long as normal. It was extended 'cos our platoon wasn't considered to be up to scratch. I can't speak for the others, but I'd have to admit that I was pretty rubbish, but that's 'cos I had absolutely no interest in it whatsoever. Havin' said that, when our scheduled 6 weeks were up, I was as gutted as anyone to find it was bein' extended. Truth be told, we were all lookin' forward to bein' posted out of that place.

I mentioned that some of the so-called 'trainin' officers' were rogues. Well, this particular day when we were due to go off to the firin' range, we were told to put our best boots at the foot of our beds for inspection. I thought it was a bit strange 'cos normally we were present for kit inspections, not least so we could get a bollockin' for any faults, however minor. Anyway, when we got back my boots were gone. I was genuinely proud of those boots. I'd put a lot of time into them so they shone like mirrors and were practically as soft as carpet slippers when I put 'em on. It sounds daft, but I loved those boots. Those so called 'officers' had taken the best ones.

I hadn't done anythin' but of course it was me for the high jump. I had to go on orders in front of the Commandin' Officer and I got 3 days CB (confined to barracks) for losin' my boots through negligence. Every 3 hours, durin' daytime, I had to present myself at the guardhouse for inspection. You have to remember that I was only 18 and these guys were just a load of bullies abusin' their rank. To make matters worse, my 3 days included Saturday, so there was no way I could get out of the camp to play at the Star & Garter that weekend or go to see mum.

As it happened, the duty officer for that particular weekend was a Warrant Officer whose name escapes me, which is unfortunate because it turns out he was a decent chap. Seein' me, he asked, "So why are you here at the weekend sonny? What have you been up to?" I knew he was what you might call 'old school' so I took a chance and told him the truth, to which he said, "I don't like the sound of that at all. Leave it with me. I'll look into it and you go and get yourself a new pair from the stores on Monday. Tell them I sent you." Like I said – a decent chap. Proper Old School.

Don't think I was the only one to suffer – there were loads of incidents, especially of stuff goin' missin'. For instance, a Welsh lad brought a transistor radio back one weekend. It didn't last a day in the barracks before it 'disappeared'.

Thankfully, after our 12 weeks of trainin', in June 1952, the 24th to be precise, we were transferred to Bicester to join 16th Company. It was only about 50 miles as the crow flies, but bein' the army they sent us all round the houses to get there. We went by train to Eastleigh near Southampton, then changed to go up to Oxford, and then changed again to go to Bicester and then a lorry there to pick us up to take us to the barracks about 5 miles away.

It was a massive camp, 'home' to four different companies and, as usual, in the middle of nowhere. It was no picnic, but better than Blackdown. There was even a bit of on-site entertainment, but we had to go up to 4th Company for that. Mostly it was the prospect of 36- or 48-hour passes that offered respite. They either ran from 12 noon on Friday or 12 noon on Saturday to midnight on Sunday. Usually we'd be able to get away after a midday parade. So you see, it wasn't all bad, and talkin' of good things, one bit of good news filtered through not long after I was transferred – that old school

Warrant Officer had been true to his word. Apparently he'd laid a trap and a sergeant and a corporal whose names I'd best not mention, but both from Peckham, were caught stealin' from recruits and hauled over the coals and sent to the army prison at Shepton Mallet. I never did get my own boots back, but I did at least get some satisfaction on hearin' that.

In the '50s Bicester Camp comprised a whole series of Nissen type huts – big half-round corrugated metal things. We were billeted in them and we worked in them. As it turned out, my experience of workin' for a firm of stockbrokers was to make this part of my army career a much more cushy number than it might otherwise have been. They thought that because I'd worked in the Stock Exchange then I must be a bright young thing. Wrong! – but then again, I wasn't goin' to disillusion them. So, havin' arrived at Bicester, in effect I was put with the 'elite' and billeted in the HQ Hut. We all worked in the Camp Offices, but really makin' me a clerk was a big mistake because I'd never been a clerk in my life. They thought because I'd worked at the Stock Exchange in an office, I must be the right material, but I wasn't at all. Bein' a clerk in an office just wasn't me, but it was a much cushier number than regular soldierin' or workin' down the Depot. Lookin' back, it was one more reason to thank my lucky stars for bein' put with such a wonderful foster mum as Aunt Raithby. After all, if it hadn't been for the helpin' hand her sister's daughter, Katie had given me, I'd never have landed that job at the stockbrokers, never in a million years, and then my army career might have been a very different story. Don't misunderstand me though – it wasn't all that cushy – it was still the army. It wasn't civvy street.

Army life revolves around routine – which didn't really suit me. The day would start at 6.45 am with 'reveille '. Basically, a bugler givin' us a wake-up call. Most of the lads would be up and off to the ablution block and then to breakfast before the first compulsory action of the day – we had to be on parade at 8 am – no excuses. As for me – often as not when reveille sounded, I'd pull the blanket over my head and try to get another half hour in. Bein' only 18, I could get away with shavin' every other day and I didn't always fancy breakfast. All the huts used as sleepin' quarters had a fireplace in them and stacked up beside it was a big pile of metal bowls – shiny aluminium. Quite nice things really. Anyway, the idea was that you picked up a bowl and took it down to the ablutions block for a wash. The ablutions block had toilets and taps but no showers.

This particular mornin' about a month into my time at Bicester, I started the day by sayin', "Won't somebody go out and shoot that bleedin' bugler!" or words to that effect. Rather than gettin' myself up and out of bed, I rolled over and said to one of my mates – "Do us a favour. Bring me a bowl of water back with you." Sure enough he did and so havin' grabbed a few extra minutes kip I was able to have a quick wash in our hut. Finishin' up I just kicked open the door and threw the bowl of water out. BIG mistake. Water takes a bit of time to travel through the air before it lands. A split second really – but time enough for me to have regrets – yet powerless to intervene in its trajectory. My bowl of water spread itself out – shimmerin' – before drenchin' the Regimental Sergeant Major. I could see it happenin' but there was no way I could stop it. For once in my life I was rendered speechless. Standin' there in the doorway open-mouthed whilst the Regimental Sergeant Major looked first at me, then down at his soakin' clothes, then back at me. The look on his face told me he wasn't best pleased – to put it mildly – but he didn't 'lose his rag'. In fact he was quite calm as he ordered me to "go and stand outside his office – now!"

With that, he turned his bike around and went back whence he came. Unbeknown to me, until that day that is, the RSM was in the habit of takin' a shortcut on his bike from his married quarters, through the gap in the hedge close to our hut and on to his office across the camp. Just my luck for him to choose that particular moment to be passin' by our door.

As you can imagine, the rest of the lads thought it was hilarious, but equally, they were all agreed that I was really for the high jump this time. I was a cocky so-and-so, used to gettin' in and out of scrapes, but even I wasn't goin' to get away with drenchin' the Regimental Sergeant Major. Standin' outside the RSM's office I had plenty of time to reflect and just so you get the picture, outside his office really was outside – in full view of the camp. This was no office block with corridors – it was a corrugated nissen hut like all the rest. As I say, I had plenty of time to reflect. Ok, it was a freak accident, but I should never have been washin' there in the first place and the RSM of all people. They might even view it as assaultin' an officer – a really serious offence with 'heaven knows what' consequences.

As it turned out, lady luck hadn't deserted me altogether because when the RSM returned about three quarters of an hour later he just said, "You'd better get yourself inside sonny or you'll get wet!" It had just started to rain and if he'd been the vindictive sort he could have kept me standin' out there in the pourin' rain. Me havin' soaked him, it would have been understandable, but he didn't. He wasn't goin' to let me off the hook altogether though. He kept me standin' in his office in silence 'till midday. I was burstin' to apologise and to try to explain, but you have to remember in the army you don't speak to an officer unless you're spoken to. You can't just start up a conversation. So for me – more time to reflect – lots of it and all the time feelin' more than a little uncomfortable.

There I was, this 18-year old, still wet behind the ears, ponderin' what this war veteran had in store for me. The RSM was 50 years plus, 'old school', strict, but, as it turns out, fair. By noon he decided he'd had enough of me clutterin' up his office and he packed me off with a flea in my ear but no further disciplinary action. Lucky or what?

That night, back in the billet, there was disbelief that I'd got away with it. Somehow I had and, as you can imagine, the whole episode didn't do my reputation amongst the lads any harm either. I was already known for my duckin' and divin' and narrow squeaks and somehow comin' out smellin' of roses – but this was somethin' else. The consensus was that when the RSM had got home to change, his wife must have burst out laughin' and made him see the funny side of it. Whatever the case, I was probably the first and last private in the British Army to throw a bowl of used washin' water over a Regimental Sergeant Major. To have got away with just a stern tickin' off was more than lucky. I even got a bit of celebrity status from it. As you can imagine, that kind of news spreads through the camp like wildfire. Mind you, I got a few jibes as well, such as, "Don't stand too near Jack – he has a habit of throwin' water over yer", or, "Is it true yer goin' into the movie business Jack – followin' in the footsteps of Charlie Chaplin". The cute ones amongst you will have noticed I was back to bein' Jack in the army. Well, for starters, it fitted the image I was tryin' to cultivate in there – 'Jack the lad.'

*

I mentioned earlier that the army day proper started with parade at 8 am. Occasionally, the Regimental Sergeant Major would take parade

– usually if he had some important announcement or other to make. Most often though, he'd skip parade and go straight to his office and parade would be taken by Warrant Officer Steer. He was Ok, but he used to try to give us new recruits a bit of a hard time. He'd go on about how useless we all were, especially when we didn't all get to attention at the same time. He was probably right. We probably were a bit useless – but then most of us didn't see ourselves as career soldiers. We were just tryin' to make the best of our compulsory National Service. As I've told you, at the time, there was trouble kickin' off in Korea and W.O. Steer was fond of threatenin' to get the lot of us sent off to Korea if we didn't shape up. Company Orders were posted up on the notice board every night. It was your duty to make sure you read them to see what, if anythin', applied to you – no excuses. The funny thing was that one night when some of the lads and I went to check on Company Orders, who should be listed as bein' posted off to Korea – none other than W.O. Steer! We had a good laugh about that, but doubtless W.O. Steer didn't see the funny side of it, 'cos bein' posted off to Korea was no laughin' matter.

We'd been transferred to Bicester in June 1952 and towards the end of July I was told to go and stand outside Major Ward's office but, as was typical with the army, given no explanation as to why. Major Ward was the Company Adjutant. He more or less ran the place. I was a bit apprehensive, but I didn't think I was in any trouble – well, no more than usual - and as it turned out, I wasn't. Far from it. Once inside, rather than keep me standin' to attention, he told me to sit down. To start with I thought it must be bad news from home because mum was in hospital down at Epsom and dad wasn't all that well either. But, havin' sat me down all friendly like, he started sayin' he'd been goin' thro' my records. I thought he was goin' to tell me I'd have to come out of the offices because I wasn't up to scratch, but it wasn't that either. He produced a letter from Major Jarman, Director of Music, Ordnance, and went on to explain that he knew the major personally and that the letter was askin' for his help in locatin' a percussionist. "Now," he said, "I think you could be just the sort of chap he's lookin' for" ...... "am I right?" "You're dead right, Sir." ... I could hardly get the words out fast enough.

I was already beamin' from ear to ear when Major Ward announced he was goin' to give me a 3-day pass and followed it up by sayin' he didn't care what I did so long as I got myself down to

Hillsea Barracks in Portsmouth for the audition and came back and told him how I'd got on. So you see – far from bein' in trouble, Major Ward was handin' me a ticket to salvation. He told me to get my stuff together and be ready for 4pm and he'd order a tilley to take me to the station so I could catch the 5pm train. I caught the train, but only as far as London. I never went down to Hillsea Barracks that night at all. I went home first to check on dad and see how mum was. Thankfully, everythin' was alright, at least as alright as it could be, and I caught the mornin' train down to Portsmouth.

When I got to Hillsea they found me a bed in this particular barrack room and told me to be ready for an audition at 1 pm. No way was I goin' to mess up the chance to spend the rest of my army career playin' with the Ordnance Band – I was goin' to nail that audition. And I did. A chap called Pat Dimmock played the piano, somebody else played the saxophone and of course I played the drums. Remember the name – Pat Dimmock – because he was to become somethin' of an inspiration. He was big band mad and could play any instrument you threw at him. An amazin' bloke. He knew Johnny Dankworth, who, like Pat, also came from Walthamstow, North London. They used to knock about together as kids. Anyway, it turns out they already had a very good military band percussionist called Webb, but he couldn't do dance band work and the other one, a chap called Skinner, was leavin'. He'd done his time. I played about five or six numbers and I must have done Ok because the director of music told me there and then that they'd take me on but the band were just goin' off on tour and Skinner wasn't leavin' 'till October so I'd have to go back to Bicester 'till their tour was over and then they'd send for me to go and join the band down at Hillsea.

Back at Bicester, I couldn't wait to tell Major Ward the good news. The only downside was that I was goin' to have to wait until September to get started. Mind you, as things turned out, the intervenin' two months were pretty cushy. My success had made me somethin' of a celebrity. All the blokes were talkin' about me ….. "You know Jack's goin' into the military band." Even more amazin', suddenly, rather than bein' ordered about, I was bein' asked if I'd mind doin' this or that and, in particular "if I'd mind workin' in the Quartermaster's Store" lookin' after all the ammunition, etc. Would I mind! …… a cushy number if ever there was one. Much better than tryin' to be the clerk I wasn't, or 'soldierin' which definitely wasn't me.

The munitions depot was a good 20 minutes hike, but once up there I was my own boss. I'd had no trainin'. I'd no idea what I was doin' or what I was dishin' out. They didn't realise how unsafe they all were – leavin' me in charge. Fortunately, there were no real incidents. In fact everythin' went swimmin'ly. The only fly in the ointment was this warrant officer. We didn't seem to hit it off very well. I got the impression it was because he knew I was bein' posted off to join the Ordnance Band in Portsmouth. I don't know, but maybe he was a bit jealous. Whatever, I was surprised to say the least when one day he comes up to me and asks if I would do him a favour. "I've never told you," he said, "but I'm a pianist and I play at the REME Camp down the road (Royal Electrical Mechanical Engineers). Could you bring some of your drum kit back from London this weekend? We've got a dance next Friday and I'd like you to play with me." It turns out he was billeted at the REME Camp but worked in our camp as a Quartermaster, bein' excused other duties because of a condition which meant he couldn't wear boots! Anyway, come the Friday we played at this dance together and we both enjoyed it.

After that we got on well – not for long, mind you, because the followin' week I was off down to Portsmouth to join the band. I didn't see him again then for another eight months – until our band, the RAOC Staff Band (Royal Army Ordnance Corps Staff Band) came up to Bicester to play for a General's Inspection Parade of all Troops. That was a 3-day affair.

On the first day everyone is on parade and the General arrives to inspect the troops. Whilst he is walkin' round, we are playin' music – stuff like Greensleeves. The main inspection over, all the officers stand on a podium and the troops march past, hopefully in time, to us playin' a marchin' tune. Colonel Bogey was probably the troops' favourite.

The day before the main event, we'd usually do a 'dress rehearsal' so the troops would get used to marchin' to music. Normally they weren't too bad and would fairly quickly get the hang of it. Not always though and one particular day the Director of Music got really fed up because they just couldn't keep in step. Unusually for him, he lost his rag a bit and said, "Right, that's it. We're not playin' any more until you lot get it sorted. I'll just give you the drummer." I could have just tapped out a simple 'left-right, left-right' but I thought I'd just jazz it up a bit so I gave them a bit of Glen Miller. Picture it - there's me playin' solo and the rest of the band in hysterics. Now I should explain, the reason the lads are killin' themselves laughin' is 'cos here I am playin' the St Louis Blues March, which, as I say, is more or less a Glen Miller number. If you know your music, you'll know it's a bit swingy, which the troops liked, but it has an off beat in it which really threw them and at first had 'em practically trippin' over themselves. I'm not sure Major Jarman was quite so amused, but he let me get on with it and, unorthodox or not, the troops responded and within a few minutes they were marchin' okay more or less in time. Then Major Jarman got the whole band playin' some classic marchin' music and hey presto – they got it and next day, far from bein' a fiasco, the parade went just fine.

If I'd stopped to think about it, I suppose I'd been stickin' my neck out a bit playin' Glen Miller, but by this time I'd developed a good relationship with the Major. Other percussionists had let him down in the past and he'd already let me know that I was "a handy bloke to have around", I guess because I could play dance band music as well as all the military band stuff. I'd been lucky bein' posted to Bicester. For both Major Jarman and me it had been a case of right bloke, right place, right time.

It wasn't all military band stuff. Quite often, the day after the main parade, a few of us, usually 8 or 12, would play as a dance band, often at Officers' Mess do's. When they're all dressed up they look like proper gentlemen but, you know what they say - "looks can be deceptive". When their wives were present, generally there'd be a reasonable amount of decorum throughout the evenin'. When they were on their own, things would often be very different – especially once they'd got a few drinks inside 'em. Then it would be a much more raucous affair turnin' practically riotous at times and men gettin' stripped naked was not uncommon. For me, early on, seein' what went on was a real eye-opener. The really raucous do's were usually when men were bein' posted or new officers bein' 'welcomed' in. There were times when things got so out of hand that the Old Man called a halt, took us out and we just left them to it. More often, before things got that far, he'd take his leave and the Band Sergeant Major would take over. By the early hours, somethin' approachin' civility would be restored and breakfast would be served up to the officers at 1 am.

Whenever ladies were present, proceedin's would run more or less smoothly. We'd set up as a six-piece band playin' soft 'background' music whilst the officers and their wives were havin' their meal. As a drummer I'd be more or less caressin' the drums and cymbals with my brushes rather than tappin' out the beat. The ladies would retire whilst cigars and brandies were served and then, normally, they'd return and we'd set up in Dance Band format and play 'till maybe 1 am. Then breakfast would be served – not for us, but for them. Not a bad life in the army – for the officers that is. For the squaddies – well, that was quite a different story. Talk about chalk and cheese. Toil and privilege.

Some of the bigger camps had theatres – they were all called 'The Globe' and then we'd do a concert for all the troops. The officers still had the best of it, mind you, with all the front rows bein' easy chairs reserved for them and their wives. The first half of the concert would be fairly serious, military type stuff and in the second half we'd do Big Band numbers – all the latest stuff which always went down really well, especially with the troops. You have to bear in mind that the big bands like Glen Miller and his orchestra were the 'pop stars' of their day.

I remember it was October time the followin' year when I returned to Bicester with the Band. Rather cold it was, and at times more than a bit foggy. I still knew quite a few of the blokes there and I'd been lookin' forward to playin' for some of my old mates. You see they'd never actually heard me play. Generally they'd fared pretty well and some had even been made up to Sergeants. As a conscript, advancement up the ranks wasn't somethin' I gave any thought to, but amongst the regulars in the band I know it was a bit of a sore point. As a band member, the chances of advancement were much more limited than amongst the regulars generally.

Anyway, enough of that. I travelled the length and breadth of the country playin' with the RAOC band and enjoyed every minute of it. Some venues stick in the memory, like Longtown, which is near Gretna Green. The place itself was nothin' special – in fact it was a bit of a 'God-forsaken place', but I guess bein' near Gretna Green was a bit of a bonus. When 'on tour' we'd usually get time off to walk around and, as you can imagine, we took the chance to go into

Gretna Green and see the Old Blacksmith's Shop, which was, to say the least, an unusual, but world-famous weddin' venue. Mind you, we didn't have much luck findin' out a bit more about it other than what was written up. We might as well have landed on Mars. We could barely understand a word the locals said!

Back at the barracks I went up on stage before the rest of the band to make a few adjustments to my drum kit. There I was, mindin' my own business, when this squaddie starts whistlin' at me from the wings. "Hey mate ...... when's this bleedin' concert finish then? They're makin' us all come and tonight was my night off. There's only one girl in this place and it was my turn tonight!" You have to laugh, don't you – but, as I told him, there was nothin' I could do about it.

Anyway, we played the concert and as usual it seemed to go down a storm. After, there I am again on stage packin' up some of my gear when lo and behold there's this same squaddie back in the wings. "Psst – hey mate. I just wanted you to know that was bloomin' marvellous. I really enjoyed it. I wouldn't have missed it for the world." So there you go – that just goes to show that behind every cloud there's a silver linin'. Like the squaddie, you just have to be receptive to it. Better than sex though – now that really is an accolade. Mind you, no doubt his 'turn' would have come around again pretty soon, whereas it would be a long while before the band showed up again and when all's said and done, Longtown Barracks was right out in the sticks – they had nothin' in the way of entertainment up there. So I guess it's little wonder we went down a storm.

Another venue springs to mind, not so much for what happened, more for where it was. If you remember, when I was in the CLB a couple of times we went to summer camp on the Isle of Wight. My memories of it were idyllic, includin' long warm, sunny days. Amazingly, when tourin' with the Band, on one occasion we were sent to play on that very same campsite, except conditions couldn't have been more different. A battalion of boy soldiers were camped on the site and we were due to play for them in a big marquee set up for the purpose.

It was already rainin' when we got there, but then the heavens opened and it really started to rain. When I say rain, I mean persistent torrential rain, the like of which I'd never seen before or since. The marquee had duck-boards, but the water was flowin' in torrents under and over 'em. No way were we goin' to be able to play that evenin' and standin' around all night in this marquee wasn't my idea of fun, so I suggested we borrow some capes and take ourselves down to Sandown. I told 'em I'd been before as a kid and knew the way.

To be honest, there wasn't that much doin' in Sandown either, so we didn't stop long and headed back. The rain barely let up the whole night and it was cold with it. I can't remember gettin' any sleep at all. We just sat playin' cards. Come mornin' we weren't just tired, but chilled to the bone and not relishin' havin' to go and play in the church as arranged. The 'Old Man' had been tucked up in a hotel somewhere, but he could see the rest of us weren't in good shape and it was still pourin' and cold with it. A lorry arrived to transport our gear, but thankfully the Old Man pulled the plug on it and instead we were dispatched to the ferry to take us back to Portsmouth.

Once on board we headed for the bar and got stuck into the whiskies to try and warm us up a bit. Leastways that was the general idea. I never was one for drinkin' much, but these whiskies were goin' down a treat and did seem to create a bit of a warm inner glow. I guess I must have got a bit carried away because I can distinctly remember sayin' to Tommy Carter, a clarinet player and, as you'll learn, the 'money lender' in the band, "When's this damn thing goin' to get goin'?" The thing was, I might have had a warm inner glow, but I was still soakin' wet and perishin' cold. You could have knocked me over with a feather when Tommy grinned and said, "What do yer mean? We're just pullin' into Portsmouth Harbour." I hadn't realised we'd even set off! Mind you, I was mighty glad to find we were nearly back and it wouldn't be long before I could get into some warm dry clothes. Only trouble was, those whiskies might have numbed the cold a bit, but not bein' used to drinkin', I paid for 'em later.

Here I am givin' you a flavour of what happened when we went on tour and yet I haven't told you anythin' much about Hillsea and my time there, so I'd better put that right.

First off, Hillsea, unlike many barracks, wasn't in the middle of nowhere. It was in Portsmouth. It wasn't just a collection of nissen huts either. The billets were proper brick built affairs with toilets and washin' facilities. No more havin' to trek from one nissen hut to another in all weathers to get a wash and shave in cold water. As an added bonus it was near the sea. Best of all, it was the HQ for the RAOC military band – and I was one of two percussionists. It was as far removed from Deepcut as it's possible to imagine. Talk about landin' on my feet. It was paradise – at least it was to me.

A lot of the band members, includin' Major Jarman – the 'old man' – as he was affectionately known, were married and either lived in married quarters or in their own homes with their families in Portsmouth. Bein' a big naval base, a good few in the band were ex navy, havin' been in marine bands before and most had transferred so they could be with their families more. From a band of about 45 musicians, there were only eight single blokes plus two boy soldiers livin' in the barracks. When I say livin' in the barracks, I should explain we were actually on the perimeter and we could get in and out without enterin' the barracks proper at all. Our billet was a series of first floor rooms above the army dental centre. We had a sergeant who had his own room and the rest of us shared 3 or 4 to a room. The two boy soldiers – they would have been 15 or 16 – shared a room next to the sergeant where he could keep an eye on them. Boy soldiers in the band were more or less chaperoned – we all looked out for them. The regulars didn't get that sort of treatment, but the Band was like one big family. You really belonged – it was lovely.

One of the boy soldiers was a cornet player. His family lived in Portsmouth, so he would go home sometimes, but most of the time he preferred to live in the barracks with the rest of us. The other one – Nobby Clark his name was – played the tuba or euphonium as we used to call it. Years later Nobby became a Band Sergeant Major. Army life must have suited him 'cos he finished up doin' about 40 years service.

In case you're wonderin', we did get paid for doin' military service. The pay was rubbish compared to what I'd been gettin' at the stockbrokers, but at least we did get paid. Pay day was always Thursday afternoons about 2pm for us in the band. Young officers would do the handin' out, sat behind tables set up in the 'multi-purpose hall' at Hillsea. We'd have to form an orderly queue at a discreet distance. When it was our turn we'd march forward, arms swingin' stamp our feet, salute and shout out our roll number, In my case "22647453 Sir", and then hold out one hand with our pay book. Providin' all was well, the pay would be handed over and the book returned. We'd salute again, right turn and march out of the hall. All very ordered, all very military. Well, after all, conscripts or not, band or not, we were all in the army and that's how things were done.

As I've tried to explain, bein' a member of the RAOC Military Band was special. The work – if you could call band practice and playin' music and doin' concerts work – well it was special and so was the camaraderie and the banter that existed between us. I was popular with the lads, not least for my wicked sense of humour. I could always see the funny side of life and apparently had this knack of makin' funny things seem that bit funnier.

When stationed at HQ we had a decent social life too. Ok, it would have been better if I hadn't been goin' back to London every weekend to the Star & Garter on a Saturday and to go with dad to see mum on a Sunday. Even so, when we could, on a Friday night, four of us would go off to the Savoy Dance Hall in Portsmouth. Tommy Carter – the 'money lender' in the Band, always acted as our banker for the night. We'd give him 10/- each and he'd sort the whole thing out. We'd usually start by goin' down to the Rosemary Café for an evenin' meal – about a ten minute walk. It was a café by day, but transformed into a cosy little restaurant at night. An evenin' meal would cost about 2/6 and it made a change from army food back at the barracks. At about half seven we'd catch a bus to the Savoy Dance Hall and Tommy would pay our admission fees – about 3/6. When we arrived the House Band would be playin' and there'd be enough left in the kitty for a couple of drinks.

Friday night was 'radio night' which in those days was a live broadcast. The 'guest band' would play from around 8.45 'till 10.00 pm and then again from 11 – 1 am. When I say 'guest band' I should explain that we were treated to some of the really top notch bands – the likes of Joe Loss, Ted Heath, Cyril Stapleton, Jeff Love, Teddy Foster, Jack Parnell – the real stars of the day. I loved just standin' listenin' to them, but durin' the evenin' we'd split up and try our luck askin' the ladies for a dance. We'd always be in civvies, which, thinkin' back, was a bit of a disadvantage. Portsmouth bein' a naval base, there was always a big contingent of 'matelots' – sailors in uniform – to compete with us and, as the sayin' goes …….. "All the nice girls love a sailor!" All things considered though, we didn't do so badly, but for me at least it often didn't go beyond a few dances. I could never ask a girl out at the weekend because, as you know, I always went back to London. You couldn't blame them for thinkin' that was a bit odd and maybe they even thought I was just spinnin' them a line and really I was seein' some other girl or married even. Sometimes I'd get lucky though and she'd agree to go to the pictures with me on a weekday night.

We'd get our night out at the Savoy about once a fortnight and we'd make the most of it. The lads and I would generally be amongst the last to leave just after 1 am. The good thing was there were always special buses laid on. They were normal Corporation buses commissioned by the Savoy to take its patrons home. It was included in the admission price so it didn't matter if we were spent up by then. They'd take you more or less anywhere in Portsmouth for free. O' course if you were escortin' a girl home it might mean you'd have a long walk back to Hillsea afterwards, but then hopefully she'd be worth it.

Saturday mornin' was always band practice then just after mid-day I'd be on my way – hitch hikin' up to London. I'd put on an old battledress, that somehow I'd 'forgotten' to hand in when leavin' Bicester, for hitch-hikin. People would stop for a man in uniform. I've only got a couple of photos of me in the army and in both I'm in that battle dress, the reason bein' that I was just goin' off hitchikin' up to London when some of my mates called me back to be in a 'farewell' photo. Pete Gill, the guy on the far left, was goin' off to Mons for officer trainin' and the point was to get a group photo before he left. No prizes for guessin' that I'm the one with the snare drum. Pat Dimmock, who I've told you could play more or less any instrument, is on accordion behind me. Believe it or not, that's also me messin' about with Titch Cocker's trombone and, before you ask, no I couldn't play it. As usual, the photos are at the end of the chapter.

I used to carry that snare drum in a bag mum made specially plus a case full of cymbals to and from London every weekend. The rest of my kit was at the Star & Garter, but the snare and the cymbals were part of my kit for doin' more private jobs durin' the week down in Portsmouth. My hitchikin' journey would start with a fourpenny bus ride from just outside the barracks to Portsdown Hill. That was on the main London Road. I'd start walkin' and, whenever I heard a car comin', the thumb would come out. Sometimes the journey would take as much as 4 hours, but on a good day I could be in London in an hour and twenty minutes!

Hitch hikin' you met all kinds of people in all manner of transport. I'll just tell you about one because it was especially memorable. As I've said, wearin' my regulars' battledress uniform, I'd usually get a lift no problem, but this one particular Saturday I'd been stuck on the A3 near Petersfield for quite some time. There wasn't much traffic and what there was didn't seem keen to stop and I was gettin' desperate and thinkin' if I don't get a lift soon I'm goin' to be late for my spot at the Star & Garter. Then my prayers were answered and how! This Roller glides to a halt beside me and, as luck would have it, he was goin' all the way to Putney. I'm sayin' he. It was actually a couple, well to do, but very nice with it. I'd never been in a Roller before and to be honest I was a bit awe-struck. I think they must have been Lord and Lady somebody or other because they were clearly loaded and very well spoken, but they didn't say and I didn't like to ask. Whoever they were, they were takin' their own strawberries to the tennis. I guess even for them, Wimbledon strawberries were too much of a rip-off. As we glided along – 'cos that's what you do in a Roller – you glide, the smell of the ripe strawberries in this big basket beside me mingled with the smell of leather. That's not an everyday experience or one you forget in a hurry, especially since they didn't just let me smell 'em, they told me to help myself. That wasn't all. There was this drinks cabinet in the back with an open bottle of champagne and yes, you've guessed it, I was told to help myself to that as well. Of all the lifts I've ever had, that was the best. Talk about samplin' how the other half lived.

No matter what I was ridin' in or who I was ridin' with, folk always wanted to know why I was goin' up to London. Most thought I must be goin' up to see a girl, but curious why I was carryin' a snare drum. Typical of me, I'd get the old violin out and lay it on a bit thick. How army pay was a pittance and I was goin' up to London to earn a few bob playin' the drums. Hitch hikin' was fun and saved me about twelve and six a time dependin' on where I was dropped. This couple dropped me at the top of Putney Hill and I caught the bus from there, still smilin' at my stroke of luck. Sometimes I'd have to spend about another sixpence on bus fare to get me right home. But Portsmouth to central London for less than a shillin' – that can't be bad, can it?

Speakin' of London and stickin' with the theme of dances and chasin' after the fairer sex, durin' my first summer with the RAOC Band I had two weeks leave. Truth be told I enjoyed the life so much I could have skipped the leave, but anyway, nothin' for it but to go back to dad in London. As usual I hitchhiked wearin' my uniform. Hitchhike in civvies and you could stand there all day, but in uniform I'd usually get a lift in no time. How times have changed. Servicemen today would be just as likely to find themselves a target for terrorists. But there I go gettin' on my high horse and digressin' again. The point is, I was home and at a bit of a loose end, so I decided to go down to the Festival Gardens in Battersea Park.

As I've told you, the Gardens had been created in 1951 as part of the Festival of Britain Centenary celebrations but I hadn't had much time to enjoy 'em then. Some of the main attractions were still goin' strong in '53, includin' the funfair, the Vauxhall Beer Gardens and my favourite, the Dance Pavilion. I was music mad and that's where the dance bands would play. I was on my own and I'd decided to go in uniform, in part because I thought I might stand a better chance with the girls, but mainly because I was proud as hell of my brass lyre RAOC Band badge which I'd polished so it glinted like gold against its red base backin' cloth. I wanted to identify with the bands. As a kid I suppose you could say I'd idolised 'em. Now, I wanted 'em to see that I was one of 'em. I got there around 5 pm. It was a weekday – I forget which – but Nat Allen and his band were playin'. I knew they'd be playin' alternate hour slots with Arthur Copperfield and his band. They were both good bands, very good. Later Nat Allen would become resident band at the Savoy and Arthur Copperfield went on to play at the Café du Paris. As I say, I was band music mad and I was lookin' forward to a good night just standin' listenin', but as it turned out, fate had somethin' different in store for me that night.

The band had only played maybe 2 or 3 numbers when this yankee sailor walks in with a girl on each arm. I was just thinkin' 'typical yank', lucky so-and-so, when one of his girls gives me the eye and walks over, introduces herself and engages me in conversation. I was stunned. So stunned that, try as I might, I can't for the life of me remember her name. Nothin' like that had ever happened to me before and I remember thinkin' to myself, "blimey, I must try wearin' my uniform more often'. As I told you we'd always worn civvies to the Savoy back in Pompey.

We had a fair few dances and at some point the yankee sailor and his girl disappeared. To be honest I would have been more than happy stayin' in the Dance Pavilion all night, listenin' to the bands, dancin' and chattin' to 'my girl'. Well she was now. After all, she had left the yankee sailor to come over to me and now he was nowhere to be seen. Trouble was, she had other ideas. I got the impression she was a bit older and a good deal more experienced than me. I was 19 with my tongue hangin' out! She got her way – of course she did. Well, it's the way of the world, isn't it? Young, unattached men fallin' over themselves to please a lady. So it was that we left the bands and went on every type of ride there was – her favourites more than once. We stayed together the whole night and were amongst the last to leave at lockin' up time – 10.30 pm I think it was. She was a real looker and bein' that much older and more experienced than me, to be honest I was a bit in awe of her. I felt a bit out of my depth, which maybe accounts for why instead of escortin' her home, I just called a taxi for her.

For me it was only about a 15-minute walk back to dad's in Gambetta Street. I was walkin' on air and once I got to bed with our Dinky tucked up beside me as usual, I got to goin' over the night's events and thinkin' – 'has this really happened to me?" It seemed so unreal – more like what you'd see at the movies. Next day though, it was back to reality. I still loved my fishin' – second only to music, it was my big passion in life. I'd planned to go fishin' and I didn't change my plans. I didn't try to contact my 'dream girl' from the previous night. We'd had a great night, but maybe it was best to leave it at that. Anyway, I'd be back off to Hillsea in a couple of days and my weekends were already fully committed what with band practice, the Star & Garter and mum. Not to mention my other 'private' jobs. I had no time for courtin'.

Talkin' of 'private' jobs, if I say so myself, I was quite good at this promoter lark albeit on a fairly small scale. Whilst most work came by way of recommendation and word of mouth, I was pretty savvy, pretty businesslike. I wanted to be on stage performin' but also arrangin' things behind the scenes, gettin' in the work, sortin' out the venues. A bit time consumin' sometimes, but I got a buzz from both sides of the job. Of course, bein' in the army, very often I'd be somewhere I shouldn't have been, but that was me – a bit of a chancer I suppose, but most definitely a survivor.

Many was the time I'd be 'playin' away', but not in the sense you're probably thinkin'. When I was in the army, I wasn't even goin' steady, never mind hitched – I just didn't have the time. When I wasn't rehearsin' or playin' with the lads at some army function or other near Hillsea or on tour, very often I'd be organisin' a band to play at some private function or other mostly back in London and that was in addition to my regular Saturday night spot at the Star & Garter. Sometimes I'd put a 3 or 4-piece band together for a function, but I wouldn't attend in person. I preferred to if I could, but that wasn't always possible.

That might well have been the case with Betty Lilley's weddin' reception, but her mum, who was a neighbour and friend of mum's, especially wanted me to play, so I got a stand-in for the Star & Garter and did the weddin' gig.

Now here's a little memory test for you. Does the name Betty Lilley ring any bells? No? Then take a look at the photos at the end of Chapter 4 and see if that jogs your memory. The doll in a box! Anyway, like me she'd done a bit of growin' up since then had Betty and now she was knockin' on mum's door askin' if I'd play at her weddin'. She'd done rather well for herself too had Betty. She was marryin' the son and heir to the Rolls Royce Washin' Machine Company. Quite a fancy affair I have to say and me and my band, well, let's just say we didn't disappoint.

I provided the music and organised a 4-piece for the occasion. Doris on piano (she lived at Clapham Junction). She was good and very reliable, so I used her a lot. If Doris was available she was always my first choice piano player. Len McCauken, (from Stottham) on accordion, and Douggie on saxophone. It was a memorable day music-wise, startin' and endin' well. People cheered when my band walked in, which, as you can imagine, always gave us a lift and I guess helped inspire us to put on a pretty special performance.

Some of the guests hadn't danced in years, but they soon found their feet and it was clear everybody was enjoyin' themselves and the atmosphere was great. Believe me, that's the best feelin' when you've put together a band to play at a weddin' or any gig come to that. We played all the popular stuff, quicksteps, waltzes, foxtrots and all the 'get together' dances like the Gay Gordons, Palais Glide and of course the Lambeth Walk...

It wasn't a late do, which was just as well, because unusually that weekend I was due to play with the army band at Southampton on Sunday mornin' to welcome in a troop ship from Egypt, so I needed to catch the last train out of Waterloo that night to get me back to Portsmouth ready to go over to Southampton with the rest of the lads in the mornin'. All was goin' well, congratulations all round from proud parents and the rest and we were packin' up not long after 10.30 pm. Trouble was, when I got outside, this thick London fog had descended. When I say thick, I mean really, really dense - much worse than any fog you get today, a real 'pea souper' smog. I could barely see in front of me, so there was no way I was goin' to get to Waterloo. It was a pain, but I wasn't too worried. I'd just go home for a bit of a sleep and get up at 3am and go to Waterloo then, to catch the early mornin' milk train to Portsmouth. I'd still be in time to go with the rest of the lads over to Southampton to play the troop ship in.

You know what they say about good intentions and the best laid plans? I didn't wake up! I overslept and not by a bit – it was nearly 8am when I came to. This time my 'playin' away' was goin' to get me into hot water – scaldin' more like. Failin' to get back on duty to play the troop ship in was bad enough, but it was worse. Before I'd left on the Friday, the Band Sergeant Major had entrusted me with the Director of Music's dress sword and baton. I'd packed them inside my drum accessory box, which I was supposed to ensure went over to Southampton with me in time for our performance. On such occasions the Director of Music was always resplendent in full regalia and there'd be hell to pay when he found himself with no dress sword or baton. This time I'd be for it and no mistake. I'd missed the train and, as a result, literally missed the boat.

Rushin' back now wasn't goin' to help any so I just went over to see mum as usual and caught the afternoon train, gettin' me back to Portsmouth just after 5pm. I was bracin' myself for the worst, but as it turned out, lady luck was still lookin' out for me. When I caught up with the lads, Sheriden informs me, "We never played a bloody note." It turns out they'd had dense freezin' fog down in Southampton as well, so dense they could barely see the ship, much less the troops gettin' off. The whole event had been abandoned without a note bein' played – not even the National Anthem, nothin'! The fog had saved my life – well my bacon at any rate.

I didn't get off scot-free though. My absence had been noted. I had to go before the Adjutant to explain myself. In such situations, the best thing is to come clean, well, more or less, and grovel. "I'm terribly sorry Sir. I was caught in dense fog in London and couldn't get to the train." I missed out the bit about bein' on a good earner, playin' at the weddin' and then oversleepin'. As it was, I might still have found myself bein' put on orders and locked up for a spell, but as luck would have it, the band were off up to Carlisle on another job the next day and really they needed me to play, so that was it. I more or less got away with a slap on the wrist and a warnin' not to do it again. That went in one ear and straight out of the other because of course I did do it again, not once or twice, but lots of times. Ok, I was a bit of a chancer, but you had to be to make the most of life's opportunities and, in my case develop as a musician whilst makin' a fair few bob on the side.

Word soon gets around, and I did a fair few weddin's on the back of that Rolls do. Some I'd do a bit cheaper, to help them out. It all depended on who they were and their circumstances. I got asked to play at a fair few reunion do's as well. It wasn't that long after the War and retired veterans liked to get together now and again. Most times there'd be wives and sweethearts and dancin' involved, but they all liked to listen to a bit of nostalgia with war-time favourites like Lily Marlene and Tipperary and I was only too pleased to oblige.

Time flies when you're enjoyin' yourself and before I knew it, it was 1953 – Coronation year. In the days leadin' up to the main event, our band, along with maybe 50 or 60 other military bands, were mustered in Hyde Park. The logistics were a bit of a nightmare and in particular they had a job feedin' us all. Orders went round to reduce the numbers and sadly, as a relative newcomer, I was one of the ones asked to stand down in favour of a chap called Webber (Webby), who I have to say was a brilliant percussionist and, if you remember had been with the band when I joined. He went on to play with the Scots Guards – the crème de la crème of Military Bands. And so it was that rather than bein' centre stage, I spent Coronation Day back at Hillsea Barracks, Pompey, listenin' to coverage on the radio. A bit of a let down, but then again, you can't have everythin' and in truth I was still countin' my lucky stars that I'd been given the chance to spend my national service doin' somethin' I loved rather than square bashin', or worse still, riskin' my neck out in Korea.

Before I leave the subject of the Coronation, there's a couple of things I want to tell you and maybe have a bit of a dig at the politicians whilst I'm at it. Dad was staunch labour and none too pleased by the results of the recent elections. Uncle Vic was conservative and the two of them would always end up arguin' about politics whenever they got together. In temperament I was much more like Uncle Vic, but politics didn't really interest me. I was pretty neutral. Anyway, to get to my point, you remember my visit to the Festival Gardens in the summer of '53 and my fond memories in particular of the Dance Pavilion? Well, although I haven't mentioned it, amongst the Festival Garden buildin's there was also this Riverside Theatre which at its peak was runnin' as many as six shows a day, includin' music hall, dancin' and festival follies – a bit of a throw-back to Victorian Times.

Unlike many of the Festival buildin's, the Theatre had been designed to last and its construction carefully thought out to allow it to be moved and re-erected elsewhere if necessary. Sadly this was not to be the case. Politics would intervene. Despite bein' home to the world premiere of a 3D colour film of the Coronation, shortly afterwards, on Saturday Oct 13th to be precise, the Theatre was closed by the new Conservative Government. Its leader, Winston Churchill, whilst in opposition, had denounced the Labour Government's Festival of Britain as "a monstrous waste of public money". Bein' an ordinary 'member of the public', I beg to differ. Anyway, not long after the Riverside Theatre, along with most of the other Festival buildin's includin' my beloved Dance Pavilion, was demolished and cleared, never to re-appear. Fortunately some of the gardens and features like the Guiness Clock were retained and can still be seen to this day. But, insofar as the dance bands went in the Pavilion, it was goodnight and goodbye for good.

Naturally 1953 is best remembered for bein' Coronation Year and certainly at the time it was the major cause for celebration, not just in the capital, but throughout the country, it was celebrated by the masses. Talkin' of masses – for the workin' men at least, football was the major source of sportin' entertainment and Wembley was regarded as more or less a fortress. England bein' beaten there – the home of football – it was practically unthinkable. But in 1953, the unthinkable happened. England were beaten at Wembley, 6-3 by Germany. Not a lot of people remember that – or maybe they just choose not to.

Whilst all this was goin' on I was still in the army, in theory at least, doin' my national service. I was also still visitin' mum. Just Sundays now – with dad. I never missed except when the band was on tour. As I've said, I'd normally hitch goin' up to London, but comin' back on a Sunday evenin' I'd take the train. Sometimes, if I sensed he needed me, I'd go back to London first with dad, but mostly I'd catch the train from Epsom to Guildford and change there to the main Portsmouth line. That way I could be back for around 6 pm in time for a bit of a drink with the lads. It wasn't so much the drink I needed, but the camaraderie and banter to lift my spirits. Mum's problems I kept to myself. With hindsight, not givin' myself the outlet of talkin' about them with anyone except dad was maybe not good for me, but it's what I did, until now – until John got me to open up to him.

Mum was hospitalised – institutionalised – for more than five years in all. Before and throughout my army career and well beyond. In all that time there were highs and lows. Sadly more lows, but focussin' now on the highs. As I've told you, mum was a voluntary patient, technically free to come and go as she pleased and so, when she was feelin' well, sometimes she'd take it into her head to bring herself home for the weekend. Before her illness, mum had always run the household – been in charge of the finances, not least payin' the bills. Although spasmodic and irregular in the extreme, part of the motivation for mum's 'weekend excursions' seemed to be to check on dad – whether he had remembered to pay the rates or whatever. Mum had problems, big problems, but from time to time that part of her brain seemed to function normally.

Saturdays were always hectic for me, especially when in the army. First gettin' back home, then havin' time to catch up with dad and get myself washed and changed in time for my performance at the Star & Garter. Dad liked fish on a Saturday and often as not I'd be just in the throes of gettin' myself ready for work when he'd say, "You wouldn't mind just poppin' up Lavender Hill for me, would you?" – for herrin's or kippers or whatever he fancied. This would generally be around 4.30 pm because we'd normally eat around 5.30 pm. Whenever mum did come back, invariably, as dad was about to dish up, there'd be a key in the door and I'd say, "Hang on dad, I think we've got a visitor." And sure enough, it would be mum come home. How she ever managed it, I'll never know – first gettin' on the right train in Epsom and off in Clapham Junction and then the right bus either the 77A, 168, or 169 to either Queenstown Road or Silverthorn Road and always managin' to arrive just in time for tea. We didn't call it dinner or supper back then. Dad would always find her a herrin' or whatever and she'd stop the night. Durin' tea, I'd have to watch the clock a bit and very often end up havin' to bolt my food a bit in order to catch the bus. Like it or not, I'd just have to leave them to it because I had a commitment to work at the Star & Garter. I just couldn't let them down, but if truth be known, I didn't want to – I loved it there. If I had the chance now, I'd do it for free.

Next day – Sunday – we'd always have an early lunch. It had become our routine to make time for our hospital visits. When mum ventured home, we still stuck to our routine and we'd go on our hospital visit as usual except this time we'd be takin' mum back with us rather than just visitin'. Contrary to what you might expect, she was always fine about goin' back, she wanted to. Nevertheless, I'd always go back with them both because mum was unpredictable and you never knew when she might have 'a bit of a turn'. Sometimes without warnin', her eyes would glaze over and her whole demeanor would change. It was worryin' and you could almost say frightenin' at times.

I spent one and a half years playin' and often tourin' with the RAOC Staff Band and I loved it – I really did. I loved everythin' about it. The practices, the concerts, the pomp and ceremony, the camaraderie – the like of which I'd never experienced before – or since. The banter and the humour in the band, especially behind the scenes – it was amazin'. It was a joy to be part of it. Just thinkin' about those times makes me choke up inside and my eyes well up with tears. I'm 83 now and lookin' back, I wished I'd signed on, but I didn't, and no amount of wishin' will change that. If the band had stayed based in Portsmouth, then maybe I would have, but we didn't.

About 6 months before I was due to be de-mobbed, some idiot in the Corps decided our HQ should be transferred to Deepcut. I ask you – Deepcut! Of all the God-forsaken places they could have come up with, it had to be the worst. The same place I'd done my initial trainin' – the middle of nowhere. To say it was unpopular with the

Band is an understatement. As I've told you, many of the band had families and houses in Portsmouth – includin' Major Jarman, the Director of Music – and in a very real sense, Hillsea was home. Rumours about our Band HQ bein' moved had been circulatin' for about a year. Major Jarman had been resistin' it, but in October 1953, about the same time the government were busy ravagin' the Festival Gardens, it finally happened – we were transferred up to Deepcut. The 'Old Man' had been fightin' a rearguard action, holdin' out for suitable facilities before he'd move. In the end they converted a buildin' specially for us into a pretty decent band room. After that the die was cast and, like it or not, we were transferred. We were in the army, so as far as the Band members were concerned, there was no discussion, no consultation. We were goin' and that was it.

We all felt the loss of bein' turfed out of Hillsea, but in truth it was easier for us single blokes. The married lads livin' in married quarters could transfer to Deepcut, but most had houses and families in Portsmouth and for them it was either a case of sellin' up or makin' the best of bein' separated. Ok, they could usually manage to get home at weekends, but that's hardly the same as what they'd been used to. There was a good deal of bitterness, I can tell you. The band were allotted two barrack blocks on Frith Hill, which is directly opposite, just across the road from Deepcut proper. They were two-storey brick built blocks with toilets and ablutions on each floor. They were quite good by army standards of the day and we probably had the 'Old Man' to thank for that, but nothin' could replace Hillsea, especially for the married men.

In the first week most of the lads, especially us single blokes, went out most nights to cheer ourselves up or drown our sorrows. Joe, one of the sergeants, was married with three kids. He was a real family man and takin' the enforced separation hard. By Thursday we said to ourselves, "We can't just keep leavin' Joe. He's well down." He needed takin' out of himself, so we decided to give him no choice. "You're comin' with us tonight – no arguments." I'd cut my teeth at Deepcut, so I knew there was a reasonably decent pub – The Garibaldi. By road it was a fair old walk, but I told them I knew a short cut through the woods at the back of the barracks. Leastways, I thought I knew it. It's funny how different things can look on a dark, misty night 18 months down the line.

Joe was gettin' on a bit – in his early '50s. A good bass player – brass and strings – and a good dance band player too. Ex marine. I was 19 goin' on 20, still green around the gills by comparison, but as far as Deepcut was concerned, I was the one with experience, so I guess I was a bit cocky. Leastways I was when we set off. Deep into the woods I was a bit less cock-sure of myself and when we encountered this bog, the lads, understandably, began givin' me grief. Long story short, we did eventually get through the woods to the main road and The Garibaldi, but not before gettin' our shoes and trousers plastered with mud. We weren't wearin' boots. You only wore army boots on parade. I don't exactly recall, but I guess havin' finally made it to the Garibaldi the drinks were on me. I would have needed to make amends.

Next day, all seemed forgiven, even though we had to spend a good deal of time cleanin' our shoes and washin' and ironin' trousers – by hand. No washin' machines in those days. The lads weren't just goin' to let me forget it though. From then on I became known as "Short cut Wattley!"

I don't want to dampen the mood, but there was somethin' that happened back at home around this time that, like it or not, I have to tell you about. The trouble with pets is you become attached to 'em, which in many ways is good, but inevitably, no matter how well you look after 'em, one day they die. Our Dinky died whilst I was in the army. I came home one weekend to find dad had taken him in a sack to Battersea Dogs Home to be cremated. In truth, I was too involved, too busy with my new life, playin' in the army band, at the Star & Garter and dashin' off to visit mum to be overly affected by it, but come bed-time, well that was never quite the same with no Dinky lyin' there beside me. It was then that I felt the loss.

After a few weeks at Deepcut, things began to settle down a bit. I suppose we all thought, we can't change it, so we might as well make the best of it. The Garibaldi became quite a popular haunt – with those of us who drank, that is. A chap called Jimmy Buck joined us around this time. He was a studious sort – a nice chap, if a bit serious. He didn't drink, so he never had occasion to visit the Garibaldi. He was a brilliant musician, though, a top drawer French Horn player of the day. He'd been taught by Dennis Brain, a well-known and highly respected French Horn player. Jimmy was so good that even as a teenager he'd already played with one of the Philharmonic orchestras in civvy street, but, like the rest of us, he had to do National Service. At least with his pedigree he went straight into the Band and he got regular dispensations to play at venues like the Albert Hall. Irrespective, like all army musicians, he had to play more than one instrument. Jimmy played violin and he was good, but his French Horn playin' was different class. He was a joy to listen to.

By the time Jimmy joined us, quite a few of my mates had got themselves second-hand bikes, mainly to cycle over to The Garibaldi. For some reason, my 'shortcut' wasn't that popular, not even with me, but then again it was winter. I never did get myself a bike, but Jimmy had a beauty – chrome lights, dynamo, everythin'. Top o' the range, it was. Anyway, this particular night when Jimmy was away, the lads announced they were off up to the Garibaldi. I said I'd give it a miss – it was freezin' out and I didn't fancy the walk. They suggested I borrow Jimmy's bike – he was away, but they were sure he wouldn't mind. I was a bit dubious, but then again it was only a couple of miles – what harm could it do? What harm indeed?

As I said, it was freezin' out so we were well togged up – great coats, peak cap – everythin'. Once out on the open road I was enjoyin' myself – speedin' along, as you do when you're young. Comin' up to the Garibaldi there's this steep hill. I'm still not quite sure what happened – maybe I was goin' too fast, maybe I hit a patch of ice, maybe I just braked too hard. What I do know is that all of a sudden I was flyin' through the air – me one way, the bike another. O'course the lads thought it was funny until they saw the state I was in. They finished up practically carryin' me into The Garibaldi, where the landlady did a sterlin' job patchin' me up. Back then nobody wore cycle helmets. There were no such things, but it was a good job I was wearin that peak cap and a great coat. They saved me from serious injury. I was limpin' about for weeks, but no real harm done.

I wasn't lookin' forward to explainin' to Jimmy about the damage to his bike, but he took it in good part. I guess he could see the funny side and o'course I did pay for the repairs – new mudguard and the like. Mind you, I never did 'borrow' that bike again or anybody else's come to that.

When my 2 years National Service was up, I decided to leave the Army and see if I could make my livin' from music out in civvy street. I was in no hurry to leave though. In fact I did an extra five days before I thought I'd best go and explain to the band Sergeant Major and the Director of Music that my time was up and I should already have left the army! I remember Major Jarman sayin' to me, "You never did sign on, did you John? I don't really blame you ... I'm going myself shortly." In reality, as far as the RAOC Band was concerned, me leavin' was a minor blip. As contracts were up, musicians came and went all the time, but Major Jarman leavin', now that really was momentous. Quite literally the end of an era. It was the 'Old Man' who'd first formed the band and seen to it that it had blossomed through the War and beyond. I didn't ask, but I guess it was the move to 'Deepcut' that decided it for him. I often sit here reminiscin' to myself. Thinkin' what happened to the Old Man and to all my mates in the Band. Sadly, I've never seen any of 'em since. Not to speak to that is. But Jimmy Buck – I have seen him a time or two – on the telly. Playin' at the Albert Hall and other venues. We all knew he was destined for bigger things.

Lookin' back, despite the early setbacks, for me, my time in the army was, in many ways, the makin' of me. I'd dreaded goin' in but as it turned out, I wouldn't have missed it for the world. Most of all, it gave me the opportunity to really develop as a musician – somethin' I would never have had the time or opportunity to do in civvy street. Mind you, if I'd ended up in Korea instead, I'd have been in a right state and I'd be tellin' you a very different story about what army life had been like for me. But I was lucky and then, as now, I knew it.

Some of my army mates. Me on snare drum and Pat Dimmock on accordion. Pete Gill, on the extreme left, playin' trombone, was off to Mons for Officer Trainin'. We wanted a group photo before he left.

Me playin' Titch Cocker's trombone – well, posin' with it 'cos I couldn't actually play the thing.

CHAPTER 7

Music Was My First Love

When I came out of the army I thought I'd try and make music my full-time career. As it turned out, Pat Dimmock, who if you remember was the pianist and all round musician who'd played at my audition, came to the end of his 9-year contract at the same time, and he and I decided to join the newly re-formed Aldershot Palais Dance Band. Pat could play more or less any instrument, but he was a particularly talented saxophonist. After 9 years Pat felt he'd had enough and wanted to pursue his real passion – dance band music. The Palais had been refurbished and there was a real buzz about the place, which felt great. We felt like we were part of somethin' special. It was a new beginnin' for the Palais and a new beginnin' for us as professional musicians.

We started on 8th March 1954 – four days after leavin' the army. Before that though, I headed back to London to formally wind up my career at the Stock Exchange, collect my P45 and say goodbye to all my friends. Leavin' the Star & Garter was more difficult. They'd been especially good to me and I'd had some great times there, but somehow I needed to be out of London for a while. I was 20 – no longer a teenager – and perhaps for the first time I felt in control of my own destiny.

Bob Potter was our agent at the Palais. He'd been responsible for re-openin' the place. There was another dance hall in Aldershot, but, strange as it may seem, I never went there. I never needed to. The Palais was a roarin' success and I was part of it. We'd normally be an

8-piece band with a chap called Gordon as our singer. He was a semi-invalid with a deformed back, but boy could he sing. He would stand on stage and the audience probably didn't know he had a disability problem, but if he went any distance he'd need a wheelchair. It had an electric motor – a forerunner of the electric scooters that you see everywhere today.

Bob Potter was clever, you'd have to give him that. He had this brightly coloured van which, like all his literature, proclaimed that "all his musicians were broadcastin' musicians". That wasn't a con. That was true, because by recruitin' ex military band musicians, he could be pretty sure that at some stage they'd have played on radio, as we'd done fairly regularly. Perhaps I should explain that in those days the BBC would start broadcastin' at 6.30 am and the first half hour would always be a military band playin' live. It was always live, not recorded. We'd go up to London on the early train from Portsmouth to be sure of bein' at the Paris Studios in Regent Street for 6 am, givin' us time to set up. That was the downside, the very early starts, havin' to leave Portsmouth at around 4am but it was worth it. For once I wasn't moonlightin'. It was all official and above board – sanctioned by the army. I loved it – not just the playin' but the braggin' rights that went with havin' played on radio and what's more we got extra pay for it, so it was win, win all round.

In a sense, by joinin' Bob Potter, our timin' couldn't have been better. Either he or his dad, I'm not sure which, had bought the Aldershot Palais. It had been run down and closed for years, but the total refurbishment was completed just as we joined him. It was March 1954. I was young, single and ambitious. We'd do three nights at the Palais – Thursday, Friday and Saturday. He didn't have a licence for Sundays. Normally we'd be an 8 or 9 piece band and the dances were very popular. When I say dances, this was the 1950s when dancin' meant proper ballroom dancin'. None of this jigglin' about on the spot stuff. The jive though, that was just comin' in and the jivers would be up by the stage, but always to one side where they wouldn't get in the way of the ballroom dancers. In those days, management were very strict about it. If the place was too crowded, or there was insufficient room, then the jivin' would have to stop.

On Sundays Pat and I would join a bigger outfit, generally an 18-piece band, to play at the California. That was a holiday leisure complex with chalets, a boatin' lake and entertainment includin' a circus. It had a really big dance floor which didn't just cater for holidaymakers. It was very popular with folk from Readin'. It was always a late night affair and in addition to the band we'd usually have a singer, and not just any singer, but the chap who normally sang with the well-known Billy Turnant Orchestra, both in London's West End and on the radio in Variety Bandbox. It was work, but it didn't seem like work. We never rehearsed, we just improvised on the night, but that didn't seem to be a problem. We went down a storm and, just as much as the dancers, we were havin' a ball.

Occasionally we'd get Mondays, Tuesdays and Wednesdays off, but most often we'd be playin' on one, two or all three nights, mainly at one or other of the American camps in the area. In particular, we had a regular spot at the American base at Newbury, Berkshire which was always a really late night for us. Once a month, we played at the English Air Force Base at Bracknell. There we'd just be a 5-piece band, but we were so popular, even the officers queued to get in. For them we played mainly modern jazz, which was becomin' increasingly popular.

Before I go any further, I ought to tell you a bit about where I was livin', who with and what we got up to. The army had been providin' a roof over my head for the last 2 years – Ok, 2 years and 4 days to be precise, but now I was on my own. I needed accommodation and I needed it fast. I'd been askin' around without any joy, so I resorted to lookin' for ads in shop windows. As luck would have it, there it was – an ad for full board at 21 Halimont Road, Aldershot. It turned out to be a decent neighbourhood – rather posh really – and the house itself, spotlessly clean. So that was it – that was me fixed up. The old man of the house was a retired sergeant major in his 50s I'd say, but his wife seemed much older. He'd recently retired and they'd only just started doin' B&B. When I say retired, I mean from the army, but now he'd got himself a part-time job as a 'tally man', collectin' payments house to house for Jays furniture store. I was their second lodger – a Mr Timothy Healey had been there about a fortnight.

A bit reserved at first, within a few days of my arrival, Mr Healey seemed to come out of his shell. We shared a sense of humour and increasingly spent some of our spare time together. Nothin' special – things like walkin' the owner's dog or on a sunny summer's evenin' watchin the tennis in the park for an hour or two. It was a good standard and drew quite a crowd. Whilst watchin' the tennis, often as not we'd be havin' a laugh and a joke about where we were livin' and especially the food situation. That needs a bit of explanation.

My rent was two pounds ten shillin's a week, but that included three meals a day. To be honest I think runnin' a lodgin' house was too much for the old dear. She seemed to spend most of her time doin' housework and preparin' or cleanin' up after meals. What's more, she was chancin' her luck a bit offerin' board because she wasn't the best of cooks, but the biggest problem was the portions – they were always too small. Maybe for someone her age they were ok, but I was 20 and needed feedin' up a bit. As it was, I was always starvin'. Breakfast was just cereal and toast, and lunches were small so by mid-afternoon I'd be off buyin' food to keep me goin' 'till dinner in the evenin'. I was partial to kippers, so I was pleased when the old lady announced it was "kippers tonight". I should have known better. Rather than a pair of kippers, she served up half a kipper each plus bread and butter. I was so hungry I was wishin' she'd left the head on! Tim and I had a good laugh about that. Take a tip from me – whenever you can, it's much better to laugh than to cry.

My band work was more or less exclusively in the evenin', so I was often at a bit of a loose end durin' the day. I'd not been there long when the old man asks if I'd like to accompany him on his rounds and I thought, 'Why not?' So off we go in his Austin 7. We made a couple of quick calls in town and then he heads off into the countryside and pulls up outside this big posh house, right out in the sticks it was. Now here I am sittin' in this car, gettin' a bit hot and bothered 'cos it's a sunny day, and the time goes on ….. and on ….. and on. After what seemed like hours later, he comes back out lookin' a bit red-faced and flustered. "Sorry about that," he says, "took rather longer than I'd thought." I don't know about collectin' money – I reckon he was 'fillin' his boots' at the same time. If you ask me, what he wasn't gettin' at home, he was gettin' on his rounds! Maybe his wife was a bit past it, but there was life in the old dog yet. Bit of an eye-opener, that little trip.

Tim never told me the full story, but I got the impression he'd walked away from a bad marriage. He'd had a good job in the shoe industry in Northampton, but the industry was in decline and now he'd taken a job as manager of Timpsons shoe shop in Aldershot and, like me, he was livin' as a lodger. Rather sad really because, unlike me, he wasn't just startin' out, he was in his late '50s. He was nearin' retirement.

Mind you, as I say, he still had a good sense of humour and we had some good banter together. The old man especially liked a drink and on a Friday he'd take his wife out for the night and accordin' to Tim, they'd be a bit worse for wear comin' back. I never saw 'em myself because at that time I'd always be out playin' with the band. Even so, two Fridays in particular are memorable for very different reasons.

I'd picked up this gadget from somewhere. I'm not even sure what it was, but if you put it between the bulb and the holder, it made the light flash on and off. Anyway, Tim and I thought it would be a laugh to put it in on a Friday and see the old dear's reaction when they rolled in with a drink or two inside 'em. Of course I was workin' at the Palais, so I wasn't there to see it, but accordin' to Tim, as usual they came back a bit giggly and struggled to get their key in the door. Switchin' the light on, they couldn't fathom what on earth was happenin'. They were all over the place, so havin' had a bit of a laugh to himself, Tim decides to be their knight in shinin' armour. He takes the bulb out, slips the gadget into his pocket and replaces the bulb. Hey presto – problem solved. The old dears were ever so grateful and none the wiser as to our little prank.

On another Friday, the old dears went off out a bit earlier than usual and I decided to have a bath before goin' off to work. There was a big gas geyser at one end of the bathroom, which you had to light to get hot water. To light it you had to use a lighted taper. I'd never done it before because the owners had always done it for me – but how difficult could it be? Quite difficult as it happened. Try as I might, I couldn't get this thing to light. Tim was in his room, so I thought I'll ask him if he could give me a hand to light the thing. Typical of Tim he comes out with, "I don't know what you'd do without me – you must think I'm your nursemaid" – all in fun o' course. Anyway, Tim goes into the bathroom to light it and I goes off to fetch a towel. Next thing, there's this almighty bang and Tim comes staggerin' out, black as night. The geyser was hangin' off the wall and the window was blown out. I guess in tryin' to light the thing, I'd let loads of gas escape and build up, so if anyone was to blame, it was me, but Tim wasn't the sort to apportion blame. We just spent the next half hour cleanin' up as best we could. Then Tim told me to get myself ready and clear off out to work and leave him to smooth things over with the old dears when they got back. I can still hear him sayin', "Go on – clear off – you've done enough damage for one night!" and I can still see him standin' there in his blue serge suit and now not so white collar and tie. I never did get that bath. Somehow the prospect of a cold bath in a bathroom with the window blown out didn't have much appeal. In the followin' weeks we'd often laugh about it, but to be honest, neither of us thought it was all that funny at the time.

Before I get on with tellin' you about my music career, there's one more thing I want to tell you about my digs – Wendy. The old dears had a daughter called Wendy. Now, I got the distinct impression that mum and dad thought I was just the young man for their Wendy and I think she had her eyes on me too. She seemed to make excuses to come knockin' on my bedroom door. Trouble was, she just wasn't my type at all – a bit plain and well, borin' if you ask me. I got the feelin' a bit of an atmosphere was beginnin' to develop and not just Wendy, but mum and dad were none too pleased by my lack of interest.

Life has taught me that whenever things are gettin' a bit difficult, somethin' usually turns up to rescue the situation – and so it did – in the form of a third lodger. I didn't take to the bloke – too snooty by half for my likin', but with his arrival the atmosphere lifted. He and Wendy hit it off and soon got together, which was a lucky break for me. It got me off the hook.

The food – or lack of it – apart, those digs suited me fine. They were clean, I could walk to work and I had my own key, so comin' in, in the early hours, after a night at the Palais or wherever I'd been playin' wasn't a problem. That was a big plus for someone like me. Digs where you could come and go as you pleased were few and far between. Then of course there was Tim. He and I were good company for one another. So, as I say, those digs suited me and I stayed there until gettin' my own place, some nine months later in December '54. When the time came for me to leave, I was excited about movin' on. The reason for that will become clear later. But, I was sorry to be sayin' goodbye to Tim and the feelin' was mutual and it showed. He was wellin' up – he got rather emotional. I'd never had quite that effect on anyone before and even now, lookin' back, it brings a bit of a lump into my throat. I can't dwell on it though. I need to get back to my narrative.

As I've said, my digs bein' close by, I used to walk up to the Palais. I'd always play there on Thursdays, Fridays and Saturdays. Durin' the rest of the week we'd have jobs all over Hampshire and Bob Potter would take us around. Sundays though – in the beginnin' at least – they were still reserved for mum and dad. I'd often be a bit shattered followin' a late Saturday night at the Palais, but after a bit of breakfast, I'd always get myself down to the train station in Aldershot so as to be 'home' with dad for a quick lunch before headin' off to the Hospital in Epsom to see mum. It was 1954 now and she'd been 'institutionalised' for 4 years. As time went on, she was feelin' better and more confident in herself and her impromptu visits back home became more and more frequent – but I'll tell you more about mum and her progress later. For now, I need to tell you more about my burgeonin' career as a professional musician and some of the things that happened to me on and off the stage.

As I've told you, I used to play Thursday, Friday and Saturday nights at the Palais, plus special occasions. I'd been there about four months when this girl started sittin' on the side of the stage on a regular basis. A looker she was, and I realised it wasn't the band in general she was interested in – it was me. We'd smile at one another and pass pleasantries and maybe chat a bit between 'sets'. By 'sets' I mean three numbers, because we'd normally do three waltzes or three foxtrots or three quicksteps or whatever with maybe a minute's break between each. And yes, it was ballroom dancin' in those days – what I'd call proper dancin'. There was an order to it and even the youngsters had a semblance of grace and poise. None of this handbags on the floor and just jiggin' about doin' your own thing more or less on the spot – that came later. Mind you jivin' and jitterbuggin' had made its way across the pond and was gainin' in popularity. It was still a minority thing though, and only tolerated by ballroom management provided it didn't interfere with the dancin' 'proper'. That meant it was confined to a small space, usually to one side of the stage.

As it happened, this girl, Cynthia her name was, always came with a friend called Gertie amd Gertie used to spend most of the night jivin' – whenever the music fitted, that is, but I never remember Cynthia jivin'. She would often be asked to dance though, but it was noticeable she would always come back and sit on the side of the stage beside me. This was the second time a girl had come chasin' me. Remember the girl in Battersea Park? What's more, this one was persistent. She kept comin' back and I guess I was flattered. It wasn't the traditional beginnin' for romance of boy asks girl for a dance, show her a few moves, whisk her off her feet, give her the chat and see where it goes from there. Then again, I was there to perform, not dance. I was up on stage doin' what I loved best and when it was clear this girl was interested, I guess I did turn on the style with a bit of flashy drummin'. I was nothin' if not a showman.

After about a week of this, she must have wanted to move things on a bit because out of the blue she suddenly said, "I thought you might have asked to walk me home by now!" That night, naturally I did – well you can't refuse a pretty girl, can you? Truth be told, I didn't have much experience with women. Before the army, I always seemed to be workin' and in the army – well, you know the story there. Weekends I was always committed, so there'd been no real opportunity to develop a relationship much beyond a few one night stands.

Anyway, after that we quickly became an item, Cynthia and I, – goin' steady as they say, and she rarely missed a show. Mind you, as what might now be termed a 'groupie', she got reduced price admission. Thinkin' back now it makes me smile. Here I was, this experienced fisherman, but it didn't occur to me at the time that now it was Cynthia who was doin' the fishin'. I was the fish and I was well and truly hooked and she was reelin' me in.

Women change our lives, don't' they? – or at least they did in my day. Suddenly your life is not your own – your priorities change – they have to. Now there were two important women in my life and somehow I had to share my time between them. I had to show them both I cared. So it was that my dutiful weekly visits to see mum (and dad of course) became fortnightly. Cynthia wanted me every Sunday – but we compromised on fortnightly. As far as mum was concerned – it wasn't as bad as it sounds. My goin' steady coincided with a decided upturn in mum's condition and she was makin' more and more frequent visits home on a Saturday night. I think it was more or less a spur of the moment thing, although she always seemed to walk in around the same time – about 5.30 pm – in time for tea. We called it tea in those days rather than dinner or, if you want to be really posh, 'supper'. Rightly or wrongly, I thought that it might be good for mum and dad to have more quality time together without me bein' there. Maybe that would encourage her to discharge herself from the hospital and stay home permanently.

Now, before I go on to tell you more about my developin' relationship with Cynthia, I need to briefly mention Z Reserve. The thing is, although I'd left the army, the army wasn't finished with me yet. As part of National Service, in addition to the 2 years we had to do a further 3 stints of two weeks each. It was called 'Z Reserve'. I suppose you could say they were like 'refresher courses'. I'd left in March 1954 and I got my call-up papers again wantin' me back in the August that same year.

The 'refresher courses' were supposed to be about keepin' us sharp for soldierin', not playin' in an army band, but I was lucky because I didn't get sent back to Deepcut – for me it was Portsmouth, more or less where I'd been billeted with the band. No music this time though. Along with all the rest, it was back to square bashin', the rifle range and all that. The trouble was, unlike the rest of the 'squaddies', I'd spent most of my time as a conscript playin' in a band, not messin' about with a rifle, so compared to most of 'em I'd have to admit I was a bit useless at regular soldierin'. I'd still got my 'band lyre' – my badge of honour you might say, and I wore it proudly on my return. The squaddies were curious about it – "What's that on yer arm, Jack?" O'course that was my cue to give em' the whole story. That lyre was, and still is, my most prized possession.

With me back again from 'soldierin', Cynthia continued to follow the band – well, me really – and on my nights off we'd generally be together. In those days if you weren't goin' to a dance, then the cinema was the place to take a girl, and so the Odeon in Aldershot was a place I got to know really well. Mostly, like any courtin' couple, there we'd be kissin' and cuddlin' in the back seats, missin' half the film except not this one particular film. 1954 saw the premiere of 'The Glen Miller Story'. Now that was one film even Cynthia couldn't distract me from. Louis Armstrong was in it and James

Stewart played Glen Miller. Although he came to England, I'd never been lucky enough to see Glen Miller perform live but I loved his music. Lots of the top bands played it includin' Joe Loss and his Orchestra. Havin' got Glen's permission, Joe adopted one of Glen's most famous numbers – 'In the Mood' as his signature tune. I saw Joe lots of times includin', if you remember, at the Savoy in Portsmouth, when I was in the army.

As for 'The Glen Miller Story', in my book it's an all time classic. I've seen it a good few times includin' with Sandy my daughter in America. Now that is me, really gettin' ahead of myself, but you'll come to know Sandy later, much later. Ok, it's an old film but I'd say it's one that's stood the test of time. If you get the chance, try and see it. Early on, Glen goes into this pawn shop and buys this second hand trombone. He starts a band but things get rough and he has to pawn it again. I won't tell you any more, except it features some of Glen's all time greats and ends, as Glen's real life story did, with Glen in a small plane leavin' an airfield in Bedford to join the rest of his band for a performance in Belgium.

On my Sundays with Cynthia we'd often go down to Southsea or Portsmouth. Of course, I knew that bit of coast from my time at Hillsea Barracks. We didn't do that much – just sat on the beach mostly – but it was somewhere to have a bit of quality time together. Later, you'll see a photo of Cynthia on the beach in her bathin' costume. In fact, Cynthia was happy doin' very little. Even so, she was often drowsy on the train back home as if we'd had a really hectic day. We didn't know it at the time, but later, much later, we were to find out that she suffered from pernicious anaemia and that's why she got tired so easily.

When I first met Cynthia's parents, Les and Flossie, they were livin' in a three bedroom house in Aldershot, 50 Belle Vue Road to be precise. Les was a Dover lad. He'd been born in one of the little white cottages under the cliffs near the harbour. When Flossie met him he was a young man – you might almost say for her, a 'toy boy', workin' at a big nursery in the town. Whether it was love at first sight, I can't say, but they were smitten with one another enough for them to elope to London together with Flossie's kids in tow. They settled in Finchley, but Flossie's husband, a Mr Wingfield-Hill, refused to give her a divorce and so unbeknown to everyone, Flossie and Les were never officially married. To all appearances they were man and wife, but legally they weren't. In fact, the bigamous relationship didn't properly come out until after Flossie's death in 1969, but even then she was buried with 'Flossie Gould' written on her coffin plate. But that's all in the future and for now I need to continue tellin' you about how things were in 1954.

Although Cynthia always thought of Les as her father, along with her two elder brothers – both Harolds! – and sister Monica, she grew up with the name 'Wingfield-Hill'. Cynthia had three younger brothers, – Tony, John and Mickey. I think Tony and John were Les's, but I'm not sure. Anyway the family had moved to Aldershot durin' the War, around 1940. It was a brand new house for rent and Aunt Beatie, Flossie's sister, had found it for them. Flossie saw it as a means of gettin' evacuated from the bombin' where they lived in Finchley, London.

Durin' the war, Les had been a tank engineer fightin' with Montgomery. Havin' successfully come through the North Africa campaign, includin' the decisive allied victory at El Alamein, Les went with Montgomery into Sicily and then Southern Italy where, at a place called Arkangelo, his wartime exploits came to a sudden end in a near death experience. Les was standin' by a disabled tank explainin' to an officer why he couldn't get it movin' because he needed additional parts. Durin' the course of the conversation, he and the officer literally changed places and then, almost immediately the officer was hit by enemy shellin' and killed outright. Les was badly wounded by flyin' shrapnel, resultin' in his leg havin' to be amputated, and towards the end of 1943 Les was sent back to Engand for convalescin' before bein' invalided out of the army.

Flossie had once worked with Marie Lloyd as a gaiety girl and when war broke out, with husband Les away fightin', Flossie and sister Beatie decided to do their bit by entertainin' the troops with their song and dance routine. Trouble was, Flossie, always outgoin' and flamboyant, did a bit more entertainin' than she should have done with a certain Canadian soldier. The result was Mickey. This much I know. What I don't know is how Les first reacted to the news. All I can say is that by the time I knew them, when first courtin' Cynthia, Les was dad to Mickey just as he was to all Flossie's other children, includin' Cynthia, irrespective of who had actually fathered them. Mind you, whilst Les was dad in the household, there was no doubtin' that Flossie wore the trousers! She ruled the roost, did Flossie. There was no doubtin' that!

Flossie's first husband had been a chap called Darling, but he was killed in the First World War. Her second husband, a gentleman called Wingfield-Hill, was, we believe, Cynthia's actual father. Flossie, always a colourful character, had, as I told you eloped with the children and Les, then only 18 years old, and settled first in London and later in Aldershot, where, as I've told you, they'd moved to escape the bombin' durin' the Second World War.

As you can imagine, I thought it was somewhat unusual to have one son called Harry, the eldest, and then another called Harold, but then again, Flossie was an unusual woman. I never saw much of Harry, but I did learn that he too had somethin' of a chequered past. Apparently he'd been a deserter durin' the War. You couldn't blame him. Young recruits were treated like machine gun fodder. To help cover his tracks he had changed his name to Lloyd and to get by he worked as a farm hand. He never got caught. When I was courtin' Cynthia, all the rest of the family worked for the army in one capacity or another – except Cynthia herself and her mum who was gettin' on a bit and Mickey, who was still at school. It used to amuse me how Mickey would come down the hill from school brazenly smokin' yet still in short trousers!

Flossie and Les were quite happy about me courtin' Cynthia. Not every parent would have been so pleased to find their daughter was goin' out with a professional musician – not with the reputation we had. Maybe Flossie's background in showbiz made a difference or maybe it was just me. Like me, she was a proper Londoner and loved talkin' about London and the old days. What's more, I like to think I was presentable and a decent sort of chap and truth be told, I barely had time for courtin' Cynthia, much less chasin' after any others. On the other hand, Cynthia was her mother's daughter and a bit flighty, so I had to be on my mettle.

Did we have sex before marriage? We were human – of course we did – but this was the days before the pill so we were careful. We had to be. This wasn't mum's era, the late 1920s, when you could literally be drummed out of town for gettin' pregnant out of wedlock, but nor was it like it is today, where more or less anythin' goes. Even if a girl was goin' steady, gettin' pregnant out of wedlock was still frowned upon. At least if you were goin' steady and your girl did get caught out, or thought she had, you could always get married on the quick and doubtless many did.

In September, when we'd been goin' steady for just 3 months, I popped the question. Maybe that was a bit premature, but I guess I didn't want to risk losin' Cynthia. As I've already said, she was a bit of a flirt in those days. Well, after all, she was still young and fancy free. Cynthia still hadn't met my parents, so we decided to go up to London for a few days – Thursday to Saturday – to celebrate our engagement and meet dad. Although she'd lived in North Finchley as a little girl, her parents had never taken her 'up town', so Cynthia was lookin' forward to it. It was all new to her. Even the underground was a whole new experience, and I was in my element, brimmin' with confidence, showin' off a bit.

I'm not sayin' we were saints. We were passionate and hot-blooded like any young couple, but there was none of this sharin' a bed at dad's. Cynthia was on the put-me-up in the front room and I had my old bed in the back room, but it felt a bit empty not just because my girl was in another room, but because, as you know, I'd always been used to sharin' that bed, with Dinky. Dad was workin' in the daytime and I didn't want him comin' home and cookin' for us. Everythin' had to be just so with dad and I didn't want him goin' to a lot of bother on our account. What's more, we wanted to be up town and out and about – not sittin' at home in Gambetta Street. Cynthia wanted to see the sights and, truth be told, I wanted to impress her and show off a bit. Even in '54 the Festival Gardens in Battersea Park were still quite a sight and bein' only a 15 minute walk, they had to be on our agenda. Sadly, the Dance Pavilion was long gone, but there were still beautiful floral displays by day and colourful fountains at night. On the Friday night we went up to the Palladium to see Norman Wisdom. As I say, I wanted to impress Cynthia, so we had front row seats.

I know I'm digressin' again, but I think I should tell you a bit about Norman Wisdom, not least because like me he was a 'Londoner', born in Marylebone in 1915. We had somethin' else in common too – the army – but I'll come to that. In case you never saw him, he was a little bloke – only 5'2", but take it from me, he had a BIG stage presence. His trademark was his 'gump' look and 'accidental' trip. On stage he always wore a tweed cap askew with the peak turned up. His jacket and trousers were too small for him and his collar was all crumpled and his tie always awry. His act always included his unmistakeable trip up and stumble routine. Followin' in the footsteps of Chaplin, he was a master of physical slapstick comedy but, that wasn't all, he played the trumpet and he wasn't a half bad singer either. His theme song, with which he closed our show, was "Don't laugh at me 'cause I'm a fool".

By 1954 Norman was already a big star, but still on the rise. His first film "Trouble in Store" had been screened in '53, but don't go thinkin' that success had come easy. He hadn't been born with a silver spoon – far from it. A poignant joke he was fond of tellin' was, "I was born in very sorry circumstances – both of my parents were very sorry!" You know the sayin' "many a true word", well that would have been pretty near the mark in Norman's case. He had an elder brother and the family lived in one rented room. His father could be violent and, havin' been at one point disowned, Norman was largely brought up in an orphanage before runnin' away at the age of 11. In 1930, at the age of 15, he enlisted as a drummer boy in the 10th Royal Hussars and served in India as a bandsman. He learnt to play trumpet and clarinet and he became army flyweight boxin' champion! It was in the army where his performin' abilities were first appreciated – in particular the ability to make people laugh. He left the army in 1946, havin' worked in a command bunker in London through the War years. Success as a performer in civvy street was more gradual than instant, but by 1952 his career really began to take off. One of his most famous quotes which I particularly want to share with you because to an extent it resonates with me, was, "I owe everythin' to the army".

I think you can see why I wanted to tell you a bit about Norman but that's enough of me digressin' and I'd best get back to my own story. Suffice to say that Cynthia and I really enjoyed the show. Havin' plumped for the early performance, the night was still young when we came out, so I continued to show Cynthia some of the sights. That included a stroll down Soho. Back then Soho was really quite respectable by day, but come nightfall it was totally transformed, becomin' very 'racy'. It was a real 'eye opener' for Cynthia and I impressed upon her that she must never tell dad.

Fortunately she didn't, but nor did she just forget it. She'd often bring it up when we were socialisin' with friends – even years later.

Back in Aldershot, Cynthia got wind of this furnished flat becomin' available in the High Street, No 143 to be precise. At the time flats were like gold dust and Cynthia wanted me to snap it up before it went. The trouble was, couples didn't just live together in those days. It just wasn't the done thing, but this flat was too good an opportunity to miss, so we decided to take it and set an early date for our weddin'. And so it was that Cynthia and I were married on 18th December 1954 – only about 6 months after we'd first met. I guess you'd call it a 'whirlwind romance', but the fact is, or rather was, that people did seem to tie the knot younger in those days. With my fortnightly visits to Epsom, obviously Cynthia knew about mum and I'd tried to explain her condition, but they'd never actually met. Whilst a mental hospital is hardly the ideal place to take your future bride to meet your mum, with the weddin' loomin' I thought there was nothin' for it but to bite the bullet and take Cynthia along with me. Sad to say, come the day, mum wasn't on good form at all and it was obvious she didn't really register who Cynthia was, much less that we were about to get married. Knowin' mum, if she'd been herself she'd have been straight out of that place and off to the church to make sure it was clean enough! Ok, maybe that's a bit of an exaggeration, but, really, in better times that's how mum was – a stickler for cleanliness and never happier than with a bucket of water and a mop.

Worse was to come. In December mum's condition took a further nose dive and she couldn't attend our weddin'. It wasn't just her mental state. Havin' picked up an infection, she went down with bronchitis and was bed-ridden in the 'hospital wing'. Of course I went to see her just before the weddin' and I was shocked to see just how much she'd gone backwards again. The infection didn't help, but havin' thought she was makin' good progress, it was the deterioration in her mental condition that was most worryin'. I don't know, but now I think maybe they'd given her another course of electric shock treatment. The medical staff never used to tell us anythin' about the treatment they were givin' her or how she was gettin' on. It was always a case of just seein' for ourselves when we got there and, as I've told you, it wasn't until much later that I read about the effects electric shock treatment could have on patients. Whatever the reason, mum was far from herself and I don't think she even recognised me. Words can't express how upsettin' it was to see mum like that. Here I was, about to get married, and I'm not convinced mum even knew.

Cynthia and I were married in St Joseph's Catholic Church, Alexander Road, Aldershot. I wasn't a catholic, but I knew the buildin' well because it was only just down the road from the Palais where I played and Cynthia and I had first met. As a non-catholic, I was required to attend a series of classes prior to the weddin' – a sort of crash course in the Catholic faith. I was obliged to marry into the faith – there was no question of Cynthia defectin' to C of E. Mind you, Cynthia had already defected once – she'd been Jewish originally. As a condition of our marriage, I also had to agree to bring our children up in the Catholic faith. It wasn't a case of 'if we had children'. As far as the Catholic Church was concerned, it was our duty to do so. Not that it mattered because we wanted children anyway.

The actual ceremony was at 2.30 pm, December 18th, 1954. It was a chilly day, but that didn't put a dampener on things. I thought Cynthia looked beautiful in her dress and folk said we made a lovely couple, but you can judge for yourself if you look at the photos at the end of the chapter. The chief bridesmaid was Cynthia's best friend, Gertie. She lived with her mum and dad opposite Les and Flossie, Cynthia's parents. Whilst mum wasn't well enough to attend, I did have the support of dad and our Roy who'd flown home from Kenya to be my 'Best Man'. True to form, Roy turned up resplendent in his best blue army uniform, but I suppose you could say the day didn't start out all that well because he had to 'knock me up'! That doesn't sound too good I know, but I did have an excuse. I'd been playin' at a private function the night before out at Risley, where the rifle academy is, or at least it was. Pat and I had both been playin' as part of an 8-piece band. As we were packin' up at about 1am in the mornin' I made the mistake of sayin', "It's alright for you lot – I'm gettin' married in a few hours." O'course that set 'em off, didn't it. I got, "He's gettin' married in the mornin' ...," the full works. As it happened, luckily, it wasn't in the mornin', it was 2.30 pm in the afternoon, which was just as well because I felt like I needed a bit of shut eye.

Once Roy had got me up and about, generally I think you'd have to say the day went well, really well, except for one more 'hic-cup'.

Bein' Cynthia's best friend, I knew Gertie quite well. Even so, I'm afraid on my weddin' day I got a bit too close to Gertie. No, not in the way you might be thinkin'! Les and Flossie had no money for weddin's, so I was payin' for everythin' – the service, the licence, the reception, even Cynthia's dress, which in case you're wonderin', I hadn't seen before the day. Ok, I had a limited budget but everythin' was organised or so I thought, but you know what they say about the best laid plans. To save a bit we didn't have hire cars or fancy limos. Les would drive his daughter to the church and Cynthia's elder brother Harold was to take me. When I first met him I remember thinkin' he didn't look a well man. Days before the weddin' he was very yellow – just like a Chinaman. Come the day, Harold was too ill to attend our weddin' and certainly too ill to drive. That left me in a bit of a predicament. Nothin' for it but to hitch a ride with the bridesmaids. Only trouble was, their car was already full, so that's how I ended up gettin' a bit too close to Gertie, I finished up arrivin' at the church on Gertie's knee! When I stop to think about it now, she should have hopped out and sat on mine, but on the day that's not the way it happened. We must have looked a sight – arrivin' at the church all crammed in together, but a little thing like that wasn't goin' to spoil our day, and it didn't.

At least I got there on time, if a bit squashed and crumpled and the ceremony itself went without a hitch. Harold apart, Cynthia's family were all there – mum Florence, dad Les, who of course gave her away and her other five brothers and sisters – Monica, Harry, Tony, John and Mickey. Like most Catholics, they were a big family. Florence had had at least ten children includin' several still births. As for Harold, I'm afraid he wasn't just ill, he was really ill. Sadly, within a few weeks he died of liver disease. He was just 34.

When it came to, if I say so myself, the weddin' service itself went well and, after pausin' for some photos, some of which I've included for you to see, we headed off for the reception at the local Bakers! Well I was on a budget. As you can see from the photos, it wasn't the most beautiful of days, but at least it wasn't rainin' and it was December after all. Despite the weather, our weddin' photos are pretty good, don't you think? That's because we were lucky. I probably couldn't have run to a professional photographer, but Cynthia worked for one and he took the photos and presented us with the album as a weddin' present. As you can imagine, I still treasure it.

Before I go on, I'll just tell you about some of the weddin' photos. The one with Dad, Roy and me was taken before the service. The way I'm standin', I think I was a bit nervous. Roy looks good in his dress uniform, sportin' his medal and sergeant's stripes and Dad, resplendent in his Anthony Eden hat, looks just the same as he would if goin' off to work except for the button hole. The first group photo has Cynthia and me flanked by Roy and Gertie with Kajic and Stephka, Monica's kids, holdin' hands. In the main group, we've been joined by Dad, Les and Flossie. That's a real collector's item – a photo of Dad outside without his hat! In the next photo, the lad on crutches is Cynthia's brother Tony who had septicemia at the time. Cynthia's elder sister Monica with husband Jeff are at the back and either side of Mum, Flossie is her brother Mickey and Margaret, her brother Harrold's daughter.

Ok, where I'd arranged for our reception wasn't exactly the Ritz, but when I say it was at the local Bakers, it wasn't a 'tuppeny ha'penny' affair either. They sold bread and cakes downstairs, but upstairs they had a lovely café/restaurant which they hired out as a private function room on such occasions and I have to say they did us proud. The food was plentiful and lovely and they'd dressed the tables really nicely. Cynthia had made the cake so all I had to pay for was for them to do the icin'. And then of course there was the reception itself. It hadn't been a big affair. Mainly close family and a few special friends, so only about 20 people, but receptions are never cheap, are they? Amongst the guests were two special mates from my army band days – Tommy Carter and of course Pat Dimmock. It had been an eventful day to say the least, with a few surprises along the way, but the biggest and nicest surprise came when I went to pay for the reception. The owner took me to one side and said, "You don't owe us anythin' son – go on, on your way." I was 21, just startin' out in married life. I had, give or take, just 21 pounds saved up in the Post Office. To say I was pleased, and that he'd made my day, was puttin' it mildly.

I'd had enough money saved for the weddin' but goin' off on honeymoon, even for a few days, well that was just 'pie in the sky'. I did have a couple of days off though and so the very next day after gettin' married, I took Cynthia, now my wife, over to meet Aunt

Raithby. It wasn't to her old house where I'd been fostered as a child because, as I think I told you, around 1940 whilst I was in Ardingly, Aunt Raithby moved to a council house, No 123 Norbury Avenue, Croydon. The years were takin' their toll, but Aunt Raithby was still very upright, very prim and proper. She was still dear old Aunt Raithby. I haven't recounted any of my visits as a man, so perhaps I should explain that, as I'd gotten older, havin' welcomed me in, she would sit me down with a cup of tea and always a chocolate biscuit. Then she'd prop herself up at the table and standin' there across from me would proceed to tell me all the news about everybody in the family I'd known as a child. When Cynthia and I arrived it was just the same on this and every subsequent visit. From that early age of just 8 months until the day dear Aunt Raithby died, she remained a constant in my life and even now I have to thank my lucky stars that I was placed with such a kind and carin' lady as Aunt Raithby. She wasn't an Aunt at all, but to me she was more than any real aunt could ever be. She was a surrogate mum – constant, dependable, always there for me. A truly wonderful human bein'.

Our flat at 143 High Street, Aldershot was our first home together. It was rented furnished – all second-hand stuff of course and at two pounds fifty a week it was pretty expensive, especially since we didn't exactly have the place to ourselves. The whole time we were there, I suppose you could say we had non-payin' guests, and judgin' by the sound, lots of 'em. Of a night time you could hear 'em scamperin' all over the ceilin'. As a musician playin' mainly in a dance band, most of my work was at night. Rather than be stuck in on her own, often as not Cynthia would come with me. We'd get back from the Palais around midnight or later, dependin', but despite the hour, we'd be ravenous for a sandwich and a cuppa. Our sittin' down to a midnight snack was pretty much always a cue for one of our uninvited guests to make an appearance. This cheeky little beggar would come out from behind the dresser and sit waitin' for the crumbs. Some women would have gone spare, but Cynthia was alright about it until one day when I was lookin' in the mirror over the fireplace to do my hair before goin' out. I got a bit too close and stood on the fender. There was this almighty squeal which made us both jump and then this defeanin' silence. I lifted the fender, gingerly, and there he was – our four legged furry friend, squashed, dead. . I was sorry, but this was one of those times when 'sorry' couldn't mend it.

Talkin' of things that couldn't be mended has made another little incident pop into my head that happened durin' our first week of marriage. We broke the bed! OK, maybe it was gettin' quite a bit of use, but it's not like I was jumpin' off the top of the wardrobe or anythin' like that. It couldn't have been up to much. Even so, it was a bit embarrassin' havin' to go and tell the landlord. I was expectin' a 'right ribbin', we bein' newlyweds and all, but he didn't bat an eyelid, just replaced it with another, but still second-hand bed. I think he owned a lot of property so maybe to him it was just 'par for the course'.

Cynthia and I didn't plan on havin' a big family, but we didn't waste any time in gettin' started. Within a few weeks Cynthia was pregnant. Doubtless the Catholic church would have been pleased that we were 'doin' our duty' – not that duty had anythin' to do with it as far as I was concerned. It's just that we wanted a family and couples tended to have children whilst the mother was much younger than tends to be the case today. If you ask me, in many ways it's the natural thing to do with women bein' in peak child bearin' age in their early '20s. Waitin' till they are over 30 or even 40, as often happens today, tends to create complications, increasin' the risk for both mother and child. We didn't want that.

So now there I was, just 21, a married man with a lovely young wife expectin' our first child. I certainly wasn't 'little Jack' anymore, in fact to most folk, Cynthia included, I was now John but, much more than that, I was no longer single and carefree – I had responsibilities. Livin' in a furnished flat, most things we needed were provided by the landlord, but not stuff like cutlery and saucepans. I only mention it because I remember goin' out buyin' saucepans just before we got married and the thing is, they must have been good because I'm still usin' one of 'em after all these years!

Bein' in the High Street, you could say we were in the thick of things. It was an upstairs flat above a 'tally shop' with, would you believe, an undertaker on one side and a fish and chip shop on the other. An odd sort of mix, don't you think?

The 'tally shop' was an office where folk came to pay off instalments for goods that had been sold 'on tic'. Any youngsters readin' this probably won't have a clue what I'm talkin' about, so I'd better try to explain that in those days, for most people, money was scarce and few would have enough to buy expensive items like furniture or maybe even suits and shoes and rather than waitin' for them whilst they saved up enough, they'd pay a deposit and then have the use of whatever it was whilst payin' off the rest in instalments – weekly, fortnightly or monthly – dependin'. Inevitably, buyin' things 'on tic', as it was commonly referred to, would cost more than payin' for goods outright, but it was a way of bein' able to have and use whatever it was, much sooner than waitin' 'till you'd saved up enough to buy it outright.

As for the undertakers, we had a bit of 'inside information' about them which may surprise you. The thing is that one of Cynthia's brothers worked for 'em for a while and accordin' to him they used to stand the dead bodies upright propped against the wall to wash 'em. Bein 'stiffs' I suppose they could. It's amazin' what goes off – or did.

You could say the fish shop was handy, but at times the smell used to drive us mad, especially when we didn't have the money to go buyin' any. What drove us more mad was the sound of this record player, the reason bein' they only seemed to have one record and kept playin' it over and over and over. 'Rosemary I love you' it was. In the end Cynthia and I would go around singin' it. We couldn't help it – it was ingrained on our brains.

Our flat was fine, but it was expensive and ideally we would have liked our own place – preferably with a bit of garden for when the children came along. Livin' in the same town, we saw a lot of Flossie and Les, Cynthia's mum and dad. In particular they'd come round once a fortnight to sample one of Cynthia's culinary specialities – a sort of suet puddin'. She'd make this great big roly-poly puddin'. One half would be plain and the other half would have raisins and currants in it – like spotted dick. They'd have their meal at home and come to us just for this suet puddin'. I guess they must have liked it a lot because it was always the same puddin'. Flossie liked hers plain with golden syrup and Les always had the currant side with custard. Cynthia and I would have whatever was left, but the whole thing would always get eaten. I wasn't always there. Sometimes I'd be out workin', but when I was we'd all sit chattin'. Cynthia and Flossie would exchange gossip, which was fine, but now and again Flossie would get a bit agitated, moanin' about us two for not havin' this or that. The 'tally man' business, particularly buyin' stuff from catalogues on HP, was already rife in Aldershot, and as I've told you, we lived on top of one, but it wasn't for me. I'd have to keep puttin' my foot down or Flossie would have had Cynthia buyin' all sorts of stuff that we didn't really need and definitely couldn't afford. I never did subscribe to HP – not then, not ever. Mum had taught me well in that regard. I think so anyway.

Flossie was the Matriarch of the family and used to gettin' her own way, but now that I was married to her daughter, I needed to show that I could stand up for myself and wouldn't be pushed around. I suppose it was more symbolic than anythin', but I remember early on sayin' to Flossie, "You're in my house now – so take your hat off," and she did. In fact she always did after that. It's only a small thing, but I think it was one of the ways in which I was able to earn her respect, which I could see would be important or she'd walk all over us. As for me and Cynthia, we didn't argue much. If you ask me, 'rowin' never helped any relationship. Rather than get into a heated argument, I'd take a different tack with Cynthia. I tended to back off and give us both time to calm down. If you think about it, if you keep silent you can't say the wrong thing or hear yourself sayin' somethin' you'll later regret. That's my philosophy anyway.

I was gettin' plenty of work as a musician and the money was pretty good. We weren't just playin' at the Palais. Pat and I were gettin' plenty of other work, especially in the various military bases, includin' the US bases at Newbury and Bracknell. Pat was very serious about his music – he lived and breathed it. Gettin' to and from gigs could sometimes be a bit of a problem though, so Pat splashed out and bought an old station wagon. Now I should say that Pat was a bachelor and did all his own washin' and ironin'. He was very particular about his appearance, but somehow always contrived to get it a bit wrong. He'd call to pick me up and say to Cynthia, "How do I look?" She'd often have to laugh because chances were he'd have gone and spread brylcreme on his shirt or somethin' similar that needed sortin' out. In case you're wonderin', "What's Brylcreme when it's at home?" In those days most men used Brylcreme to hold their hair in place. Dreadful stuff when I think about it. Made greasy marks on everythin' it touched, settee backs, pillows, you name it and somehow Brylcreme managed to get on to it and mark it. Makes you wonder how it ever caught on, but it did. Every barber sold the stuff, along with "somethin' for the weekend!"

As well as Newbury and Bracknell, there was another big US Airforce base near Aldershot. For the life of me I can't remember the name, but no matter, although, thinkin' about it, I'm pretty sure it was off the A287 at a place called Odiham. The point is, we'd play there fairly regularly. Popular we were. I'm mentionin' it mainly because somethin' odd would happen at least once and often twice durin' the course of the evenin'. We'd be playin' away when all of a sudden this terrible, deafenin' roar would go up. It would go on for maybe ten minutes or more and then fall silent again. We were expected to keep playin', which we did, but I doubt anybody could hear us over that racket. I'd always assumed it must be planes startin' up for take-off, but I could never fathom why so many and goin' on for so long and why every time we played. It would be years later when I was workin' at the North East Surrey College of Technology before I got the answer. A Wing Commander Brown joined us as Chief Administrator for Nescot and I happened to be chattin' to him one day when the topic came up. He'd been C.O. all over the place and was able to tell me all that noise was down to manoeuvres – at the ready preparations associated with the Cold War. The mid 1950s in particular was a time when apparently some of the air bases were on pretty constant high alert. And there we'd been, a dance band, entertainin', oblivious.

There's no doubt we were popular with the Yanks, so much so that they'd already be queuein' up to go in when we arrived. Trouble was, the work was at night and already that wasn't goin' down too well. Cynthia had fallen for me as a performer and she loved to see me up on stage, but she didn't like bein' left on her own in the flat. That's why, very often she'd come with us and two particular occasions stick in my memory.

The first would have been around February 1955. It was freezin' cold, about 1 am in the mornin' and we were on our way back from the American Airforce Base at Newbury. Cynthia and I were in the back of Pat's station wagon. All of a sudden this bloomin' great stag jumped out of nowhere straight over the bonnet. Cynthia screamed. It's a good job she wasn't far gone or the shock might have started her off there and then. I yelled, 'Blimey, did you see that?" Pat was nonplussed. "What's up? I never saw anythin'." I always knew his eyes weren't so good because he wore special glasses when playin', but I never thought they were that bad. How he could have missed seein' somethin' as big as that jumpin' across the screen beggars belief. Were we safe bein' driven by this man? Cynthia wasn't so sure and ever after she was a bit nervous bein' driven about by Pat.

The second was a few weeks later. We were doin' one of our regular stints at the Palais and that particular night we were doin' Be Bop type music. I loved doin' that. I was really in my element. We had piano, drums, sax and a string bass and together we created a good sound. Our pianist sang as well – a bit like Ella Fitzgerald. In the interval we'd generally go to the cafe upstairs for a cuppa and a fairy cake. Honestly, I'm not jokin' – we rarely had alcohol durin' the breaks in those days. Anyway, this particular night Cynthia was up there chattin' to George Magee – our string bass player, whilst I was gettin' the drinks. She always liked chattin' to George. I overheard some of the conversation, which went somethin' like this: "You've really got to talk to John. You've only been married a short while but your marriage is never goin' anywhere unless he does somethin' else. As it is, John just lives for his music." That wasn't somethin' I wanted to hear, but it struck a chord and the seeds of doubt had been well and truly sown – I guess with both Cynthia and me. You could say his words hit home like a poison dart which slowly but surely took effect. It was still early days though and I did so love my music. I really came alive when performin'. I was never more alive than when I was up on that stage. What's more, it was our livelihood.

Not long after, Pat and I got an unusual request – to play in a circus! Baker Bros Circus to be precise. They used to over winter at the California Leisure Complex near Readin'. It wasn't a big circus, but they had some talented performers. Not least Hampee the Clown. They used to team up with Bertram Mills to do special Christmas performances at Olympia. Then Hampee would work with Coco. He'd dress up like a tramp but with a clown's face – a bit like one of Charlie Chaplin's guises. You might think clowns are a bit simple minded – but you'd be wrong – very wrong. Hampee was a very intelligent man. Durin' the war he'd been assigned to an intelligence unit charged with interrogatin' important German prisoners.

We didn't exactly jump at the chance to work with the circus. In fact we ummed and aahed about it for a while, but then we thought, 'What the hell. It'll be a bit of an adventure'. And so it proved to be. We both revelled in it. We worked up a basic routine for 'em, but there was also a lot of improvisation needed . I liked workin' with Hampee best. We got on well because he liked the way I could improvise and quickly work out how best to interpret and project what he was doin' in his 'performance'. I guess like all great performers, he wasn't one for stickin' rigidly to any script, so I always had to be on my toes, ready for anythin'. But I was young and quick and good at anticipatin' and he appreciated that. Whenever he made a move I had to reflect, emphasise or dramatise it in music, which was challengin' and fun. Part of the act included an explodin' car, which always went down well. Of course we knew it was goin' to happen, but Hampee was always full of surprises and his unpredictability kept us on our toes. He generated feel good factor and sympathy rolled into one. You couldn't help but empathise with him and laugh along. Mind you, Hampee himself, he never so much as smiled – always completely deadpan – when performin' that is. When, eventually, I left the circus, I hadn't expected to see Hampee again but, as things turned out I did, and even though it was a good number of years later, he spotted me in the audience and made a point of comin' over after to 'catch up'. But, that's all in the future.

Whilst for the Winter Season the circus was based at the California, the owners also took the show on the road and they wanted Pat and I to go with them. Really they wanted us to 'muck in' like the rest of 'em and help dismantle and set the thing up, but Pat wasn't havin' any of that. We were the musical accompaniment and that was as far as it went. We were with them about 2 months, visitin' such places as Marlow on Thames, Maidenhead, Luton and Bedford. Bedford sticks in the memory because it was there the monkey got loose and ran away. It was a well-trained performer ridin' bare-back on a pony doin' somersaults, backflips and everythin'. What it didn't do, it seems, was come back when called. Picture the scene: there was this little monkey dashin' down the street – very fast it was – and half the circus chasin' after it. Then there was this woman on the pavement in hysterics. I can see her now – clear as day. I never could resist a bit of a joke so I said to her, "It's alright you laughin' missus – it could have been the tiger!" You should have seen her face. We never even had a tiger. At one point the monkey bolted into a house, but they couldn't catch him and he was off again. He was just too quick. They tried everythin' but in the end they had to shoot him 'cos they just couldn't catch him. The circus folk were very upset. They brought him back and buried him. It was all very sad.

It would have been around May 1955 when I got offered and decided to take this week long job playin' with the circus, still mainly as back-up to the clowns, creatin' atmosphere and a sense of anticipation in the crowd. By now Cynthia was quite heavily pregnant, so I'd 'ummed and aahed' a bit before agreein' to go. The circus was performin' near Luton at the time and, as things turned out, bein' popular they extended and needed me an extra day. This was in the days before ordinary people like us had phones, but somehow I needed to let Cynthia know. I had a brainwave. I thought, nothin' for it, I'll phone Aldershot Police and get them to call round with a message. I played the poor pregnant wife home alone card and it did the trick. They didn't tell me where to go or give me a lecture on wastin' police time. They dutifully relayed my message. Try doin' that today. You'd be lucky if anybody answered the phone, much less did you a service like that.

Bein' away quite a bit, when I wasn't workin' I was always lookin' for somethin' to please Cynthia. In the early 1950s, very few ordinary workin' folk had a car, but Cynthia's father, Les, did and so did Monica's husband Jeff. Occasionally we'd go on family outin's, often at my instigation. One particular time springs to mind. One sunny Saturday in, I think, May 1955, we decided to go on a fishin' trip-cum-picnic to Cut Mill Pond, Guildford. Beautiful it was – a shimmerin' expanse of water in a woodland settin'. Cynthia's sister Monica and her Polish husband Jeff came too. He was no fisherman, but I set him up with a spare rod and tackle and I got him to cast out and then set his rod on a 'rest' whilst I set to fixin' my own rod. It was a bakin' hot day, so I'd taken my shirt off.

I'd barely got started puttin' my rod together when Jeff pipes up, "John, me float's gone." I set to helpin' him and after a gargantuan struggle, we finally landed this amazin' big carp. I know this is a 'fishy' story, but really, this thing was absolutely massive. Bein' Polish and somethin' of a virgin fisherman, Jeff wanted to take the thing back home for dinner. Right enough, it would have fed a small army, though I'm not sure how it would have tasted. Anyway I had to explain it was a sport and the done thing with fresh water fish was to put 'em back. We did, but I'm not sure he was all that happy seein' it swimmin' off – especially after all the effort it had taken to land it.

Amazin' though it was, that huge carp wasn't the only reason I remember this particular trip so vividly. We packed up around 4 pm because I had a band job that evenin'. Back home I got myself washed and changed, but it was difficult. Why? Because like a fool, havin' had my shirt off all day, I'd let myself get badly sunburnt, and I do mean badly. It had been hot and sunny all day, but I suppose bein' next to the water I hadn't realised I was burnin'. Now I was in agony – I really was – but I had a job to do. When Pat came to pick me up I was in a right state, but I clambered in and somehow I got through the night. My playin' must have been all over the place, but at least I didn't let them down. I learnt my lesson though. I've never let myself get burnt like that again. Once was enough.

Throughout 1955, Pat and I frequently went on tour with the circus. We'd share a caravan and usually we'd be away Tuesday 'till Sunday then we'd be off back to Aldershot whilst the circus packed up and moved on to the next venue. Then we'd re-join 'em when all the hard work had been done. As you know, I'd not been long married, so you can imagine, my bein' away didn't go down too well with Cynthia. I guess part of the problem was that musicians had a bit of a reputation for philanderin'. I wasn't 'playin' away', leastways not in that sense, but Cynthia wasn't to know that. To make matters worse, my job with the circus wasn't the only reason for my bein' away for more than a few days at a time.

When I finished tellin' you about my army career, I think I told you that after gettin' married, apart from Pat, I'd never seen any of my army mates again since leavin' the army. That's true, but you'd be forgiven for thinkin' I meant at the end of my two years National Service. If there's any of you readin' this old enough to have done National Service in the 1950s, then you'll know that it wasn't quite over when your two years were up. If you remember, I've already mentioned that for the next three years you'd become part of what was known as 'Z Reserve'. With that in mind, when your two years as a conscript were up, you still kept your two uniforms to use when called up again as Z Reserve. For most conscript squaddies, that meant two battle dress uniforms, both the same except one of 'em would have seen a lot more everyday use than the other. In the band we didn't have battle dress uniforms – we didn't need 'em, but I'd still kept mine. As you know, it's what I'd used for hitch-hikin'. In the band we wore CD's – rather like First World War uniforms they had buttons right the way down. Rather smart they were. I thought so, anyway. One was what we called 'a set of blues' that we wore when playin' in public. For Z Reserve though, I used my old battle dress uniform. After all, apart from hitch-hikin', it hadn't seen much use. The idea was that for each of the three years followin' your two years National Service, you'd get called up for a further two weeks a year 'refresher trainin', except I don't know anyone who was sent for more than twice. Maybe some were and they just gave up on those they could see were useless at proper soldierin' – like me!

Anyway, as you know, I'd been called up again in August 1954 – a bit soon I thought havin' only left in March - and now, as we got to August 1955 my call-up papers came again. It was a bit of a nuisance really because the pay was poor and havin' not been married long, I was already in a bit of hot water for keep bein' away for days at a time with the circus. By August Cynthia was heavily pregnant with our first child and neither of us were happy about me havin' to leave her on her own for a fortnight.

Fast forward for a minute to the summer of 2015 and I'm movin' house at the moment. Well, I am 81 (leastways I was then) and bein' on my own I thought it was about time I downsized. I can practically hear you sayin' "it's a bit late for that" and if you're not then you should be. Mark my words, it is, so don't leave yours so long. Anyway, the point is when you're downsizin' you tend to spend a lot of time sortin' through stuff you'd forgotten you'd got and I've just come across a whole batch of letters I wrote to Cynthia when I was away on 'Z Reserve'. It seems I wrote every day bar one and my Cynthia thought enough of 'em to keep 'em. Readin' 'em, they're full of nothin' really, but they were important enough to Cynthia for her to keep 'em, and now I can't bring myself to throw 'em away.

Back to my narrative. Right, so what have I got to tell you about Z Reserve? Well, for starters it wasn't hard graft. In fact, in truth for me it was a bit of a holiday really because I had more free time than anythin' else. My letters to Cynthia don't really reflect that, but then – well, I think you can understand why. It wasn't just the amount of free time I had, it was where I was posted that made it more like a holiday for me. Back to Hillsea – now how lucky was that. I'm sayin' Hillsea, but it was actually the ground opposite, but that was near enough as to make no difference. For my first stint in 1954 we had been in tents, but that was fine because we had lovely weather. In fact, if I remember right, we spent a lot of our time on Southsea Beach sunbathin'!

August 1955 was a bit more eventful, so I'll focus more on that. This time we were assigned to a particular group of huts. Nothin' unusual about that, except these were filthy. How and why that came to be I don't know 'cos squaddies are normally made to keep 'em pretty much spotless. Maybe it was done on purpose – a sort of welcome back present from the regulars who generally regarded us part-timers as several rungs beneath 'em. Maybe it was just to give us somethin' to do in our 'spare time'. Whatever, we had a real job to clean 'em up. It's all recounted in my letters home.

As you know, Cynthia was about 7 months pregnant and before leavin' we'd talked about her comin' down to Southsea with her mum and dad for a day as a bit of a break. Even so, durin' the second week when we were on the range, havin' shootin' practice, I got a real surprise. This bloke drives up to the rifle range with a message for me from back at camp. My pregnant wife was here to see me.

As you know, in my army career, I'd barely touched a rifle. Those around me were in more danger of bein' hit than the targets, so it was a relief all round when Cynthia turned up and I was allowed to go and see her. I bet not many blokes can say they've had a pregnant woman rescue 'em from army rifle practice.

Havin' been told I could clear off, I hopped into this Tilly Van, a sort of jeep with a canvas cover on the back, and got chauffeured back to base. Cynthia was there, not with her mum and dad, as I'd expected, but with Babs and her daughter, Margaret, then about ten. Babs had been married to Harold, Cynthia's brother, the one who'd died shortly after our weddin'. Their marriage had been a funny set up. I'll tell you about it in a minute.

Anyway, it was lateish afternoon, so I took the three of them down to South Sea Beach and we strolled along the front. After, we only had time for a bite to eat before I had to put them back on the train in Portsmouth Station. They were headed back to Aldershot, not to our flat, but to Les and Flossie's. With her bein' pregnant, we'd arranged for Cynthia to stay with her mum and dad whilst I was away and as it happened Babs had gone to stay with them too.

Now, although I'm digressin', I can't resist tellin' you about that 'funny set up' with Babs and Harold. For a start, Cynthia's family were a good sort, but, as you've probably gathered by now, unusual with it. Babs had been married to Harold, one of Cynthia's brothers – the one who was ill and sadly died just after we married. Harold had big ideas, but none of 'em ever came to anythin' and he never had any money. He was rather quick-tempered and a bit strange. I think he was 'all there' but he used to sit readin' kids' comics. Anyway, their marriage was a strange set up because most of the time they lived apart. Harold lived at home with Les and Flossie and, whilst Babs would come and stay with him for the odd fortnight now and then, most of the time she'd stay in Finchley, London, with her mum and dad. Now, I should explain that as well as not havin' their own home to go to, one of the reasons Babs stayed with her mum and dad was to help out with her mentally handicapped sister. She also more or less looked after her parents – got their tea and everythin'. She was just that type.

Anyone could see theirs wasn't much of a marriage, so it was no surprise to anybody when shortly after Harold died, Babs got married again to the chap who'd been lodgin' with her parents in Finchley for some years. He worked in the city. I never really got to know him because I never saw that much of him even when we went over to see Babs and the rest of them. Lovely family they were – very welcomin'. Used to make a real fuss of our three kids. Babs' sister must have been about forty, but she acted like a child and used to run around and play with our three. Harmless she was, but she could never go out anywhere on her own. There I go again, not only digressin' but jumpin' the gun, mentionin' our three kids when we haven't even got one yet! Back to August 1955 and Z Reserve.

As usual, one of the first things the Instructors would do next day was go through all the targets and in most cases tell us how useless we were. As it happened, I'd thought I'd been doin' quite well before Cynthia arrived, but it seems the only hits I'd scored were on the blokes' targets in the next bay! The Instructor had a bit of a sense of humour 'cos he shouts out, "Oh, and by the way Wattley, if we ever get you out on the range again, get your wife to come down and take you out of the way before you do any damage!" O'course all the lads were laughin', but I didn't mind. I'd had my day out with Cynthia and, in case you're wonderin', that was the only day I didn't write home.

Next day I was wanderin' about at a bit of a loose end when I heard a band strikin' up. I knew where they'd be playin' so I made my way into Hillsea proper and there they were, the RAOC Band playin' for a General's Inspection of the regular troops. It felt strange seein' another drummer in my place and I've got to admit I was a bit envious of him. Although it was a couple of years on, I knew most of the band because they were regulars. I got chance to catch up with them after and learn there was a dance on in the all-purpose hall at Hillsea the followin' night. So that was me fixed up for Friday night as well. Not too bad this Z Reserve. They say that 'a change is as good as a rest' and really Z Reserve was both for me. I didn't tell Cynthia that though. Some things are better kept to yourself.

One of the jobs we had when back in Aldershot was playin' with Billy Turnant's singer at the California. He was quite a well-known band leader often on the wireless playin' on Variety Bandbox on a Sunday night. As I've told you, Bob Potter used to get us the work and so it was that on one particular Sunday I asked him if I could have the night off. Cynthia wanted me to go to Bognor with her family. I wanted to be a good husband and you have to remember I'd only just got back from Z Reserve and I'd often been days away with the circus and at other times often out 'till 2 am in the mornin'. In those days the California was a very popular venue and, to say the least, Bob wasn't best pleased. I clearly remember him sayin', "I bloody told you – you should never have got married." He wasn't goin' to make it easy for me, but as I say, I wanted to be a good husband and so I went anyway. After that, things started fallin' apart between my manager and me.

It had all been very quick. I'd met Cynthia and we were married just a few months later in that same year, 1954. We were very young – especially Cynthia – and I suppose it was all a bit too quick really, but she was a good lookin' woman, she was choice. I thought so anyway. Now she was pregnant and I'd be leavin' her about 7 o'clock at night and often not gettin' back 'till the early hours. She didn't like it and I didn't feel right doin' it so I started askin' for more days off and that didn't go down well with Potter. When Cynthia was almost full term, I had this blazin' row with Bob Potter. I can't recall the date or even what the row was all about. Maybe I've just blocked it out on account of what it led to. Long story short – I got in touch with Jeff – who if you remember was Monica's husband, Cynthia's brother-in-law, and asked him to come over in his car, collect my kit and take it over to Potters Music Shop in town and see what he could get for it. I'd bought it from them. It was practically new. As you know, we were livin' in this furnished flat in the High Street, No. 143. It was a three-storey buildin' and we were on the top floor, so I'd left my drum kit on the ground floor in the communal entrance area ready for collection.

Jeff and Monica, Cynthia's sister, lived a good few miles away and he'd made a special journey over to do the job for me. He was good like that, a lovely bloke. When he came we chatted for a bit. I think he wanted to be certain I was sure, but although I told him I was, when it came to it, I just couldn't go downstairs with him to help load up. I tried not to let it show, but in truth I was overcome with emotion. I was really choked up. I could barely breathe. It was like my heart would stop – like it was literally bein' wrenched out of me. I wanted to be a good husband and a good father and I resolved to make that my priority, but before Cynthia, those drums had been my great passion in life. My first love. They were more, so very, very much more than just a piece of kit that I played for a livin'. I'd put my heart and soul into my playin'. I loved it. I loved it so very, very much. Words can't really convey how I felt. Lettin' go. Sayin' goodbye to that part of my life was the hardest thing I'd ever had to do. It was then and it still is. Recountin' it for you now is painful, even after all these years I just can't stop the tears.

Cynthia on the beach at Southsea or Bognor – I'm not sure which.

Portrait photo of 'Cynbo', my nickname for Cynthia, taken at 'Airborne Pictures', the professional photographers where she worked.

Dad in Anthony Eden hat with his two sons – Roy resplendent in his army dress uniform with sergeant's stripes and me, taken just before goin' into church for my weddin'. Dad is dressed exactly as he would have been if goin' out to work. Always the same.

The bride and groom – Cynthia and yours truly.

Cynthia and me with Gertie, Cynthia's best friend, my brother Roy and Kajic and Stephka, Cynthia's sister Monica's children.

Now we've been joined by dad and Cynthia's parents, Flossie and Les. A real collector's item this one — Dad outdoors without his hat.

Flossie with son Mickey on the left, Monica and Jeff behind and son Tony (who had septicaemia at the time) and granddaughter Margaret.

329

Cynthia and me cuttin' the cake at our reception.

CHAPTER 8

Life After Death

Ok, I know it's an odd title and no, I didn't actually die again, but when Jeff drove off, with him went my music career. That was it – the end of an era - the shatterin' of my dreams. My music, that had died, and with it, somethin' inside me, deep inside had died and for a long, long while, I'd feel bereft. Don't misunderstand me, I don't mean all the time. I didn't sit mopin'. I didn't dwell on it. I got on with life and tryin' to be a good husband but, now and again, that feelin' of loss would take me unawares and I'd be overcome by it. In case you're wonderin', I did play in public again, but not for 13 years. Even then, it was for one night only – but I'll come to that later, in the sequel. For now, I don't want to dwell on givin' up my music any more. I need to push it to the very back of my mind – where it's been lyin' dormant in wait for so many years. I need to move on.

It's a while since I gave you a proper update on how mum was farin', so before I go any further, I'd better put that right. As you know, mum was too ill to attend our weddin', but I'm glad to say that over the course of the followin' six months she improved greatly. Her visits home became more and more frequent until finally, in September 1955 I think it was, she decided she was well enough to stay home permanently. It was a big relief all round and I certainly didn't miss the Sunday trips to Epsom. It's probably not a very nice thing to say, but dad wasn't really much use when mum came out of hospital. He wasn't welcomin' or anythin'. He never showed any emotion. I suppose I didn't just want him to be pleased, I wanted

331

him to show he was pleased, to maybe say, "Mum's back – let's have a party!", but there was none of that. It was just a big anti-climax and mum just had to slot back in and get on with it.

For me at least, it was good to have mum home and for a while I harboured hopes that in time she'd be back to her old self, but deep down I suppose I knew it was unlikely. Mother was home with dad, but she was rarely the same mum I'd known and loved. Don't misunderstand me, I still loved her, of course I did, but she was different. She was unpredictable and still prone to actin' strangely. I could cope and for want of a better phrase, I knew how to handle her. Cynthia on the other hand couldn't cope at all and didn't like to be left alone with mum. Then again you must remember Cynthia was still only 19.

Our baby was due towards the end of October, but out of the blue at the beginnin' of the month mum arrived in Aldershot "to help out". Cynthia wasn't best pleased. She just didn't feel comfortable with mum around. Oblivious and unperturbed, mum set off around the shops to buy things for the baby. Even Cynthia couldn't help but be pleased about that. Funny thing was though, a few weeks later we got all the bills! Mum had done the shoppin' but left us to do the payin'! It's just the way she was now – not really mum at all.

Anyway, mum had been on her shoppin' spree on the Saturday – 1st October as it happens – and next mornin' she took herself off to church. Bein' a Sunday mornin', Cynthia and I were havin' a bit of a lie-in. Actually we were both sittin' up in bed smokin'. I know that sounds terrible, but back then most young people smoked. No-one realised the dangers – not least to the unborn child. I smoked quite a few, but not nearly as many as Cynthia who was on at least 50 a day.

Mum hadn't been gone long when Cynthia's waters broke. We didn't panic, but when it's your first – well these are anxious times. I went down to the phone box and called for an ambulance. It probably wasn't very long, but in the circumstances it seemed to take ages to arrive. I wanted to go with Cynthia, but then there was mum to sort out. As it was, the ambulance was just speedin' off when mum came round the corner. She wanted to stay to help out, but with everythin' that was goin' on I just didn't feel I could cope with mum as well, so I was firm and packed her off back to London. I knew that Cynthia wouldn't have been happy to find mum still with us when she came out of hospital with our new baby.

Victor – that's what we called our little boy, wasn't born straight away. In fact he didn't enter the world until later that night – 6 pm, October 2nd, 1955. By this time I was in the hospital, but there was none of this encouragin' or even lettin' the husband be present at the birth. It was all very Victorian. You were lucky to be allowed to sit and wait in a corridor. Victor only weighed 5 lbs and had been born several weeks premature. Now we'd think the heavy smokin' had somethin' to do with it, but back then nobody made the connection, not even the medical staff.

It's difficult to describe how I felt seein' our new-born son for the first time. I guess it was a mixture of joy, pride and relief that everythin' had gone Ok. Victor was very small, but perfect. And he was ours. Our very own baby boy. A tiny bundle. A livin', breathin' miracle.

Next night, naturally I went visitin'. It's a visit that sticks in the memory, but not for the reasons you might think. Aldershot Hospital has been pulled down now, but I can still picture the maternity ward. It seemed to go on forever. As I walked in, the sister – or matron in charge – I'm not sure which, greeted me with the words, "Thank goodness you've come. We've had such trouble with your wife." I followed her down the corridor, all the while worryin' that Cynthia was ill or not copin' well, but when we came to this bed with screens round it, I got a bit of a shock. In other circumstances I might have started laughin'. Behind the screens there was this poor woman in bed, very distressed she was. The sister says, "Come on dear, quieten down now – your husband's here." I just stood there takin' in the scene and when I didn't move to comfort this stranger the sister turns to me with, "Are you alright?", to which I replied, "No, not really – this isn't my wife!"

In fact we'd walked right past Cynthia's bed, but I hadn't noticed in my haste to keep up. As you can imagine, Cynthia and I had quite a laugh about that, but it wasn't the only bit of humour to mark my first visit. I'd got there early so it was a good while before the bell went, but then of course, along with the other visitors, I had to leave. With all the excitement of our new baby I suppose my head was up in the clouds as I skipped down the stairs. It wasn't until I got outside that I remembered I'd forgotten the dirty washin'. In those days husbands were expected to take away dirty nappies and vests and bring clean ones back next day. Anyway, as a dutiful husband, I went bouncin' back up the stairs and into the ward to collect the dirty washin'. Trouble was, with visitin' time bein' over, by this time half the women were out of bed, half naked, breast feedin' and so on. The way some of 'em started screamin' you'd have thought I was molestin' 'em instead of just fetchin' some washin'. The Sister was on to me in a flash – "Get out of my Ward. I've had enough trouble with you." It was no good arguin', but in truth I hadn't been any trouble. She was the one who'd made the mistake, but it was her Ward and I didn't want her givin' Cynthia grief so off I went, washin' in hand, 'my tail between my legs'. You have to remember that Sisters ran their wards with a rod of iron in those days and woe-betide anyone who challenged 'em.

Being so small, Victor needed special attention and in particular he had to be fed six times a day. In those days it was quite normal for mother and baby to stay in hospital for at least a week before bein' sent home. Cynthia and Victor came home after ten days.

I was glad when they were home, not least because I didn't have to keep runnin' the gauntlet past the Sister at the Hospital. Victor was a lovely baby in the daytime, but he turned into a little terror at night. We never got any sleep. Part of the problem might have been that Cynthia had to stop breast feedin'. She had a problem – mastitis I guess it was – but I can't remember the term bein' used at the time. She'd only been home a couple of days when she went into a sort of coma. Very frightenin' it was. Fortunately I was on hand to call a doctor. From day one, a nurse had been callin' in to check up on mother and baby, but the frequency of her visits increased after that. Within a couple of days though she called a halt. Cynthia was too ill to try to continue breast feedin'. It was a Sunday. The nurse had powdered milk supplies with her, but not bottles. Fortunately Cynthia remembered her mum still had a baby's feedin' bottle and measurin' jug at home.

I walked over to her mother's house – about a mile and a half – and went in to find them all watchin' Sunday night at the London Palladium. I'll never forget it. They barely turned round as I recounted our problem and nobody moved. Flossie, Cynthia's mum, just told me which cupboards to look in. So I just helped myself and set off walkin' back home thinkin', "that's grandparents for you. Not exactly dotin', these ones". If you remember, Les had a car. Later he'd become very supportive and helpful, but not at that early stage in our relationship. Thankfully Victor took to the bottle pretty well. I guess he was hungry - poor little mite. Then we tucked him up in his drawer hopin' for a good night's sleep. Some hope. It would be a long time, a very long time, before Victor obliged us in that regard. You're probably thinkin', "what's all this about a drawer?" Well, the thing was, Victor was too small for a cot. He was much safer and more snug bein' tucked up in a drawer!

There's lots more to tell you about our family life, but before I do I need to go back a few weeks, before Victor was born, to when I'd sold my drum kit. With it went my livelihood. Our furnished flat was two pounds ten shillin's a week, which was quite pricey for Aldershot. With my drums gone and with them my income, my first priority now was to get myself a regular job with regular income and regular hours. I needed a job quickly. Luckily I had no trouble gettin' one. In fact I started with Southern Electric that same week. I was assistant to this surveyor measurin' for pylons. Not exactly a vocation, and to be honest I pretty soon realised it wasn't for me. What's more, I didn't like the bloke I was workin' for. The pay was only 7 pounds a week – enough to get by, but that was about all. Worst of all I had an early start and was away from home all day, leavin' Cynthia to cope on her own. I only stuck it for a couple of weeks before gettin' a job with a firm of local builders and decorators, Snuggs & Co.

Snuggs & Co were well-known and respected in Aldershot. A traditional family firm. I was too old for an apprenticeship, but Mr Snuggs was a decent old chap and willin' to give me a try. He put me with the decoratin' team doin' wallpaperin', paintin' and decoratin'. I didn't know the first thing about it. I'd never done any, so it was a case of learnin' on the job. As it happens, I took to it like a duck to water. It was still only 7 pounds a week, but I was doin' somethin' I enjoyed and I felt I was acquirin' some useful skills and usually, I wasn't away from home for quite so long. Mr Snuggs was proud of his reputation. His motto might have been, "If a job is worth doin', it's worth doin' well." That attitude extended to every aspect of the service we provided. I remember one time he gave me a bit of a tickin' off, but not in front of the customer. That would never do. I was scrapin' wallpaper off in this hotel and I asked one of the staff if they could lend me a bucket. He took me on one side and made it very clear that I was never to ask a customer for anythin' I required to do my job. "If you want anythin' then you go back to the depot for it and next time, before you leave the depot in the mornin', think about the job in hand and make sure you've got everythin' you might need with you on the van."

That little incident apart, the job was goin' quite well, but the money wasn't good – enough to get by but that was about all. There was no real future in it. No chance to save to better ourselves. It was the end of October 1955, Victor was still just a few weeks old and havin' been so premature, wasn't the easiest of babies. Havin' had to give up breast feedin' Cynthia still wasn't feelin' too well and strugglin' with Victor. Mum had come visitin' to see if she could help out. I have to say she seemed much better in herself, she didn't have any turns and was as near normal as she'd been for a very long time, almost like my mum of old. She offered to have us come up to London to stay with them where she could help out with Victor and I should have more chance of gettin' a better paid job. I thought it would do mum good too – give her a greater sense of purpose and self worth. Cynthia still had reservations but she had to admit mum seemed fine and what's more, we wouldn't have to find the two pounds ten every week for rent.

We talked about it and decided, all things considered, we should give it a go, so we gave notice on the flat and packed up all our stuff into boxes and on November 5th 1955, Les came in his car to take the three of us and all our worldly goods off up to London. At that time we had no furniture of our own so all our stuff went in his car, no problem and off we went to mum and dad's in Gambetta Street. It wasn't ideal, givin' up our own place to move in with parents, but we thought so long as I could get a better paid job in the city, we'd be able to start savin' and fairly soon be able to get a place of our own.

Whilst she could see the upsides, Cynthia was apprehensive about movin' in with her in-laws, so it was important to try to relax her a bit. Bein' November 5th, parents and kids were lettin' fireworks off in the street, so while mum and dad minded Victor in the back, I took the opportunity to have a bit of quality time with Cynthia watchin' the fireworks from the front room window. It was an upstairs flat remember, so we had a good view. She liked that and I think the distraction helped a lot with the settlin' in.

Cynthia and I had the spare room (my old bedroom) and the front room to ourselves, so we had some more or less 'private space'. It wasn't ideal because for a start we weren't sleepin' together. If you remember, my room was a box room only just big enough for a single bed. Cynthia had a divan bed in the front room. At least that was a step up from the 'put-you-up' bed Roy and I used to use. Back in my old bed, it wasn't just Cynthia I was missin' because, as you know, Dinky had died. The bed felt empty without my feline companion. Dinky had been one of a kind. Mum and dad never had another cat.

Despite my best endeavours, almost from the outset there were tensions in the house. Dad had little patience with children. He'd never been very good when Roy and I were young and he was that much older now and if anythin' even less tolerant. On the other hand, mum was in her element. She loved lookin' after Victor. Trouble was, she was maybe a bit too possessive and a bit too quick to tell Cynthia how to do things. Times had changed and Cynthia had her own ideas and the three of them didn't always gel together at all well. In particular, mum's old-fashioned remedies for baby complaints like colic didn't go down well with Cynthia at all. It was a case of "you're not givin' my baby this or that". As the days went by, tensions were risin'. On the one hand Cynthia was nervous of mum and didn't like bein' left alone with her in case she had one of her turns, and on the other they weren't just a generation apart, their ideas of how to spend time were worlds apart. Cynthia liked to sit and read a women's magazine, which to mum was a total waste of time. Mum thought she should have been out there on her hands and knees with a bucket of hot water scrubbin' the front step. At times there was more than a bit of friction and there was me, like 'piggy in the middle' tryin' to keep the peace, tryin' to mediate and smooth things over. The trouble was, for much of the time I was at work.

Speakin' of work, before I go any further I need to go back a few weeks to tell you how I came to get a job. Dad was a great trade unionist and he told me the first thing I had to do was to go and sign on at the Labour Exchange. We'd arrived on the Friday night and so first thing Saturday mornin' Cynthia and I went out together with the intention of me signin' on. We left Victor with mum and were glad to have a bit of time on our own together. At that time the Labour Exchange were makin' temporary use of this big house on Cedars Road, more or less opposite Clapham Common. Cedars Road was full of big, stately lookin' properties. In former times it was where all the gentry had lived. They all had in and out drives – for horses and carriages originally. Whilst of stately proportions, this place had been let go a bit inside. It was a bit seedy really. What's more, the place was packed. We were shocked. There must have been 50 people already waitin'. Cynthia and I sat there for maybe as much as an hour feelin' more and more uncomfortable. Then we just looked at each other and decided this was no place for us and we walked out. We were never goin' to get seen anyway. I never did sign on – in fact I never have and it's a bit late to start now!

Cynthia and I walked round for a bit to get the atmosphere of that place out of our system and to enjoy a bit of quality time together. When we got back, rather than upset dad, I'm afraid I told a bit of a 'porky pie'. On Monday I went down to the main Labour Exchange on Battersea Park Road. I couldn't see anythin' I thought was really suitable but they did send me for an interview at a paint factory. If I were honest, I wasn't that keen, but in the event they wouldn't take me on anyway. They said I wasn't suitable – havin' worked for a firm of stockbrokers and at the Stock Exchange, they felt I was too much of an academic and wouldn't fit in. Whilst workin' on the factory floor of a paint factory wasn't what I really wanted to do, at least it would have been a job and what's more, it would have been in walkin' distance from home – 9 Elms Paint in York Road off Battersea Park Road. It wasn't to be though.

That night when dad got home from work to find I still had no job, he was really on my case. I'd intended to go back to the Labour Exchange next day anyway, but dad made it pretty clear what his expectations were regardless. I saw the same woman. This time she asked if I'd be interested in workin' for London Transport. Apparently they'd just launched a new recruitin' drive. I didn't come back with a job - not yet anyway – but at least I had somethin' to tell dad and mum and Cynthia of course – I had got another interview.

Next day, Wednesday, I had to go up to the London Transport HQ at Chiswick. It was a funny sort of interview. They just seemed to look me up and down and gave me a pretty basic mental arithmetic test. I'm sayin' me, but actually there were about 30 of us, all would be bus conductors or 'clippies'. I passed and that was all there was to it. I was in – that is provided my two weeks trainin' went well and I wasn't goin' to screw that up. On my way home I remember feelin' pretty pleased with myself. I'd got a job and it wasn't just any old job. It was with a big organisation with possibilities of promotion. Ok, for now the most important thing was I'd be earnin' – but on top of that I felt it had prospects.

On the followin' Monday I had to report to Clapham Garage for my two weeks trainin'. In those days it was a very big and very busy bus depot. Now it's a museum, so you can go and see it for yourself if you like.

Practically the first thing they did was to give me a temporary pass which was good for all London Transport – buses and underground. That was a pretty valuable perk and it re-inforced a sense of belongin' right from the start. I was to be trained as a conductor and I was assigned to an instructor called Mr Heath on route 155. Quite a busy route really – Wimbledon to Westminster takin' in Stockwell, the Embankment and Blackfriars Bridge and comin' past the Houses of Parliament on the way back.

It was over sixty years ago, but I can remember that first day like it was yesterday. We pulled out of the depot at 6.15 am so we'd only been workin' about threequarters of an hour when we got to Wimbledon around 7.00 am. Bein' mid November, it was still dark. We pulled up, switched off and the driver and Mr Heath started walkin' off. I didn't know what was goin' on. "Don't look so worried – just follow us." So I trotted along behind them into this little café and they bought me a cuppa tea and a sausage roll. We had about a ten minute turn around. As we came out I remember thinkin', "What nice people. They won't even take any money off me." I already felt I was settlin' in and beginnin' to enjoy myself. Not a bad job this – a tea break after less than an hour.

Before I go on, I think I'll just describe my day and the route in a bit more detail. I'd got to Clapham Garage just before 6 am because I knew I had to sign on by 6.05 am. Then I had ten minutes 'preparation time' – makin' sure I'd got my ticket machine, float and everythin' I needed ready to go out with the bus at 6.15 am. The buses had an A and a B route. A was into the city and B towards the suburbs. We were startin' on B – I guess because it was less busy and would give me a better chance to get settled in. I'll quickly run through the main stages, but bear in mind there were lots of request stops in between. The first stage was Clapham Common Tube Station – the Plough, which is where we picked up my first ever passengers. We'd been goin' about a minute.

I thought I'd got the hang of the ticket machine pretty well, but I was probably all fingers and thumbs and way too slow. As the day went on, I soon realised how the pace had to pick up – it got manic at times. Anyway, after the Plough we went all the way alongside Clapham Common to Clapham South and then downhill towards Balham (underground and rail station), then Henlys (named after the newsagents) on to Tootin' Beck and Mayfair Cinema, where lots of passengers clambered on, past Auntie Annie's House (although I hadn't time to look out for her) to Tootin' Broadway and on to Colliers Wood (underground station) and South Wimbledon (underground station) and then we took a right and wiggled our way round to Wimbledon Rail Station, which was a very busy place, but also our terminus, so everyone got off there, hopefully havin' been issued with the right ticket. This is where we took our ten minute break and went round the corner to the little café. There was a locker on the bus, but I was instructed to take everythin' with me – just in case.

Our ten minute break over, as we walked back to the bus, Mr Heath told me he's got a very important piece of information to tell me on the way back to the garage, but for now I need to focus on issuin' tickets to all the passengers who'd be waitin' at Wimbledon Station. That was our first stop on the way back – Wimbledon Station, in the High Street and sure enough we picked up a lot of passengers there. I was too busy to go ponderin' on what the important information might be because although we were runnin' the same route in reverse, now that we were on the 'A' route goin' towards the city, there were a lot more passengers waitin' at each stop.

Although I didn't realise it at the time, not bein' familiar with the route yet, when we were a few minutes before Merton Garage (which would become familiar as another Bus Garage), Mr Heath decided to impart this 'important information'. "At Merton Garage you'll pick up a very important passenger. You might recognise him, but he won't speak to you – not good mornin' – nothin'. He'll just go upstairs and sit down. When you get to him he'll just flash this gold badge at you. You may have been introduced to him as a new recruit – He's Mr Fairbanks, the Chief Depot Inspector at Clapham. Get to him in turn, but try to get to him smartish." Over time I came to realise he hadn't been checkin' up on me especially – that was his normal journey to work. He lived near Merton Garage. Anyway, that was it really for my first day – indeed my first week – runnin' back and forth to Wimbledon time and again. By the end of that week I reckon I could issue the right tickets with my eyes closed – well, maybe not, but I did feel I'd mastered the route pretty well.

London buses were all double-deckers and as a conductor I'd be up and down stairs all day. If I wasn't that fit when I started – I pretty soon would be. Durin' my two weeks trainin' I learnt how to issue tickets, collect the right fares, identify and deal with fare dodgers and work as a team with the driver – makin' sure everyone was on board before ringin' the bell and that those who wanted to get off had done. The bell of course was the signal to the driver to move on. You couldn't afford to hang about – you had a timetable to stick to and woe-betide you if you didn't. There were Inspectors – 'jumpers' as we called them – hoppin' on and off buses all the time – lookin' for fare dodgers, but by the same token tryin' to catch you out if you'd missed any or issued the wrong tickets to passengers who had paid.

The 'jumpers' were the bane of our lives, particularly when it was rush-hour and the bus was packed and passengers gettin' on and off the whole time, some of 'em avoidin' eye contact to try to avoid payin'. If a jumper came on and he noticed you hadn't collected a fare within 2 stages, he could book you for that. Then you'd have to report to the Chief Depot Inspector to explain yourself. I soon learnt that you didn't want to be havin' to do that too often or you'd pretty soon find yourself pickin' up your cards and walkin' out the door for good.

I'm not sure I should be tellin' you this, but I was also instructed in the art of 'fiddlin'! Don't get me wrong, we're not talkin' major crime here. Anyway, this is how it worked: the bus is always busy and most times you just can't get round everyone before they want to get off. Now and again there might be as many as a dozen top-deckers comin' down the stairs and you have to grab fares off 'em before they get off. There's no time to issue all these tickets and when they've gone you just ring up six. So now you've got, say, six tuppeny fares in your pocket for which no ticket has been issued, and that's the basis for your daily 'float'. As my instructor explained – strictly between us mind you, I needed a float to cover daily expenses. For a start at the end of each shift you have to count and check in all the takin's for the day and that has to tally exactly with the value of tickets issued – the weighbill. We'd carry money bags. Blue for copper and green for silver. Part of our job was to count and bag all the money. Five shillin's per bag in the case of copper. The cashiers just weighed the bags. There wasn't time to count – not unless the weight was suspect. Any discrepancies and you'd have to make it up, in theory from your own money, but in practice from your 'float'. The other important daily expense was the driver - let's call him Harry. Now, as my instructor explained, you're a team. You have to look after Harry. When it comes to your break, Harry might need a sausage roll and a sarni, so you'll need a float – but as I say, that's between us.

Before I move on, I'd like to give you a visual picture of Mr Heath, my instructor. He was a replica of Tommy Trinder. I can see him now standin' at the back of the bus chewin' gum, keepin' an eye out to see how I'm shapin' up. He rarely moved from that spot 'cos from there he could see me downstairs or upstairs via the mirror and he'd be on hand to collect any fares from passengers I'd missed before they got off, some of which would become our 'float'. A decent bloke was Mr Heath. He wasn't there to trip me up. He wanted me to succeed.

So that was it really – that was my trainin' in a nutshell. The week after my two weeks probation/trainin' I was allocated a driver, Ron Lucas, and then, well, Ron and me, we were now a team. I suppose as far as the company were concerned, it's more correct to say we were a crew. Just to be clear, we'd always work together on every shift irrespective of the route – there was none of this 'choppin' and changin'. I'm maybe makin' it sound a bit simpler than it was. To do the job properly you had to master the fare structure p.d.q. You needed to know the stagin' structure and relevant fares off pat so as to issue the correct value tickets for the journeys made. Again the 'jumpers' would be down on you like a ton of bricks if they found you'd issued incorrect tickets. There was always a list of fares posted up in the bus, but that was really intended for passengers' reference. As a conductor on a London Bus you just didn't have time to keep consultin' fares lists. What's more, as a crew workin' out of Clapham, we chopped and changed routes all the time, so whilst I started on route 155, the next week I might be on 37, 45, 137, 181 or any one of the nine different routes operatin' out of Clapham, and that's not countin' the special rush-hour services. So there was a lot to learn because to do the job you had to know all the stops and prices on all those routes.

Although you could be assigned to any route and generally I worked a different route each week, normally you worked as a team, with the same driver week in, week out, except on overtime. Workin' rest days you were paired up with whoever was available. I was lucky because, as I said, for every day work, I was assigned to a driver named Ron Lucas. He'd just been transferred from Battersea Garage, but what he didn't know about buses and gettin' a bus around London wasn't worth knowin'. Ron had been a Japanese prisoner of war and I noticed he walked a bit strangely, possibly as a result, but I didn't like to ask.

In addition to the 'brain' work, there was a PR/Enforcement role too. You had to be on hand to help all the old folks, pregnant women and mums with babies and toddlers. And then o'course there were all the drunks, troublemakers and fare dodgers. Drunks and troublemakers were the worst. I found humourin' em was generally the best policy, but occasionally you had to get tough and throw 'em off the bus. These days if you tried to physically escort someone off a bus, you'd probably get done for assault, but things were different back then.

Fare dodgers, they were ten a penny – we'd get 'em all the time. Often as not they'd sit there lookin' out of the window, usually with money in their hand, but never offerin' it unless I challenged them. Most would cough up then, no bother, but some would still try it on with somethin' like, "Oh, I'm gettin' off at the next stop", to which I'd reply, "'Course you are – but you still gotta pay first."

Some customers couldn't speak the language even or maybe they just pretended they couldn't. Another common fare dodger trick was to ask for a threehalfpenny, which was the lowest fare in those days. If they were still on for more than two or three stops I'd know what they were up to. When we were really busy they'd have a better chance of gettin' away with it 'cos there just wasn't time to follow 'em all up and the clever ones, I guess they knew that. Whilst you were arguin' the toss with an awkward one, three more customers might be hoppin' off who would have paid if you'd gotten round to 'em. What I'm tryin' to say is that we did the best we could for the company. I was proud to be part of London Transport and so I did the job to the best of my ability and that included dealin' with difficult customers. I didn't just take the soft option and turn a blind eye. Pretty much all human life travelled on a London bus. Young, old, rich and poor and everythin' in between. You were always on the go and you could say there was never a dull moment.

I've got lots more I want to say about my life as a 'bus conductor' but before I do I think I should tell you about how things were goin' at home. On the one hand Cynthia was pleased I had a job and with no rent to pay we were startin' to save for a place of our own. On the other hand it was shift work and she was bein' left at home with Victor and mum all day. Mum meant well and for most of the time she was more or less normal, but she could be a bit overpowerin'. Cynthia, remember, was still only 19.

We'd been livin' with my parents in Gambetta Street for about 6 weeks when, long story short, Cynthia announces she's had enough. We talked about it and decided it would be best if she took Victor back to Aldershot to stay with her mum for a bit. For Christmas at least. Obviously I didn't want them to go, but we agreed it would be for the best. I told her not to worry – I'd sort somethin' out. I'd get us a place of our own. I had no idea how I was goin' to do it, but the intent was there. And, of course I'd go over and see them whenever I could – on my rest days. But even that wasn't straightforward. I was in a quandary. If I worked my rest days, or some of 'em, the overtime made a very big difference to my take home pay and we needed all the money we could get if we were goin' to save for a place of our own. I tried to strike the right balance, but as you can imagine, it was a case of damned if you do and damned if you don't. I couldn't win.

I was workin' so I couldn't accompany 'em, Cynthia and little Victor that is, but I'd explained to Cynthia how to get to Aldershot by bus and train. She caught the 168 to Clapham Junction fine, but Clapham Junction was then the biggest rail station in the world and I guess can be very confusin' if you're not used to travellin' by train. You probably know what I'm goin' to say – Cynthia got on the wrong train and finished up at Guildford. Fortunately, in those days stations had porters on hand to help young ladies in distress. Apparently they carried baby and pram literally across the tracks so as to get Cynthia to the right platform in time to catch the train for Aldershot. They'd be a bit late, but at least they got there safe and sound.

Mum was really cut up about them leavin'. In particular, she'd really enjoyed havin' Victor around. Truth be told, I think dad was glad to see the back of 'em. He'd never had any patience with us as kids. Mum had done all the bringin' up. Now he was much older and old for his years. Havin' a young married couple in the house with a baby that regularly cried at night had been a strain. It was somethin' he could do without at his time of life and he was more than happy to have some peace and quiet.

I was enjoyin' my new job and gettin' on well, but as you can imagine, bein' apart from Cynthia and our baby took the shine off things. As luck would have it though, they'd only been gone a day or two when mum comes back from Beaties – the corner shop at the top of our street – with the news that the old lady who lived in No 25 had died. No 25 was next door to Beaties. I don't want this to sound callous, but it was an amazin' stroke of luck – not that the poor old dear had died – but that mum had been in Beaties and picked up the news. Although it was the corner shop, she hardly ever shopped there. She preferred the Co-op for the prices and the divi and she always said the food was fresher there. What's more, she wasn't one for gossip and Beaties was the hub of local gossip. Mum only ever went there once in a blue moon. Luckily, this was one of 'em.

I think I told you that mum had bought her house in 1948. Now she saw the opportunity for me to buy 25 and 25A from the same landlord, Mr Kesley, who still owned a lot of property round about. What's more, whilst we wouldn't be under the same roof, Cynthia, Victor and I would still be livin' in Gambetta Street. Whilst I didn't know the lady who'd died by name, I'd often seen her walkin' up and down the street to and from the shops on Lavender Hill. I think she was a widow. Even in the 1950s widows often continued to wear black and this particular lady was very Victorian in her dress. She was always in black right down to her gaited black boots. I was sorry that she'd died, but, as mum said, it was an opportunity for me and I intended to make the most of it.

Mr Kesley lived in Eden Bridge, Kent, near to Mr Churchill. He had an office in Clapham Junction and whilst doubtless he had a number of staff, he liked to collect the rents himself. I knew he came down Gambetta Street every other Monday. He always wore a leather satchel to put all the money in. No way could an elderly gentleman do that today. He'd be mugged for certain. You might try to convince me that lots of things have changed for the better, but bein' able to walk the streets in safety isn't one of them. Anyway, I made sure I was home when Mr Kesley came collectin'.

I stopped him in the street and told him I was interested in buyin' 25 and 25A and could I look around. He looked me up and down and said he'd be back in half an hour when he'd finished his collections. True to his word, he came back and showed me round No 25. The upstairs, No 25A, was tenanted to a widow, Mrs Crout and, as it turned out, even the downstairs was bein' sub-let to a chap called Arthur who it seems had been more or less lookin' after the old dear for some time before her death. As I'd expected, the layout was more or less the same as mum's place and what's more, it was immaculate – clean as a whistle. Perfect.

I got the old violin out and told Mr Kesley my story. About my wife and new baby, the situation at mum's, about Cynthia havin' taken Victor off to her mother's in Aldershot, and about my new job with London Transport. I think maybe he felt a bit sorry for me. Anyway, he said the place was mine for 1050 pounds. I didn't say as much, but I remember thinkin' at the time that maybe the 50 pounds was for my cheek for askin'. The price was for both by the way, No 25 and No 25A. They had separate front doors, but they were always sold as pairs in those days. I didn't know where I was goin' to get the money, but I was all for shakin' hands to seal the deal. All I could see was Cynthia, little Victor and me back together, settled, happy in our own home.

Mr K wasn't goin' to pour water on my dream – he was too decent a bloke for that – but he did bring me down to earth a bit. "The first thing you need to do young man is sort out your finances. You need to get yourself down to Battersea Town Hall and ask about a mortgage." He'd give me time. There was no rush, but the 50 pounds – that he wanted in cash as a deposit. I didn't have fifty pounds, but Roy did and he was happy to loan me the money. That's what brothers do – help one another when they can.

I went to Battersea Town Hall. The good news was they'd grant me a mortgage. The bad news was, they'd only give me 600 pounds. Deflated doesn't describe my emotions as I went to explain to Mr K that I couldn't go ahead. "Oh well," he said, "That's it then, isn't it." Then he smiled. "I'd better lend you some money." I don't know whether you're countin', but here again was an instance when lady luck was right there with me, pullin' me back from the brink of disaster. I already knew Mr K was a decent bloke, but he was a businessman too and this was no business decision. I guess he just felt sorry for me and decided to give Cynthia and me a helpin' hand. "So, now that's two mortgages you've got son, so you'd better get yourself off to work and earn yourself some money." He gave me a red record book and instructions to send him 4 pounds a month to his home in Kent, not to his office. This was between us. It was no business transaction. It wouldn't have made business sense. It was more of a gentleman's agreement.

Thinkin' about it now, Mr K was takin' a risk. Quite what he could have done if after a few years I'd just stopped repayin' him, I really don't know. As it was, every month Cynthia or I went up to the Town Hall to pay the mortgage and for the next ten years – till 1965 – I sent a postal order to Mr K's home. Sometimes it was a bit of a struggle and from time to time I'd have to tell Cynthia that she couldn't have the new curtains – or whatever it was she was hankerin' after 'cos there wouldn't be enough left to pay our mortgages. But we managed. In fact lookin back, I think we managed pretty well. There I go, gallopin' ahead of myself again when we haven't even bought the place yet, so, back to 1955.

If you remember, we weren't just buyin' one house, we were buyin' two – well, flats really, an upstairs and a downstairs and with them, tenants. So, as regards income, there was my wages plus rents. When we took over, Mrs Crout was payin' sixteen shillin's and eleven pence a week for upstairs (No 25A) and Arthur was payin' two pounds for his room at the back, plus a bag of coal and eggs and bacon for his breakfast. A strange arrangement, but it suited him and it would be a much needed boost to our income. I would guess that Arthur was in his fifties. He worked on the railway as a checker down at 9 Elms. The old lady had cooked his breakfast before he went off to work and I told him Cynthia would do that. She was still at her mum's and I suppose really I should have checked with her first, but I was on cloud nine and lookin' at the world through rose-coloured spectacles. As for Arthur, I think he was quite relieved that he could stay on and didn't have to think about movin'.

In practice, sortin' out everythin' to do with our new house, includin' all the paperwork and legalities, took the best part of 3 months, so before I go any further, I'll just take you back a bit to Christmas. When I first started on the buses, we used to work what were called 11 day fortnights. In theory that meant I'd get 3 days off every fortnight. In practice though I'd maybe take only 1 or 2 days off every fortnight because, as I've told you, if I worked my rest days it would make quite a difference to my take-home pay. I wanted to save for our future, but I was also missin' Cynthia and little Victor and there was no way I was goin' to miss spendin' our first Christmas together. Fortunately I got both Christmas Day and Boxing Day off, so I took myself over to Aldershot. Cynthia and I shared a put-me-up in the front room and Victor was with us in his pram. He was still too tiny for a cot. As usual we didn't get much sleep with Victor, but that didn't really matter – we were together and that was the main thing. Les had tried to make it a bit more festive for us by puttin' up a tree. That was good of him and I'll always remember it, not least for the fact that it only had three workin' lights on it! This will probably sound ungrateful, but I remember thinkin', "Next year I'll make sure I do better than that. And I did – although as the years went by it was Cynthia who was the main instigator of Christmas decorations. She loved our house to look festive at Christmas.

As luck would have it, that year I got New Year's Eve off as well and that's when I first experienced Flossie's New Year tradition. Les had to go outside and, on the stroke of midnight, he had to open the door and throw four lumps of coal down the passageway. That was strange enough, but the funny thing was he'd not been sat down again more than five minutes when Flossie pipes up, "Don't just sit there Les. Get that coal cleared up!" I had to choke back the laughter. I was still fairly new on the scene and I didn't want to get the wrong side of Flossie. I'd already learnt that she could have a real sense of humour one minute, but cross her and she could really 'clean you up' – that's a cockney expression. In other words – give you a right goin' over, a right tellin' off. Over the years I became skilled at knowin' how to handle Cynthia's mother. She had a big family, but all of 'em said, "There's only one person in the family who can tame Flossie – that's Johnny Wattley.

Over the next couple of months, I tried to strike a balance between the need to earn and therefore work as much as possible and the desire to go over to Aldershot to see Cynthia and baby Victor. It wasn't easy and either way I couldn't win. It was durin' this period of unwelcome separation that the Christenin' was arranged so, come what may, I had to be there for that. We arranged to have our Victor Christened at St. Joseph's Church on Alexander Road, the same Catholic Church where we'd been married. There's a photo of Cynthia, Victor and me taken on the day of the Christenin', if you want to turn to it now. Look closely, you'll see that my eyes in particular look rather dark and that's because the day didn't start off too well. I'd worked the Saturday and then gone over to Flossie's for the night. Next mornin', the day of the Christenin', Cynthia and I decided to take a bath together, to save time as much as anythin' but it turned into a bit of a disaster. Unbeknown to us the water heater in the bathroom was faulty and leakin' fumes and the pair of us were nearly overcome. That's why my eyes look black and somewhat sunken in the Christenin' photos 'cos I was still sufferin' from the effects! To add insult to injury, Flossie had found us on the bathroom floor and accused us of havin' a bit of 'how's yer father' when we should have been gettin' ready! Sometimes, life's just not fair. We had to have the doctor out. A lady doctor and whilst I don't remember the details, I distinctly remember her sayin' we'd been lucky!

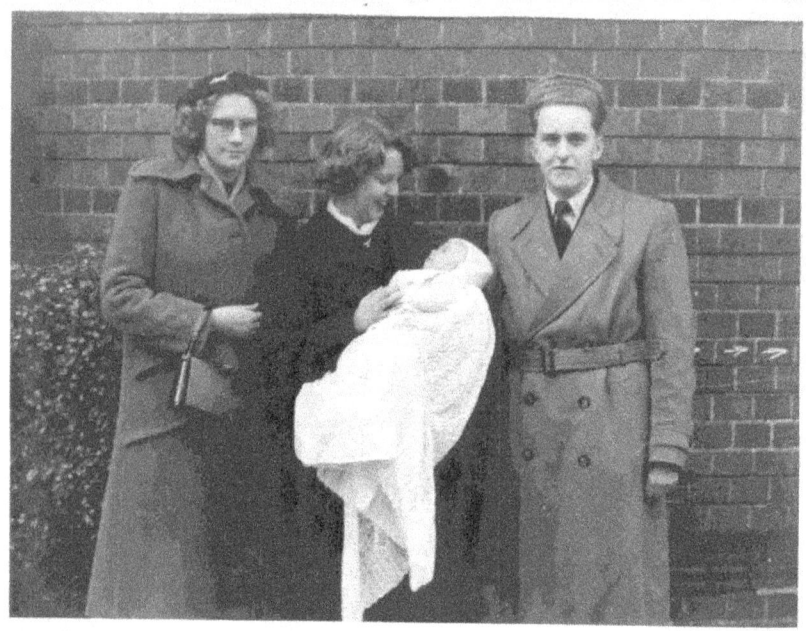

Cynthia with baby Victor, sister Monica and me outside St Joseph's Church, Aldershot on the day of Victor's Christenin' My eyes are still dark from bein' gassed!

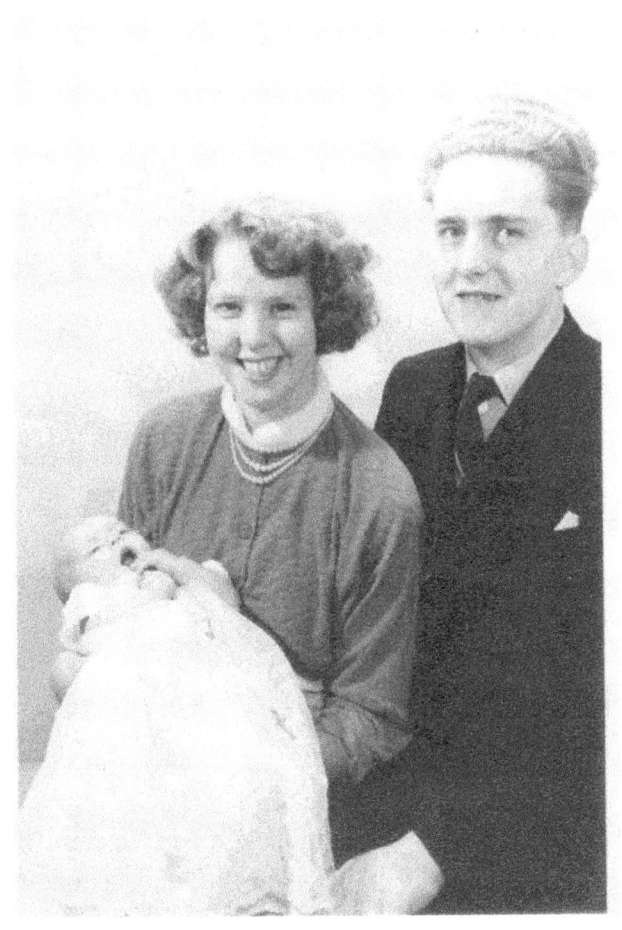

The proud parents, Cynthia and me, with Victor in his christenin' gown.

CHAPTER 9

Now We Have A Home Of Our Own

I got the keys to our new home in March and the first thing I had to do was go and buy a bed so I could get Cynthia and Victor back from her mum's and we could move in. I remember I went over to Brixton to buy it and it cost 26 pounds, which was a lot in those days. I could have got one cheaper, but I wanted a good one. I didn't want it breakin' on us like our first bed together in Aldershot! Remember that? I paid cash for it. In those days HP was still rather frowned upon, at least it was in our family. I know that mother would never have even considered havin' anythin' on HP. In our house – by that I mean mum's – you either had the money to pay for somethin' or you saved for it until you did or you went without. That's another thing that's changed in society today, and not necessarily for the better. Too many young people in particular buy whatever they want on credit cards without givin' enough thought to how they're goin' to pay for it later.

Although I'd had the keys for a few days, the actual completion date, when we could move in, was March 26th, 1956. It's a date I'll never forget because it's the day Cynthia, Victor and I were re-united. I had my family back together again and for the first time, we were in our very own home. Luckily for us, the old lady had left a table and chairs and one or two other bits and pieces and no relatives ever came to collect any of it. We didn't have a lot, but we had each other and our baby and we were happy. Life could hardly be better.

Arthur had his own bed and a few pieces of furniture in the back room and he had his own little fireplace to burn his bag of coal, so I think he was quite cosy in there. He worked on the railway. He was a proper bachelor, but always very clean and smart. He kept himself to himself and was certainly no trouble to us. What he paid in rent included Cynthia keepin' him supplied with bacon and eggs for his breakfast. Fortunately for Cynthia, he'd decided to cook it himself on the gas stove in the scullery at about 6.30 am every mornin' before goin' off to work. The smell was really temptin' but Cynthia and I rarely had a cooked breakfast ourselves.

Other than that, when he came home from work he'd go straight through to his room and he'd go out quite a lot in the evenin' – I guess to a pub - I'm not really sure. Our arrangement might have gone on for a long time had it not been for one small fly in the ointment – Victor! As I've told you, he was a lovely baby in the daytime, but he could be – no, he was – a little so and so at night. He seemed to save all his cryin' for the night time and it wasn't just Cynthia and I who suffered. Arthur could hear him too. He put up with it for a while, fair play to him, a long while, probably thinkin' things would improve, but when they didn't, finally, after about nine months, he decided to move out and go and live with his sister. We'd be sorry to lose the extra income, but you couldn't blame him. In case you're wonderin', it would be two years, two long years! before we got a decent night's sleep with Victor. He didn't just cry, he weeed for England too. We ended up wrappin' him in a tablecloth rather than just a nappy.

As you know, we also had a tenant upstairs, Mrs Crout. Her 16 shillin's and eleven pence rent came in very handy although sometimes I used to think: "I'm spendin' more on replacin' sash cords than I'm gettin' in rent!" They were forever breakin' or comin' adrift. We reckon a combination of the war and the window cleaner was to blame. I'd better explain. When the doodlebug dropped – you know, the one that nearly did for me – it took out windows right up and down Gambetta street as well. That's how powerful and destructive these things were. Anyway, we reckon that when the war time repair crews were sortin' out the windows in No 25A, they didn't match up the sash cord weights properly. We think some of the windows had the wrong sized weights in 'em, makin' 'em unbalanced and prone to damage. As for the window cleaner, well Mrs C had him come once a fortnight. We were the landlords, but we couldn't afford it, a window cleaner that is. I used to do ours standin' on a chair. Anyway, Mrs C's window cleaner didn't use a ladder. He'd climb half out of the window and, sittin on the cill with his legs inside, he'd clean them from there. He was a bit heavy handed and especially if the sash stuck, he'd send it crashin' up or down as the case may be. It was the combination of that and maybe some of the weights bein' on the heavy side or unbalanced that tended to do for the sashes. If I happened to be in at the time I'd hear it go and I knew it wouldn't be long before Mrs C would be knockin' on the door wantin' it repaired.

Les and Flossie – Cynthia's mother and stepfather, would come up to London to see us practically every other weekend. Sometimes they'd stay over Saturday night, especially if there was any work to be done. Cynthia would spend time with her mum and Les and I would get together for a bit of male bondin'. He was older than me, but much younger than Flossie. We enjoyed each other's company and, often as not we'd be workin' on one project or another on the property. Les was quite handy and he made this special 'weighted mouse' to run inside the sashes and pull down the cords so we could either replace them or re-attach the weights. If you recall, Les had lost a leg in the war, so I was the one sittin' out on the cill. At first it would take us most of the mornin', but over the years we did it that many times we became quite professional at it. What's more, now that we had a place of our own, my decoratin' skills I'd picked up when workin' for Snuggs & Co came in very handy. I'd do all the paintin' and ceilin's and Les would do the paperin'. He was a dab hand with wallpaper. We made a good team and the banter between us and the laughs we had made it enjoyable. Not a chore at all.

Before I go on to tell you about our growin' family, I think I should try to paint you a picture of what our little home at 25 Gambetta Street was actually like and how we improvised a bit to make best use of the space. The photograph at the end of the chapter, taken in 2015, shows the outside to be not so very different to how it looked back then. We called it our house, but really I suppose it would have been more correct to refer to it as two flats. Ours was the ground floor, No 25, but if you remember, they were always sold as pairs and our tenant, Mrs Crout, lived at No 25A above. As now, there were two front doors. Ours was the one on the right. Over time, the internal arrangements have been modified somewhat to incorporate modern amenities – in particular a bathroom and an inside toilet – but there were no such luxuries back in the 1950s. Our neighbours on one side were Mr & Mrs Green – Grace and Arthur to us – and on the other Beatie's shop. Both would be significant in our lives, so I'll tell you more about them later.

Inside the front door there was a long passage with doors off. The first on the right opened into the "front room" which really should have been just that – the main sittin' room – to be used mainly when visitors called or at Christmas and other special occasions. To us it was far too precious to be kept for such limited use and right from our first movin' in, it was, and remained, our main bedroom. The room where Sandy, our third child would be both conceived and born, but that's in the future, so I'll come to it later. The second door on the right opened into what we called our 'second bedroom'. It was rather small and whilst it might have taken a double bed, it would have been very cramped in there. Towards the end of the corridor on the left there was a built-in cupboard and on the end, facin' you, a further door leadin' into the kitchen which, with its open fire range, was quite cosy and we used it as our main livin' room.

Another open corridor led off the far end of 'the kitchen' and within that a door on the right led into the scullery which was equipped with a gas stove, a sink and a free-standin' copper. The copper had 3 legs with a gas burner under it connected by a flexible red rubber hose to a gas point on the wall. It took ages to heat up and come to the boil so, to save money, most of the time we didn't use it. Only on special occasions like when Sandy was born as you'll learn later. There was just a cold water tap in the sink, so for washin' up or for havin' a strip wash in the sink, we always just boiled the kettle. That sat on the gas stove. There were no electric kettles in those days. From within the scullery, a further door led out to a yard and a small bit of garden. Off the yard there was a small brick built outside toilet. Not exactly luxury, but at least it wasn't shared. No 25A had its own toilet upstairs. I'm sayin' it wasn't shared, but whenever we had tenants stayin' with us in No 25, it was shared with them.

As you know, when we moved in, Arthur occupied the back and final room, also accessed from the rear 'open passage'. Just to be clear, when I say open I don't mean open to the elements – just that the passage led direct off the kitchen with no door. Lookin' back, old

Arthur's room was pretty meagre and sparsely furnished with just a bed, a chair and a small foldin' table, but at least he had his own small fireplace and it seemed to suit him. Arthur bein' a 'sittin' tenant', we hadn't really ventured in there until after he'd left, when we discovered that despite the little fireplace, it was really rather damp.

As you'll no doubt have noted, there was no bathroom in the house – just a galvanised tin bath hangin' on the wall in the yard. I'm sayin' a bath but actually there was a small one as well we used for the kids. Mostly we'd bath the kids in the scullery sink but sometimes in summer we'd bath 'em outside in the small tin bath. There's a picture of me bathin' Victor in the back yard that you'll see later. Cynthia and I would have a bath in the kitchen/livin' room in front of the fire, which sounds quite romantic, but in practice it was such a palaver fillin' it from the kettle and then strugglin' to empty it, that baths weren't exactly a frequent occurrence.

I never remember Arthur takin' a bath. I think he used to have one at his sister's in Lavender Hill where he'd usually go at weekends. For a strip wash or just a wash and shave, he'd use the sink in the scullery as we all did – takin' it in turns. When he was young, Cynthia would 'bath' Victor in the sink. I can still see him sittin' on the drainin' board havin' his hair rubbed dry with a towel. Basic, very basic but, happy days, well in summer, but maybe not so great in winter. That's because of course there was no heatin' in the scullery so it could get cold, really cold in there. Kids today won't know what I mean when I say that sometimes 'Jack frost would paint ice pictures on the window'.

When I wanted a really good bath, I'd go down to Latchmere Baths in Battersea. As well as a thorough cleansin', I'd get some exercise thrown in because Latchmere Road was a good half hour walk round the 'back doubles' (side streets and back streets). I'd usually go on a Saturday mornin'. I knew it well because I used to go there when I was in the army and home for the weekend to play at the Star & Garter. I had to get spruced up for that now, didn't I? If you look back at that photo the management had taken of me to put on the billboard outside I hope you'll agree that I scrubbed up pretty well in those days. I could have passed for a film star, don't you think? …. Well, in my dreams!

Cynthia was 'lucky' because right from the off we had a Hotpoint washin' machine with a mangle on top. I say 'lucky' because in the 1950s there were still plenty of housewives doin' their washin' in a dolly tub. Although our 'house' was really a flat, dryin' the washin' was no problem because we had a washin' line out in the back yard. A good job really because, with a baby like Victor, there was always plenty of washin'. Nappies, nappies and more nappies! None of those handy disposable things that mothers have these days. They don't know they're born. Speakin' of washin', some time in the mid to late 1950s, I don't remember just when, mum splashed out on a Rolls washin' machine and spin dryer. Luckily for us, they'd got this special offer on and it came with this free Frigidaire Fridge. Mum already had a fridge and so she gave it to Cynthia and me. It was our first fridge and it must have been a good one because it lasted donkeys' years. We couldn't wear it out.

As you know, Mrs Crout kept Les and me busy repairin' her sashes, but that wasn't all. One day she comes to me and says the toilet seat is broken. I went to look and sure enough the wooden seat was broken right across. When you've got tenants, you have to expect to do repairs. It comes with the territory, but at the time it seemed to be one thing after another with Mrs Crout. Fortunately we were insured, so I thought at least this time we won't have to fork out for the repair. A builder came, who co-incidentally was also a councillor. The repair was no problem, but he also started askin' questions like, "How much was she payin' for upstairs?" I told him and he said, "No, that's not right. She should be paying at least two pounds." Bein' a councillor, he sent me some forms and, long story short, that broken seat turned out to be a blessin' in disguise because as a result Mrs Crout did agree to pay more which came in very handy.

I never knew her exact age but Mrs Crout was quite elderly and so I suppose it was no great surprise when, about two years after we'd become her landlord, she died. Because she'd been a sittin' tenant when we bought the pair, I'd hardly set foot inside 25A except to do repairs. Now it was vacant I could have a proper look around and I could see it needed a good goin' over to get it into a fit state for re-lettin'. As ever, Les was happy to give me a hand and between us we did the whole place up over about a month, mainly at weekends. As well as decoratin' we decided to take the range out and put in a normal fireplace, givin' the new tenant the option of continuin' with a coal fire or puttin' in a gas fire. There was a toilet, but back then, still no bathroom.

Once it was ready, I advertised it in the Evenin' Standard at £3 per week. Some folk in the street thought that was scandalous. On the grapevine I got to hear I was bein' dubbed another Rackman for overchargin'. Steep or not, it didn't take long for new tenants to arrive, who were happy with the rent. It was a mother and daughter from Luton who'd been commutin' back and forth every day and were only too happy to have found a suitable place in London. If you ask me, I was only chargin' the goin' rate. It's just that new tenancies didn't arise in our street very often and folk were behind the times.

Whilst Les and I were busy workin' on our house or upstairs, Cynthia and her mum would be havin' a fine old time together. When they weren't out shoppin', they'd be sittin' chattin'. The pair of 'em could talk for England. Flossie missed London and liked catchin' up on all the gossip and just as much she liked Cynthia takin' her up town to savour the atmosphere. I suppose you could say, once a Londoner, always a Londoner, but the London she hankered after wasn't to be found in the likes of Oxford Street. The pair of 'em were much happier goin' up to East Street Market in Woolworths Road, just before the Elephant & Castle. It was famous then and still goin' strong I think. A bit like Petticoat Lane.

Victor would often sit playin' with his toys on the floor whilst we worked, but sometimes, if he was gettin' a bit bored and maybe a bit fractious, I'd pop him round to Grace & Arthur's next door so we could get on a bit faster – with no distractions. That didn't just suit us. Victor was happy to go round and Grace and Arthur loved havin' him, so everybody was happy.

Come tea time, Les and I would go down the jellied eel shop – Harrisons, down the Wandsworth Road. It was a bit of a way, so we'd go in Les' car. We'd take a basin and get it filled up and come back with pie and eels. It was mainly a treat for Flossie – she loved her pie and eels did Flossie, and you couldn't get 'em back in Aldershot.

Whilst Les and Flossie would drive up to London nearly every fortnight to see us, less often we'd go to Aldershot to visit them and, havin' no car, we'd go up on the train – Cynthia, me and little Victor. Les would always take us back in his car, which was really good of him and typical of Les. Except this one particular time we'd left it a bit late and so I was already on edge because I had an early start the next day. Not to worry though, because we were headin' home now, that is until we reached the Hogg's Back on the A31 Farnham – Guildford Road, when we came to a grindin' halt. There we were, in the dark, pretty much in the middle of nowhere and my heart sinkin' at the thought of not gettin' home or to work in the mornin'.

At that time, what I knew about cars would fit on the back of a postage stamp with space to spare. Luckily Les was just the opposite. He just got out, lifted the bonnet, shone a torch and pondered for a minute before calmly sayin', "Oh, I see – have you got a sixpence, John?" I searched in my pockets and gave him one. He just filed it a bit, then stuck it in somewhere – don't ask me where – and then asked me to start her up. Hey presto, away she went. A bleedin' marvel was Les, a brilliant engineer and mechanic. He said it was a temporary job, but whatever he did we had no trouble all the way to London, and nor did they on their trip back.

Eventually though, that particular car fell out of favour with Flossie and this time even Les couldn't salvage the situation. To be honest though, she did have a point. Thanks to Les, mechanically it was probably very sound, but there was no gettin' away from it – it was old – and underneath the bodywork had shot it. Rustin' away or not, Les still liked it and wanted to keep it, but once Flossie had made up her mind, like it or not, that car was goin'. She put it nicely, I'll give her that, but Cynthia and I had hardly walked in the door before Flossie turns to me and says, "John, do me a favour will you. Take Les out now and come back with a new car. There's a hole in that thing out there right under my feet and I can see the road when we're goin' along." She wasn't for havin' it patched up and Les didn't protest.

So that was it. Off we went to the nearest dealer and Les looked around for somethin' he thought Flossie would like and came up with this Westminster. Four hundred pounds it was. A lot of money in those days, but for Les I think it was more about pleasin' Flossie than anythin' else. At this stage in my life I still knew nothin' about cars. I was a conductor on the buses and still hadn't learnt to drive. All I can say is it looked good and when we got back, it did the trick with Flossie. My havin' gone with Les was useful in one respect though. I couldn't be of any help when checkin' over the mechanics, but then Les was a real expert and needed nobody's help in that regard, but he was a very meek-mannered man and useless at bargainin'. Havin' paid over the £400 I really think he would have just driven off and left it at that. It was down to me to negotiate a price for his old car. He was just goin' to leave it, but I got him £50 for it. Whether that was a really good deal I couldn't say, but one thing's for sure, it was £50 more than Les would have gone home with if I'd not been with him.

I've no photos of Les or Flossie except the sepia ones you saw that were taken at our Weddin', but the image I'd like you to picture of Flossie when out in that new car is of a lady not unlike the Queen Mother. She'd even often be wearin' powder blue clothes and that wave, I'm tellin' you, Flossie had that same wave. I never knew the Queen Mother, but looks and mannerisms apart, I doubt she and Flossie had much else in common.

Flossie was a proper Londoner and loved talkin' about London and especially the old days. She wasn't the only one. Remember Gertie – Cynthia's best friend who offered me her knee on my weddin' day? Well, as sure as eggs is eggs, whenever we went visitin' we'd hardly be sat down before there'd be a knock at the door and there would stand Gertie's mum wantin' a shillin' for the gas. She was an Irish woman and good fun and it was obvious that what she really wanted was all the news from London and she wasn't leavin' with her shillin' till she'd got it.

Before I forget, I'll just tell you another little story about my time with Cynthia's family. I'm goin' back a bit to the summertime, a few months after we'd moved in to our new home. I'm sorry I can't remember when exactly - only what happened.

Cynthia's family had taken this chalet over down in Haylin' Island for a week. They all went down – Flossie and Les, Monica and Jeff and their three kids and Cynthia's brothers, John, Tony and Mickey. I put Cynthia and little Victor on the train so they could join them for the week. For me it had to be work as usual. I couldn't afford to take a whole week off without pay, but as it happened, I'd worked it so my rest days that week were Saturday and Sunday so I could get one day down there. The Sunday would be spent travellin' back, but at least Cynthia, me and little Victor would be doin' it together. Cynthia had been a bit nervous about makin' the journey down on her own. As the week wore on, I thought, wouldn't it be nice if I could turn up and surprise them a day early?

I thought I'd try askin' for the Friday off so I could spend a couple of days with them rather than just the Saturday. I got nowhere with the under management. Just a blanket, "We don't do days off", so I thought I'd change tack and request to see the Chief Depot Inspector – Mr Gold Braid himself. I knew that askin' for a day off so I could join my family at the seaside wasn't goin' to cut it. I didn't want to come away empty-handed again, so I decided to come up with a more 'reasonable request' and sure enough, it worked.

I was on mornin' shifts, so the first train I could get was the 5 o'clock from Waterloo, so it was quite late when I got to Havant Station – already dark. That was Ok though because I'd decided I'd better let them know I was comin' and so Les met me in his car and Cynthia was with him because Victor was already asleep with Flossie babysittin'. They'd even saved me some dinner.

They all knew I'd said I couldn't get the time off, so they were all wonderin' how I'd managed to wangle the extra day. I didn't let on for a bit, but Flossie was like a dog with a bone. She just wouldn't let go. She was determined and one way or another she was goin' to weedle it out of me. When I told her she didn't want to know – well, that just made her more determined, so in the end I just came out with it. "Well, if you must know, I'm buryin' you tomorrow!" Not much shuts Flossie up – but that did. The poor woman was dumbfounded. Lucky for me everybody else thought it was hilarious and Flossie, she was a good sort, she soon came round and didn't take offence. I don't suppose I was quite the 'blue-eyed boy' for a while, but long term I was still the one she turned to for advice. That wouldn't be the last of it though – that story got recounted time and time again, whenever there was a family gatherin'.

I know it was a 'porky pie', but the bosses were none the wiser and nobody got hurt, so no real harm done really – except of course I did lose a day's pay. Funeral or no funeral – it was no work, no pay in those days. It was worth it though. This was our first 'family holiday' and I didn't want to miss it altogether. My family were, are, important to me and I wanted them to see that.

The chalet they'd hired was right on the beach, so more or less perfect for a family holiday. The weather continued to be kind to us too, with warm, sunny days. I know that probably sometimes I look back through 'rose-coloured spectacles', but really and honestly it seems to me that our summers were much better, much warmer and more reliable than today. Mind you, if I was honest, sun, sand and sea weren't really my thing – it was just bein' there with Cynthia and little Victor that were so special, so important to me.

So far I've told you a bit about our new home and its occupants, but to complete the picture I need to at least start to tell you about our neighbours on the one side, Mr & Mrs Green at No 23 and on the other Beatie's Shop, No 27. Before I do, I want you to understand that this was a time when you knew pretty much everyone in the street and they knew you but, if you were lucky, your near neighbours weren't just mere acquaintances, they were real friends – folk you could rely on, turn to – like an extended family.

Lookin' back, I can see that we really fell on our feet when I bought that house. As so often in my life, it wasn't just pure chance, it was down to mum keepin' her ear to the ground and lookin' out for me. If you're lucky, you can buy a house, but no amount of money can buy good neighbours and yet good neighbours can make all the difference to how you feel about livin' in a particular place and we dropped lucky, really lucky, havin' the Greens, Grace and Arthur, for neighbours. Right from the start, Grace in particular was especially good to us, to Cynthia, baby Victor and me, and over the years, as our family grew, so did the amount of time and help she and Arthur were to give us. But that's in the future. For now they were just warm, friendly, welcomin' neighbours and that I can tell you made such a difference.

I'd known Grace a long time because she'd worked at Heathbrook School on the non-teachin' staff. Originally she'd been a dinner lady, but progressed to general non-teachin' duties, helpin' with readin', first aid, playground duty – that sort of thing. To Cynthia and me though, she was always 'Auntie Grace'. She wasn't an Auntie at all, but she was to us on account of all the fuss she made of our Victor in particular. She loved havin' him round and even took him off with them for weekends to stay with Sheila, their married daughter, in Croydon. It gave us a bit of a break and Victor loved goin'.

Beatie's, No 27, was the corner shop at the very top of our street. Before the war, it had been a sweet shop, the Candy Store we called it, but it had got bombed out. By the time I moved in next door, the shop had been rebuilt and Beatie was runnin' it as a general store.

She sold everythin' – well almost, from firewood under the counter to bacon on top. There were no fridges or freezers in those days, so fresh or perishable products had to turn over fast and be delivered on a regular basis. Bacon, for example, would be delivered three times a week by a boy on a bike. Bread would come in daily. That would be delivered around 6.30 am by 'Mr Wonderloaf.' Come rain or shine he'd just leave it outside in big plastic bread trays. Beatie only sold sliced bread, which fortunately came in a blue waxed paper wrapper. I say fortunately because, if it was rainin', the bread might be standin' out a while before Beatie fetched it in. She'd open up at around 7 am and about the first thing she'd do would be to put out this gob stopper machine which would stand outside on the pavement whenever Beatie's was open.

It was a real old-fashioned 'front room' type corner shop with atmosphere. Beatie never had a till. She'd itemise and reckon everythin' up on strips of paper and keep all the cash in a drawer. Today she'd be robbed in a flash, but back then Beatie was a respected member of the community, providin' a valuable service and nobody ever robbed her. She'd give customers the bit of paper with all the reckonin' on to check when they got home. It was always right.

I'd known Beatie since childhood because as a kid, sometimes mum would send me to Beatie's if we'd run out of somethin', but I don't remember her ever goin' in there herself. That's what made mum havin' gone in Beatie's and found out about No 25 becomin' empty so remarkable. I can't be certain, but the more I think about it now, the more I reckon mum went in there specially to ask. She knew Beatie's was the hub of local gossip and if anybody would know about a property becomin' vacant, Beatie would. Mum was a 'Co-Op' shopper at what she always called 'the stores'. It was practically unheard of for her to get groceries from anywhere else. She was very thrifty and she didn't mind walkin' further to get what she thought was better value and of course they gave divvy. Every customer had their own divvy number, in mum's case 456173. You gave your number whenever you bought anythin' and then twice a year you'd get money back in the form of a dividend. By the way, mum's number, I've not found it written down somewhere. It's just one of those bits of useless information that's stuck in my brain for all these years. I guess I went shoppin' for mum often enough for her divvy number to be imprinted on my brain for good – like it or not.

As for Beatie, she'd stand in that corner shop from 7 am 'till 7 pm and even then people would go knockin' her up sometimes long after she'd closed. She always kept the bacon on the counter where folk could see it. Back bacon, ready sliced it was. That shop sold anythin' and everythin'. Stacked on the floor in front of the counter were bundles of firewood and to one side of the shop was this big barrel of vinegar which Beatie sold loose by the pint or half pint. You took your own bottle and she'd fill it up. Inevitably, little bits got spilt and over the years this permeated into the wooden floor. It gave that shop an unmistakeable distinctive aroma and if I concentrate I can smell it now. Pungent, but not unpleasant, just distinctive. If you're old enough to have been in a shop sellin' loose vinegar, you'll know exactly what I mean – unmistakeable, unforgettable.

That's enough of home life for a while - back to the buses. If you remember, I told you my driver was Ron Lucas. He'd just been transferred from Battersea Garage. Ron had a rough time durin' the war. He walked a bit strangely, possibly as a result of havin' been a Japanese prisoner of war. He never talked about it, but everybody knew. He was a union man and a very knowledgeable chap. What Ron didn't know about buses and London transport wasn't worth knowin'. Another thing everybody knew about Ron was that he'd transferred from Battersea to Clapham so he could keep an eye on his wife, Betty. They were like chalk and cheese. Ron was rather serious and straight-laced whereas Betty was the life and soul and well – a bit flirty. She'd been a clippie on a tram durin' the war and by all accounts had been carryin' on with her driver for years. He was now drivin' buses and Betty was still his clippie.

I liked them both – Ron and Betty that is. I had a lot of respect for Ron and well – Betty was one of those women you just couldn't help likin'. She could be forceful and generous and not just with her favours. If our breaks co-incided, we'd often sit together in the canteen. There were no set times for breaks. Sometimes you could be on the road for five hours without a break. Another time you might break after an hour. It just depended on how the schedules went and whether there was a crew in the garage waitin' to take over. One break time I happened to mention that I'd taken this old fireplace out and when I could afford it I was goin' to install one of those new Cannon Gas Fires. They were all the rage back then. Next day Betty walks up to me, takes hold of my hand and shoves twenty-five pounds into it sayin', "Pay me back when you can – no rush" and before I could say anythin' she turns tail and walks off again.

That was Betty – generous to a T. I never could see what she saw in her fancy man though. Too snooty by half for my likin'. Thanks to Betty, Cynthia and I got our trendy gas fire straight away and although Betty got her money back, it did take a while. Twenty-five quid was a fair bit of money in the 1950s and it took some savin'. I didn't tell mum. I'm not sure she would have approved.

As I've told you, my first everyday route was the 155 Wimbledon to Westminster. In case you want to follow it on the ground or on a map, I'll quickly run through it. From Wimbledon we'd go up to Kennington and from there we'd basically run in a circle clockwise or anti-clockwise dependin' on the schedule. Typically we'd go along the Causeway to Westminster Bridge, over the Bridge to Westminster, past Big Ben and right along the Embankment, past Charring Cross, right over Blackfriars Bridge to St George's Circle and the Elephant & Castle and on back to Kennington. As a conductor workin' out of Clapham Garage I got to be very knowledgeable about London because we had nine regular routes plus special rush-hour buses all runnin' out of Clapham Garage. When I worked my rest days I could be assigned to any one of those routes.

Certain buses were renowned for potential trouble and our late 155 from South Wimbledon to Clapham Common was one of 'em. By late I mean that all bein' well, we'd be runnin' in to the depot at around 12.15 am. Saturday nights were often a problem 'cos when the Wimbledon Palais turned out, there'd often be more people standin' at the stop than we could take. In case you're interested, chances are Oscar Raybin and his orchestra would have been playin' there. We were only supposed to take 5 standin', but we knew it was the last bus so we'd try to pack in as many as possible. We had to be careful though, and not just because of the Inspectors. Irate folk didn't realise that the extra weight with passengers standin' top and bottom had a big effect on how the bus would handle. There was no power steerin' in those days and the driver would have a real job turnin' the wheel and would often have to stand up to get enough leverage. We'd do our best, but there were limits, and sometimes we'd just have to leave some. Stoppin' them boardin' wasn't easy and they knew when I rang the bell we'd be movin'. I'd be standin' at the back and I'd have to be careful not to get dragged off.

To compound matters, a good number of the late nighters would be drunk when they boarded and there was always a danger some of 'em would turn nasty. I used to find that humourin' em was the best way to avoid trouble. One night in particular when there was some fisticuffs, I remember sayin, "Come on now, don't do that ... I haven't collected his fare yet!" That diffused things. There was laughter and everybody cheered. If I'd tried to break it up physically, things could really have got out of hand. I'm makin' light of it, but to be honest we really dreaded that late nighter.

I worked as a conductor for about 18 months before applyin' to become a driver. It was now 1957. I couldn't drive and I didn't even have a licence, but in those days they trained you on the job. I'd never driven anythin' so if I was accepted, I'd have to learn to drive on a London bus! That's another thing you couldn't do today.

Before I tell you how I got on, I'll just take a little break from work. You might have noticed, I haven't taken many, but then that's how things were for me in those days. Mind you, I don't think all work and little play made me a dull boy!

As you know, Grace and Arthur were good neighbours – in fact they were the best. They were always helpin' us out. I remember one evenin' in particular, out of the blue, Grace came round and said, "It's about time you two had a break and took yourselves out for the evenin'." Victor didn't need askin' twice. He loved goin' round to 'Auntie' Grace. I think they spoilt him rotten.

It was about 6.30 pm and, bein' rather a dull evenin', to start with I don't think we were as enthusiastic as we might have been. On the plus side, at least it wasn't all that cold and it was a chance to get out together, which with me workin' all the overtime I could, didn't happen all that often. We decided to go down to the Festival Gardens in Battersea Park. As you know, the Festival had been back in 1951, but the gardens and some of the attractions kept goin' for years after. It was now 1957 and the really memorable thing that night, and the reason I'm tellin' you this, is there was a fairground and we decided to wander around it just soakin' up the atmosphere as much as anythin'.

Cynthia and I were never really that much into fairground rides, not least because they were mostly over in a flash and expensive even back then, so we'd pick and choose and spend most of our time just wanderin' enjoyin' the atmosphere. Lured by the prizes on offer, we did have a go on this airplane game. There was no skill involved – no more than there is in roulette. It was just down to chance. If the plane landed on your destination ticket, you won, simple as that. The thing is we did, so we had another go and won again and then again! We went home happy and laden, with a decent dartboard, a set of saucepans and, both bein' smokers, 50 Players cigarettes. The reason it's so memorable is because I don't think we'd ever won anythin' before – or since! The thing with 'fairground' saucepans though, as we soon discovered, they don't last long. They looked Ok but, when it came to usin' 'em, they weren't a patch on the ones I'd bought back in Aldershot. Now they were good pans because, as I've told you, I'm still usin' one of 'em today!

It was 1957. I was 23 – young, even for a conductor, but I was ambitious and I had a young family to provide for and two mortgages to pay. So I applied to become a driver. Ok, I wasn't just young, I'd never driven anythin' beyond a push bike, so maybe I was a bit of a chancer, but what's the worst that could happen? They could say no. But they didn't. I got accepted on to the three week driver's trainin' course. I'd got my foot in the door. Don't get me wrong, I wasn't the first conductor lookin' to progress to a driver and I wouldn't be the last, but I was probably the youngest and the least qualified as regards any drivin' experience. Well, you can't get much less than none!

Most of the course was practical – on the road – but we started with a couple of days classroom work back at Chiswick HQ. It was all pretty straightforward – Highway Code, that kind of thing. Then there was a day manoeuvrin' a bus around the depot – gettin' used to the size of the thing, changin' through the gears, reversin' and so on. Scary stuff really for a complete novice, but nothin' compared to that first trip out into London traffic. It was a busy old place even in those days.

For open road work we had an instructor to every three candidates. I had a Mr Butcher. He worked out of Sidcup Garage, but for trainin' purposes he'd come up to Clapham and we'd take a bus out from there. Our day would start in the canteen. Every garage had its own staff canteen. It was the hub of the place. A simple thing really – but I loved the atmosphere in there and the sense of belongin'. Mr Butcher would arrive at 9.00 am and we'd be there waitin' for him. The first day we were nervous as hell – leastways I was. Practically shakin' in me boots inwardly, but outwardly – well that was bravado. There were four of us in the bus – three trainees and our instructor. We'd take it in turns to drive – about an hour each. Our day would finish around 4 pm and once we'd left the depot we'd be drivin' around London all day except for our lunch break. On the subject of lunch, that would be the first task we'd be set each day – decidin' where to have lunch! I don't know what the other instructors were like, but he was good – Mr Butcher. He wasn't just good at instructin', he was good at puttin' you at ease, gettin' you relaxed. Even so, that first time behind the wheel, I'll never forget it. I'd never been so frightened in all my life. Not then. Not since. It's a good job I didn't have my 'dicky heart' and thankfully, I still had a strong bladder back then.

So, what was it like? Well, for a start there were no dual controls – nothin' like that. It was a standard bus. The only difference was the window at the back of the driver was missin'. Once we got in that cab, it was down to us. Mr B would stand or sit behind us where, in theory at least, I suppose he could lean over and grab the wheel if he had to. My first time out, I remember he stood behind me for a while, I guess 'till he thought I'd got the hang of it. After that he sat down. His confidence gave me confidence, if you know what I mean.

I remember the very first time we got on the bus Mr B told us not to worry. He was there to help us. He knew how we felt – he'd been there. Whilst he was good at puttin' us at our ease, there was no messin' about. It was all serious stuff. We had three weeks to learn and it was his job to make sure we did. He instilled the basics into us and then gave each of us ample opportunity to hone our skills and grow in confidence as we went along. On gettin' in the cab, the first crucial thing was to check the brake was on before startin' up the engine. There was no ignition key – it started by pullin' a lever above your head. What's more, London buses had pre-select gears and so there was no clutch as such. All you had to do was press a pedal with your left foot. At the time Daimler cars had a similar arrangement. It was more or less the forerunner of automatic cars. So, in that sense, these big lumberin' red giants were pretty state of the art. What they didn't have, not in the 1950s, was power steerin'. That didn't really matter while we were learnin' with an empty bus, but as I was to learn later, it could be a real problem when you had a full load. To turn a corner then I'd have to stand up to get enough leverage and even then, I'd have a job.

I mentioned that the first task of the day was decide on where to have lunch – dinner as we called it then. Say it was Plumstead Garage – then Mr B would take us through our paces en route to land us there around midday. We were runnin' 'Out of Service' but we'd still have to use a combination of bus routes. You couldn't take a double-decker just anywhere, especially if there were any overhead bridges in the way. As time went on, we grew in confidence but we knew that at the end of the three weeks there'd still be a drivin' skills session back at Chiswick to pass before a final day when we'd be independently examined by some big wig from London Transport. Whilst the three of us were all gettin' on pretty well, we were all a bit worried by the prospect of the tests on the final two days.

They say time flies when you're enjoyin' yourself. Take it from me, it also flies when you're concentratin' hard, tryin' to impress. And so it seemed like no time at all and we were into our penultimate day and our drivin' skills session at Chiswick HQ. We needn't have worried. It turned out to be a bit of fun really. Somethin' to give us experience. It didn't seem to matter whether we were good, bad or indifferent. We all three passed. So what was it, this skills test? Well, the main part of it was on the skid pads. The idea was to show us what would happen if we came across sheet ice and had to brake. The pads were soaked with hosepipes and we had to drive onto them and then brake hard. When you do that, what happens is the bus starts turnin' round and round and round and you've got next to no control over it. Brake hard on real ice on a busy London street and you'd do the same, ploughin' into and takin' out whatever is in the way. It was as much about teachin' us what not to do as what to do.

Next day was our final day – our big test out on the road. We still had our instructor onboard, but this was all about impressin' a big wig test inspector. He boarded at Chiswick and I have to say he certainly looked and sounded the part. Very smart. Gold braid on his cap and badges all over the place and when he spoke, very formal, very correct, very posh. His demeanor, his 'presence', that in itself was un-nervin'.

I was first one up and in a way I was pleased – better to get it over with. Once I was underway, I soon got the better of the 'butterflies'. I'd been drivin' for a while and feelin' it was goin' fine until I came to Hammersmith Broadway. In front there was this old boy with a cap on on a bike. I can see him now, clear as day. He stuck his hand out, as if he was intendin' to turn right, but then disaster. He lost control, fell off and, although I braked hard, he still finished up under my bus! I know my first thoughts should have been of him, but in truth they weren't. I thought, "Oh no, just my luck. No way am I goin' to pass this now. It's back to the ticket machines for me, for the foreseeable at least."

I'd braked so hard and so sudden that my four passengers had been practically catapulted out of their seats. As for the old boy, he'd only just slid under the front. He wasn't hurt – in fact he was more worried about retrievin' his cap. I was still in the cab. A bit shaken, and, if truth be told, downcast, and more so when Mr Gold Braid comes up to me and says, "Right, driver, get down and go and sit in the bus". I remember thinkin', "Oh no. This is it. He's had enough of me drivin'. Here comes the bad news," but no, it seems Lady Luck was right there beside me yet again because what he actually said was, "Very commendable driver. A wonderful emergency stop. We look forward to having you join our team of London Transport Drivers." If he hadn't been a bloke I could have kissed him – well almost. I don't really remember anythin' much about the rest of the journey when the other two candidates were drivin'. I couldn't wait to get back. I couldn't wait to get home to tell Cynthia ... and mum and dad and anybody else who would listen!

Me bathin' Victor in the back yard of our house, No 25 Gambetta Street.

Sadly, I haven't been able to locate a photo of Vivian as a baby. When we were havin' a sort-out, I think the girls took the ones of them. I don't want to leave Viv out though, so here's one Sandy found of the three of them together. We think it's taken on an outin' up town with Nanny Wattley. A street photographer with a monkey used to ply his trade outside Clapham Junction. Viv's the one huggin' it.

Little Sandy, aged about 18 months, sittin' on top of the garden wall at the back of our house in Gambetta Street. Reminiscent of 'Humpty Dumpty' don't you think?

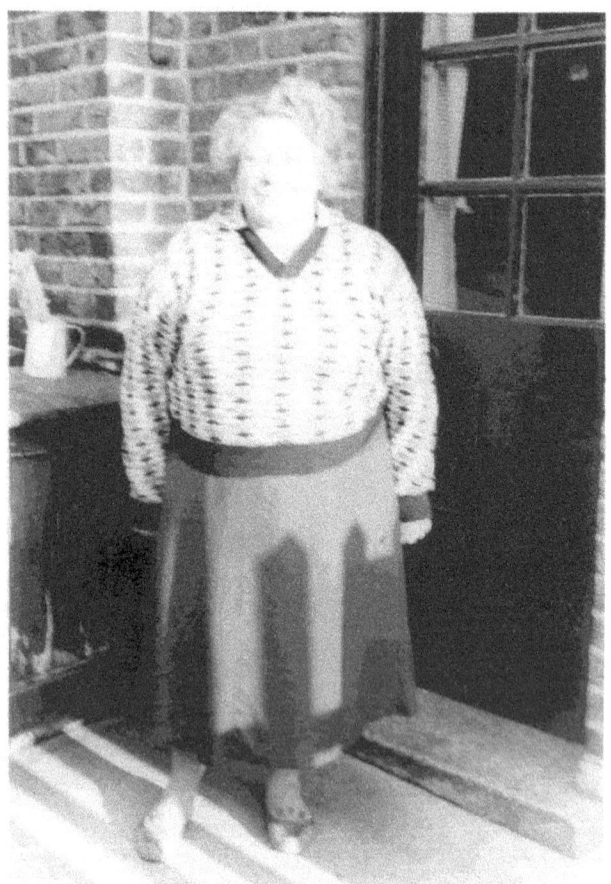

Mum on the 'flat' as we called it (upstairs balcony) of 15A Gambetta Street. As you can see, mum had put on a lot of weight in hospital.

CHAPTER 10

Drivin' A London Bus

The very next day I took a service bus out on my own from Clapham Garage. A route 37. I say on my own – obviously I had a clippie, a woman called Marge, but the drivin', that was down to me now, no instructor standin' behind, just me. As you can imagine, I was a bit nervous at first, but my main emotion I'd say was pride. I was a cocky little so and so and proud of myself for steppin' up and becomin' a driver. I knew the route because, of course, I'd been over it time and again durin' my 18 months as a conductor. Marge was a nice woman and although much older than me, we got on well. She'd been around a bit includin' workin' on the trams durin' the war. In more recent times she'd had a run of bad luck and things weren't workin' out well at home. Her husband had left her. Mind you, she wasn't one to dwell on her troubles. She was a good sort was Marge.

It wasn't just the workin' classes or the regulars who boarded the bus, in fact at times, it felt like all of London was spillin' in and out of my bus. They came from all walks of life. Sayin' that, weekends were different. We had a different clientele. Weekdays was mainly takin' people to and from work with a huge increase over the mornin' and evenin' rush hours. Saturdays, the bus would be full of the 'gadabout' Saturday crowds, includin' a fair smatterin' of tourists and the first hints of the 'cosmopolitan look' which long since has swamped what in my day was the local white populace.

Summer Sundays could be really busy on the 37's. Whole families – well, mums and kids mostly, would get on at Peckham and take a run out all the way to Richmond – about an hour's ride. They'd pile out and sunbathe on the banks of the Thames near Richmond Bridge and the kids would swim in the river. For many Londoners it was a bit like goin' to the seaside and probably as near as most of 'em ever got.

As a driver I didn't tend to have that much contact with the passengers, but two spring to mind because I guess they must have made a bit of an impression and yet the funny thing is, neither of 'em actually boarded, leastways not at the time. As it happens, both were well-to-do ladies, dressed very posh, and both spoke to me or tried to when I was stuck in heavy traffic. I'd usually have my window down you see because we'd been taught that our ears were nearly as important as our eyes for helpin' to avoid accidents.

One was when we were stuck outside Selfridges waitin' to get into Oxford Street and this lady catches my eye and says, "Just a moment driver .... Just a moment, I want to get on your bus." I smiled – well, you have to, don't you, and answered with what might have sounded like sarcasm, but wasn't really intended to be, "You'll have to go up the other end dear. You can't get on this end," and then realisin' we weren't even at a stop, "but you can't just get on when I'm in traffic. You have to go to a bus stop." If you've never seen a '50s bus, perhaps I should explain that passengers boarded and exited at the back not the front like they do today.

The other old dear was in Oxford Street itself, so still a 'well to do' area and by the way she spoke, so was she. Speakin' with 'a plum in her mouth' she says, "Excuse me driver, can you tell me if the seats upstairs are upholstered?" It was full downstairs and I don't think she was goin' to risk gettin' on without checkin'. I don't know, but judgin' by her concern, she must have thought it was all spittoons and sawdust up there! There wasn't time to reply properly before I had to move on, but since we weren't at a stop she couldn't have boarded anyway.

When you worked on the buses you worked by the clock. Now that I was a driver, it was my responsibility to make sure our bus was on time, or as near as we could be and so Cynthia went out and bought me a pocket watch. I got into the habit of checkin' the time every ten minutes or so to see how we were runnin' against the timetable. If your bus was 3 minutes or more behind schedule, the 'jumpers' could report you for that. They'd be more lenient durin' peak periods – the so-called rush hours – because they were always extra busy. What you couldn't do was run early. Get caught runnin' more than 3 minutes early and you'd risk bein' booked by the 'jumpers' and then you'd have some explainin' to do to the Chief Traffic Inspector. Not somethin' any of us drivers relished. Transgress once too often and you'd be out of a job. They didn't mess about in those days.

Drivin' in really heavy traffic was no picnic, but now and again it did have an up-side. Stickin' to timetables, bein' on time was paramount for the company, but even the 'jumpers', London Transport Road Traffic Controllers to give them their proper name, knew there were times when it was just impossible to keep to schedule or make it up once you'd fallen behind. At such times they'd board and tell you to turn at one of the designated spots – like Swiss Cottage – rather than complete the route. You couldn't just turn a London Bus anywhere, but turnin' was sometimes the only way to get back on schedule. Now both as a conductor and a driver we used to like it when we were told to make a turn before the terminus. With any luck, it might mean we had as much as a twenty minute impromptu break at the designated turn around – plenty of time for a smoke, before pullin' off again so as to start back on schedule at that point on the return route.

Whilst keepin' to the timetable could be a bit of a bind at times, I had a good deal of admiration for those who worked it all out and organised it. It was really very clever the way all the services and all the crews with all their breaks were factored in. All in all, a very complex operation and yet it worked – it worked like clockwork.

Breakdowns apart, all through the workin' day the buses never stopped – only the crews. If we were due a break or comin' off shift, then we'd stop at Clapham Common Depot or, to be more precise, in Clapham High Street more or less opposite. As I say, the whole operation worked like clockwork. It was all down to timin' to avoid delays or down time. As we pulled up, the change-over crew would be there, waitin' on the pavement.

There were about nine different routes workin' out of Clapham Garage and you needed to know all of 'em because from one week to the next you never knew which route you'd be assigned to. Routes have changed now and have become much shorter, in part in response to increased traffic volumes. Back then on the 155's for example, we'd go from Clapham High Street to: Clapham North; Stockwell, the Oval (home of cricket), Kensington, from where services would alternate either going to Elephant & Castle or Lambeth North. If Elephant & Castle, it would then be St George's Circus, Blackfriars Bridge where we'd go left over the bridge and then left again onto the Embankment (that's where the toilets were where mum found her penny – remember that?)

Before I go on, I'll just mention somethin' that happened one Sunday around lunchtime. It was very quiet goin' over the bridge that day, so I had plenty of time to look around and there on the parapet was this bloke sprawled out – dead or I'm a Dutchman. I'm tellin' you, I saw all of life and death whilst drivin' a London bus. I'm afraid 'witnessin' accidents was practically an every day occurrence and amongst them there must have been a fair smatterin' of fatalities, but this poor chap looked as if he'd just keeled over. As luck would have it, if there is such a thing in the circumstances, on the other side I could see this policeman, so I pulled the bus over and in a calmish tone, told him he'd got a fatality to sort out on the bridge and, before I could get roped in, I was off again. It's not like I'd seen anythin' happen and I didn't want to get involved with witness statements and coroners 'cos, as you know, it was a case of 'no work, no pay' on the buses in those days. It was a shame for that bloke, but it's not like I could have done anythin' to help him now.

So, back to my route: we'd go all the way along the Embankment past Cleopatra's Needle until eventually we'd get to Westminster Bridge with Big Ben and the Houses of Parliament in front of you. Then it was left over the bridge to the opposite bank with County Hall on one side and St Thomas's Hospital (where if you remember I died) on the other and then on down towards Lambeth North and then on back to Kennington to pick up the outward route again – goin' on what we called the 'B Route' now of course towards Clapham Common back out of London. The 'A Route' was the route into London.

I'll just take a break from tellin' you about me at work to tell you about what was happenin' at home and how Cynthia was farin'. With Arthur gone and with him the rental income, we were findin' it a bit difficult to make ends meet.

Money was always short. I know what some of you must be thinkin' – so why didn't the pair of you give up smokin' then? Nowadays I'd have to agree it would be the obvious economy to make, but things were different back then. For a start, smokin' wasn't the pariah it is today and nobody thought they were doin' themselves harm, possibly irreparable harm, by smokin'. Everybody smoked. It was the done thing. Socially, you almost had to smoke to be accepted. I never smoked as many as Cynthia, perhaps because workin' I just didn't have as much time on my hands, but together we probably got through more than a dozen packets every week.

Anyway, we talked about the possibility of Cynthia gettin' a job – in part because it would get her out of the house. She was young and bein' cooped up in a small place with a young child all day created pressures of its own. At that time in her life, Cynthia needed another outlet. We'd talked about the possibility of her gettin' a job, but with Victor, now a toddler, at home, that seemed out of the question. There was always mum, livin' just up the road, but the mum Cynthia knew wasn't the mum of old. It was the one who had been through the mill of the mental institution. Cynthia just couldn't entrust the care of our Victor to mum for long periods on a regular basis. But, as so often in my life, it was mum lookin' out for me that made the difference. I told mum we were hard up and could do with another tenant to replace Arthur. We didn't really need the back room, but we did need the income. Mum put the word out and as a result one day Lily came knockin'.

Before I go any further, I should perhaps explain who Lily was and to do that I need to take you back to when mum and dad first moved into Gambetta Street, or maybe even earlier. Originally, the whole street had been built to house railway workers. With comin's and goin's over the years, by the time we arrived in the street, it wasn't so much of a railway community anymore, but even so, a good many of the residents did still work on the railway and that included mum's next door neighbours, the Lark family. Mr Lark senior lived upstairs with his wife, son Ron and daughter Lily. Their other son, George, lived downstairs with his wife. George was a boxer. Nobody messed with George. He liked a bet and his wife would be off up the street every day to the bookies for him. The interestin' thing though was their cat Tony would always follow her all the way up and all the way back. Tony was Dinky's mate. They didn't fight, they got along fine together. Maybe it was a case of mutual respect.

Now I know I'm digressin', but one thing I must just mention is that Mr Lark was a driver of the famous Golden Arrow steam train, which was a luxury 'boat train' service between London and Paris. I was never lucky enough to ride on it, but apparently passengers were taken to Dover, where they'd be transferred to a ferry for the crossin' to Calais. Then they'd join the French equivalent, the Fleche d'Or, to take them on to Paris. It was a steam service, but apparently it 'ran like clockwork' – luxury travel, with rarely any delays. The London to Dover link, which Mr Lark drove, took just 98 minutes. This was the 1950s remember. Amazin' when you think about it.

Anyway, that was Lily, mum's neighbour's daughter, and it seems, that whilst I was in the army, Lily got married to another George and they were livin' somewhere in North London, but didn't like it. Even today, north and south Londoners often don't see eye to eye and back then even more so. Lily wanted to come back south of the river. Trouble was they didn't have much money, so we came to a different arrangement which suited us both. Lily, George and their little boy would move into our back room. No money would change hands, but Lily would look after Victor durin' the day so that Cynthia could go out to work. London Transport were still recruitin' and she fancied followin' in my footsteps so to speak by applyin' for a job on the buses. As well as helpin' to pay our mortgages, Cynthia wanted some extra money so she could buy stuff for the house – new curtains – that kind of thing, and I thought maybe we could even save a few bob.

In those days folk really did shove any extra cash under the mattress. It was quite common. There were banks, of course there were, but as I recall, in the 1950s and 60s only wealthy people had bank accounts. Ordinary people like us shoved money under the mattress or, more sensibly, used the Post Office for savin', assumin' they had anythin' left over to 'put away for a rainy day.' It wasn't really until the 1970s that banks became accessible to ordinary people and even then it was a kind of enforced marriage. Where they could, firms started payin' monthly and wages became salaries which were paid direct into a bank. It made sense, but really I think it was about business becomin' more efficient, makin' employment more cost-effective.

Generally the four of us, Lily and George, Cynthia and me, we rubbed along quite well, but every arrangement has its little drawbacks. George's dad worked at Billingsgate Market, so he'd often bring fish home – usually fresh salmon. Very nice you might think – except we shared the scullery and they used to stink the place out. Sometimes I'd only have to open the front door and the smell would hit me. I shouldn't be complainin' because we usually got our share and overall, them bein' with us was a good arrangement and not just because of the child mindin'. They hadn't been there long before they discovered woodworm in their room – lots of it. As luck would have it, Lily's brother was a carpenter. He didn't just renew all the floorboards, but some of the joists as well. It would have cost a packet, but lucky for us, he never charged us anythin' – not for labour or even materials. To be on the safe side, we burnt all the infected timber in the back yard. I might have tried to salvage some for firewood, but he told us that's how most woodworm comes in – via bundles of firewood – so I wasn't goin' to risk any more of that.

Cynthia got a job as a 'clippie', no problem. After two weeks' induction at Chiswick, which was classroom work, Cynthia joined me at Clapham Garage, except we didn't see that much of eachother because we fixed it so that generally we were on opposite shifts. They didn't allow husband and wife teams anyway, so Cynthia never clippied for me, not even when we worked rest days. I was pleased when Cynthia got teamed up with Arthur Shoulders. A steady sort who I knew would look after her. He was a good bit older than me, but I knew him well from the fishin' club. He'd been a tram driver before and had loads of experience.

It's just occurred to me that I haven't told you anythin' about the fishin' club – the London Transport Fishin' Club – so before I forget, I'll just put that right. I was so busy workin' on the buses or on the house that I didn't get much time for recreation, but as you know, I was fishin' mad, so I did join the work's fishin' club.

Doubtless durin' the war but certainly in the post war era, lots of people kept chickens in coops in the back garden or even just a yard includin' the Faggs, the people who lived in No 15, below mum and dad in Gambetta Street. They kept chickens, mainly for the eggs. All those chickens needed feedin' and so, as a result, there were a good number of seed chandlers in London, which was handy for fishermen like me. A favourite bait combination I often used when out with the London Transport Fishin' Club was hemp seed and elderberries. When in season, I'd gather the berries direct from the bushes. Otherwise I'd have to buy 'em from a fishin' tackle shop by the jar in some sort of preservin' liquid. The hemp seed I'd buy by the 1lb from the seed chandlers. It wasn't any good used direct. I had to boil it 'till it split, revealin' the white seed inside. The trick was to toss some hemp seed into the water to attract the fish. They seemed to go mad for it. Maybe it doped them a bit. I don't really know. All I needed then was some elderberry on the hook and I was away. I had a lot of success with it. Mind you it was a young man's way to fish. You had to be workin' all the time. None of this puttin' a line and float out and sittin' ponderin' while munchin' a sandwich. Sadly now I can't even manage that. It's all the gettin' to and from that's too much for me. Like my music, I just have to fall back on my memories. Havin' said that, John's offered to take me. He wants to see me catch a fish and show him how to catch one so, you never know, I might just get those rods out again. There I go again, digressin', daydreamin' about what might be, when I'm supposed to be tellin' you about my time on the buses.

I'd not been drivin' long – about 6 months - when the powers that be decided to shut Clapham Depot and transfer us to Stockwell. Then we were 're-mated' and instead of Marge I was teamed up with a 'new' clippie, Helen. When I say new, I mean new. She wasn't just new to me, she was new to the job and at 22, even younger than me. No problem though. She turned out to be an A1 clippie and a real looker to boot. A beautiful young Irish girl was Helen and she knew it. You could tell by the way she walked around holdin' her head up high but at the same time lappin' up all the admirin' glances. Now don't go makin' assumptions. We were work mates and that's as far as it went. I'm just sayin' that she was beautiful. I wasn't blind and you couldn't help but notice her hour glass figure. Because we were a young crew – in fact we were *the* young crew – the rest of them called us the 'two puppies'. No matter, we were good on the job and worked together as a team for about 4 years.

Unfortunately, when they shut Clapham and transferred us all to Stockwell, Cynthia got re-assigned to a new driver – a young chap with 5 or 6 kids and a bit of a reputation as a 'ladies' man'. Friendly enough, but to be honest not my type at all. He had this big Zephyr and he kept offerin' to lend it to me if ever I should want to 'go for a ride', but I didn't want to get that close, so I never did take him up on it.

I've already told you that Cynthia could be a bit 'flighty', especially in her younger days, so I had to keep an eye out and an ear to the ground. There were always rumours circulatin' round the garage, but half of 'em were probably unfounded and most of 'em amounted to nothin' really. Some of 'em were about Helen and me and I knew for sure there was nothin' in that. I wasn't one for payin' any attention to 'tittle-tattle'. Even so, when some of it concerns your nearest and dearest, then you begin to sit up and take notice. With Cynthia now teamed up with a bloke not much older than me who already had six kids of his own and a reputation as a 'ladies' man', I felt I had to be on my mettle so I kept an eye out and an ear to the ground. Cynthia gettin' moved away from Arthur, a steady bloke with his eyes on the job, to this character, who really fancied himself, wasn't exactly welcome news.

Cynthia worked on the 77A route, which ran between Raines Park and Kings Cross. Sometimes we'd work the same shifts, but very often we'd be on opposite ones. I might be on at 6 am workin' through 'till 3 pm or earlier if I was lucky and Cynthia might get the 4 pm 'till midnight shift. Our least favourite was probably the 7 am – 7 pm split shift slot and although split shifts coverin' the rush hour were a bit deadly, we liked them financially. The first shift would be 7 am – 10.30 am and then back again for the 4 pm – 7 pm evenin' rush hour. The good bit was we'd get paid for a full 12 hour shift even though we'd be at home for half of it in the middle.

Unlike Clapham, when workin' out of Stockwell Garage you didn't chop and change, you worked the same regular route and so, unless I was on overtime, I'd be drivin' my regular No 2 route. Occasionally I'd run the No 2A out which only ran between Norwood and Victoria, but mostly it was the No 2 which ran between Golders Green and Crystal Palace. Comin' out of Stockwell, we'd often as not take off on what we called the 'B Route' goin' out towards the suburbs. That would be Stockwell, Brixton, Coal Harbour Lane, Herne Hill, Tulse Hill, Norwood, and then on to Crystal Palace. There we'd turn and generally have time to take a 3 or 4 minute comfort stop and speedy cuppa. Then it would be back on the return 'A Route' towards the City and sometimes we'd get another tea break at Stockwell and other times we'd just carry on to Vauxhall, Victoria, Hyde Park Corner, Hyde Park (from about 1960. Prior to that it was up Park Lane) to Marble Arch, down Oxford Street and left into Portland Place, up to Baker Street, past Lords Cricket Ground, to Swiss Cottage into Finchley Road, Childs Hill into Golders Green where we'd turn, hopefully havin' had time for a comfort stop and a cuppa in the London Transport Café. The return journey to Stockwell would be the reverse of the inward route except goin' down Park Lane itself rather than along the edge of Hyde Park.

Once, when I was just drivin' past Baker Street Station, I came close, a bit too close, to a 'ghost' from the past. Well not exactly a ghost, in fact far from it. A larger than life character would be a better description. It was Brian Mickey – remember him? The compere from Granada Theatres I told you about seein' as a kid. If ever there was a chap who was larger than life, it was him. A massive bloke with a personality to match. But that particular day was very nearly his last because I very nearly killed him. He must have had somethin' on his mind and been in a tearin' hurry because he came rushin' out of the station and straight into the road in front of me. Because he was so massive, I could hardly miss seein' him, but I had all on to stop before hittin' him. Talk about a hair's breadth. My heart was in my mouth and my passengers were probably all over the place. As I looked down thinkin', "bloody hell", I saw it was him – none other than Brian Mickey. I'd not seen him in years, but it was definitely him. He barely gave me a second glance as he just hurried on oblivious to how close I'd come to squashin' him all over the road.

The funny thing is, my only other really close shave with a pedestrian was another celebrity, Tito Burns, and funnily enough it was on that same stretch of road, just a bit further up. Now to me, Tito Burns was a famous 1940s and 50s band leader. What I'd call a 'bop accordionist'. He ran a live band, but I'd mainly heard him on the radio. His band, the Tito Burns Sextet, recruited several of London's leadin' young musicians, includin' drummers Tony Crombie and Ray Ellington and later saxophonists Scott and John Dankworth. Dependin' on your age, you probably didn't know any of that, but you might know him better as the bandleader who went on to manage risin' stars like the young Cliff Richard, The Springfields and The Searchers and promote amongst others The Beatles and

Jimmi Hendrix, or the man who became a big noise in theatre land. The thing is, he'd never have done any of that if I hadn't had my wits about me. He'd have ended his days in 1959 under a London Bus – my London Bus. Again his mind must have been somewhere else because he just stepped out in front of me without lookin'. I just had time to hit the horn as I anchored up, screechin' to a halt inches from him. But he didn't seem phased. Acted like it was normal. No histrionics. Ok, he side-stepped a bit, but didn't really break his stride as he turned and looked up at me with that characteristic grin on his face, emphasised by the moustache he sported in those days, and gave me a wave in thanks I guess.

Helen and I would sometimes be paired up for overtime jobs as well. One time we were drivin' an early mornin' shift on the No 37 route. It was about 6.30 am and we pulled up at a stop the other side of Richmond Bridge. There was nobody much else about and it turned out this Air Hostess had overslept and was runnin' half an hour late. She was bound for London Airport, but relyin' on us to get her to the underground airport link at Hounslow. Helen would help anybody in trouble – she was that sort of lass and she came up to the cab and asked me if maybe we could do somethin'? Stickin' to timetables was the be all and end all with London Transport. As I've told you bein' just 3 minutes early or late was a bookable offence if you were caught. At that time in a mornin' though, we could be pretty sure there wouldn't be any 'jumpers' about and, at that time, on that route, there wasn't much in the way of traffic to hold you up or passengers come to that, so I just grinned and told 'em to 'hang on tight'. I really put my foot down to get to Hounslow in record time, so hopefully that young lass made her flight.

Hounslow was our turn-around where we'd normally get a short break – more of a comfort stop than anythin', but we were more than twenty minutes early, so we needed to lay low and filter back out on schedule. Fortunately there were still no 'jumpers' about so Helen and I were able to creep up to the canteen above the garage and keep our heads down. With time goin' on, it was gettin' busier now and with all the comin's and goin's nobody seemed to notice, so no harm done and hopefully we'd got that young lass out of a jam. Goodness knows what would have happened if we'd been caught. Three minutes either side of schedule was a bookable offence with consequences. Twenty odd minutes – well that was just unheard of.

Once we were back on the road it was soon becomin' manic as usual as the mornin' rush hour got underway and in truth, even back then, in reality the frenzy lasted for much longer than just an hour.

That was by no means the only out of the ordinary incident that happened when doin' overtime. One that springs to mind didn't so much involve riskin' my job as my life – or so I thought. As it happens, again I was drivin' the 37 route. I can't remember the date, but that doesn't really matter, the point is I had a nasty, heart stoppin' experience. Dependin' on the schedule we'd been given, goin' out on the B route, we'd either turn at Richmond or Isleworth or go all the way through to Hounslow and turn there. Anyway, this particular day we'd just turned at Isleworth and, as luck would have it we had about five minutes stand time before havin' to head off back into the city on time. That was enough for a smoke. I never smoked when drivin'. Some did, but I never did, but like most everybody else, drivers and conductors, about the first thing I'd do when we had some down time, was light up. I'd barely stubbed it out before this mist started descendin'. Bad news because, I knew from experience, the chances are it would get worse, much worse, the nearer we got into the city. Sure enough, as we headed towards Richmond it was gettin' thicker, much thicker.

It was afternoon, about 4 o'clock time, as we approached St Margaret's Station – that was a stop on Southern Rail – when this damn great jumbo jet suddenly appeared out of the mist, flyin' low. When I say low, I mean low – very, very low – only just over the houses and headin' straight for me with its wheels down. I'm not jokin'. I nearly had a heart attack. I thought, "This thing is goin' to crash and take me with it." At such times they say your whole life flashes before your eyes – but in my case there was no time for that. This thing was comin' right at me and instinct took over. I put my foot to the boards and yes, I ducked – as if that would have done any good! I thought if I can just get underneath it before it comes down takin' my bus with it. I confess I wasn't really thinkin' of the passengers. There just wasn't time. In a heartbeat I was under and thankin' my lucky stars. As for the passengers, surely some of 'em must have seen the thing. For the most part though, all they would have experienced was me acceleratin' like mad in the gatherin' fog. What they thought of that, goodness knows. After a bit, I eased off, but I didn't stop. I still wanted to put as much distance as possible between my bus and me and the fall-out when the thing crashed. I'd expected to hear this massive explosion behind me but nothin', I heard nothin'.

To say I was shaken up is puttin' it mildly, but I just carried on drivin', gettin' calmer by the minute. I was certain there was no way that thing was goin' to land. It had to crash. It was so very, very low, there was no way it could have made it to Heathrow. But it must have. Somehow it must have got back up because I never heard any more about it. There was nothin' on the news, nothin' in the papers, nothin'. It was as if I'd dreamt it, but I hadn't, believe me, I hadn't.

Helen and I took our breaks together and Helen used to take my advice about a lot of things, but not her love life. Eventually she married this Irish bloke called David. Very good lookin', no doubt, but a scoundrel. He led her a merry dance, not least with his gamblin', especially the late night card schools. Eventually in 1963 Helen had a child, but because of all the trouble she was gettin' at home, she didn't feel she could cope with it and came to ask Cynthia and me if we'd look after it – in effect adopt it. We didn't. We felt sorry for her, but we'd got our own family to look after and for us three was enough. We didn't want to start again lookin' after someone else's baby.

Here I go again gettin' ahead of myself, talkin' about 1963 when I've not finished tellin' you about the '50s. I need to take you back a year or two and tell you a few more things that happened when Helen and I were workin' on the buses.

Whilst workin' out of Clapham, I'd become very knowledgeable about London because of all the different routes we worked on. Now, in a sense Stockwell was easier because there we worked the same specific route week in, week out, in our case the No 2 route, but we still had to know all the other routes because if we wanted overtime, that is if we wanted to work our rest days, we could be assigned to any route operatin' out of Stockwell, and there were half a dozen of 'em. Once, when I was on overtime I was drivin' a 169, so not my usual route, and dad got on my bus at the Lavender Hill stop on Queenstown Road. Nothin' strange about that, except he got on escourtin' this woman and the pair of 'em sat down together, more or less behind my cab. I'd spotted them but they never saw me. They got off together at Vauxhall. That mean't they were changin' to another bus and goin' on to the West End. Knowin' dad, they were probably headed to some political meetin' or other – but you never know! Whilst it seemed to me that dad was predictable and stuck in his ways, it's just possible he was a bit of a dark horse!

Helen and I might have been the young kids on the block, but we were a good team. Even the bosses thought so, or they'd never have left us together. We didn't always do things by the book though – especially me. Preparin' for my Cynthia's 21st was a case in point. I wanted to make it a bit special and one thing I wanted to do was surprise her with a birthday cake. Even if I could bake, makin' it at home would have ruined the surprise, so I ordered it from Websters, a famous bakers in South Wimbledon. They were next to the tube station and you could see 'em from my bus icin' cakes upstairs. I'd made an impromptu stop the week before – just long enough to pop in and order it. I stopped again two days before the big day to collect it and to tell the truth, I got a surprise myself. Massive it was, but I have to say they'd done a beautiful job. That cake rode round beside me in the cab until my shift was over all the time me prayin' I didn't have to brake hard. I knew I'd be home before Cynthia because she'd still be workin' her shift on the buses but, even so, I couldn't risk her seein' it at our house, so I gave it to Grace next door to keep 'till the day.

On the day itself, Cynthia bein' on 'middle shift', I knew she'd be back around 7.30 pm so with me finished and home by lunchtime, I had time to prepare. It wasn't a really grand affair. We would only be six – Grace & Arthur, Cynthia's sister Monica, husband Jeff and the two of us, but hopefully the surprise made it memorable. I know it might seem awful, but I didn't invite mum and dad because Cynthia was always nervous and wary of mum as she was prone to havin' one of her turns if she got a bit excited. It was Cynthia's special day and I didn't want anythin' to spoil it. When Cynthia came in, we all burst into song – she's 21 today, key of the door and all that. I'd got this lovely buffet all laid out ready and my special cake, that had pride of place.

In London, all the crews worked pretty hard. There weren't really any cushy routes. Ok, some were busier than others and some could be positively manic at times, but it was swings and roundabouts really. Havin' said that, as a driver I did my best to give Helen as easy a time as I could, especially if I could see she was a bit under the weather. We neither of us rang in sick unless we really had to 'cos, as I've explained, in those days it was a case of if you didn't work, you didn't get paid – simple as that. As a driver I didn't want to be leader of the pack. That wouldn't do at all, or Helen would be shattered at the end of our shift. But I did need to be ahead of the game, know how to duck and dive a bit. Playin' second fiddle, now that was good. If you're a bit confused, and don't understand my meanin', then maybe I should explain that to give Helen a bit of an easier time I'd try and run in close behind another bus. That way it would pick up most of the passengers. At times, that might put us a bit ahead of schedule but passengers didn't really suffer because services were so frequent that nobody had to wait more than a few minutes for a bus in London. I just had to watch I didn't get too far ahead and risk fallin' prey to the 'Jumpers'.

Most of the time though, Helen and I ran a pretty tight ship so as to keep more or less on schedule. Even so, as I mentioned earlier, sometimes delays were inevitable due to factors beyond our control, like the time we were stuck for an hour outside the Dorchester without movin'. I've come back to that because it wasn't just memorable for the long delay. Somethin' much more interestin' happened. The rush hour had already finished, so normally we'd have been runnin' pretty much on schedule. We'd come from Golders Green, through the West End and into Park Lane. As I say, it was there we got held up outside the Dorchester for the best part of an hour. We were approachin' Hyde Park Corner and eventually we did get through and down to Victoria, to Stockwell and on to Brixton. Talkin' of Brixton, we had a bit of a joke amongst the drivers: We'd say if you kept your window open you could hear Winifred Atwell playin' as you went through Brixton. Anyway, from Brixton it was on to Herne Hill and then Crystal Palace where we turned round. Normally we'd have taken a comfort break at Crystal Palace, but by now we were runnin' nearly an hour and a half late, so we just turned and got on our way.

On our return route I got caught short at Herne Hill. I wouldn't make it back to the depot, so I pulled in at a stop near Brockwell Park where I knew there were some toilets. I switched the engine off. If ever I did that, Helen knew where I would be goin'. As I walked towards the toilet, I saw this big Daimler type car with this rather large gentleman bein' supported by two chaps, one on either side. I could see they were smartly dressed, but I didn't take that much notice. I was more interested in gettin' to the toilet 'cos I was burstin'. I was still standin' there doin' what you do when these three characters came in and it was then I realised who this rather large gentleman was. None other than Mr Winston Churchill! Not every day you take a leak next to a former Prime Minister, War Leader and possibly the most famous face in Britain. In other circumstances I might have asked for his autograph, but this was neither the time nor the place and the way he was havin' to be supported, he'd obviously had a few. Surreal or what?! We came off for our break at Stockwell. As you can imagine, I couldn't wait to tell Helen the story.

I saw a lot of things whilst workin' on the buses, particularly whilst I was drivin'. You get a good view sittin' up there in that cab. I saw a lot of accidents, sometimes before they happened, but I was powerless to intervene. We saw a lot and yet we saw nothin'. That's because of the unwritten rule amongst drivers, conductors and clippies on London Transport. It was a sad state of affairs, but the fact was if you saw too much, then you didn't earn a bean because as you now know, the system was 'no work, no pay'. Simple as that. Spendin' days in court bein' a good citizen was somethin' we couldn't afford.

As a London Bus driver you didn't just have to keep your eyes open, but your ears peeled to avoid bein' in an accident yourself. One of the things that had been drummed into me whilst learnin' was that a big part of drivin' in the city was hearin'. Obviously you had to keep your eyes on the road constantly on the look-out for the unexpected, especially pedestrians steppin' out, but what you didn't see you might hear. You might get an audible warnin' of whatever. That's why, despite the advent of aircon, I've pretty much always driven with my window down. Old habits die hard I guess. Mind you, I've paid a bit of a price for it because as a result I've got this 'rodent ulcer' on my right temple. It's a form of skin cancer caused by the sun. Now at 83, they've decided I've got to have the thing cut out, but the hole will be so big that I've got to have a skin graft taken from my chest to avoid spoilin' my good looks!

Talkin' of good looks, if there are any Matt Monroe fans readin' this, you may be interested to know that Matt was drivin' London buses at the same time as me. If I remember rightly, he drove one of the No 27's out of Richmond Garage. Of course that was before he became really famous and because our paths didn't cross that much, I can't say I knew him well, but we all knew he 'did a bit of singin' on the side!

Come 1957, Prime Minister Harold McMillan was tellin' us all that, "We've never had it so good." Well, that depended on your circumstances. With two mortgages to pay and a young family to keep, to make ends meet, I'd often work my rest days. Overtime was well paid and that extra day, it made a lot of difference. This particular day I was drivin' a 181, Victoria to Streatham. At Victoria the road was wide, wide enough to turn a bus round. About the only place in London where you could – officially at any rate. So, there I was, pulled up at the side of the road with the engine runnin' waitin' for a break in the traffic and an opportunity to do a U turn. Up in front there were some parked cars. All of a sudden this woman steps out from between 'em straight into the traffic. Right up into the air she went and back down headlong into the tarmac. I knew she'd be a gonner and that was confirmed later. I guess her mind was elsewhere and she just wasn't thinkin' where she was. I suppose we've all done it, but not in such a dangerous spot or with such serious consequences. Very sad all round – for her and for the driver. You couldn't help but feel sorry for him – he had no chance – no time to react before he hit her. There were loads of witnesses, so I just got on with my job and tried as best I could to put the incident out of my mind. You never do though – not completely – not somethin' like that.

Usually when I did overtime, it was with another conductor or clippie, but this particular day that springs to mind they were short of both a driver and a conductor on the 37's, Hounslow to Peckham route, so Helen and I were doin' overtime together. I don't remember the date, but it was winter and there was snow on the ground. We were comin' from Peckham and just after East Dulwich Hospital there was an old girl standin' at a request stop. She had a white fur coat on to match the snow! I remember that makin' me smile. I pulled in. I could see she had a brown paper bag in her hand. Now I should tell you that as a bus driver, your mirrors were your best friends. You could see everythin' in those mirrors – not just activity on the road, but the passengers as well. As the old dear went to board the bus, I was checkin' on her in the mirrors before pullin' off. One second she was there, next she just disappeared. She wasn't onboard. Helen was upstairs collectin' fares, so I knew she wouldn't have seen anythin'. Havin' given the woman time to board and get seated, she'd rung the bell for me to go, but I hesitated. I had this premonition. Where's the old girl gone? Had she tried to board the bus or just walked behind us? Somethin' wasn't right. Rather than drive on, I switched the engine off and got down out of the cab. A good job too. As I walked towards the back of the bus I could see her head stickin' up from under the bus! She must have slipped tryin' to get onboard and slid right under the platform at the back. Fortunately beyond the wheel or I'd have killed her if I'd tried to move off.

With the engine off, Helen came down to investigate and together we pulled the old dear out, rather like a sledge. She was lyin' stranded in all this ice and snow. We got her onboard and sat her down on one of the long seats. You might think she was badly shaken up and in a bit of a state, but not a bit of it. All she was interested in was retrievin' her bag of tomatoes! She was worried some of 'em had got squashed. We retrieved the bag – what was left of it, but had no time to go searchin' for all the tomatoes. We were already runnin' late. As it was, the old dear got off at the very next stop – Herne Hill. Helen and I were happy she was Ok, but she was still goin' on about her lost tomatoes. She must have been in her '80s. She should never have been out in such weather – especially not just to get a bag of tomatoes. She was a tough old stick though – you've got to give her that. This was one time Helen and I made out a report of the incident. We had no choice. Half the bus had noticed and taken an interest in the old girl's welfare.

So that's two incidents I've recounted for you that happened in the vicinity of Herne Hill – the old dear and my encounter with Mr Churchill. They say things happen in threes, so I'll tell you another one before movin' on. It was November time and we were in the midst of one of those 'pea soup' fogs you've probably read about but never experienced. Sometimes it would just descend on you almost out of nothin'; other times there'd be this thickenin' mist that might come to no more and just disperse, but often as not would gradually turn into this dense chokin' smog. We called 'em 'Pea Soupers' on account of their thick grey green, swirlin' consistency. Nowadays, people see a bit of fog and think it's the same, but trust me it's not, not by a long chalk. I suppose if you've never experienced it, it's nigh on impossible to imagine just how bad it was. So, take it from me –

we're talkin' dense fog – very, very dense smog.

You don't get real 'pea soupers' now, but back then everybody had coal fires and it was all the smoke trapped and minglin' with the fog that did it. Anyway, we were comin' back from Golders Green and when we got to Stockwell this Traffic Controller hops onboard. At times like this it was really up to the driver to decide whether it was safe to carry on. Helen was concerned and the Controller admitted a number of drivers had already called it a day and run in, but he also said, "It's up to you John but I'm told it's not too bad the other side of Brixton." We had a good few passengers still onboard so I told Helen, "We'll get rid of this lot by the time we get to Brixton and then turn at Herne Hill rather than goin' on all the way to Crystal Palace." I should explain that Crystal Palace would mean goin' another 5 or 6 miles up the road into an area renowned for bein' very bad when there was fog about. Another thing you need to understand is that you couldn't turn a London Bus round just anywhere – there were designated points where it was both possible and allowed.

So, we get to Herne Hill, where I'd intended to turn, but standin' at a stop more or less opposite what I now thought of as the 'Churchill Toilets', was this chap and a young woman with a baby. I slid the glass across in the cab, intendin' to explain that owin' to the conditions we were turnin' back, but before I could get started this chap gets his two pennorth in first. "You blokes are all the same," he said, "I've been waitin' over an hour for a bus," to which I replied, "Can't you see the situation – do you want to have a go" – openin' the door. "Come on, jump up." Jokin' apart, the young woman looked a bit distressed. Apparently she'd been visitin' her mum's and was tryin' to get home – to West Norwood. Helen looked at me as if to say, "Don't do it John," but I said, "We can't leave that girl with such a young baby," and I told her to get in. I was thinkin' that could be Cynthia and our Victor stranded here, but, as the bloke went to climb onboard, I more or less shouted, "Oh no, not you – you're walkin!" I guess he was lookin' daggers at me, but I couldn't see on account of the fog. "You're walkin' in front of the bus with a flare. I can't see a thing from up here and unless you carry a flare up front for me 'till I can, we're goin' nowhere." Fair play to him. He seemed in his element then – I guess seein' himself as a knight in shinin' armour.

In those days flares were kept in a box under the luggage compartment. Sometimes they were so old they wouldn't light, but this one lit straight away. Practically everybody carried matches or a lighter in those days because most people smoked. Once lit, it would burn for ages. It gave off a special neon type light which illuminated the area just in front of the bus. I could see the bloke carryin' it clearly, but as regards the side of the road or the middle of the road – I'd no idea – it was lost in a dense smog. There could have been a herd of elephants for all I knew. The headlights weren't especially good at the best of times, but in thick smog they were worse than useless. They just made a bad situation worse.

Even in a pea souper, the fog used to swirl around, so now and again the visibility improved a bit and then I'd get this chap to hop on the back whilst I speeded up. Part of me wanted to make him walk all the way to teach him a lesson for bein' so rude, but luckily the practical side won over or we'd never have got there. As it was, with him hoppin' on and off, walkin' and ridin', it still took us a good 40 minutes longer than normal to reach Norwood. Not surprisingly, we didn't pick up a single passenger en-route. Not one at any of the stops. Everybody else knew all the buses would have stopped. I don't recall seein' another vehicle either. It was just too dangerous to be out. As for our would-be passenger, now that the girl and baby had got off, I think the gloss had worn off carryin' the flare and even he could see it was time to call it a day. He was goin' a bit further, but we were turnin' around and headin' back. I'd gone as far as the designated turn-around and I wasn't prepared to risk goin' any further.

On the way back, Helen obliged with the flare whenever necessary. Again there were no passengers to pick up and by the time we got back to Stockwell there were no inspectors to be seen. No-one. All long gone. I suppose I'm blowin' my own trumpet, but that young mother was lucky it was me behind the wheel. We'd been the last bus still operatin' and so far as I could see, the only vehicle on that stretch of road. If you ask me, her mother should have kept them with her for the night, not sent her daughter home in such weather with a young baby and all.

In those days thick fog in central London was a fairly regular occurrence. We always did our best to keep goin' for the passengers, but when the fog turned into a real pea souper, with such limited visibility, progress was slow and delays inevitable. I'd be much longer in the cab so more prone to gettin' caught short. One night, in really dense fog, I had to stop near Marble Arch. It must have been around 10pm. I'd always turn the engine off so Helen would know where I'd gone. I struggled to find the toilets in the fog. Bear in mind though, they were underground so not much to see. Worse than that, comin' out I got disorientated and came up the wrong steps on the Bayswater Road side, except in the fog I couldn't tell where I was. It took me a good half hour to find my bus! When I did, there was poor Helen cryin' her eyes out with two coppers sat either side tryin' to console and sort her out. The fog was worse than ever and the passengers had given up and gone. I decided our bus was goin' no further. With no passengers there was no point now and it was just too dangerous. Helen soon came round to see the funny side, but I never did live that little episode down.

Fortunately the real London Pea Soupers are a thing of the past. Bein' behind the wheel in one was no picnic, I can tell you, but drivin' my bus on a normal day, I loved it. Yes, the traffic could be a right pain at times, but that apart, we had some fun, Helen and I. As I remember, my first couple of weeks as a driver were a bit stressful, but once I'd got used to it, a London bus was a lovely thing to drive. Funnily enough, when in April 1965 I eventually got a car with a normal gearbox, it felt very strange – like learnin' to drive all over. For a long time I used to think – give me my London Bus any day. It was big, bulky, but beautiful to drive and up high in that cab – I was king of the road. Leastways, it felt like I was. Maybe I'm romancin' a bit - lookin' back with rose-coloured spectacles – but I don't think so. The only problem – I was always tired. In part that was on account of the steerin'. By the time I was clockin' off, I knew I'd put in a shift, especially if we'd been busy. With a full load and no power steerin' it was all I could do to turn the wheel and I'd often have to stand to get enough leverage on corners. But for me the real problem was the shifts or 'turns' as we sometimes called 'em. That's what would beat me.

The early shifts – they started any time between 4.00 am and 7.00 am and then I could be finished as early as 10.30 am or as late as 1.30 pm. It was swings and roundabouts. It all depended on the schedule I was on. The spread-over shifts – they were both the worst and the best. The worst because it was a long day – startin' at, say, 7.00 am and not finally finishin' until 6.30 pm or even later. The best because we'd get paid for the whole day includin' the hours in the middle when we weren't actually workin'. Startin' at 7.00 am I'd probably be home by 10.30 am, but then I'd have to be back at work by 3.30 pm to finish at 6.30 pm or a bit later. If I'd been a bit older, maybe I'd have rested in between, but I never did. I was always on the go, doin' one job or another at home, so it made a long day.

The middle shift was probably my favourite – startin' at 10.30 am and finishin' at 7.00 pm. The late shift I didn't like at all – not least 'cos I'd have been on the go all day before goin' to work. In theory it was 4.30 pm 'till 12.00 am, but in practice the last bus wouldn't be runnin' into Stockwell until more like ten to one in the mornin'. If you were on lates, you could ask to go on the staff bus, which left the depot around five minutes to one, but that went all over London and as often as not I'd opt to walk 'cos that was quicker. I only ever drove the late staff bus once, takin' all the other drivers home. To be honest, once was enough. I got back to the depot around 2.00 am and then there was still the walk home and work again next day.

Whilst we had passes for London Transport which helped with gettin' to and from work, on earlys the buses wouldn't have started – or not enough of 'em to make it worth hangin' around – and on lates they'd have finished, so either way it was a case of walkin'. On a good day I could walk it in about half an hour, but it extended the day and wasn't what I wanted in the early hours whether goin' to or worse comin' back from work. Earlys and lates apart though, I'd use public transport to get me most of the way to and from work. Either I'd get a bus in Queenstown Road to Clapham Common and take the underground from there to Stockwell or, more often, I'd walk up Silverthorne Road and if there was no bus in sight, I'd start walkin' down Wandsworth Road. There were four routes on that stretch so it wouldn't be long before I'd hear a bus comin' and stick out a hand. When you worked on the buses, there was never any need for waitin' around at a stop. After a good mile, we'd be approachin' Lansdown Way and I'd give the driver a couple of bells just to remind him to slow down so's I could jump off. Goin' on to the stop would mean havin' to walk back and there was never any time for that. I'd always be cuttin' it fine. Only about a quarter mile walk and I'd be in Stockwell Garage and with any luck more or less within the ten minute time slot I had between signin' on and takin' my bus out.

In the summer it was light at 6 am and I remember this particular day it was an especially lovely sunny mornin' – you know, the type that give you that 'glad to be alive' feelin'. I couldn't swear to it, but I'd say it was 1958, but it doesn't really matter. The point is I was walkin' up Landsdown Road on my way to work and passin' this bomb site. I know you must be thinkin' that was a long time after the war, but there'd been so many of 'em that there were still a good few bomb sites still around, even then. Anyway, somethin' caught my eye glistenin' in the early mornin' sun. Well, I couldn't just walk on by, could I? I had to investigate. Turns out it was three big beautiful plates cum dishes stuck upright between bricks. Obviously they'd not been there since the bomb dropped, but there they were stickin' up out of a bomb site, so I thought, shame to leave 'em there to get broken and they are on a bomb site so 'finder's keepers'. They were big though, so there was no hidin' 'em. Arrivin' at Stockwell they caused a bit of a stir before I even got 'em into my cab. I remember especially the controllin' inspector sayin', "Come prepared have we John?" I didn't bother tryin' to explain to anyone. I just shrugged it off, but I was pleased with my plates. Beautiful matchin' ones they were and sturdy too. Even so, I was glad when the shift was over and I could take 'em home. I'd got nothin' to wrap 'em up in to protect 'em in the cab and, all the while, I been worried they'd slide and break before I could rescue 'em.

That particular day I was doin' an overtime job on the 88's and those plates went in the cab with me to Acton and back about three times. That meant they'd done a fair few trips round Trafalgar Square had those plates and on two different buses 'cos we'd changed buses after our lunch break. I needn't have worried 'cos they had a charmed life those plates. We used 'em for years and years and at Christmas they were great for the turkey. When it came to down sizin' recently, I'd still got 'em!

Cynthia and I, we both enjoyed our jobs with London Transport but doin' 11 day fortnights plus overtime was tirin' not least for Cynthia because although she did much less overtime, as a clippie she was runnin' up and down stairs all day and she had this undiagnosed health problem that made her tired even without all that exertion . And so it was that in May 1958, Cynthia and I got a welcome break from work that I need to tell you about, although that's not how we saw it at first, because it was then we had the biggest all-out strike in

London Transport's history.

There hadn't been any decent pay rises for London Transport Workers since the War Years. As is often the case, talks between the Union reps and the bosses were headin' nowhere until a tribunal ruled that 36,000 transport workers in central London should get pay rises, but the 14,000 workin' in the outer suburbs were to get nothin'. London Transport accepted the findin's, but the Union refused. They wanted money for all 50,000 workers, includin' a partial re-distribution of money bein' offered to us 36,000 central workers. London Transport refused and the Union, led by Frank Cousins, called an all out strike. Despite some misgivin's, all 50,000 answered the call and overnight all services ceased. Most of us – the 36,000 – stood to gain nothin' from the strike, but it was all about solidarity in those days.

In truth, 'the writin' was on the wall' from the outset when the underground workers refused to come out with us. If they had, the capital would have come to a standstill. As it was, many of our passengers could just switch to the underground and the bosses felt – indeed they knew – they had the upper hand. After the first week or two it was becomin' clear that a quick solution was very unlikely and a right wing organisation callin' itself "The People's League for the Defence of Freedom" got permission to run skeleton services in and around the capital usin' a number of old buses. Some strikes – the most successful ones – gain momentum from the level of support amongst ordinary people. Ours wasn't one of 'em. It was deeply unpopular with the public, especially those whose daily routine was bein' disrupted and with it their livelihood threatened. What's more, as the strike dragged on, so the discontent grew amongst the central London crews, who, when all's said and done, stood to gain nothin'.

Whilst from time to time I made a token gesture, to be honest I didn't see the point of wastin' my time on the picket lines. I was never politically motivated and there were plenty of 'bodies' there anyway. What did I do? I decided to be pragmatic and practical and look on it as an 'opportunity'. The outside of our home, Nos 25 and 25A Gambetta Street, needed paintin', but hitherto I had neither the money to pay for professional decorators nor the time to do the job myself and I couldn't afford to take time off work because as you know, on the buses it was a case of 'no work, no pay'. Now, suddenly, I had the opportunity. I didn't have to go to work every day – I couldn't and yet I was gettin' paid – Four Pounds and Ten Shillin's a week strike pay. In fact it was better than that. Between us, Cynthia and I were gettin' nine pounds a week because as I've told you, when the strike was called, Cynthia, was workin' as a clippie. For us, the strike, it wasn't hardship, it was manna from Heaven. Mind you, we were the lucky ones. Most families only had one lot of strike pay comin' in and for them it was a different story.

To do the decoratin' of 25A, the upstairs flat, I needed a triple extension ladder. I used to hire it from Cayless in Broughton Street. They didn't just hire 'em, they made 'em. It was wooden with metal supports and ropes and I'm tellin' you, that thing was heavy. Broughton Street is beside Prairie Street – you know, where we lived for a while after bein' bombed out of Montefiore Street. About a quarter to a third of a mile walk, which might not sound that far, but you try walkin' it carryin' a triple extension ladder. It wasn't just the weight, it was an awkward thing to manoeuvre along pavements, around corners and across roads, especially Queenstown Road, which was always very busy. I bet I was a comical sight, but it didn't seem at all funny to me. I was always in desperate need of a cuppa and a sit down when I got home with the thing. It wasn't cheap. It cost seven and sixpence a week – more if you kept it over the weekend. I used to pick it up first thing on a Monday mornin' and take it back last thing on a Friday. The weekends Cynthia and I would spend together. In fact, we had more time together durin' the strike than we'd ever had. In some ways it was more like a paid holiday for us. We'd usually go over to Aldershot to stay with Les and Flossie for the weekend. I couldn't face decoratin' at the weekends as well and chances are, Les and I would have ended up doin' just that, if they'd come over to us.

In case you're wonderin' what I was doin' – decoratin' that is – it was all the windows, sills, gutters and downpipes. The windows were all wooden sashes painted cream and the rest I painted maroon. If you've ever tried paintin' sash windows, you'll know how long they take to rub down, prime and paint and just how fiddly they can be to do. The two front doors, to 25 and 25A, which until now had been varnished, I painted Paris Green with black metal work and knockers. When I'd finished they looked a picture. I was especially proud of my Paris Green doors. You have to remember this was 1958 and all up and down the street lots of the houses now had painted doors rather than varnish. Fashion and tastes had changed, but if I were honest, proud as I was of my painted doors, the street as a whole never looked as nice as when all the doors were varnished as they'd been when mum and dad first moved into Gambetta Street. With all different coloured doors the street had lost its uniformity and with it, a bit of class. Havin' said that, with things as they were, I still think mine looked the best. I'd learnt to do a 'proper' paint job workin' for Mr Snuggs back in Aldershot and for a good time after fnishin' 'em I felt a sense of pride, walkin' up our street and seein' my Paris Green front doors.

I didn't just do the front, there was the back as well, where there was lots more woodwork – the toilet door, verandas and railin's. All of it needed rubbin' down, an undercoat and two top coats. I didn't skimp on the preparation or the finish. I did a proper job. Mind you, we were part of a terrace. There was no side entrance or easy way round so, before I could even get started round the back, I had to manoeuvre this bloomin' great ladder through the house! No easy task I can tell you. It's a good job I could get a pretty straight run, through the front door, down the passage, through the kitchen and scullery and out the back window bein' careful not to catch any walls or door frames. When I'd finished all the paintwork back and front, I still hadn't finished. Like most everywhere else in the City, Gambetta Street had lost its railin's durin' the war. I couldn't 'run to railin's, but I rather fancied puttin' up a fence with a garden gate. Don't ask me why, but I suppose there was a bit of 'markin' out my territory involved in that decision.

As it happened, Mickey, Cynthia's youngest brother, had left school now and although he had no qualifications whatsoever, he'd got himself a job at a timber yard in Aldershot. He came to help me make these cedarwood railin's and do you know, he'd cycle all the way over from Aldershot to do that. Leastways I thought he did but, unbeknown to me at the time, it turned out he was keen on a girl who lived just up the road in Robertson Street. Still, girl or no girl, Mickey was a big help.

We didn't make the gate, but to finish the job off, I decided to go and buy one. There was nowhere local, so I went all the way to Vauxhall to buy it. I can remember people standin' at the bus stop starin' at me waitin' for the bus with this great thing. At least I'd had the sense to avoid the rush-hour or that really would have turned a few heads. Havin' got it all fixed in position, my new fence and gate still needed treatin' but, after all that rubbin' down and time-consumin' preparation, treatin' that with oil was a breeze. I was still proud of the finished result, mind you. I could stand back and, lookin' at the front of the house, admire a job well done.

In the end the strike dragged on for seven weeks. A good job really, because it took me all of seven weeks to do all that decoratin'. By the end though, I was glad to get back to work, back to drivin' my beautiful red London Bus. Work? It was a breeze after all that decoratin'. I'm sayin' I was glad to get back to work – but not half as glad as the lads whose families had been strugglin' to get by on just four pounds ten shillin's a week. It was money - or rather lack of it - that caused the strikers to capitulate in the end. Families were strugglin' to cope and Union funds were runnin' dangerously low and couldn't sustain the strike any longer. 50,000 workers had come out on May 5th and Union bosses finally called a halt on 20th June 1958. They'd got some minor face-savin' concessions, but in truth the workers had well and truly lost, financially that is, and the Union had been all but crippled.

Cynthia and me, with our double strike pay, we'd been fine. I'd got all my decoratin' done and in between we'd had a ball, but, make no mistake, we were the lucky ones. As for the regular bus services themselves, well they'd been non-existent durin' the strike, but even after they were never quite the same. Management took the opportunity to make cost savin' cuts, especially to more marginal services in the suburbs, knowin' there'd be no appetite for further strike action. What's more, two things that happened durin'; the strike had predictably longer-lastin' effects. There'd been a transfer of passengers to the underground, some of which never came back. Their livelihoods threatened if they couldn't get to and from work, a good number resorted to buyin' a car and car sharin' became a factor. Again, many of these former passengers never returned to patronise the buses. It had been a damagin' strike all round.

Cynthia enjoyed her job as a clippie and especially the extra money it gave her. She loved shoppin' did Cynthia. Her whole life she loved shoppin'. The downside was havin' to leave Victor with Lily. She was never really comfortable with that. Not that there was anythin' wrong with Lily. It's just Cynthia was Victor's mum and really she wanted to be there for him and she had her own way of doin' things. Fallin' pregnant was the decidin' factor. It happened in early 1959 and by June the life of a clippie runnin' up and down stairs all day became too much for her. She packed it in to become a full-time mum again and shortly after, Lily and George moved out to a place of their own. They'd been with us almost 18 months and, all in all, it had been a good arrangement for all of us.

I've told you quite a bit about my home life and work, but I haven't told you much about our social life. There's a good reason for that. We didn't have either the time or money to do much socialisin'. Cynthia and I didn't go up town to the West End that often because it meant spendin' money. Money was always tight and we had other priorities, but I should say somethin' about it, about the atmosphere, because it was vibrant, excitin' and different to what you might see today. Take Leicester Square for example. It's still a mecca for entertainment I know, but back then you were surrounded by all the great cinemas. There was the Empire, the Ritz, the Warner, Odeon and Leicester Square Theatres where premieres were regularly held. TV sets were incredibly rare and for the vast majority the cinema was the focus of entertainment; the land of dreams where stars were idolised. For premieres they'd arrive in limousines and the excited crowds would be restrained by lines of policemen.

Even on ordinary days, the cinema was the place to be and there'd always be people queuin' to go in. Where there were queues, there was money to be had, a good livin' to be made. It was the most lucrative place in London for buskers and in those days, it wasn't just the odd singer or musician. There'd be a variety of singers and musicians, dancers, jugglers, escapologists and variety acts, all creatin' a marvellous atmosphere and often performin' in the road. Even back then it was busy, but the traffic just had to get on with it and skirt round 'em. It was either that or knock 'em down or, heaven forbid, get held up. I know they still have premieres today, but TV and films on disc have all but decimated the really big crowds that used to flock there and with their passin', the majority of buskers have gone the same way.

Somethin' else I ought to at least mention, because they were a real Institution, are the Lyons Tea Rooms. There were lots of Lyons Tea Rooms in the city. They were part of what made London, London. Most would be on three floors with 3 different tariffs. The middle floor would have a palm court orchestra creatin' a wonderful atmosphere, very genteel, very special. For most folk like us, Lyons wasn't an everyday thing, but havin' said that, it was an affordable occasional treat. The most memorable part was probably afternoon tea always presented just so on tiered stands with a selection of sandwiches, cakes and pastries from which to choose and served by 'Nippies', waitresses in smart uniform, who really made you feel you were somewhere special.

Holidays, well the thing is, early on in our marriage we couldn't really afford holidays away but if you read the sequel, you'll find that later on Cynthia and I took lots of caravan holidays. In fact you could say we were caravan mad. I spent a fortune on the things, but not this first one that I'm goin' to tell you about now. This was cheap and it wasn't ours, it was rented. It all started with mum chattin' to the Lollipop Lady who used to see the kids across the road to Heathbrook School where like me, Victor would be a pupil when he was old enough, but in 1958 he hadn't started school. He was only 3 years old.

This Lollipop Lady was a Maltese woman and she had this caravan in Bognor Regis which she let out. Cynthia and I discussed it and we agreed we'd take mum along with us and then it was down to me to book a week. I can't remember when it was, but it was off-season and, we thought, quite cheap. I'd had a word with Les and he agreed to take the four of us over there one Saturday and fetch us back the followin' week. That was fine except come the day, mum wanted to take pretty much everythin' barrin' the kitchen sink. She'd never been in a caravan and didn't realise they were equipped. Fortunately she was agreeable to leavin' most of it or we'd never have got in the car.

Bein' beside the river, the site was called 'The Riverside' and really quite attractive it was too. There were lots of caravans but, because it was off-season, not many of 'em were occupied.

We hadn't been there all that long when mum announced she wanted to go to Chichester Cathedral on the Sunday to see the Bishop. I should explain that she'd turned a bit religious since her breakdown. On the Sunday mornin' I went with mum to the bus stop to see her safely on her way and she said she should be back around lunchtime.

It was a lovely day and we'd been playin' outside with Victor, but we decided to eat lunch indoors. Mum was a bit late and we were gettin' peckish so, havin' plated hers up and put it in the oven to keep warm, we started ours. About half way through, the caravan door flies open and mum bursts in all of a fluster sayin, "Get hold of Victor quick – there's a gorilla outside! We'll have to go home." Cynthia and I looked at one another and I knew she'd be thinkin' the same as me – mum was havin' one of her turns. At first I tried to just pass it off and said, "Ok mum, well just sit down and have your dinner first. It's in the oven. I'll just get it." But mum wouldn't settle down – went on and on about this gorilla, so in the end, just to humour her, I got up from my dinner and went out to pretend to check. I got outside and looked first one way and then the other, intendin' to go back in and tell mum it must have gone, when I clocked it. You could have knocked me over with a feather. About three caravans up a chestnut palin' fence had been erected to make a temporary compound and, mum wasn't havin' one of her turns, there it was – this bloomin' great gorilla playin' with a ball!

I stood mesmerized for a minute and whilst I was watchin', they called this gorilla in for its dinner! Guy, its name was. Just as if it was a little kid, or rather I should say, a great big kid, it stopped playin' and went in and sat down at a table with this couple. I'd gone a bit nearer and the caravan door was open so I could see. Yet again, you really couldn't make it up!

I think Cynthia thought I was kiddin' at first, just humourin' mum, as I tried to reassure her the gorilla was Ok, it wasn't dangerous. In fact it was quite tame and civilised. It took a bit of persuadin', but eventually mum accepted we didn't have to leave. Mind you, she never would go near it. Always insisted on walkin' the other way out of the site. Never past Guy, the gorilla.

Later on I got talkin' to this couple with the gorilla and it turned out they were showmen, in Bognor for the season. Apparently their gorilla did a bit of an act on the promenade, really just a bit of rollin' around to attract attention and the real money came from folk havin' their photo taken with it. There was a bus into Bognor, but we'd generally walk with Victor in his pushchair and usually we'd walk back as well, but mum would get the bus. Walkin' both ways was a bit much for her, not so much due to her age, but bein' overweight.

We didn't let him get too close, but I think Victor was more fascinated by our near neighbour, Guy the Gorilla, than anythin'. Overall we had a lovely holiday, not least because the weather was kind to us, especially bearin' in mind it was out of season and in many ways Guy was a bit of a highlight – certainly somethin' to talk about when we got back home.

That's enough recreation and socialisin' for a while. I'd best get back to work because in the late 1950s and for a good while after, work is where I spent most of my wakin' hours. I enjoyed workin' for London transport, but it was pretty much a full time job – literally. We were workin' an eleven-day fortnight so at best that meant I'd get three days off every two weeks, but as you know, with two mortgages to pay, a young family to keep and a home to set up, I'd often work my rest days as well. What I'm gettin' at, is that there wasn't much time left for recreation with the family and even less for me on my own. As I think I've mentioned, I did join the work's fishin' club though, because I'd always loved fishin' even as a kid – remember? I know I said I'd best get back to work but, havin' mentioned the fishin' club, I think I should at least say somethin' about it. There were two sections – fresh water and sea fishin'. I was only really interested in the fresh water fishin'. I'd never done much sea fishin'.

The fishin' club was run by an old boy called Reg Cook. Believe it or not, he was the spittin' image of Reg from the TV show 'On the Buses'. He was a real character, was Reg. He drove the No 88's and whenever our buses were passin', we'd hoot to one another. Doubtless Reg would do that with all the fishin' club members, but he wasn't content with just hootin' – not Reg. He was fishin' mad was Reg and if he'd had a bit of success or he wanted to get me interested in a fishin' trip he was organisin', he'd hoot, signal me to stop, wind his winda' down and start a shoutin' conversation across the street. I remember one time he stopped me in Trafalgar Square of all places, to tell me he'd caught a one-and-a-half pound roach the day before – only on a worm! Only Reg could do that. He didn't bother where we were or how much traffic we might be holdin' up.

Another time we were on opposite sides of Oxford Street when Reg decides to try to recruit me on his latest fishin' trip. Trouble was, it was a bus trip to Dover to do a spot of sea fishin', which as you know wasn't really my bag. But Reg didn't want to take no for an answer and I could sense folk on my bus gettin' restless for me to move on, never mind the traffic backin' up behind. Anyway, I didn't want to offend Reg because he was a decent bloke and worked hard to make the club a success, so I agreed and since it turned out to be an eventful trip, I'll tell you about it.

In our Oxford Street conversation, as well as tellin' me I'd love it, Reg had advised me to take Quels or I may get seasick. Anyway, it was a nice summer's day. As always, Reg drove the bus and we stopped at this little café on the way down – very nice too. Everythin' was goin' swimmin'ly until we were on the boat. Then there seemed to be some trouble with the steerin' and we very nearly collided with this big ferry boat, but once we were out in open water everythin' seemed fine – everythin' except the weather that is. It turned from calm to chaotic in a heart beat. It felt more like bein' on a roller coaster than a fishin' boat and poor old Reg was hangin' over the side bein' sick as a dog. He literally turned green and it was all we could do to stop him goin' overboard. The weather turned from bad to worse – thunder, lightnin', lashin' rain – the lot. We'd long since given up on the fishin'. It was all about survival – about gettin' back into Dover and quieter waters. It wasn't just the weather that deteriorated – it was Reg. We all thought we'd lost him. We thought he was dead.

It had taken maybe fifteen to twenty minutes to get out there, but it took a good three-quarters of an hour to get back into Dover. It's a good job we had an experienced skipper, or we'd never have made it and it wouldn't just be Reg who hadn't lived to tell the tale. The skipper had phoned the Harbour Master to warn 'im that we were comin' in with a fatality on board. When we berthed there was a hell of a reception committee waitin' for us – harbour people, police, ambulance – the lot. They laid Reg out on the quayside and I was thinkin', "Poor old Reg. Who's goin' to tell his missus that he'd died at sea," when he just sat up! It was like some miracle. As if bein' back on terra firma had been enough to bring him round – to wake him from the dead. He seemed disorientated and perplexed at all the fuss, but his main concern was for some food. I can hear him now clear as day sayin', "Here, I ain't half hungry!" So we got him somethin' to eat and unbelievably, he was right as rain. No need to draw lots for tellin' his missus – he could tell her himself!

I never did go on another sea fishin' trip, but just to even things up, I'll tell you about one of our fresh water trips. We were goin' to Marlow, just the other side of Maidenhead, for a spot of river fishin' on the Thames, but since only four of us wanted to go, rather than take a bus, we went in this old London taxi that another chap called John had recently bought. I won't bore you with the fishy stories, but we all did well on hempseed and elderberry and suffice to say we had a great day's fishin' and were all in jovial mood on the drive back. It was a balmy summer's evenin'. Happy as Larry we were – all four of us smokin', laughin' and jokin'. That's when it happened. We were just approachin' Hounslow when the bloody thing blew up. Clouds of steam and bits of taxi went flyin' everywhere. It was terminal but, as luck would have it, we'd 'broken down' just inside the London Transport Area, so we could catch a bus home. Trouble was, an Inspector got on. All the others had their passes on 'em, but I hadn't got mine, so I had to pay and the conductor, who'd let me off, probably got hauled in front of the Chief Depot Inspector. I was sorry about that and it soured what had otherwise been a great day. We thought he was a 'job's worth' but really I guess by makin' me pay that 'jumper' was only doin' his job. Even so, the conductor, he'd only been doin' me a good turn and didn't deserve the grief.

Thinkin' back, John did well to stop that taxi without any of us gettin' hurt. Not a scratch – none of us. If you'd seen it though, you'd have thought it was hilarious – a real life Buster Keeton sketch. And that's how we saw it at the time – well, maybe not John 'cos it was his car that had disintegrated. It made for a good story back at work, but none of our fishin' stories ever topped the time we thought old Reg Cook had cooked his goose at sea!

As you've no doubt noticed, I'm a bit prone to goin' off at tangents when the fancy takes me. Before I started tellin' you some of what I got up to with the fishin' club, I was bemoanin' the fact that workin' for London Transport didn't leave me much time for spendin' at home with my young family. They meant and still do mean the world to me and yet I haven't even introduced you to them all yet, so I need to put that right.

As you know, Victor was born on 2nd October 1955, but durin' our time livin' at 25 Gambetta Street he was joined by his two young sisters, Vivian and Sandra. Vivian was born on 9th September 1959 in the Wier Road Maternity annex to St James' Hospital in central London. Unfortunately, the outcome apart, it wasn't a good experience, not for Cynthia or her baby. Cynthia had been restless in the night and by dawn it was clear things were happenin'. Childbirth is an anxious time and I was thinkin' enough's enough when Cynthia agreed we should be gettin' her into hospital. I shot down to our local phone box in Silverthorn Road to summon an ambulance.

I suppose it came fairly quickly really, but bein' anxious, that half hour seemed like an eternity. We were in the front room, which, as you know, we used as our bedroom, so I heard the ambulance comin'. No blues and twos or anythin' like that but, back then, we didn't have many vehicles comin' down our street, especially at that time in a mornin' so I knew it must be our ambulance.

It's funny the little things you remember. I'd just finished tellin' Cynthia that the ambulance had pulled up when she announces, "I'll just draw the curtains before we go then." No big deal you might think, but for Cynthia, for reasons best known to herself, that meant steppin' up on a chair and standin' on the table to open 'em. As you can imagine, given her condition, I had my heart in my mouth in case she slipped and fell. I guess that's why I remember it so vividly. Anyway, I deposited Victor with Grace and Arthur next door and off I went with Cynthia up to the hospital in the ambulance.

We arrived at St James' shortly before 8 am. Cynthia knew she was ready to give birth but the nurse told her to hold on because the doctor hadn't arrived. I should explain that they'd said a doctor needed to be present at the birth because Cynthia had been takin' these tablets. They weren't thalidomide, but somethin' similar and there were concerns about possible complications. Cynthia was gettin' more and more distressed, but rather than bein' allowed to stay and comfort her, I was ushered out of the way. How times have changed. Now husbands are positively encouraged to be present at the birth, but not in those days – no way.

I could have waited in a corridor, but rather than just sit there frettin', I decided to head back home and pick up Victor. He'd have been fine at Grace's, but somehow I wanted to have him with me at that time. Maybe I just needed to be with our perfectly formed toddler to convince me that everythin' would be fine back at the hospital.

Cynthia didn't like the hospital at all and a permanent cloud has hung over the whole experience. Vivian was born with defective sight in her left eye, which persists to this day. You wouldn't know it to look at her, but it's there. We took her to Moorfields both as a baby and as a young child, but they couldn't really do anythin' to improve matters. We'll never really know, but Cynthia put it down to the trauma of havin' to wait to give birth, which she believed was why forceps had to be used.

I'd made sure I was on 'early turns' so I would get to see Cynthia and her baby every evenin'. On the plus side, things had changed in the few years since Victor was born and husbands were no longer expected to bring home nappies for washin' every night. I'm sayin' they'd changed but maybe things were just different in London. If you remember, Victor had been born in Aldershot.

When I went visitin' that first night, I could see right away Cynthia wasn't happy. The pain of bein' made to wait for the doctor to arrive and then goin' through the trauma of a forceps delivery had left its mark and tainted her entire stay. Nothin' was right, not even the food, so every evenin' after that, I made sure I took a food parcel which would vary but with one constant – about 1lb of freshly picked tomatoes. I'd got these three tomato plants growin' in the back yard and as luck would have it, they were very prolific at just the right time.

When Cynthia brought Vivian home from the hospital, she slept in a cot in our room for the first couple of months. Victor was in his first bed by now and Vivian had his old cot. I say 'old', but there was nothin' wrong with it except the colour. I'd bought special lead-free paint, but it was a nightmare of a job. It took three coats to change the blue to pink. Cots aren't very big, but, as you'll discover if you ever try paintin' one, there's a lot of slats with a lot of surfaces and once you've done one cot, take it from me, you won't want to tackle another in a hurry. With workin' and hospital visitin' I only just managed to get it done in time for the home comin'.

Right from the off, Vivian was a bit different. Different in looks and, over time, would become very different in temperament. For now though she was the new baby in our little household and naturally, she was the centre of attention. Don't get me wrong, Victor wasn't neglected. He was our first born and as such he was – is, very special, and to Grace and Arthur next door he was, and remained, their favourite little boy.

Thinkin' about Victor, a little incident that happened to him when he was maybe 4 or 5 springs to mind. Mum used to take him to Sunday School at the Vicarage, which was next door to the Church Hall. This particular Sunday, mum wasn't very well and so Victor was sent on his own. It was only in the next street and it was safe for kids to walk the streets in those days. Anyway, Victor got as far as the Church Hall and hearin' this singin', he went in there. Apparently a group of local Jamaicans, all recent immigrants at that time, had started usin' the Church Hall for their services. It seems they were very friendly and welcomed Victor with open arms. When he got home he was full of it – this room full of all coloured people singin' and clappin' and encouragin' him to join in. At that time Victor would have barely seen a Jamaican, much less been amongst a whole room full of 'em, but they'd been friendly and he'd been happy to stay and join in the clappin'. He must have made an impression too because he told his mummy, 'They want me to go again next week'.

When I wasn't workin' I always seemed to have one job or other to do at home. There were loads of doors, surrounds, skirtin' boards and picture rails to paint and because we both smoked, nicotine stains, especially on the walls and ceilin's meant re-decoration was a pretty regular affair. Cynthia's parents, Les and Flossie, would come and stay for the weekend more or less fortnightly and Les and I would very often find ourselves decoratin'. Whilst I'd learnt to do a pretty good paint job whilst workin' for Mr Snuggs back in Aldershot, hangin' wallpaper just wasn't my thing but as I told you, Les was a dab hand at it, so I'd do the pastin' and Les would do the tricky bit – cuttin' and hangin' the sheets. We made a good team though and always got on well together. Never any cross words – just good banter between us.

Cynthia would go up town with Flossie, leavin' the kids with us. When there was just Victor, he'd often as not sit playin' on the floor with his toys. A good kid – he didn't get in the way or insist on helpin' to hang the paper! Once Vivian and then Sandy came along, combinin' decoratin' with babysittin' became a bit of a nightmare so I'd call on Grace and Arthur next door or Nanny Wattley just up the street. More often it would be Grace next door because I knew Cynthia was always very wary of leavin' the kids with mum in case she had one of her 'turns' and if Dad was home I'd be loathe to leave the kids there because kids and dad didn't really get along. He couldn't cope with the noise and especially not babies cryin', which inevitably at some time they would.

Over time we re-decorated the whole place – more than once – but I especially remember doin' Arthur's old room at the back – after Lily and George left us, which, as you know, they did just before Vivian was born. We decided it was goin' to be Victor's bedroom, so the paper we'd chosen had a blue background with aeroplanes and stuff like that on it. When we came to do it, we realised the room was a bit on the damp side, so instead of just paperin' it, we decided to line the walls first with 'Cutelea' or was it 'Katinka'. Whatever it was called, it was basically thin polystyrene on rolls. We thought this would make it warmer as well. Anyway, long story short, it took a while, but I was really rather pleased with the result. Victor seemed to like it as well – a bit too much as it happened. Kids are inquisitive, aren't they and the little so and so soon discovered that the surface was different to normal walls. He found that if he poked it, his finger would leave an impression and I guess he persisted and got really carried away because one mornin' we went in to find he'd had a 'beautiful time' managin' to pick himself a dirty great hole! I dare say he got a good tellin' off, which must have registered because after Les and I had repaired the damage, he left well alone after that.

Vivian and Victor have always been chalk and cheese. Victor had been angelic durin' the day, but our bed-time was his cue to start creatin'. Vivian was just the opposite, but at least with her we could get some sleep and it was Cynthia who bore the brunt of her tantrums whilst I was at work. As I say, Vivian was pretty good at night, I guess havin' tired herself out durin' the day, but even so, havin' a baby sleepin' in the same room, even a quiet one, still wasn't as relaxin' as havin' the bedroom to ourselves. So, after a couple of months we thought we'd try movin' her into her own room – the 'spare' bedroom just up the passage. Vivian was havin' none of that. She screamed blue murder – loud enough to wake the street up, so after a few abortive attempts and a spell back with us, we thought we'd try puttin' her in with Victor in the back room. They might have been chalk and cheese, but luckily for us, for sleepin' they settled quite well together, so that's how they stayed for quite a while.

About a year later, Cynthia fell pregnant again and right away she made it very clear there was no way she was goin' back to St James' to give birth. She was adamant about that and despite havin' a particularly difficult time, especially in the last weeks of pregnancy, she remained doggedly determined to have our baby at home. Lookin' back, and with the benefit of hindsight, most of her problems were more than likely down to an undiagnosed medical condition. It was 1961, but it wouldn't be until my Cynthia suffered a nervous breakdown in 1976 that finally it was discovered she suffered from pernicious anaemia. It was only then we understood what, on and off, had dogged her life from the moment we'd met all those years ago when I was playin' at the dance in Aldershot. Hard time or not, Cynthia remained determined, and so it was that our youngest, Sandra, was born in our bedroom, the front room of our house in Gambetta Street, with the midwife in attendance, but me still kept well out of the way. She wasn't bein' awkward. It's just the way things were in those days.

I may have been 'banished' to another room for the actual birth, but that doesn't mean the day wasn't memorable. Far from it. The day when our Sandy was born was, and remains, one of the best and most memorable days of my life. It was a Bank Holiday Weekend and we knew Cynthia was about due. By Sunday evenin' things were startin' to happen and around 9pm, Bank Holiday Sunday or not, I went down to the phone box in Silverthorn Road to summon the midwife. Whilst we were waitin' for her, there was a knock on the door and instead of the midwife it was our Roy. He'd already retired from the army. When I told him I thought we'd got a baby on the way, he didn't even cross the threshold – he was off like a shot!

Anyway, the midwife arrived on this bike and not exactly full of the joys of spring. Not a good first impression and things didn't improve when after she'd finished examinin' Cynthia she announced: "It's goin' to be a while yet, so, where do I sleep?" I hadn't been expectin' that, but with the kids tucked up asleep in the bedrooms, I wasn't about to disturb 'em to accommodate this, as I thought, 'cheeky madam'. So she had to make do with two armchairs pushed together in the kitchen. I don't think that suited her any more than havin' her there suited me, but she had to make do. The main reason it didn't suit me was because, by that time, Grace was round sittin' with Cynthia and I couldn't get through to the scullery to make tea for the three of us. It's not like we were goin' to be gettin' any 'shut eye' and a regular supply of tea at such times helps to keep you goin'. In anticipation of our baby's arrival I'd got gallons of boilin' water at the ready in the copper in the scullery, but in the end Grace went round to her place next door to make the tea.

As you can imagine, even with the midwife on hand it was an anxious time and as Sunday rolled over into Monday, the hours dragged on a bit. I don't think we were particularly tired – I guess the adrenalin saw to that – but it was about 2am when Sandy decided she was ready to be born and I had to go and wake the midwife. Cynthia was still takin' the same tablets she'd had whilst pregnant with Vivian so I asked the midwife if we should summon a doctor as well. Don't ask me why I hadn't thought to bring that up before. She took one look at Cynthia and declared, "It's too late for that. The baby's comin'. You'll never get a doctor in time." With that I was ushered into the back kitchen out of the way whilst the midwife, I guess assisted by Grace, got down to business.

As I told you, I'd got gallons and gallons of hot water at the ready, but when it came to, all they needed was about a cup full! I'd also been instructed to have a good fire goin', so I'd already got that laid in the kitchen. With things under way I went to light it, but I'd barely put a match to it when I heard our Sandy cry. That first sign of life – such a beautiful noise and one I'll never forget. At any other time a baby cryin' can create anxiety, annoyance even, but not then, not that first cry. Grace came rushin' in to confirm the good news and tell me I'd got another little girl. So in the end, doctor or no doctor, Sandy came with no trouble at all and fortunately, by the time the afterbirth and stuff was parcelled up, I had a good fire goin' ready for its disposal. With very few open fires and a raft of health & safety regulations in place now, that's a job dads aren't expected to do these days. Just as well really.

Even though everythin' went so smoothly and Sandy was born perfect and easily with no complications, I can't say I'd recommend a home birth. I still can't help thinkin' we'd have been in a right state if things had gone wrong. But they didn't and our Sandy is the livin' proof. As you'll learn later, she lives in America now, but we've always been close, our Sand' and me.

There's me, with eyes glazin' over, waxin' lyrical about our Sand' when I haven't finished tellin' you about the big event itself. I've no idea what her name was, but, for the record, I should tell you that the midwife turned out to be a very good sort. As you doubtless gathered, I hadn't thought much of her when not long after she'd arrived she wanted somewhere to sleep but when action was needed, she was in her element. After the birth she made sure Cynthia and Sandy were well and settled and, before leavin,' she apologised for bein' 'a bit sharp' when she arrived. It turns out that she'd been on duty all Bank Holiday weekend and hadn't had a proper sleep for three nights previous because she was havin' to cover for someone else who'd rung in sick. The poor woman must have been ready to drop. No wonder she wanted to get her head down, even in those two armchairs.

Grace went home, doubtless tired herself, but buoyed up by the joyous event and the part she'd played. It was about 3am and before leavin' herself, the midwife turned to me and said, "Now what I want you to do is get into bed next to your wife and both of you try to get some sleep." Baby Sandy was tucked up already asleep in her pram beside the bed. I saw the midwife out and as she left she said she'd be back to check on mother and baby at about 8am. Climbin' into bed I can remember sayin' to Cynthia that we won't be seein' her at 8am! But I was wrong – that woman was true to her word and our doorbell rang at dead on 8am! And that midwife continued to pop in regular as clockwork over the next few days to make sure everythin' was goin' fine until another midwife took over. As for us, Cynthia and me, on that first night, the pair of us went fast asleep and do you know, we never heard a murmur out of our new baby the whole night – well, what was left of it.

I was up and about by 8am. Well, I hadn't got much choice, had I? – with Victor and Vivian to see to. Mind you, fair play to 'em, they'd done their bit by sleepin' through all the excitement. As for little Sandy, she continued to be the perfect baby, sleepin' through most nights and, unlike Vivian, not bein' much trouble durin' the day. She was quite small, so we didn't move her out of her pram and into her cot for about 3 months.

Now, I'd best get back to work, not least because with another mouth to feed, and still two mortgages to pay, we needed the money. Much as I loved my job as a bus driver, I didn't like the shift work or the fact that if you couldn't work you didn't get paid. I was young, but I could see that down the line both could be a problem. I wanted security for my family so I started lookin' around for ways to, as I thought, better myself. Dad had always extolled the virtues of the Civil Service and Local Government as bein' secure jobs with prospects and a pension but I never remember him advisin' me to seek employment there. Even so, with this in mind, the first thing I tried was the Prison Service. I got an interview at Wandsworth Prison and I had to change my shift to attend, but I didn't tell anyone at work where I was goin'.

The day of the interview is one I'll never forget. For starters I had to enter through this thick iron door within a door – just like I was goin' to be put away for 25 years. Surreal and, to tell you the truth, rather dauntin'. There were three of us bein' interviewed – two middle-aged chaps and me. One had come out of the navy and the other was a London ambulance driver. We were given no explanation or warnin' of what to expect. I think part of the interview was seein' how we'd react. There was always a chap in the background with a pad makin' notes. The first thing they did was to have all these prisoners file past us – I guess to see our reaction. They were queuein' for their baccy rations and papers - a rough-lookin' bunch who made it pretty clear they didn't take kindly to bein' observed by we three. I was thinkin', "What have these guys done to be in here?" The situation and the atmosphere, it was all a bit unnervin' really.

The next thing we had was a dictation class which lasted about three-quarters of an hour. I assume they were testin' our literacy skills, maybe to see if we were capable of writin' down an interview with a prisoner. Then we had a session where we were each given the opportunity to ask questions. A bit unusual really because as yet we hadn't been asked to explain why we wanted to join the Prison Service. Anyway, I remember the navy chap didn't so much as ask a question as make a statement. He said he wanted to work with young offenders. The reason I remember it so well is because the response he got wasn't what he wanted to hear. Basically he was told he was too old and the only one of us three candidates who might be suitable would be Mr Wattley – me.

Next came the big interview with the Prison Governor – one at a time. Sittin' in were two experienced prison officers and a psychiatrist

– so we had four of 'em to face. To be honest I can't remember much about the interview except I know I tried to maintain eye contact with whoever was speakin' and mostly with the Governor whenever I was answerin' questions. All this took place in the mornin' and I can't remember havin' any lunch, but I suppose we must have done because we were in there all day.

In the afternoon they took us down through and underneath the prison to the hospital wing – to give us a very thorough medical. I'd been a bit concerned about that, but I passed quite well I thought. They didn't seem worried about past ailments like asthma or even bronchial pneumonia. The fact that I'd got over 'em seemed good enough to give me a clean bill of health. I was just sittin' thinkin' how well the day had gone and that I think I'm in here – I'm goin' to be a prison officer, when the prison doctor beckoned me over. "There's just one more thing, sir. Can you step up here." He wanted to measure my height, but I wasn't worried about that – Cynthia had already measured me when we filled out the application form so I knew I complied. Except I didn't! "I've got some bad news for you, Mr Wattley – I'm afraid you're too short. You're half an inch too small to join the Prison Service." It seems Cynthia had measured me wrong. I had a lot of hair in those days and the way I combed it gave me a bit of extra height and she'd measured the top of my hair and not my scalp. I'd put myself through all this stressful interview when no matter how well I'd done, I had no chance. Deflated doesn't describe it.

By the time I came to leave though, back out through this heavy metal door within a door, back out into the outside world, I felt this great sense of relief. It was like I'd just been let out from a prison sentence. I was free and glad to be catchin' the bus home. Despite the perks – sick pay and a good pension, I consoled myself with the thought that maybe the prison service wasn't for me anyway. A few days later I got this official sorry letter explainin' they couldn't offer me a job in the Prison Service because of my height. I'd all but forgotten about it when, about three months later, I got another letter invitin' me to re-apply because now they'd relaxed the height restriction. I thought, "Blimey – they must be keen on me. I must have made a bit of an impression." Trouble was there was a downside. The letter also explained that I'd have to go to Wakefield Prison for 3 months as part of my trainin'. That did it for me. I just didn't relish bein' away from Cynthia and our three children for so long and so I didn't re-apply. Thinkin' about it now, I wonder what sort of prison officer I would have made. Could I have coped with the confinement and the abuse from prisoners? You have to go into a real prison to experience what it's really like and, to be honest, lookin' back, I think once – one day – had been enough for me.

I feel like I'm on a bit of a roll, tellin' you about my job seekin' exploits, but havin' just got out of prison, so to speak, before I go on I think I'll take a break to make a long overdue confession. It's another 'fishy story' which started out all innocent as a trip to Trafalgar Square with the kids to feed the pigeons and ended up with me commitin' a 'crime'! Cynthia had asked me to take the three of 'em, so I agreed to go one Sunday afternoon. I think she wanted a bit of time to herself. Mind you, I wasn't goin' to buy the little packs of pigeon food they sold round about – not at sixpence a time. I knew those pigeons would eat practically anythin' and a big bag of rice would do the trick for a fraction of the cost.

Once the kids had got bored with pigeon feedin', I'd still got loads of rice left and wanderin' through St James' Park I tossed a bit into the water. The fish went mad for it. The water was positively boilin' with 'em. Rather than carryin' it home, I thought I might as well give 'em the lot. We went home and I never thought any more about it until I glanced a headline in the Daily Mirror the next day - "Hundreds of fish dead in St James' Park". It seems my rice 'treat' had backfired and expanded in their stomachs. I felt really bad about killin' 'em, but until now I've kept quiet about my part in it. I didn't want prosecutin'. The fine would have been a heck of a lot more than if I'd bought the pigeon food the street traders made a packet from by sellin' to the tourists. Now, with that old skeleton out of the cupboard, I'd best get back to job huntin'.

As you know, dad worked for Battersea Borough Council, but although he'd often extolled the virtues of workin' in the public sector, funnily enough I never remember us talkin' about the possibility of me gettin' a job in local government. In the event, it was actually a friend of a friend who sowed the seed. Their two children had both got jobs with the LCC Education department on the non-teachin' side and that inspired me to write and apply for a position as a 'school keeper'. I didn't hear anythin' for a while, but eventually I got a letter invitin' me for an interview at County Hall. It was a big imposin' stone buildin' beside Westminster Bridge. A massive place and a bit of an intimidatin' place to go for an interview when you're not used to big offices. If you go to London you can stay in it now because part of it has been converted into a Marriot Hotel!

My interview was in 'Establishment 5', which was basically that part of the buildin' dealin' with education. Come the interview itself, despite the intimidatin' surroundin's, I reckon I came across as pretty confident and self-assured. It took place in a boardroom-type situation with quite a few interviewers and me positioned around this huge boardroom oval table. I can't remember the details, but I'm pretty sure I gave a good account of myself. One thing I do remember was at the end askin' if they wanted me to wait outside, but the chairman said no, we'll write and let you know. Although I already knew about them, still the most memorable aspect of the interview was when they explained about the key benefits of sick pay and a pension. I didn't let on, but they were the main reason I'd applied in the first place. Back home naturally Cynthia wanted to know how it had gone? Whilst I thought it had gone quite well, the fact was I didn't really know. They'd not given me any indication either way. It was a bit of an anti-climax.

Days turned into weeks and I didn't hear anythin'. I thought it was a bit rude. If they didn't want me, they should at least have written to say so. Then again, with an organisation that big, I guessed it was easy to get lost in the mêlée. I thought they'd just forgotten all about me. Undaunted I kept lookin' for other outlets to better myself and I thought an Inspector – I guess that would be a step up. So I applied. I loved my London Bus, but I didn't want to be a bus driver on shift work for ever. Mind you, I wasn't sure I'd relish bein' an Inspector. They weren't exactly the most popular members of the London Transport Team, not with the staff, not with the passengers. Then I thought, I might as well at least give it a go, if nothin' else, it will be good interview practice.

As you can imagine, I didn't let on to any of my workmates that I'd applied to be an Inspector and I was hopin' I wouldn't get recognised when I was called for interview, up at the Depot in Kilbourne, at the top of Edgeware Road. Come the day of the interview, I was surprised to see how many applicants there were –

about a dozen of us. I was still uncertain about it, so I was glad I didn't know any of 'em.

I needn't have worried. I wasn't offered the job anyway. They thought I was a bit too young. To be fair, they were nice about it. Well, as nice as it's possible to be when you're rejectin' somebody. They told me not to think it had been a waste of time because they'd made a note of my interest for future reference and I should think about applyin' again in a few years' time.

It's never nice to come away from an interview without a job offer, but on this occasion I think I was more relieved than disappointed. It had made my mind up for me. If I was goin' to move onwards and upwards from bein' a bus driver, then I'd be better findin' somethin' outside of London Transport.

I was still scoutin' around lookin' for suitable job opportunities when a knock comes on the door which turned out to be a job opportunity, but not for me – for Cynthia. It was Beatie and long story short, she didn't look at all well. She wanted to know if Cynthia would go in and cover the shop for her. I knew it had to be pretty serious for Beatie to leave that shop and come askin'. She wasn't one for givin' up easily wasn't Beatie so I told her to get back and I'd send Cynthia round straight away so she could take herself off to bed. I told Cynthia not to worry about the kids. I'd sort them out. Sad to say, but Beatie never really recovered. Cynthia's 'coverin' for a bit' went on for 4 months while Beatie was in and out of hospital and throughout all that time, Cynthia worked the same hours that Beatie had – 7 am 'till 7 pm, but livin' next door, at least she didn't have to deal with the after-hours knockers as well. Maybe Charlie dealt with them or maybe they just got the message and stopped pesterin'.

As you know, it was a shop that sold pretty much everythin' - cotton, bootlaces, bread, anythin' for dinner, sticks, vinegar by the pint and bacon. I've told you Beatie didn't have a refrigerator in the shop and now that Cynthia was runnin' it, we got to know a lot more about some of the goin's on. She'd come back with stories about maggots in the bacon and how she'd have to keep gettin' the maggots out so customers wouldn't see 'em. I suppose it was a case of what they didn't see didn't hurt 'em! As far as I know, nobody ever complained. People kept comin' back for more, so maybe if the bacon was a bit on the 'high' side, it made it more tasty.

Beatie struggled on, but was never well enough to go back in the shop and sadly, after about four months, Charlie, her husband, came to tell us she'd died. Charlie worked for Harrods and he also had a part-time job as a pianist at the Waldorf Hotel. Even before Beatie was ill, he was hardly ever at home. To be honest I don't think it was just his work. I think he had a lady friend somewhere. The only time we'd ever seen him and Beatie out together was on a Sunday night. On Sundays Beatie would close the shop at 2pm and in the evenin' the two of them would go up to the Nag's Head at the top of Silverthorne Road for a drink or two.

Now Beatie was gone and a day or two later, Charlie came to me and said, "Would we like to take the shop over altogether – buy the business?" Although I knew it was quite a little gold mine at the time, and Beatie had managed to set both her sons up in business out of the proceeds, I said no. It was a lot of work, a major tie and we had 3 young children to consider. Victor was at Heathbrook School durin' the day now and Grace and mum had been helpin' out with lookin' after the other two, but that couldn't go on indefinitely. Charlie's own two sons weren't interested. One was runnin' amusement arcades and the other billiard halls. Eventually the shop was sold to strangers and the new owners gave it a total refurbishment and made it rather 'posh'. I'm not sure that was really such a good idea or that they really understood their market because it never seemed to do the trade old Beatie had done. What's more, it wasn't long before supermarkets started to appear and then, as you well know, the days of the corner shop were well and truly numbered. Just as well we never took it on.

I didn't have any academic qualifications as such, but I felt I had a wealth of different experience under my belt. I was still lookin' around, considerin' where to cast my line next, when out of the blue this official lookin' letter arrives. Fully nine months after my interview at County Hall, they sent me a letter offerin' me the assistant's job at Marion Thornton School – a girls' school no less, on Clapham Common, South Side. When I say assistant, I mean Assistant School Keeper. I suppose you could say it was a kind of trainee job – to see how I'd shape up before givin' me control at a school of my own. But I was in. I'd got my foot on the Local Government ladder. I'd landed myself a salaried job with prospects, an amazin' three weeks paid holidays, sick pay and, importantly, a pension at the end of it all. I was on the way up – or at least I thought I was. No more shift work. No more strugglin' to make ends meet if ever I should get sick. I felt I was startin' to provide a secure future for Cynthia and our three kids. I was on top of the world.

Cynthia was over the moon and I couldn't wait to tell mum and dad and everyone at work. When it came to though, by the time I came to tell my workmates, somehow some of the shine had worn off. In some ways it felt kind of sad. The 3rd November 1962 will be forever etched in my memory. I'd driven my usual route without any particular incident, but at the end of my shift, when I stepped off my bus at Stockwell Garage, it was for the last time. Helen and I said our emotional goodbyes and that was it. The end of an era – my time with London Transport. In many ways it was a sad day. I'd had some good and eventful times. I was partin' with some good workmates and whilst I wouldn't miss the shifts, I would miss my mates and that big red bus.

When that job offer had arrived in the post it had felt like a big achievement. I'd felt on top of the world but, as it turned out, I was nothin' of the sort. I'd got a lot more achievin' to do, a lot more adventures ahead. A lot more stories to tell. I left London Transport in November 1962. I was 29. I'd landed a new job with better terms and better prospects but, like my other jobs, it was to be a steppin' stone. I was still lookin' to better myself. Lookin' for the next chance. I was to move onwards and upwards a fair few times, always takin' care 'to leave the stage whilst they were still applaudin'. Mind you, you might be surprised to learn that I spent the next 25 years in Local Government and I can hear you thinkin', "Well, I bet that was a bit mundane and uneventful." Not a bit of it. I don't do 'mundane and uneventful'. I reckon I was pretty successful though. By the time I finished I had over sixty staff under me. Not bad for a former bus conductor with no academic qualifications. If you want to know more, then you're just goin' to have to buy the sequel. This is where volume one ends, 'cos I reckon if I don't end it now, then this dodgy old ticker of mine might give up the ghost before ever I get the thing published. The fact is, I rather fancy doin' a book signin'. Somewhere in the capital would be good. Hopefully – I'll see you there.

Sadly I don't have any pictures of me either as a conductor or a driver or of 'my'
London bus, but this will give you an idea of what it looked like.

Mum's house, 15 and 15A Gambetta Street. The railin's had gone in the War and having bought the place, mum had a wall built. The concrete lamp post, havin' replaced the lovely cast iron one you saw in the 1945 Street Party photo, makes me think it must have been taken in the mid to late 1950s.

POST SCRIPT

One thing I've learned is to 'always look on the bright side' because if you do, you usually find that 'every cloud has a silver linin'' and if it doesn't, then maybe you're not lookin' hard enough or tryin' hard enough to make one. Lookin' back, would I change anythin'? With hindsight maybe I should have persevered with my music career. Maybe I could have made it big - well, in my dreams! If I'd persevered, maybe I'd have formed my own Big Band. I had the audacity, but in the end maybe not quite enough drive and ambition to see it through. When I gave it up, I did it for what I thought were the right reasons. If I'd not met Cynthia, maybe things would have been different – who knows. But then again, I should thank my lucky stars because both Victor and Sandy have made a career out of music and Cynthia and I, by and large, we had a good life and me, I'm still livin' it albeit, with a new love in my life. Cynthia had three children, each remarkable in their own way. I've been lucky enough to live to see 'em all grow up and have kids of their own, so I've got a whole lot to be thankful for. I think so anyway.

Even so, I can't deny that for a long time the wrench, the realisation that I'd given up my beloved music hung like a black cloud over me, a cloud that never really went away. Leastways, not for a very, very long time, but then, as it turned out, in one important way, even that cloud had a silver linin.' That's because, with a bit of help and encouragement from me, our Victor took over where I'd left off and made a successful career out of music. That means a lot. He probably doesn't realise how much, but he will if he reads this. What's more, so did our Sandy, although, she didn't need my help to do it. You'll learn much more about their achievements and how much they mean to me in the sequel.

Is music still important to me? You bet it is. I know I'm not up to it now, but the kid inside me thinks he is, and there's many a time my mind wanders off and I'm up on that stage again, tappin' out the beat and keepin' the time. You see, as I've been fond of tellin' you, "I was never more alive than when up there on that stage – performin'." Speakin' of which, although it will feature much more in the sequel, I can't resist just tellin' you that I did get to perform just one more time, but not until 1974. It was only the once, and it had been a very long break, but it was worth the wait. It was extra special because you see, it wasn't just that I was up there runnin' the show, our band, 'The Flamingos,' was made up of Victor and his friends. To get to play on stage with your son – how special is that!

Now, at 83, I may not have my drums or the ability to play 'em like I used to, but I still have my ear. I haven't got stuck in the '50s or any other era, come to that, but if you ask me, big band music and dance band music is still the best. It's proper music, played by musicians who can actually play their instruments to compliment and blend with one another to create a sound that brings joy to your heart – well mine anyway. It's not just electronic noise or synthesised this or that. If you've never done it, do yourself a favour and tune in to Clair Teal on a Sunday evenin' 9.00 pm – 11.00 pm (BBC Radio 2) and listen to what you've been missin'. Better still, get yourself out and listen to a live band – there are still lots of 'em about – like my son's band in Devon, the Gold Coast Band, or in my neck of the woods in Derbyshire, The Ashby 'Little' Big Band or the Ockbrook Big Band. You never know, I might see you there and, before you know it, you might find yourself on that dance floor as well – it would do you the world of good. Musically, as in life, I like to think I've kept faith with my proper age, usin' and benefitin' from my many and varied experiences of life whilst remainin' forever young inside. Growin' old gracefully and fadin' away were never goin' to be my style. Ask Madge, she'll tell you.

Now, unless you're psychic, you'll be sayin' to yourself, 'Madge? Who's Madge?' Well, the thing is, I've recently moved house – downsizin' they call it, except I thought I might as well go the whole hog and move into 'sheltered' accommodation whilst I was at it. They're a collection of little bungalows – about thirty altogether and, because it's a simple fact of life that, on average, women live longer than men, almost all of 'em are occupied by single ladies. Some of 'em keep themselves to themselves, but a good few of us have regular get-togethers at least twice a week and, bein' the' new kid on the block' and a man with a sense of humour and a bit of life left in him, well, it seems I breathed a bit of new life into the place, made a bit of an impact so to speak, especially with Madge. You see, I reckon I always had the ability to make the best of whatever life threw at me, and it seems I haven't lost my touch.

So, what's my tip for a long and interestin' life? – Make sure your glass is always half full and never half empty and smile. Trust me, it's infectious. So now there we are, Madge and me, two octogenarians who've found love in their twilight years. Kind of romantic, don't you think? As well as socialisin' with the rest of 'em, Madge and I see each other every day and always have dinner together and a bit of 'quality time', if you get my drift.

You've heard the sayin', "All things come to he who waits." Trust me, that's a load of cobblers, whereas there's more than a grain of truth in, "He who hesitates is lost." When opportunities come along, you have to recognise 'em and take 'em. You have to get off your backside and make things happen. You see, if you ask me, there are basically two types of people, those who make things happen and those who just wait for them to happen. Thanks in no small measure to my experiences as an evacuee in Ardingly, I reckon for most of my life I've been the former. Eliminate risk and at best you'll under-achieve. In games, you have to take chances to have a shot at winnin' and it's the same in life. Settlin' for what was familiar, safe – at work or play – was never in my psyche, not after Ardingly, not after my time with Ma Wickens. My motto, if I had one, might be, "Nothin' vetured, nothin' gained." I've been a chancer all my life. I still am. Well, a leopard can't go changin' his spots – not at my age.

Now I'm knockin' on the door of 84, memory – memories – become more important. I'm still pretty active – well I am the 'new kid on the block' and now, in Madge, I have a new 'girlfriend', but when I find the time to sit and ponder, it's amazin' what I can trawl up. What powerful emotions can be stirred from happenin's so very long ago. When you're as old as me, they become more important you know – your memories. You have the time, the time to sit and think

— to remember. That's when you realise that life is a minefield in which memories abound. The older you get, the more there are just waitin' in ambush, waitin' to be re-discovered. Sometimes somethin' seemingly totally unrelated sparks a memory and it just leaps out at you all unexpected. That's how it is with me, anyhow. Ask John, he'll tell you. How he's managed to put this book together from all our jumbled conversations, goin' back and forth, I'll never know. But that's friends for you.

Right on cue, somethin' I haven't mentioned has just popped into my head that I think I'll share with you. I've never been invited myself, but in recent years I've noticed that a little platoon of wartime evacuees march to the Cenotaph on Remembrance Day. I can't help smilin' when I see the brown card labels with their names written on tied to their lapels with bits of string, blowin' in the wind. It's nostalgic you see and it brings back the memory of Roy and me bein' 'mustered' along with dozens and dozens of soon-to-be evacuees in Tennyson Street School playground, all of us with our labels blowin' in the wind. That memory, it's so vivid it could have been yesterday. But it's sad to think that, of our group, I could be the only one left now. I was about the youngest, you see.

Now, I think that's pretty much all I want to tell you about me before the sequel but there is one more thing I think I should share with you now arisin' from the summer of 2015 when John took me back to see some of my old haunts. It concerns the Doodlebug bomb that dropped too close for comfort in Montefiore Street. When I was tellin' you about that bomb, you have to remember that I was tellin' you about the recollections of a 10 year old. Some things that I didn't actually see, actually experience, were kept from me. When John and I went back to London in 2015, we got talkin' to Derek Green in Gambetta Street. He still lives there in the street where he grew up. If you remember, his parents, Grace and Aurthur had been our neighbours when we were livin' in number 25. Although I didn't really know 'em then, they'd been livin' in the street durin' the war, includin' when the bomb dropped. It was their brother and sister, the musicians, who were killed in the house opposite mum and dad's in Montefiore Street. Anyway, as we were reminiscin', our conversation turned to the bomb and then Derek dropped another bombshell. Unbeknown to me, it seems it wasn't just the 3 people I knew about and told you about who were killed by that doodlebug. In all 19 people were killed by it and goodness knows how many lives scarred for ever. And that was just one bomb.

Now that really is enough, probably more than enough of what's happened to me – until the sequel but, what about all the people I've told you about, the characters who featured prominently in my early life. Many of 'em will feature more in the sequel, but in case John never finishes writin' it or the Grim Reaper comes callin' or you just never come across a copy, I think I should just fill you in on the bare essentials.

Mum :

I have to start with mum, because my mother has been the single most important and influential person in my life. I know this is supposed to be an update but, thinkin' about mum, I've just realised there's somethin' I meant to tell you so, better late than never, I'll do it now.

Mum was Welsh and like many Welsh people, she had a beautiful voice. She would sing at Church Hall concerts. I can picture her now through glazed eyes, standin' with one had on the piano singin' some of her favourites like, 'Because you're mine' and 'Jeannie with the light brown hair'. I was proud then and I'm proud now. She was a special lady was my mother. She didn't always have life easy – far from it – but she made the best of life's opportunities when they came along and she was a good mum to me. Fosterin' me out at such a young age and then, havin' got me back, havin' to pack me off again as an evacuee, had been hard for her, born out of necessity, not choice.

Despite her mental breakdown, havin' finally discharged herself from hospital, mum pretty soon reverted to takin' charge of the household, to bein' dad's rock and latterly, you could almost say, his carer. Dad had been the sickly one, but it was mum who died first, all unexpected, of a heart attack in 1967. It was the same day Jonny Blake had been to 'improve' her fireplace. When she'd originally had the range taken out, she'd had this single brick fireplace built. Now she wanted it makin' double brick. She'd had the bricks for ages. I shouldn't be tellin' you this really, but the thing was, mum and I had sort of pinched 'em from a stack that had been standin' on a bomb site unused for years. We'd fetched 'em two at a time in a shoppin' bag when I was still at school and I suppose they'd been stacked out in the back yard ever since.

Anyway, when mum mentioned she wanted her fireplace improvin', I arranged for Jonny Blake to go and do it. He was a sort of 'odd job man' contractor who did quite a lot of jobs for me in school. I had a budget for repairs and could appoint who I wanted and I'd found Jonny was good, reliable and reasonable.

Dad wasn't at home when Jonny was workin' on the fireplace. Whether mum had already had the heart attack by the time he got home, I don't know, but I think it must have been dad who phoned for the ambulance to get her into hospital. What I do know is he phoned the police at Peckham Station to ask them to call round and let me know. You see, I didn't have a home phone. Not many people did in those days. It was Wally, the Community Policeman, who came to tell me mum had been rushed into St Thomas's havin' had a heart attack, but sadly, she hadn't survived. She'd passed away. I knew him, Wally. He was a decent man and he told me in as nice a way as he could, but news like that, comin' out of the blue, it's devastatin'. To say the least, it was a shock. Even so, I don't think it sank in straight away. It was so unexpected. To hear mum talk and, from all appearances, it was dad who was the sickly one. Ok, mum did have her 'funny turns', but they weren't life-threatenin', but now she was gone, and there was no chance for goodbyes, thank you's or anythin'. I don't know if you know the song "in the livin' years" but take a tip from me, if there's somethin' you feel you should say to someone, especially someone you love, don't dilly dally, say it, while you have the chance.

I needed to go and see dad – see how he was – see how he was takin' it, but first I wanted to go to the hospital to find out a bit more about what had happened and see if anythin' needed doin'. I arrived at St Thomas's near Westminster Bridge around 8pm and just parked up outside. You often could in those days. I enquired which ward mum had been admitted to and it turned out to be Nightingale Ward, ironically the same ward I'd 'died' in at the age of 13 from bronchial pneumonia. Whilst I was waitin,' my mind wandered back and I could see me lyin' there in that ward with mum standin' by my bed talkin' to the doctors and bein' given all sorts of doom and gloom about me never bein' able to work. Just goes to prove that doctors don't know everythin.' More important now, much more important, they hadn't known how to save mum from an untimely death. Today, with all the advances made, doubtless the outcome would have been different.

As it was, a nurse came out to see me and took me into an ante room and explained that mum had died of a heart attack but that she'd gone peacefully and hadn't been alone. That nurse had been with her and she wanted to tell me what mum had said in her last moments. Typical of mum, she'd been thinkin' of others, tellin' this nurse how worried she was about her husband because he was a very sick man. It seems she'd barely got those words out when she died.

I explained I was just on my way to see him, to see how he was, make sure he was Ok. I didn't actually see mum. I suppose by then she would have been transferred down to the morgue. Dad was very composed. Not that he'd ever been one for showin' any emotion. Not in front of us kids at any rate. I suppose he'd had a few hours to come to terms with the shock of it and maybe the loss wouldn't hit him for a while. There wasn't really much I could do except keep callin' in and try to be there for him and right then, all he really seemed to want was for me to tell Roy. Eventually Les and I found him in a bettin' shop in Stretham on the Saturday. Roy came to the funeral, but that was about it. It's sad to say, but he and dad just never hit it off, never could 'mend fences'.

The day after mum died, Jonny Blake came to me in my office brandishin' a poker in his hand! He wasn't for bashin' me with it, he'd come to apologise. Apparently after finishin' mum's fireplace, he'd scooped up his tool roll in a bit of a hurry to get to the next job and inadvertently he'd scooped mum's poker up with his tools and he'd come to return it. He didn't know mum had died and before I could say anythin' he went on about how she'd made him this massive plate of sandwiches on account of it bein' lunchtime, but he'd had to decline and just have a quick cuppa because he needed to get on. When I told him, he was dumbfounded. He'd left at about twenty to one and mum seemed fine. His last image was of her ploughin' her way through all the sandwiches. That was mum all over, she liked her food and never wasted anythin'. She died at about 4pm.

Mum had got her new fireplace, but she never lived to enjoy it and, ironically, that fire was never lit. Dad just put a free-standin' electric fire in there. Even that just stood there gatherin' dust because the front parlour was hardly ever used again. I suppose I must be a bit of a hoarder because I still had that fire until movin' to my warden-aided accommodation in Derby in 2015. It still worked, but it was dated to say the least and I had no room for it so, hoarder or not it had to go.

Dad :

So now, what of dad? That had been typical of mum – usin' her dyin' breath to express her concern for dad and his frailty. She may not have been quite the mum of old, but to the end, she was still that carin' person I'd always known and loved. We were close, mum and I, closer than I ever got to dad. I didn't know it then, but through adversity, I would at least get closer to dad than I'd ever been.

Adversity came, as it often does, through illness. Barely two months after mum died, dad went down with prostate trouble. It was cancer and in those days the only potentially effective treatment was to take the whole thing out. But mum was right, dad was considered too frail to be able to survive such a major operation, so all they could offer was to try to manage the illness and the pain. Part of the treatment was to give him a bag. Dad really, really didn't like that, but he had no choice. He just had to put up with it.

Sometimes cancer can be mercifully quick, but frail or not, dad wasn't one for givin' up easily. He was a fighter and I was nursin' him for all of two and a half years. Most of the time he was at home and I'd go over regularly to do meals or take meals and see to his other needs. When things got bad, as I'm afraid they did fairly often, I'd get him into hospital – Battersea General or Balham. There they'd put a catheter in and after a week or so he'd recover enough for them to feel justified in sendin' him home. Within a couple of months, I'd have him back in and that cycle would continue for the next two and a half years whilst all the while dad was gettin' gradually weaker.

Six weeks before he finally died the doctors sent him home yet again, this time with a catheter still fitted. He hated havin' that. I lit a fire in the spare room because it was cosier and nursed him in there. Lyin' on what I think he knew was his death bed, he asked to see Roy. Maybe he wanted to make peace with him before he died, but

Roy didn't go so it never happened. Dad was very weak and tired of the battle and in the last two weeks his mind started to go and he'd keep shoutin' out for me without really knowin' why. It was pitiful to see him and I thought it best to get him back into hospital, this time to Battersea General. Within a week he was dead. This may sound terrible to say, but it came as a great relief when dad finally died. It had been a long, protracted and painful illness with no prospect of a happy outcome. He was 72.

My Big brother Roy:

Roy left the army in 1960 but I'm afraid it wasn't a harmonious partin'. The army wanted to reduce costs and numbers and when Roy applied to further extend his commission, they refused. Basically, they were refusin' anyone with a poor health record and Roy had always had problems with his ears. Roy was very bitter about it and never forgave them. Now he needed a new career and decided to set up his own office furniture business in the City. As far as I could tell, it was doin' Ok, but then again, it wasn't really him. It wasn't really what he wanted. He wanted to be back in the army, but in a different outfit, and movin' up the ranks.

By the 1980s, both Cynthia and I and my brother Roy and his 'girlfriend' Eileen had retired to Lincoln. Roy smoked and drank more than was good for him, but unlike me, for a man in his late '50s, he didn't seem to have too many health problems. Nothin' serious anyway. It was a bit of a surprise when one mornin' he phoned me up to say he'd got this really bad nose bleed and could I give him some advice on what to do. I guess he thought I was always seein' the medics for one thing or another to do with my heart, diabetes, asthma or whatever. Anyway I told him best thing to do if it wouldn't stop was to get down to A & E, which wasn't far for him. They plugged him up and sent him home and to be honest, I never thought any more about it.

A week later, he had another, but this time they kept him in. I still didn't think it was anythin' serious, but by the time I got there he was on a drip and it was all happenin'. Still, there was no mention of any heart trouble or anythin' like that and I had no idea he could have a problem in that regard. I was the one with the dodgy ticker, not Roy. Mind you, later it came out that even back in his army days, Roy had experienced a bit of heart trouble. It was in his records.

Anyway, Roy was in hospital for about ten days, but I'm afraid he wasn't what you could call either a good or a happy patient. He was forever complainin' about the staff – the doctor, the sister, the nurses. Roy wasn't satisfied with any of 'em, not even with the way they dressed. I suppose Roy always had been a stickler for correct dress and he wasn't at all happy that the doctor didn't always come to see him wearin' a white coat. I don't think he trusted or wanted to be in the care of a doctor who, in his eyes, didn't even dress properly. I think he kept askin' to be discharged and eventually they told him he could go, so I went to fetch him.

I wasn't at all sure he was fit to be discharged. He seemed far from well to me and when we tried to put his shoes on, we couldn't do 'em up. His feet and ankles were swollen like I'd never seen 'em. Although I'd had heart trouble, my symptoms at this point had never included swollen feet and ankles. Now, from my own experience, I know it's indicative of heart trouble, but I didn't then, but I knew it wasn't right or a good sign, but Roy wanted to be home, so off we went. I got him in the car, but his shoes were still undone. I'll always remember that because it just wasn't Roy at all. He was always, but always so very particular about his appearance.

I took him home to his girlfriend Eileen who was livin' with him. They weren't married, but had been an item for some years. I kept droppin' in to see how he was, more or less the same as I'd done when he was in hospital, because to my mind he was no better. It was only about a week or so later that Cynthia and I went off down to a caravan exhibition at the NEC. As I've told you, we were caravan mad and always keen to see what was new on the market. We'd hardly been back in the house when we got a phone call from Eileen to say Roy had been taken back into hospital again. It was still in Lincoln, but a different one. Whether that was down to Roy expressin' a choice or just the luck of the draw, I don't know, but if you ask me, he'd have been much better off back in the main hospital where he'd been before. Where they sent him was an old complex of tired lookin' buildin's that had been used to treat airmen casualties durin' the war. It was cramped, utilitarian accommodation with nothin' welcomin' or warm about it. I don't mean it was cold in there, I just mean the atmosphere, the feelin' it gave you, the way it looked.

Roy was put on an open order ward where visitin' was allowed whenever you wanted. That in itself wasn't a good sign, but Roy seemed to be the healthiest and fittest of the lot of 'em. He was the only one up and walkin' around so I still wasn't all that worried. I just thought he needed to be in there a bit longer this time, 'till they bottomed what was wrong and sorted him out properly, before dischargin' him. Now we knew he had heart trouble, but not how serious it was, so I didn't go every day, just every other day.

He'd been in less than a week when I got there expectin' to see him up and wanderin' around, only to find he'd just had a seizure and they were all workin' on him. They'd already brought him round, but I was told he could well have another. My daughter Sandy and her American husband John were livin' in London at the time and, hearin' about Roy's deterioratin' condition, they came up and sat with him all night whilst I went home for some sleep.

I went back in at around 6 am to relieve them and about half past eight Eileen came to see how he was and told me to go off and get some breakfast. Now that Roy had his girlfriend with him, I asked her if she'd mind if I nipped home for a wash, shave and brush up to be back by 11 am. She was fine about it. At about 10.30 am, when I was thinkin' about headin' back, the phone rang. It was the hospital tellin' me Roy had had another seizure and I should try to get back quick. Puttin' the phone down I turned to Cynthia and said, "He's gone. I think Roy's gone." I was right. When I got to the hospital, staff told me Roy had died around 10.30 am.

One of the auxiliaries recognised me on the way in and came over to express her condolences. It seems she'd been there when Roy died and she told me she'd never seen a man put up such a fight for his life, but it had all been in vain. That was Roy – he'd always been a fighter. Never one to just give up. He was just 59. Just like mum, young, very young especially by today's standards, although in truth, with the effects of the drink and the smokin' and a less than healthy lifestyle, for some time, my brother had looked much older than his 59 years.

Only a couple of hours previous, when I'd left, Roy had been sittin' up in bed munchin' Rice Krispies. Eileen had arrived and I'd taken the opportunity to have a break and get cleaned up. However, it seems after I'd left Roy had been sayin' he wanted to go home and

Eileen had told him she didn't think she could cope with him at home and if he didn't want to stay in hospital then he'd have to go into a nursin' home 'till things were sorted out. The trouble was, the minute Roy felt a bit better, all he wanted was to get out of there and home and maybe bein' told Eileen wasn't willin' was a bit too much for him. We'll never know. All we do know is he got over-excited and very agitated and had another seizure and this time it was fatal. As you can imagine, Eileen was in quite a state, but as I said to her, it wasn't her fault. She'd been right. She couldn't have managed him at home as he was.

Goin' back a few days, shortly after his previous seizure, Roy had come over all serious at visitin' time. "If anythin' happens Willy, I want my name in the Daily Telegraph Obituary Column and my ashes scatterin' at Arbourfield Parade Ground. You see Willy, that was the happiest I ever was – those few weeks of trainin' at Arbourfield. As you know, I joined the wrong mob, Willy. I should have joined the Guards."

Sadly, I have to say that he was right. The Engineer Corps was never really him. He was supposed to be trained as an electrician, but that was never his thing at all. Even so, Roy was bright and he did rise through the ranks to Seargent Major, but that was never enough for Roy. He wanted to be a Brigadier and he never forgave the army for 'lettin' him go' much earlier than he wanted – before he had achieved a rank he was happy with. Roy did twelve years in the army, but I'm afraid he left very disillusioned and rather bitter. As I think I told you, they had a bit of a clear out to reduce overall numbers and those with a poor sickness record weren't allowed to re-enlist and Roy was one of 'em. He was always up the hospital with his ears. All the time he was in, he had a lot of trouble with his ears.

The past is the past and what's done is done, but I can't help thinkin' it was a shame Roy didn't stick to his guns and sign on in the Guards. I think he would have been much happier there instead of spendin' half his life weighed down with regrets and thoughts of what might have been. It's easy to see how it happened though. There he was, just a kid on his own confronted by recruitin' officers desperate to steer anyone with a bit of technical know-how into the Engineers. In truth, it was the uniforms, the pomp and the ceremony he really craved and in the Engineers he'd been a square peg all the while, which was a real shame. What made it worse, ten times worse, was later bein' refused a further commission on health grounds. He never forgave them. It left a bitter taste which persisted to his death.

Roy never lost his yearnin' for that uniform and the pomp and ceremony and back in civvy street, many was the time he'd go and stand outside the railin's at Buckingham Palace watchin' Victor playin' in the band durin' the changin' of the guard. The band would march across from Wellington Barracks, more or less opposite the Palace and once inside the parade ground forecourt, they'd form a circle and play as a forerunner to the Changin' of the Guard and then they'd play, marchin' the old guard back into Wellington Barracks. Ok, I know, I've not told you how Victor came to be in the Guards yet but I will, in a minute, I will.

Death, it's so final. I know I've more or less already told you this but it's important. Take my advice, if there's somethin' you feel you want to say, ought to say to someone, don't hesitate. Do it. Don't let the opportunity pass by, don't put it off or you may find yourself regrettin' somethin' you can't fix – ever. I never got the opportunity with mum, but with dad, I think I got as close to him as he would let me. Maybe there were things I could and should have said to Roy, but there's one more thing he said to me that I want, need to tell you, that shows what my big brother was like. You see, in some ways Roy was a bit like mum. There he was, albeit lyin' on what in a few hours, unbeknown to us, would be his death bed, and he starts sayin', "I'm very worried about you, Willy, with all the things you've got wrong with you." Little did either of us know that twenty odd years on, here I am still alive and kickin', the epitome of a creakin' door.

Roy got his wish. I made sure his name appeared in the Obituary Columns of the Daily Telegraph and Eileen, Cynthia and I went down to Arbourfield, just outside Readin', and scattered his ashes under a cherry tree beside the parade ground. Roy had died in March and it was now April 1990. The cherry tree was in full bloom, a real picture it was. I think Roy would have liked that – bein' next to the parade ground.

But, it didn't end there and much as I want to, I can't just leave it without givin' you the full story. Roy's ashes came in an urn. Nice thing it was too, but there was a somewhat comical side to Roy's last journey. I'm not sure I should be tellin' you this because you might find it very irreverent, but it's what happened so there we are. You know we were caravan mad, Cynthia and I, and would take off at any and every opportunity. Well, as it happened, there was a weekend rally at Farnham Agricultural College and Arbourfield was more or less on the way. So Roy, in his urn, travelled down the A1 in the back of our caravan.

After our little ceremony, the urn travelled on down to Farnham with us. I'd asked if the undertakers wanted it returnin' but they said no they didn't re-use 'em and would only have to throw it away. It was a nice thing that urn, but what do you do with an urn? And I didn't want to live with a constant reminder. When we got to Farnham and all parked and set up, I took the urn out of the caravan. If it had to go, it would be better sooner rather than later, but before puttin' it in one of the on-site bins, I couldn't resist takin' a last look inside. To my surprise and, if I were honest, horror, there in the bottom were a few more ashes. Somehow some of 'em hadn't come out back at Arbourfield. This bit you may not like because those last few ashes got scattered at the back of our caravan. At least I made sure that urn was empty before placin' it carefully in the bin. You've got to have a bit of a sense of humour when someone close to you dies. You'd go crazy otherwise.

As a keepsake and to keep 'em in the family, I had Roy's medals. Beautiful they were. Typical of Roy, he'd kept them pristine. Gleamin' like highly polished silver, proof coins they were on pristine brightly coloured ribbons. Just as Roy had done, I kept 'em wrapped in tissue in a box for years and I'm afraid I'd all but forgotten about 'em until Vivian, Derek, John and I came across 'em in the summer of 2015 when I was packin' up to move to Derby. I promised John I'd take 'em down to Victor's to keep 'em in the Wattley family. I know they were packed safe in a box of treasures I took with me and Vivian in the car, but when some weeks later after movin' John asked me to get 'em out so we could take 'em down to Victor's, they were nowhere to be found.

You could say that somethin' good came as a result of my brother's death, leastways I like to think what happened was, in part, a tribute to him. As you know, at that time, our youngest, Sandy, and her American husband John were livin' in London - Kingston-upon-Thames to be exact. Cynthia and I went to visit for a few days and whilst we were there, I took it into my head to drive on down to Ardingly, in part to reminisce, but mainly to see if there was still anyone there who remembered Roy and me as evacuees and to tell 'em of Roy's passin'. Cynthia wasn't keen to come, so I drove down on my own. It was a beautiful sunny day, like so many I remembered in Ardingly as a child.

I called into the church and, seein' the noticeboard just inside the arched 'open' porch, I decided to put up a notice basically to say that if anybody remembers two brothers, Roy and Jack Wattley, who were child evacuees durin' the War, I'd like them to know that sadly Roy had died. I drove slowly down through the village, takin' note of all the changes and comin' to the school, I noticed the door was open. It was a Saturday so I thought somethin' must be goin' on there. Inside a group of women were flower arrangin'. I thought I'd take a chance and just see if any of 'em remembered the evacuees bein' in the village and in particular did any of 'em remember the Wattleys? A bit cheeky really because I don't expect most of 'em were old enough to have been around durin' the war. I told 'em I'd been one of Ma Wickens' boys and that did strike a chord with one lady. She'd been speakin' to Eva (who if you remember was Ma Wickens' daughter) in the bakers that mornin' and she'd be seein' her again that evenin'! I thought about seekin' her out, but time was gettin' on and I needed to get back to Sandy's in Kingston, so I just asked to be remembered to her.

Now there are various 'committees' in Ardingly, includin' a 'history club' and they got to hear about my visit and my notice and that gave them the inspiration to try to organise an Ardingly Evacuees' Reunion. They got in touch and, as you can imagine, I was all for it. The first one was in September of that year, 1990, the year my big brother died, and very successful it was too, with around 80 attendin' includin' partners. It wasn't exactly my idea, but it was my visit on account of Roy's passin' that had triggered the whole thing off and so that's probably why I got pushed forward as our unofficial spokesman. More like a master of ceremonies really – doin' the welcome speech and vote of thanks at the end, and whatever else was needed in between. I didn't mind. In fact I loved it really. As you know, I always did like bein' 'centre stage'.

They set up a local committee who did a splendid job, organisin' things, gettin' everybody there and always puttin' on a lovely spread.

I'm sayin' 'always' because our reunions became an annual event. There's a group picture taken at that first one if you want to turn to it now. In case you're wonderin', I'm the one in the dark jacket, standin' second row, more or less central. Cynthia is to my right and Eva is sittin' in front of me, in the white jacket.

At one of the subsequent reunions, I forget exactly which year, we arrived to be told that the schoolchildren had been doin' a special project all about the evacuees in Ardingly. We were invited up to the 'new' village school to view their project work and be treated to a special concert at 3pm that afternoon. It had been a parents' open day too, so there were quite a lot of parents there as well, to greet us. There were drawin's and paintin's and neatly written script about us evacuees on all the walls and the children sang us a special song about and dedicated to us. As usual I was spokesman for the evacuees, at that time all in our 60s and 70s. I thanked the children for doin' a project on us and the village generally for accommodatin' us so Mr Hitler hadn't been able to bomb us. At one point, I persuaded a 5-year old and a 7-year old to come and join me at the front and, towerin' over 'em I explained to the rest of the children and their parents present that, "We looked just like you two when we arrived, when we first stepped off that bus at Hapstead Hall all those years ago, separated from our mummies and daddies and hopin' to be looked after by kind strangers in the village." That really struck a chord with some and I don't mean just us evacuees. One or two hankies came out, brushin' the odd tear aside.

Sadly, eventually we stopped havin' our re-unions. The thing was, Old Father Time, he caught up with us evacuees. Too many of us had either died or became too frail or unwell to make the journey. One thing I must tell you though, is that always, but always, we were lucky with the weather. We always had a beautiful sunny afternoon - just like the summers I remember as a child in Ardingly. Silly, I know, but I'm wellin' up a bit tellin' you — a sure sign that I need to be movin' on.

My Cynthia :

Even before we got married, there were times when, Cynthia and I, we both thought somethin' was wrong. Cynthia would get very tired for no particular reason, but it wasn't until 1967 that she was eventually diagnosed with 'pernicious anaemia' and started to get appropriate treatment for her condition. Havin' said that, before dischargin' Cynthia, they as good as told me, my wife 'wouldn't make old bones'. When you're both in your early thirties, that's not news you want to hear. My solution, or maybe reaction would be a better word, was to go out and buy a caravan and get on with enjoyin' life, takin' every new day as it comes. As it turned out, that would be the first of many, caravans that is, and the adventures we had in 'em, but that's somethin' you're goin' to have to read about in the sequel.

As you know, in March 1998 we 'retired' to Lincolnshire. Sadly, in 2012 Cynthia was diagnosed with cancer. I nursed her at home and it was heartbreakin' to see her deteriorate and she had other problems too that had changed her but which I won't go into. She eventually died on 8th June 2013 in Kingsmill Hospital aged 77 years. Cynthia's still with me though and I don't just mean the memories. I've got my Cynthia in a cardboard box on a shelf in my wardrobe. She's waitin' patiently for me so the kids can scatter us together. It seems that's all you get these days, a cardboard box, not a fancy urn like Roy had. My Sandy bought an urn and they're side by side on the shelf, but to be honest, I haven't dared try transferrin' 'em in case I spill any or they won't quite fit. To be honest I'd like to 'lay her to rest' now but I don't want to upset the kids so I'll leave her be.

When dealin' with difficult subjects - things that are hard to come to terms with, hard to accept - we humans resort to euphemisms. Passed away, taken from us, departed, at rest or even comic versions like kicked the bucket, pegged out, cocked her clogs, gave up the ghost, snuffed it. But, no matter how you say it, whichever you choose, they all mean the same – dead. Dead, the only word which says exactly what it means but the one people, well-meanin', kindly people, tend to shy away from. Maybe they don't realise that whatever way you say it, the finality is the same. The loss, the sense of loss and the loneliness that you feel, that I felt when Cynthia died, is real – still the same. It's a loneliness the kids don't really understand but that doesn't make it any the less real. But then again, why should they? They have their own lives to lead. In reality though, when you're left alone, when you've lost someone who you've been with for more than fifty years, you don't ever really get over it. It's nearly 4 years since my Cynthia died and now and again those thoughts creep up on me and take me unawares and for a while this melancholy takes over until I shake myself out of it.

It does get better though, and movin' on, movin' house to somewhere 'in the thick of things' rather than isolated on the edge of a village, in a place with too many memories, both good and bad, that's helped. And time, time they say is a great healer and I've come to realise that it is. More than that, I've come to realise that I still have my life to lead as well. Meetin' up again with John and recountin' my life and now findin' Madge – they've helped me to realise that, and let's face it, I'm goin' to need a new lease of life if I'm goin' to get the sequel done and dusted! When I eventually go, maybe I'll be like Spike Milligan – "I told 'em I was ill!" or then again maybe I'll be contrary and get the kids to stick a plaque over me, because, as I've told you, "I was never more alive than when up there on that stage performin'."

Speakin' of the kids, as you can imagine, they'll feature big time in the sequel, but I do just need to tell you briefly, how they've fared, startin' with our eldest, Victor.

Victor:

As you know, Victor was born in 1955, but what I haven't told you yet is that in 1970, with a little help and encouragement from his dad, Victor auditioned for the much-revered Grenadier Guards Band based at Wellington Barracks opposite Buckingham Palace. He didn't think I could, but I got him the audition and really, that was the easy bit – the performance, that was down to him. He was as nervous as hell, but passed with flyin' colours and, as a result, at the tender age of just 15 years, he signed on as a boy recruit and became the professional musician I like to think I could have been. His initial trainin' was at Purbright. At that time there was a 'school of music' attached to it – maybe there still is. Anyway, it's only about a mile and a half from Deepcut – where I'd started my own army career, so you could almost say, 'Like father, like son." Except of course I'd been a conscript and when I joined up, I had no idea, and certainly no expectation, of endin' up playin' in an army band. For me, two years out in Korea had been a much more likely prospect but, as you now know, 'lady luck' was with me and boy did I embrace her!

To be honest, I was a bit apprehensive about Victor bein' sent to

Purbright because it had a reputation not dissimilar to Deepcut. It was a tough camp. Others might say – oh, he'll be fine; it'll be good for him; it'll make a man of him. But when it's your own son – trust me, you don't think like that. As it turned out though, 'others' would have been right.

When you grow old and find yourself with time on your hands, time alone, you find your mind wanderin', thinkin' over things that happened in the past – reminiscin'. Sometimes when I think of Victor, I remember how proud I was when he was born. Such a tiny little mite he was then. In the Guards he blossomed and, if you look at the photo of him and me together, you'll see he's far from tiny now. In all, Victor did 35 years with the Guards and I'm pleased to say, if you were to ask him, he'd tell you he enjoyed every minute of it. You can't ask or hope for more than that for your son, can you? It brings tears to your eyes, well mine anyway.

In retirement Victor is still far from small. In fact, if truth be told, he's a bit too big for his own good – around the waist that is! But, jokin' apart, if anythin' my pride in him has grown with him, with all his various achievements. That's kids for you though, isn't it? No matter how big they get, you never stop bein' their dad and lookin' out for them. He now lives in Devon, with his wife Rebecca and young son Oliver. A born performer, Oliver, although only 9, he loves the stage. Maybe he takes after his grandfather? They are a very musical family and although retired, Victor hasn't hung up his sax. Far from it. He leads a dance band, The Gold Coast Band, who play at a regular venue in Bideford, but are available for hire if you need a good live band to play at your weddin' reception or whatever.

Vivian :

Vivian, a real individual, overcame livin' with one good eye to make her way in life and raise two children. After some difficult relationships she found a partner who sadly was all too quickly taken from her. Fortunately she's got a new man in her life now and they seem happy together and that's all you can hope for, don't you think? I'm sayin' new, but Derek and Vivian have been together for some 6 years now. They married just before Cynthia died and now live in Derby with her two grown-up children from a previous marriage, Paul and Amy.

Since my move to Derby, Viv is only five minutes away so she pops in most weeks and, whilst I still do all my own washin', cookin' and cleanin', one job Viv always does is change the bed for me. I really struggle with it, but she's got it down to a fine art and does it in a fraction of the time it would take me. It's good, havin' her close by.

Sandy :

As you know, Sandy is my youngest. I don't have favourites, but maybe because Sandy is like mum in so many ways, I seem to have a closer relationship with Sandy. We confide in one another more, but we have to do it mainly over the phone because Sandy lives with husband John in Kennebunk, Maine, across 'the pond' in the USA. They have 5 grown-up children – Claire, Bobby, Timmy, Emily and Edward. Whilst, in my eyes at least, Sandy is increasingly becomin' the spittin' image of Nanny Wattley, with the traits and mannerisms to match, I also like to think that, like her big brother Victor, in some ways she takes after her dad because she is an accomplished musician in her own right and works as a music teacher in the States. I wish I saw more of her, but you can't have everythin', can you.

Like I said, you'll learn a lot more about Victor, Vivian and Sandy in the sequel, but before I close, I'll just quickly tell you what became of some of the other characters in my life, startin' with Uncle Vic.

Uncle Vic :

If you remember, I told you Uncle Vic had been posted out to Hong Kong and this time Aunt Maisie wasn't goin' to be left home alone with daughter Margaret. In the event, the three of them, Uncle Vic, Aunt Maisie and Margaret were in Hong Kong for about two years or so. When they came back, Uncle Vic was posted to Bulford in Wiltshire – where all the tank regiments are, or at least they were. He knew he was comin' up for retirement (after 40 years' service), so while there, they started lookin' at places to retire to. They seemed to fancy Maidstone, but in the end finished up in Salisbury. Eighteen Castle Road to be precise. Don't go tryin' to find it because they – the Council I suppose – pulled the houses down for road widenin'.

As is often typical of long-servin' officers who've been moved from pillar to post, once out of the army, Uncle Vic didn't want to go anywhere. His allotment became the centre of his world and he just wanted to tend that. Mind you, he was very good when later I was nursin' dad. He'd come up once a fortnight on his own to see him. I used to take them both a school dinner at lunchtime so dad didn't need to bother cookin'. Amazin' when I think about it, because Ivydale, my school, was right across London, nowhere near dad's house in Gambetta Street.

Uncle Vic died in 1974, so he didn't outlive his twin brother, dad, by so very much.

Flossie and Les :

So what of Cynthia's parents, Flossie and Les? To my way of thinkin', Flossie lived a very full and colourful life and I think she was determined to get her full quota. "Three score years and ten" is what they used to say, and so it was that Flossie died in December 1969 on her 70th birthday.

Apparently Flossie had said she wasn't feelin' very well and had gone upstairs for 'a bit of a lie down'. When Les went to check on her, she'd gone. No real warnin', nothin'. Flossie died at home, about nine o'clock at night. Les phoned to give us the news, which came as a bit, no a lot, of a shock. Cynthia's mum hadn't been especially ill or anythin'. If anyone was goin' to go in the family, it was dad. We had three kids asleep in bed, so we couldn't just up and leave, so I said we'd be over as soon as we could in the mornin' – about 9.00 am. When we arrived, all the family were there assembled in the kitchen, but Les wouldn't let 'em do anythin' 'till we arrived. When it came to organisin' things, Flossie and Les had always looked to me and now it was down to me to organize the undertakers and, as it turned out, supervise them gettin' the body down the stairs. That was no easy task because she'd liked her food had Flossie and she was a big woman. The close family were ushered outside whilst they got her down. Just as well, because whilst Flossie was wrapped in a sheet, to get her down the stairs, they had to stand her upright – not very dignified, but there was just no other way.

A while later, we were doin' a bit of tidyin' up and I came across Flossie's purse down the side of the chair. We all remembered her sayin', "When I die you won't find a penny in my purse" and do you know, when I opened it up, it was just as she'd said. There wasn't a penny in it - nothin!

If you remember, in 1969 I was nursin' dad and I remember how genuinely shocked he was to hear Flossie had died. Along with the rest of us, I think he thought Flossie was more or less indestructible but, frail as he was, now he'd gone and out-lived her. Not for long though. The cancer that had been eatin' away at him would soon claim its victim and there was no amount of carin' I could do to change that.

I was there when they buried her, Flossie that is – just a bit later than my bosses at London Transport had thought! I remember seein' the plaque on her coffin which read 'Florence Gould', but as we learned later, she and Les had never actually been married. You know what they say, "there's none so queer as folk" and Cynthia's family, they were a queer lot alright, but, as I've told you, lovely with it.

Eventually Les re-married, or rather I should say married, but not to a stranger. He married Maimee, his son Tony's mother! – in law that is. That was perfectly legal because of course, although he knew Maimee well, she was no relation and she was widowed, so this time no elopin' to be done.

Monica and Jeff :

Monica, she was Cynthia's sister, and Jeff was her husband. You remember Jeff. He was the bloke who collected and sold my beloved drums for me when I decided to sell 'em. He was a lovely, kind-hearted bloke, was Jeff. You can imagine my surprise when, in 1965, Jeff turned up on our doorstep with two of his girls askin' for our help. Turns out Monica had gone missin' and he'd no idea where she was. Next day, I saw the headlines in the Daily Mirror about this woman who'd run off abandonin' her six kids. No prizes for guessin' who that was. I didn't usually take the Mirror, but I did that day. Jeff couldn't cope with all six on his own so we had the two of them thinkin' Monica would be back before long. Eventually, Monica did come back to see the kids, but she never had any of 'em back and Jeff had no real choice but to place five of the six children in a convent. Their eldest son, Kajic carried on livin' with his dad. Cynthia put Monica's behaviour down to her havin' been a skivvy for their mum,

Flossie, and her siblings and she'd just had enough. That's as may be, but, in my book, that still doesn't excuse walkin' out on 6 kids.

Grace and Aurthur :

As you know, Grace and Aurthur lived at no. 23, our nearest and dearest neighbours in Gambetta Street. We eventually left Gambetta Street in 1965. That was a memorable day, in more ways than one, as you'll learn in the sequel. It pains me now to recall that it was as much as 10 years later when we called back to see Grace and Arthur. I suppose we'd got tied up in our new lives, but even so. By then, everyone called me John, but not Grace and Arthur. To them I'd always be Jack. With her eyes glazin' over, Grace said somethin' rather movin' to me that day. "Do you know, Jack, this place has never been the same since you left. We lost somebody very important that day and I've never got over it." Tellin' you brings a tear to my eye and a lump to my throat. Grace and Aurthur hadn't been just good neighbours, they'd been the best but 'till that moment, I'd never realised I'd meant so much to them as well.

They had planned to move to Crawley New Town to be near their daughter when Aurthur retired but, in the end, they stayed in Gambetta Street, where their son, Derek had set up home, just a few doors down. The air must be good there because they both lived to a ripe old age. Gracie was 86 when she died in Battersea Hospital and Aurther soldiered on into his '90s. Very matter of fact and down to earth was Aurther. One time when I called round not long after Gracie's death, we got chattin' whilst Derek was gettin' his dad's tea, and, speakin' of Gracie, he said – "Well, that's it Jack, you can't expect to live for ever."

Characters from Ardingly :

Finally, what about the folk I knew as a child evacuee, all those years ago in Ardingly? I've told you that I still keep in touch with Eva, Ma Wickens' daughter. As I've told you, Cynthia and I were caravan mad and we'd often take a trip down that way and always make a point of callin' in to see her. On arrival, the first thing she'd do would be to phone June (Honeybun) makin' four of us for tea and cream cakes. We always made a point of takin' cream cakes. Eva's gettin' rather frail now and, havin' suffered a few falls, has recently moved into a nursin' home, but then again, she's doin' well really. She is over 90 and we still speak on the phone.

I just mentioned June Honeybun. If you remember, the Honeybuns were my first billet but I'm afraid theirs isn't a very happy story. I think I've already told you that although Mr Honeybun survived the war, he died soon after when he fell off a ladder whilst repairin' the clock up at the college. Sadly their youngest daughter Hazel died young. She was only 30 if that. Mrs Honeybun died a few years later and all three of them are buried together in the same grave in the churchyard in Ardingly. June, their eldest, fared better. She married Tinker and they continued to live in the village all their lives. Tinker died in 2002 and June has also gone now. Sadly, she died of Motor Neurone Disease about six years later.

Lastly then, *Donkey*, – an Ardingly evacuee, member of CLB and Roy's best friend. I'm pleased to say Donkey did rather well for himself. He finished up in Sevenoaks as MD of a yoghurt factory supplyin' the likes of Tesco's. I know because we met up several times at our reunions.

Well, that really is it for now. If you've enjoyed it, please visit my Facebook page and leave me a message. It would be lovely to hear from you. If you haven't, then Ok – tell me why – I can take it. You know what they say – you're never too old to learn. Whichever's the case, thanks for takin' the trouble to read it 'cos it's important to me – it's my life, or at least a good part of it. Bye for now – until the sequel.

Our first Ardingly Evacuees' Reunion. I'm standin' more or less in the centre wearin' a dark jacket and tie. Cynthia is to my right and Eva, Ma Wickens' daughter, is seated to my left in the white cardigan.

One of our subsequent Ardingly Reunions. That's me wavin' in the centre in the light trousers and dark top.

Villagers thanked for war-time care

A PLAQUE thanking Ardingly villagers for the care they gave evacuees during the Second World War is being unveiled at Hapstead Hall on Saturday.

The plaque was made by the late Aubrey Crook who, sadly, died on August 20 – the day after VJ Day. Mr Crook, an evacuee, had just visited Ardingly for the Sunday service commemorating the event and died half an hour later, while visiting a member on the village evacuee reunion committee.

He had previously attended a reunion day with other evacuees in May when another evacuee, Jack Wattley, who now lives in Lincolnshire, suggested the plaque be made to present to the village.

Residents are invited to the unveiling ceremony at 2pm when light refreshments will be served.

Newspaper cuttin's about the unveilin' of the plaque which I had suggested should be presented to the village in thanks.

Historic moment

A COMMEMORATIVE plaque for evacuees who stayed in Ardingly during World War Two has been unveiled at Hapstead Hall.

About 70 villagers and evacuees were there for the historic moment. The Rev Alex McLean welcomed everyone and introduced the widow of the late Aubrey Crook, an evacuee who had made and presented the plaque. He thanked John and Eva Newman, Scilla Thompson and Sandy Hett, whose hard work had made the occasion possible.

Scilla Thompson unveiled the plaque and said the village had loved having the evacuees as much as they had obviously enjoyed being in Ardingly.

Former evacuee Jack Wattley, who had travelled from Lincoln and suggested the idea of the plaque, said he was delighted so many people had been able to come and thanked Les Simmonds for putting up the plaque.

I'm third from the right.

Montefiore Street as it looked in 2015. Our old house, No 34, is in the terrace on the right where the skip is and the gap in the houses opposite created by the doodlebug is now a public park and children's playground. Part of the former Tennyson Street School, now flats, forms the vista at the end of the street.

Me outside Nos 15 and 15A Gambetta Street (formerly mum and dad's house) in 2015.

Me outside Nos 25 and 25A Gambetta Street, my first home of our own, in 2015.

Part of the former Tennyson Street School, now flats, in 2015.

With son Victor durin' the interval at one of his Gold Coast Band concerts in 2015 shortly before my 82nd birthday.

Playin' a couple of numbers with the band – just to show I still could!

The author, with John at a 1940s wartime re-enactment in Crich, Derbyshire, in August 2015. John went as an Evacuee and if you look closely, you'll see he's clutching his little case of belongings and wearing his name label, just as he did when evacuated from London aged 5. The cover photo was also taken at the same venue and I think neatly encapsulates John's sense of humour and zest for life. He doesn't normally use a wheelchair but there was a lot of walking involved that day and the organizers kindly loaned it to us.

You Couldn't Make It Up! is John Collins' first book. He's a retired town planner and lives in Derbyshire with his wife, Michaela. He has two sons, Nicholas and James and three remarkable grandchildren – Oliver, Bea and Thomas.

CPSIA information can be obtained
at www.ICGtesting.com
Printed in the USA
LVHW051457010819
626171LV00011B/720/P

9 781544 070520